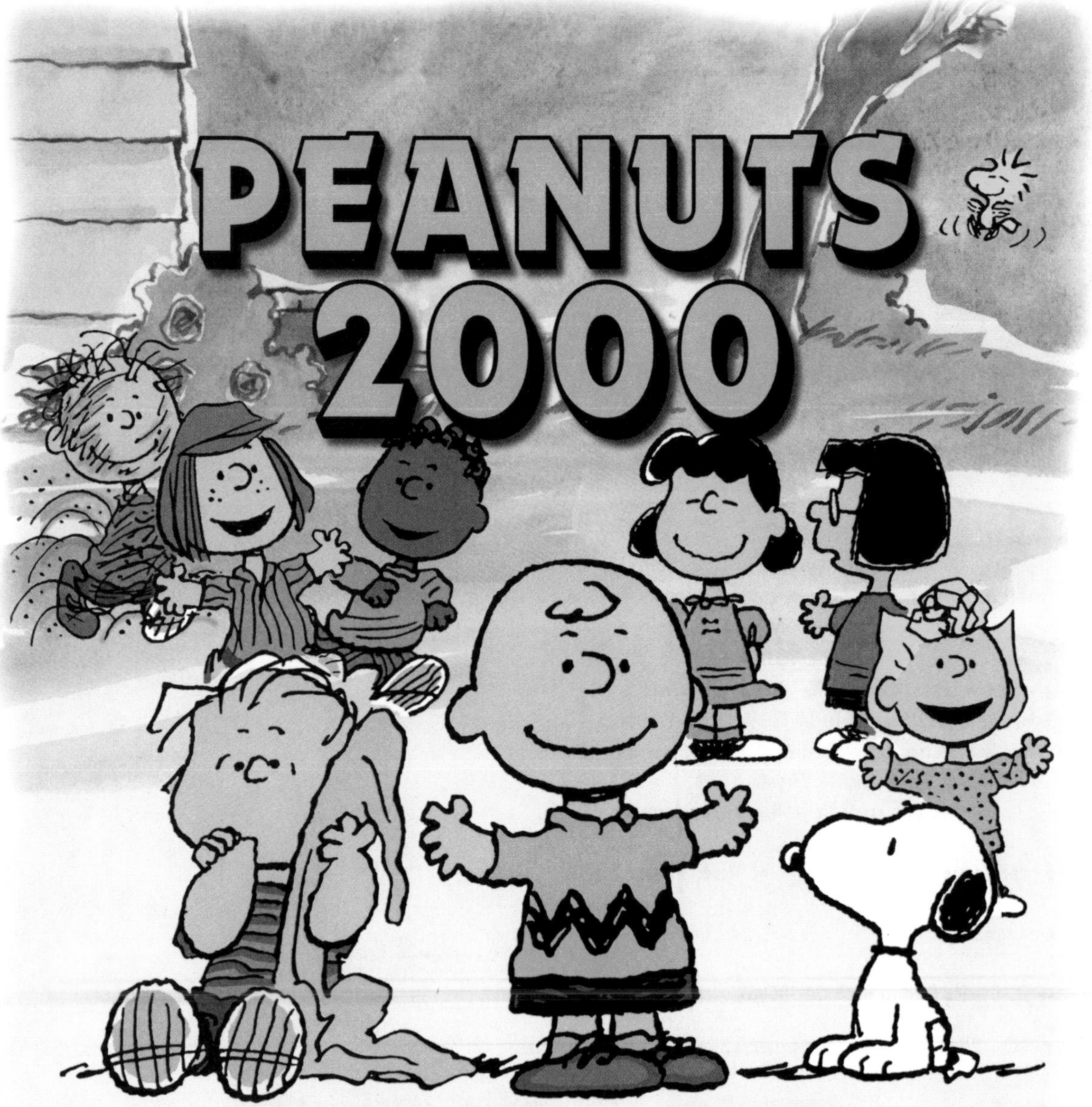
PEANUTS
2000

By Charles M. Schulz

Ballantine Books * New York

A Ballantine Book
Published by The Ballantine Publishing Group
 Published in the United States by The Ballantine Publishing Group, a division of Random House, Inc., New York, and simultaneously in Canada by Random House of Canada Limited, Toronto.
The comic strips in this book were originally published in newspapers worldwide.

Ballantine and colophon are registered trademarks of Random House, Inc.

www.randomhouse.com/BB/

Library of Congress Catalog Card Number: 00-105957

Cover design by Paige Braddock, Charles M. Schulz Creative Associates

ISBN 0-345-44239-3

Manufactured in the United States of America

First Edition: September 2000

10 9 8 7 6 5 4 3 2 1

PEANUTS 2000

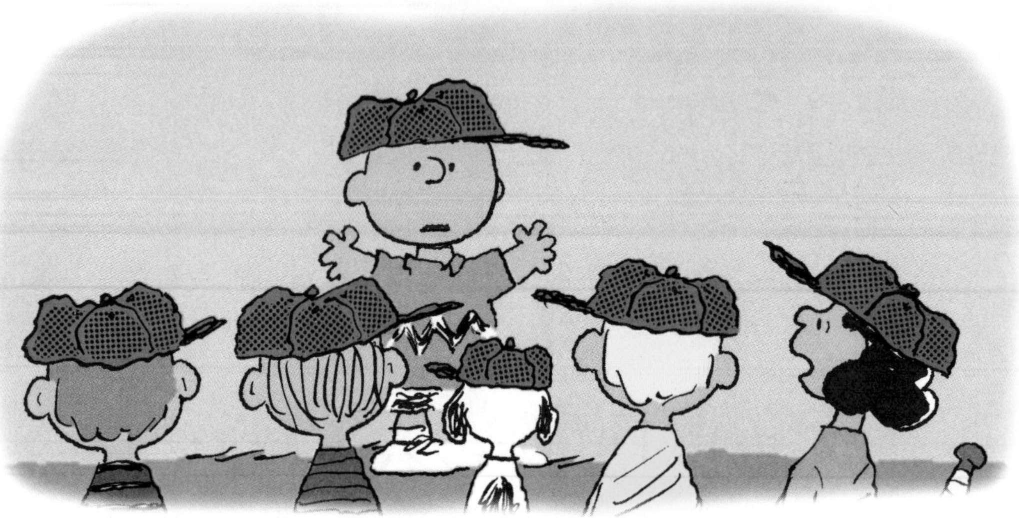

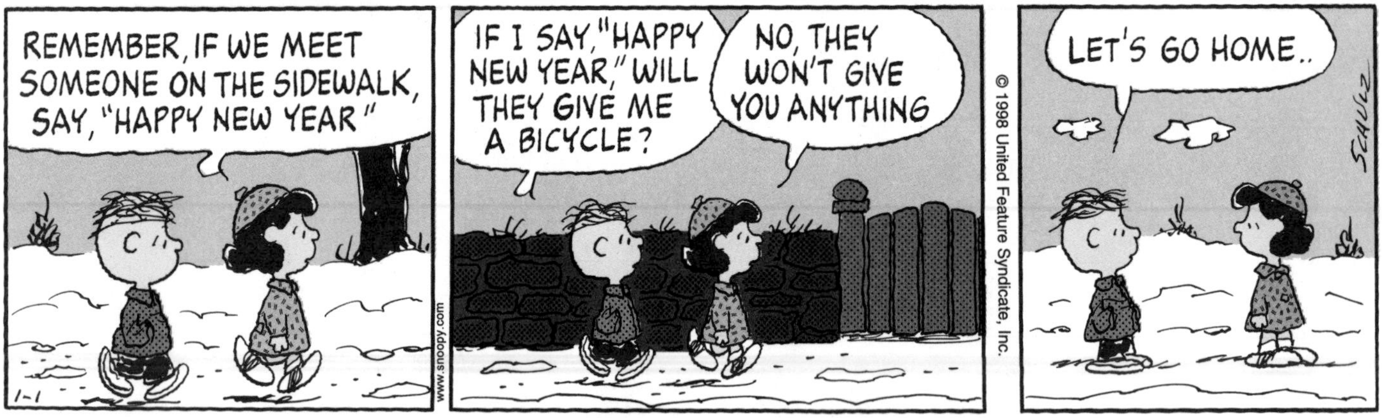
REMEMBER, IF WE MEET SOMEONE ON THE SIDEWALK, SAY, "HAPPY NEW YEAR"
1-1
www.snoopy.com
IF I SAY, "HAPPY NEW YEAR," WILL THEY GIVE ME A BICYCLE?
NO, THEY WON'T GIVE YOU ANYTHING
© 1998 United Feature Syndicate, Inc.
LET'S GO HOME..
SCHULZ

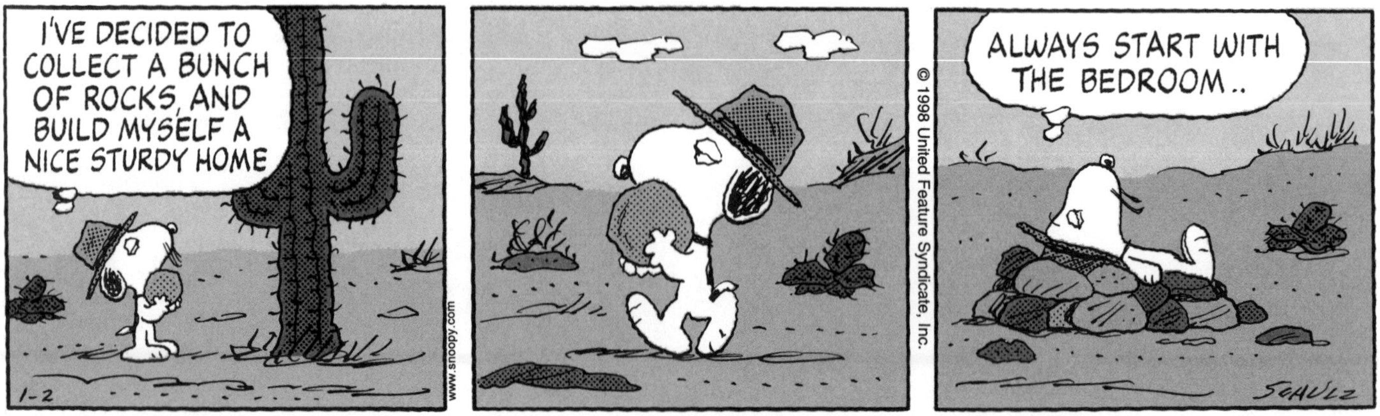
I'VE DECIDED TO COLLECT A BUNCH OF ROCKS, AND BUILD MYSELF A NICE STURDY HOME
1-2
www.snoopy.com
© 1998 United Feature Syndicate, Inc.
ALWAYS START WITH THE BEDROOM..
SCHULZ

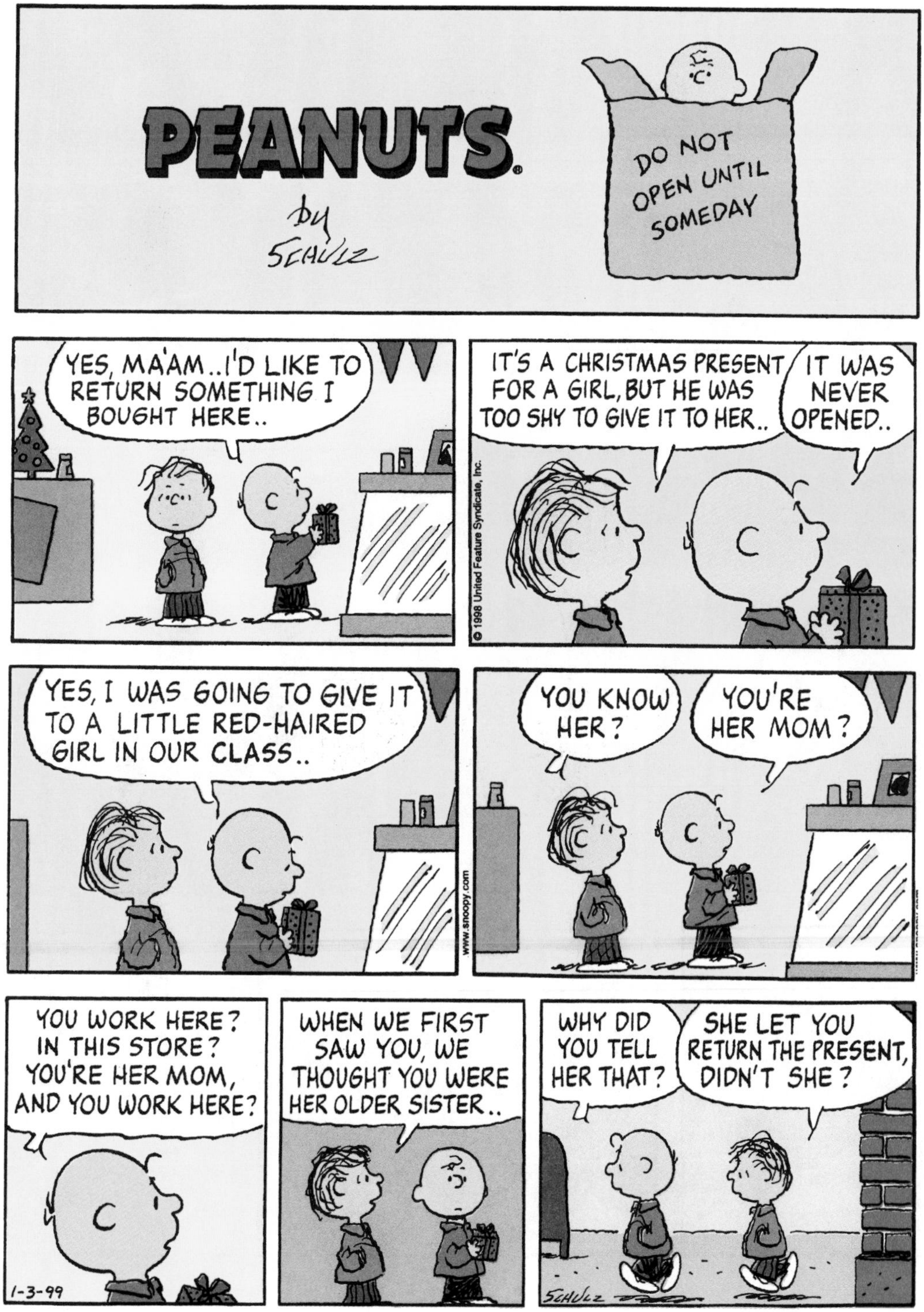
PEANUTS®
by SCHULZ
DO NOT OPEN UNTIL SOMEDAY
YES, MA'AM..I'D LIKE TO RETURN SOMETHING I BOUGHT HERE..
IT'S A CHRISTMAS PRESENT FOR A GIRL, BUT HE WAS TOO SHY TO GIVE IT TO HER..
IT WAS NEVER OPENED..
© 1998 United Feature Syndicate, Inc.
YES, I WAS GOING TO GIVE IT TO A LITTLE RED-HAIRED GIRL IN OUR CLASS..
www.snoopy.com
YOU KNOW HER?
YOU'RE HER MOM?
YOU WORK HERE? IN THIS STORE? YOU'RE HER MOM, AND YOU WORK HERE?
1-3-99
WHEN WE FIRST SAW YOU, WE THOUGHT YOU WERE HER OLDER SISTER..
WHY DID YOU TELL HER THAT?
SHE LET YOU RETURN THE PRESENT, DIDN'T SHE?
SCHULZ

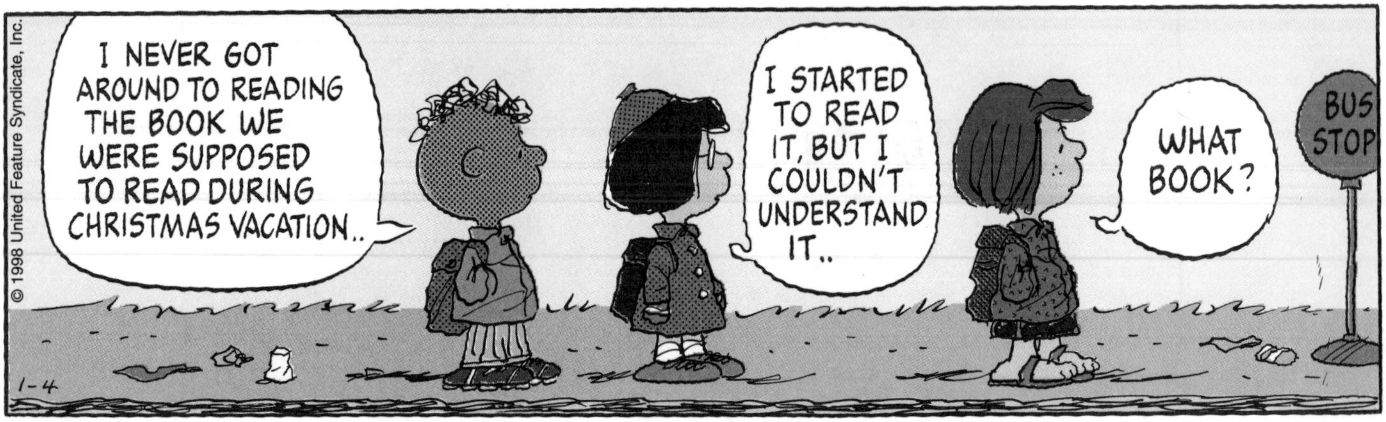

© 1998 United Feature Syndicate, Inc.
1-4
I NEVER GOT AROUND TO READING THE BOOK WE WERE SUPPOSED TO READ DURING CHRISTMAS VACATION..
I STARTED TO READ IT, BUT I COULDN'T UNDERSTAND IT..
WHAT BOOK?
BUS STOP

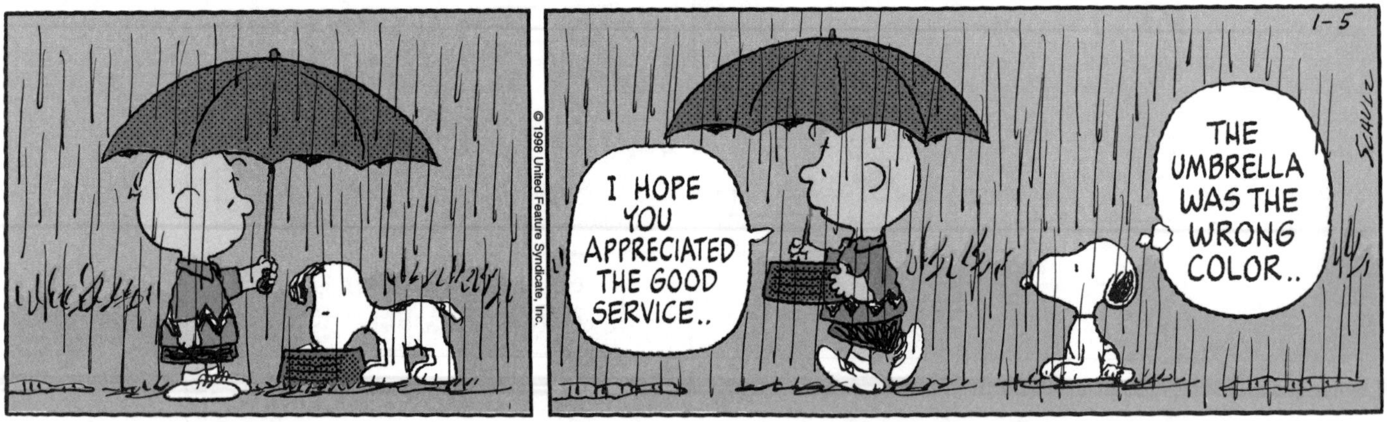

© 1998 United Feature Syndicate, Inc.
1-5
SCHULZ
I HOPE YOU APPRECIATED THE GOOD SERVICE..
THE UMBRELLA WAS THE WRONG COLOR..

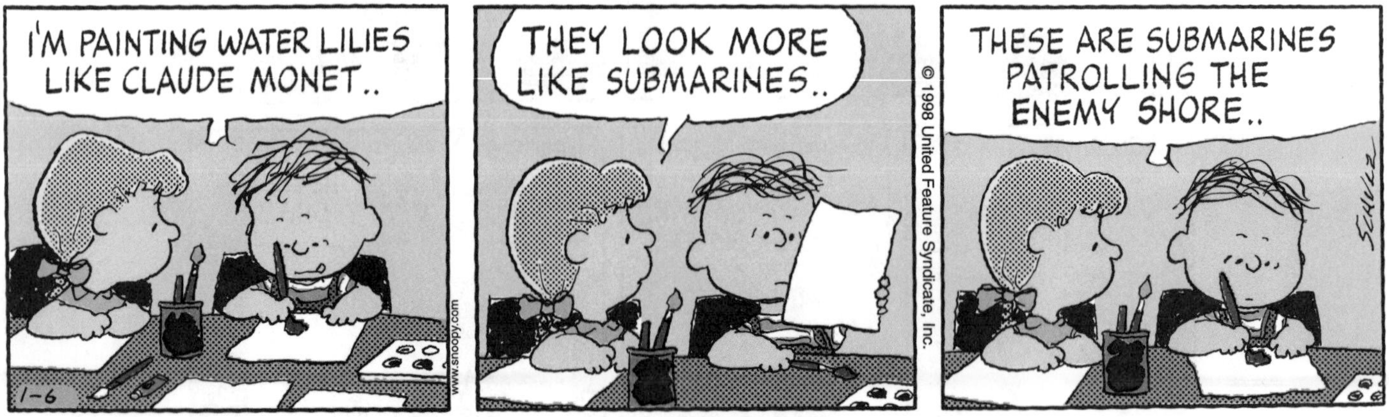

1-6
www.snoopy.com
© 1998 United Feature Syndicate, Inc.
SCHULZ
I'M PAINTING WATER LILIES LIKE CLAUDE MONET..
THEY LOOK MORE LIKE SUBMARINES..
THESE ARE SUBMARINES PATROLLING THE ENEMY SHORE..

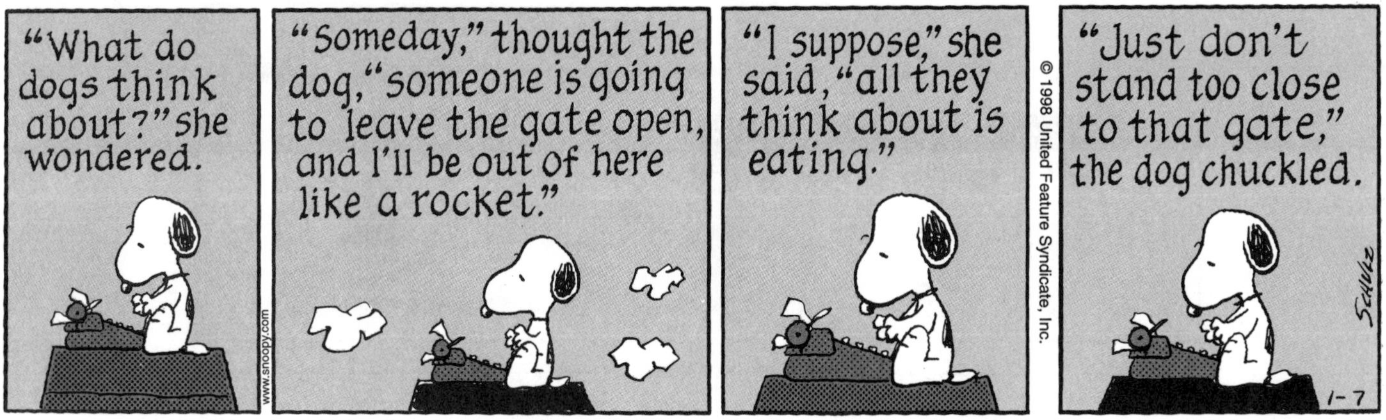
"What do dogs think about?" she wondered.
"Someday," thought the dog, "someone is going to leave the gate open, and I'll be out of here like a rocket."
"I suppose," she said, "all they think about is eating."
"Just don't stand too close to that gate," the dog chuckled.
© 1998 United Feature Syndicate, Inc.
www.snoopy.com
1-7

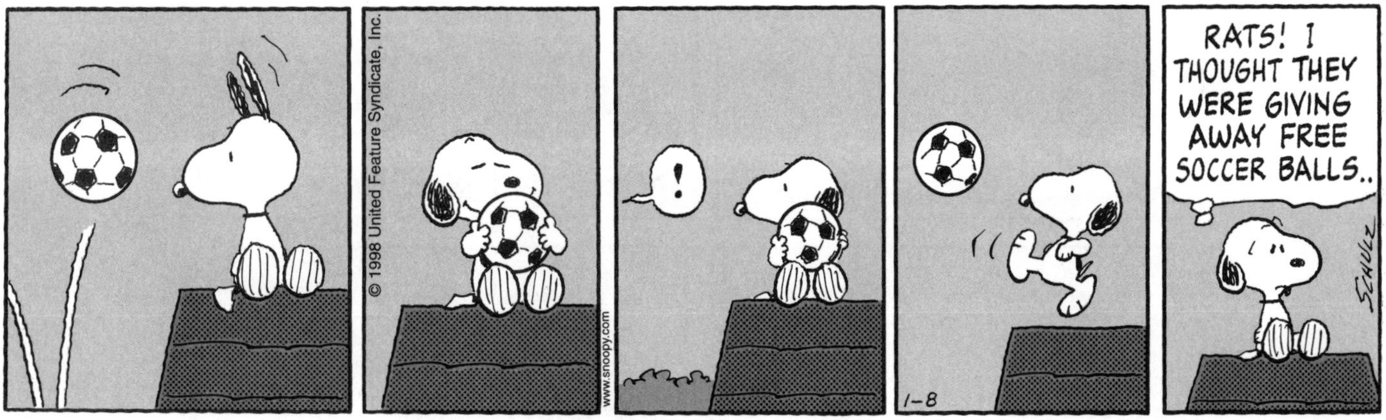
!
RATS! I THOUGHT THEY WERE GIVING AWAY FREE SOCCER BALLS..
© 1998 United Feature Syndicate, Inc.
www.snoopy.com
1-8

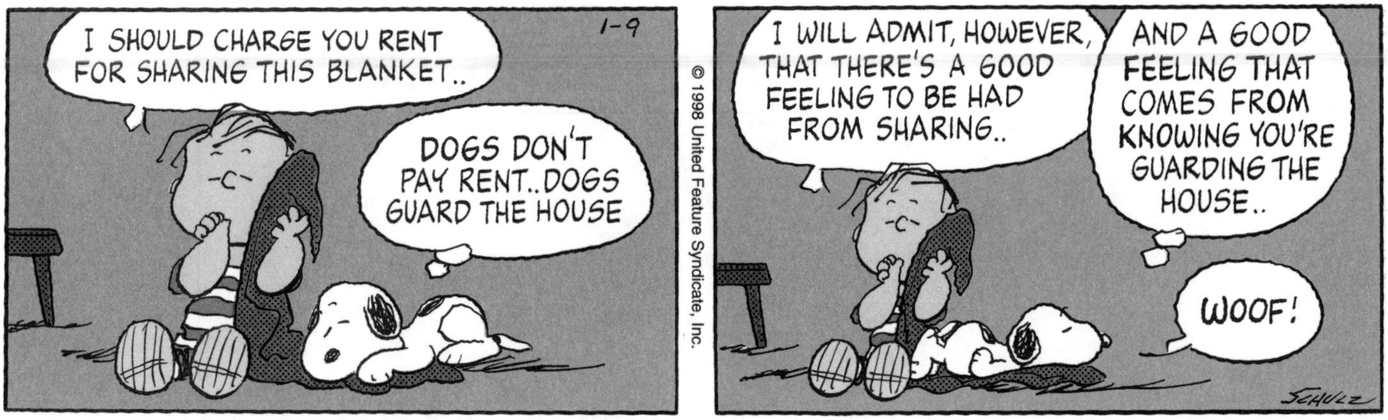
I SHOULD CHARGE YOU RENT FOR SHARING THIS BLANKET..
DOGS DON'T PAY RENT..DOGS GUARD THE HOUSE
I WILL ADMIT, HOWEVER, THAT THERE'S A GOOD FEELING TO BE HAD FROM SHARING..
AND A GOOD FEELING THAT COMES FROM KNOWING YOU'RE GUARDING THE HOUSE..
WOOF!
© 1998 United Feature Syndicate, Inc.
1-9

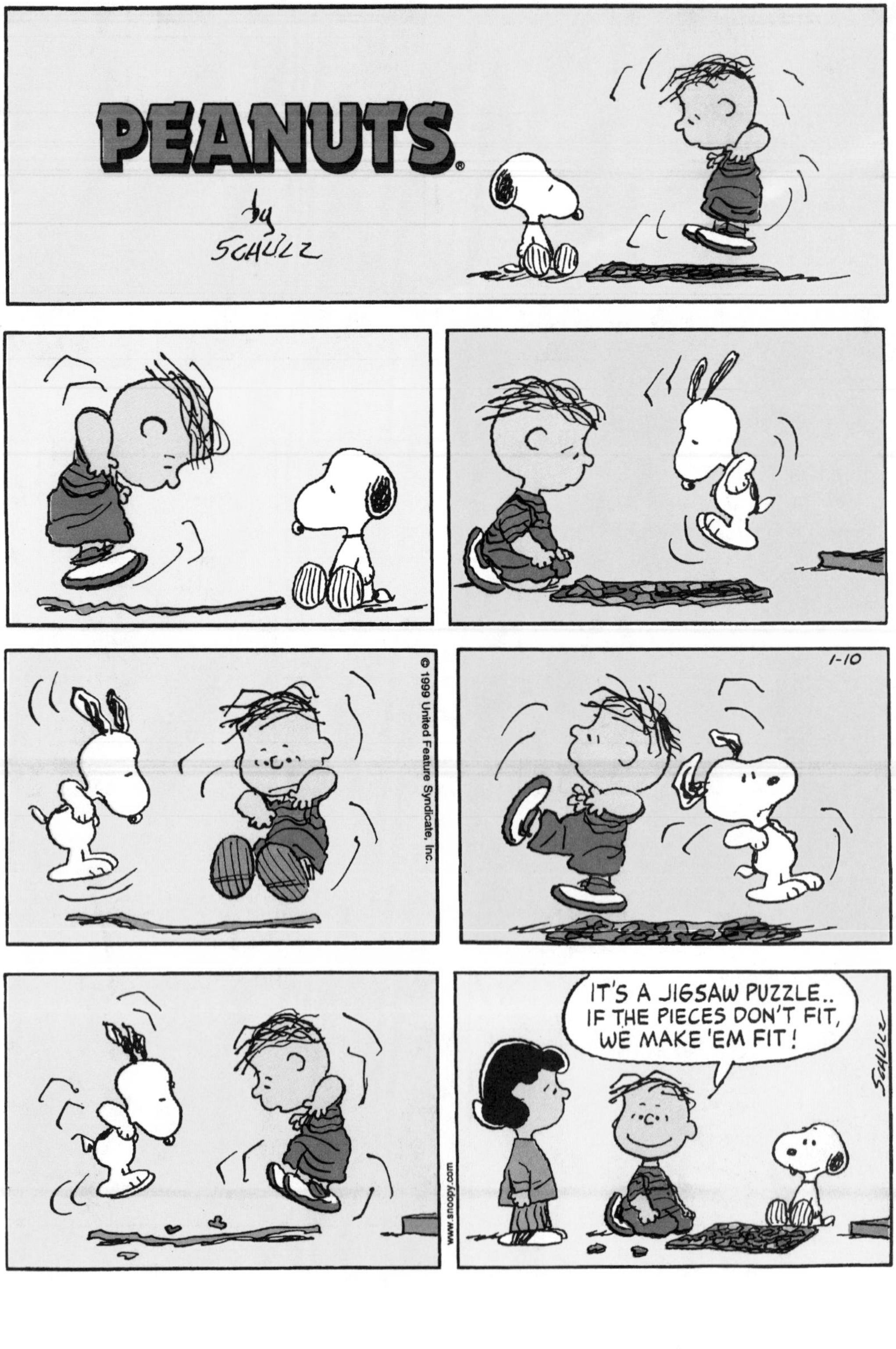
PEANUTS
by SCHULZ
© 1999 United Feature Syndicate, Inc.
1-10
www.snoopy.com
IT'S A JIGSAW PUZZLE..
IF THE PIECES DON'T FIT,
WE MAKE 'EM FIT!
SCHULZ

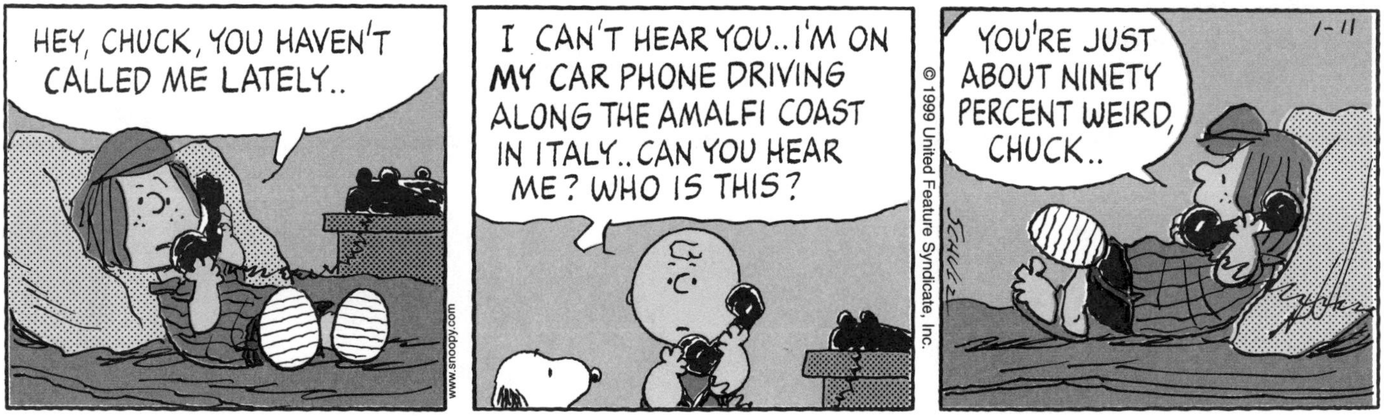
HEY, CHUCK, YOU HAVEN'T CALLED ME LATELY..
I CAN'T HEAR YOU..I'M ON MY CAR PHONE DRIVING ALONG THE AMALFI COAST IN ITALY..CAN YOU HEAR ME? WHO IS THIS?
YOU'RE JUST ABOUT NINETY PERCENT WEIRD, CHUCK..
1-11
SCHULZ
www.snoopy.com
© 1999 United Feature Syndicate, Inc.

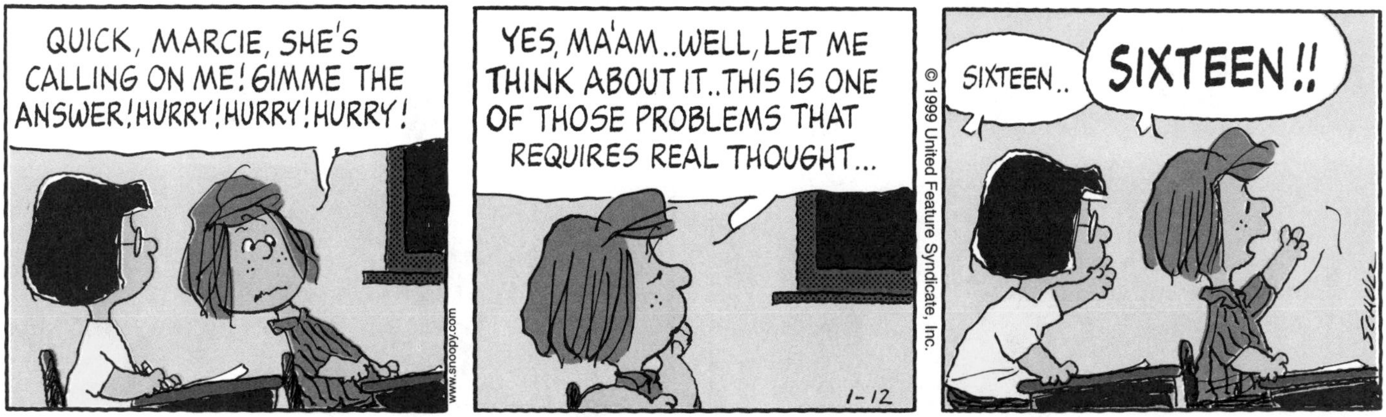
QUICK, MARCIE, SHE'S CALLING ON ME! GIMME THE ANSWER! HURRY! HURRY! HURRY!
YES, MA'AM..WELL, LET ME THINK ABOUT IT..THIS IS ONE OF THOSE PROBLEMS THAT REQUIRES REAL THOUGHT...
SIXTEEN..
SIXTEEN!!
1-12
SCHULZ
www.snoopy.com
© 1999 United Feature Syndicate, Inc.

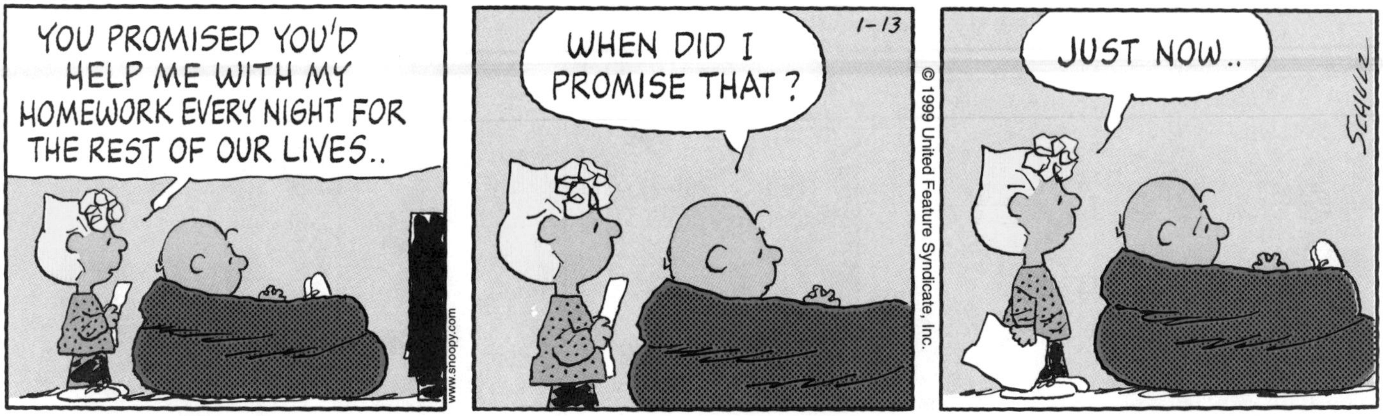
YOU PROMISED YOU'D HELP ME WITH MY HOMEWORK EVERY NIGHT FOR THE REST OF OUR LIVES..
WHEN DID I PROMISE THAT?
JUST NOW..
1-13
SCHULZ
www.snoopy.com
© 1999 United Feature Syndicate, Inc.

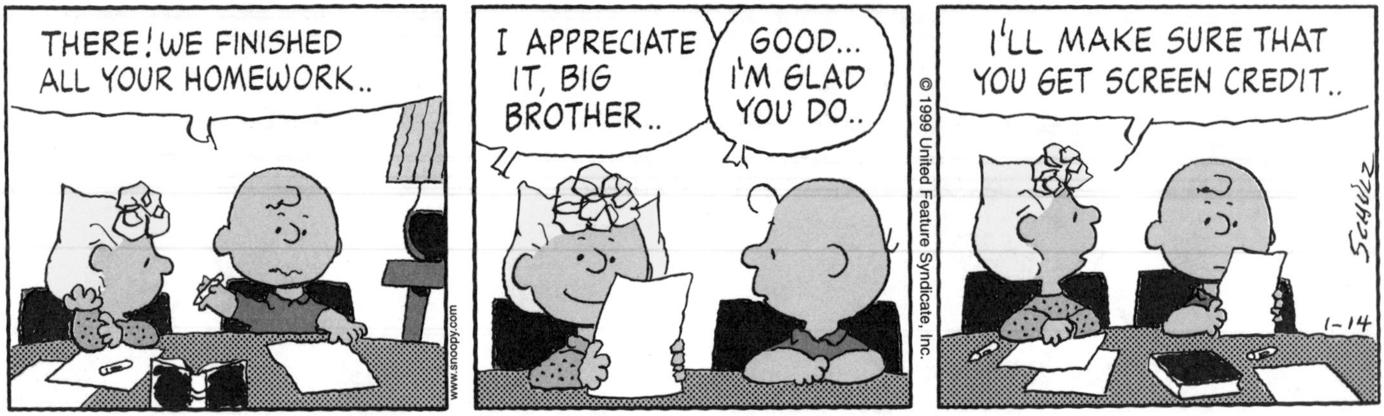
THERE! WE FINISHED ALL YOUR HOMEWORK..
I APPRECIATE IT, BIG BROTHER..
GOOD... I'M GLAD YOU DO..
I'LL MAKE SURE THAT YOU GET SCREEN CREDIT..
www.snoopy.com
© 1999 United Feature Syndicate, Inc.
SCHULZ
1-14

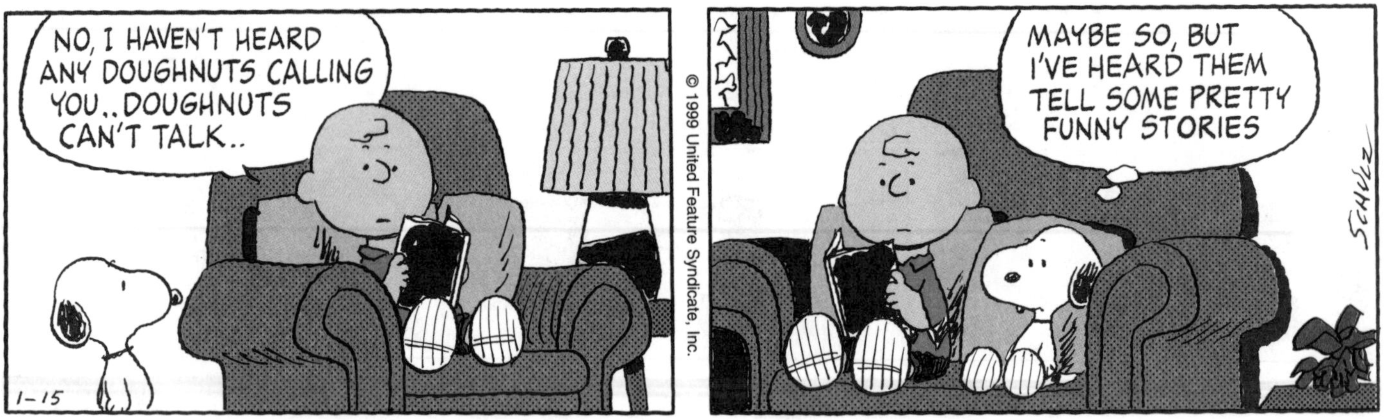
NO, I HAVEN'T HEARD ANY DOUGHNUTS CALLING YOU.. DOUGHNUTS CAN'T TALK..
MAYBE SO, BUT I'VE HEARD THEM TELL SOME PRETTY FUNNY STORIES
© 1999 United Feature Syndicate, Inc.
1-15
SCHULZ

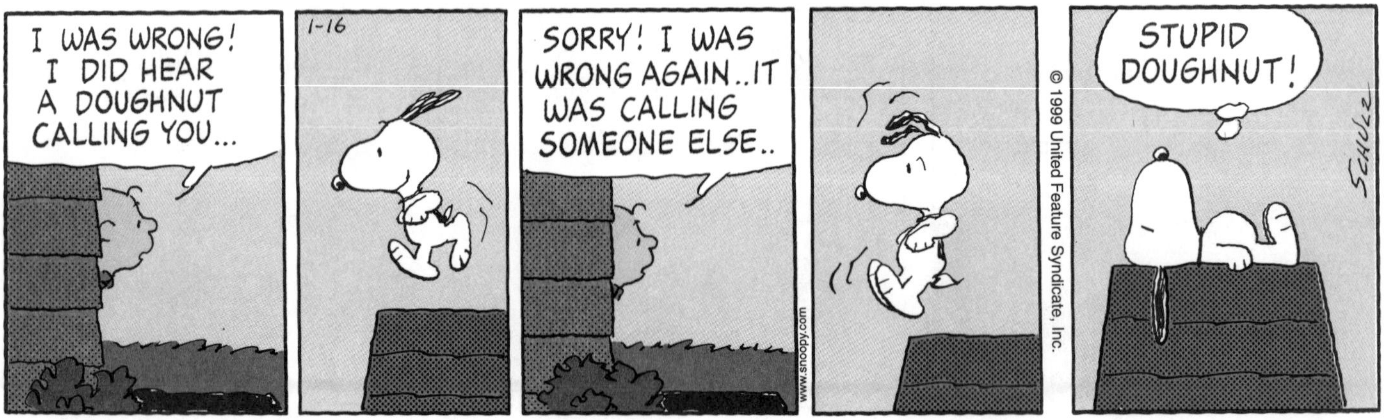
I WAS WRONG! I DID HEAR A DOUGHNUT CALLING YOU...
1-16
SORRY! I WAS WRONG AGAIN.. IT WAS CALLING SOMEONE ELSE..
STUPID DOUGHNUT!
www.snoopy.com
© 1999 United Feature Syndicate, Inc.
SCHULZ

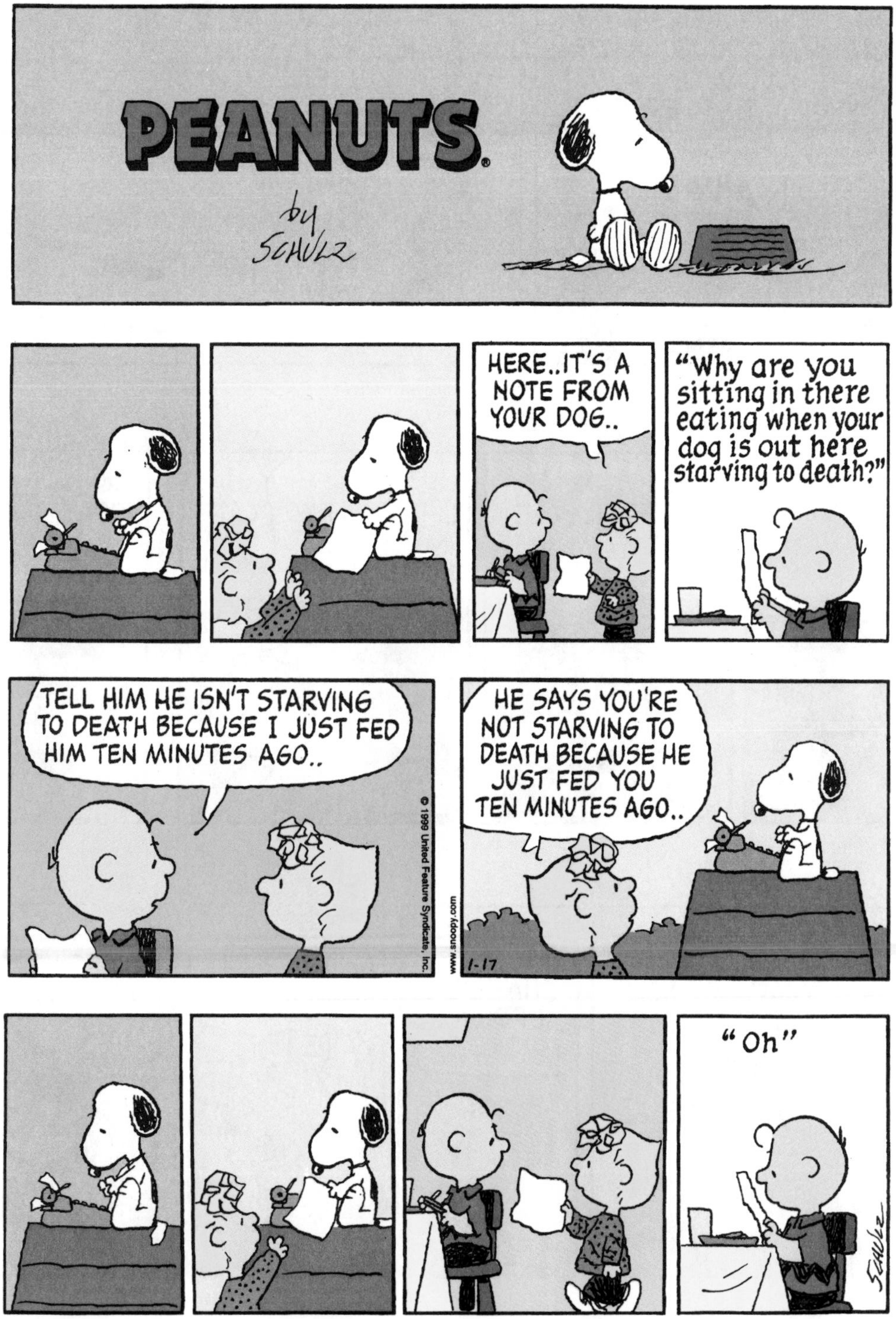
PEANUTS
by SCHULZ
HERE..IT'S A NOTE FROM YOUR DOG..
"Why are you sitting in there eating when your dog is out here starving to death?"
TELL HIM HE ISN'T STARVING TO DEATH BECAUSE I JUST FED HIM TEN MINUTES AGO..
© 1999 United Feature Syndicate, Inc.
www.snoopy.com
1-17
HE SAYS YOU'RE NOT STARVING TO DEATH BECAUSE HE JUST FED YOU TEN MINUTES AGO..
"Oh"
SCHULZ

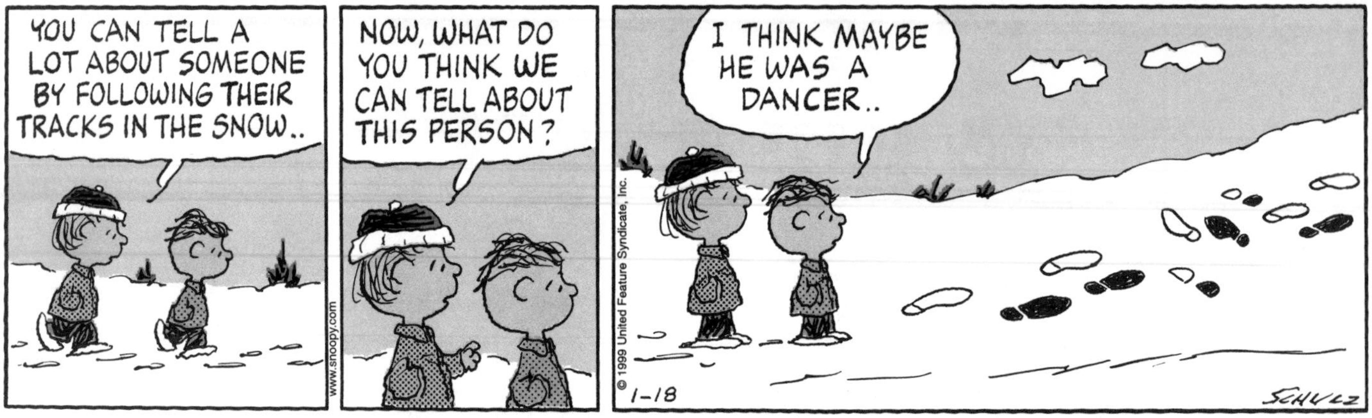
YOU CAN TELL A LOT ABOUT SOMEONE BY FOLLOWING THEIR TRACKS IN THE SNOW..
NOW, WHAT DO YOU THINK WE CAN TELL ABOUT THIS PERSON?
I THINK MAYBE HE WAS A DANCER..
www.snoopy.com
© 1999 United Feature Syndicate, Inc.
1-18
SCHULZ

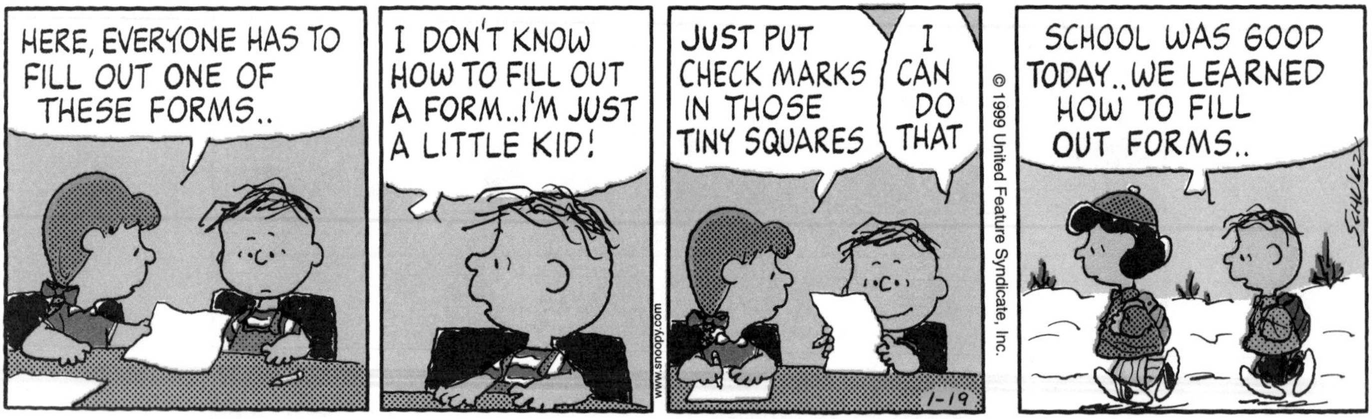
HERE, EVERYONE HAS TO FILL OUT ONE OF THESE FORMS..
I DON'T KNOW HOW TO FILL OUT A FORM..I'M JUST A LITTLE KID!
JUST PUT CHECK MARKS IN THOSE TINY SQUARES
I CAN DO THAT
SCHOOL WAS GOOD TODAY..WE LEARNED HOW TO FILL OUT FORMS..
www.snoopy.com
© 1999 United Feature Syndicate, Inc.
1-19
SCHULZ

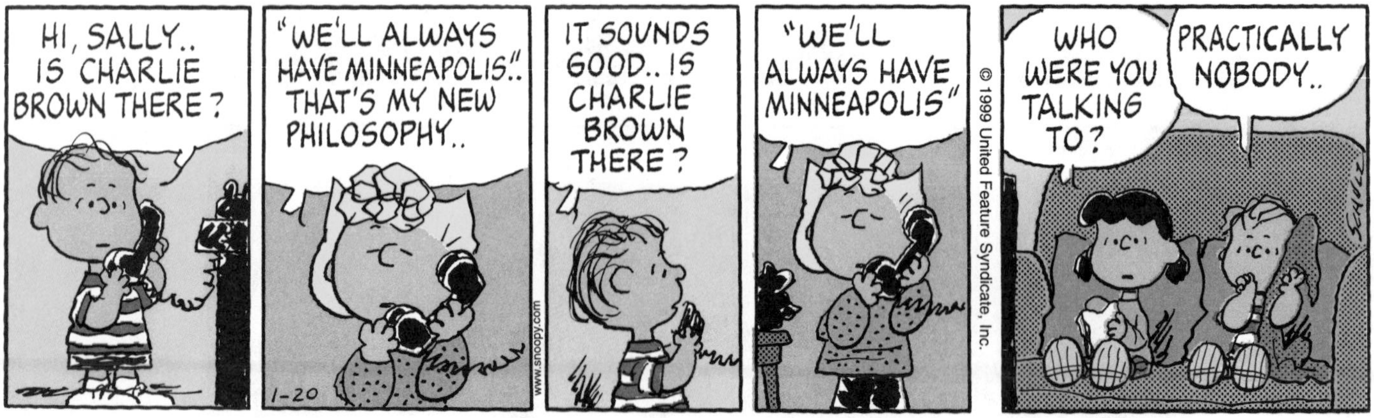
HI, SALLY.. IS CHARLIE BROWN THERE?
"WE'LL ALWAYS HAVE MINNEAPOLIS".. THAT'S MY NEW PHILOSOPHY..
IT SOUNDS GOOD.. IS CHARLIE BROWN THERE?
"WE'LL ALWAYS HAVE MINNEAPOLIS"
WHO WERE YOU TALKING TO?
PRACTICALLY NOBODY..
www.snoopy.com
© 1999 United Feature Syndicate, Inc.
1-20
SCHULZ

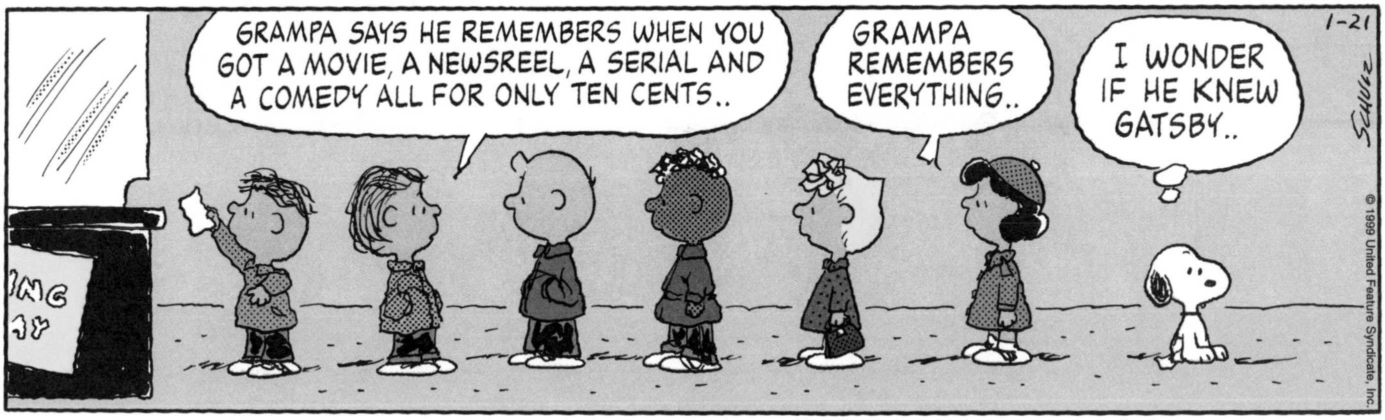
1-21
GRAMPA SAYS HE REMEMBERS WHEN YOU GOT A MOVIE, A NEWSREEL, A SERIAL AND A COMEDY ALL FOR ONLY TEN CENTS..
GRAMPA REMEMBERS EVERYTHING..
I WONDER IF HE KNEW GATSBY..
SCHULZ
© 1999 United Feature Syndicate, Inc.

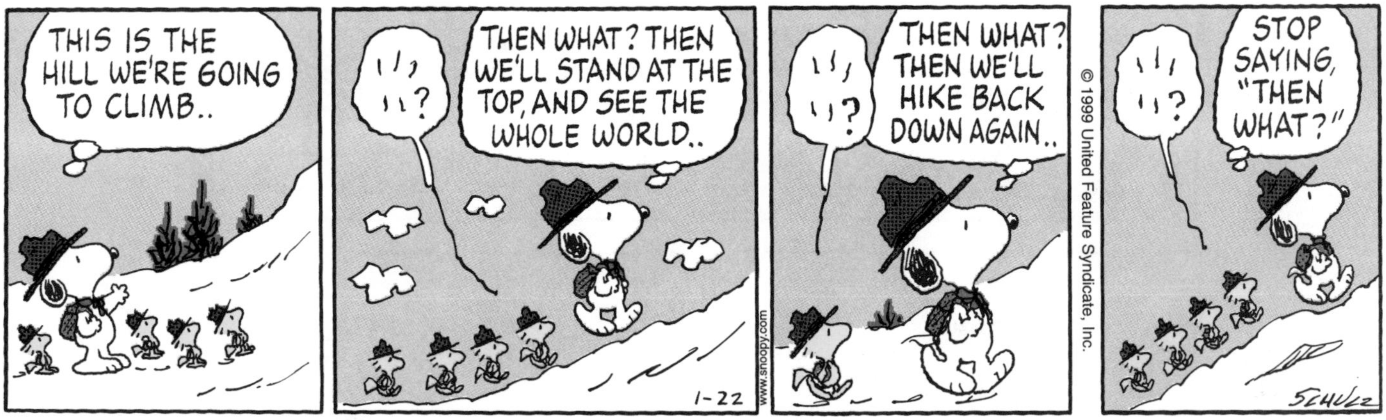
THIS IS THE HILL WE'RE GOING TO CLIMB..
THEN WHAT? THEN WE'LL STAND AT THE TOP, AND SEE THE WHOLE WORLD..
1-22
www.snoopy.com
THEN WHAT? THEN WE'LL HIKE BACK DOWN AGAIN..
© 1999 United Feature Syndicate, Inc.
STOP SAYING, "THEN WHAT?"
SCHULZ

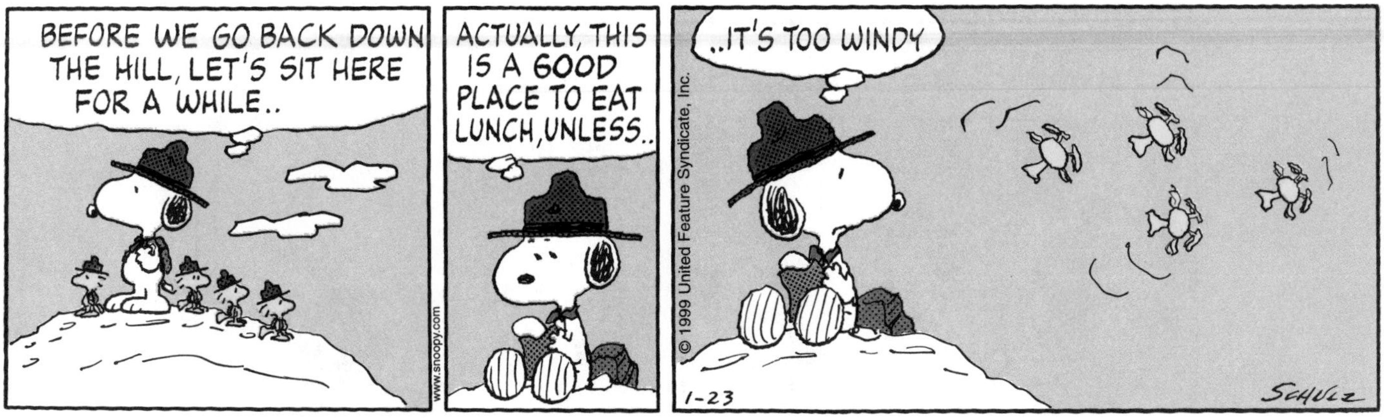
BEFORE WE GO BACK DOWN THE HILL, LET'S SIT HERE FOR A WHILE..
www.snoopy.com
ACTUALLY, THIS IS A GOOD PLACE TO EAT LUNCH, UNLESS..
© 1999 United Feature Syndicate, Inc.
..IT'S TOO WINDY
1-23
SCHULZ

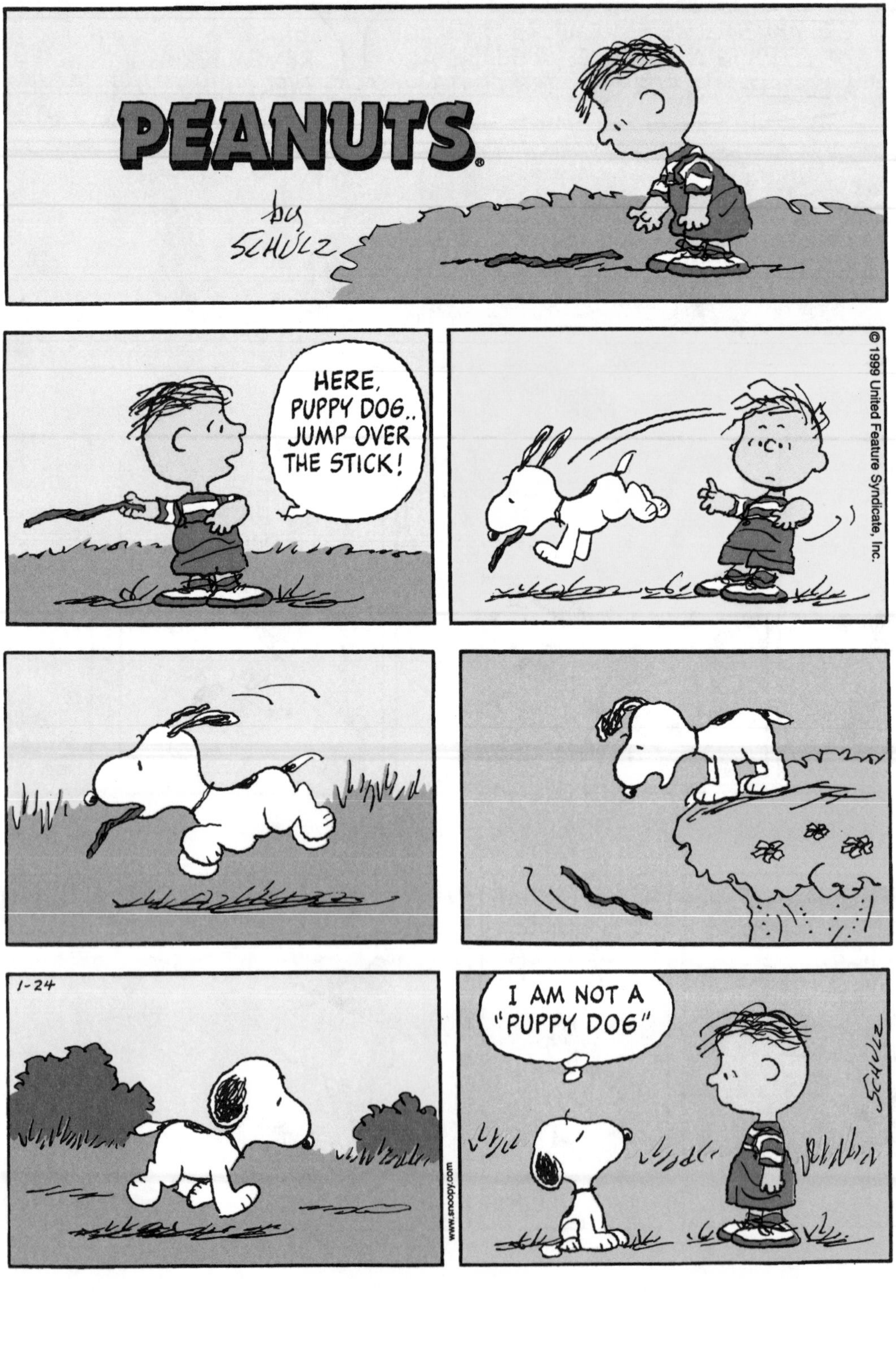
PEANUTS
by SCHULZ
HERE, PUPPY DOG.. JUMP OVER THE STICK!
© 1999 United Feature Syndicate, Inc.
1-24
www.snoopy.com
I AM NOT A "PUPPY DOG"
SCHULZ

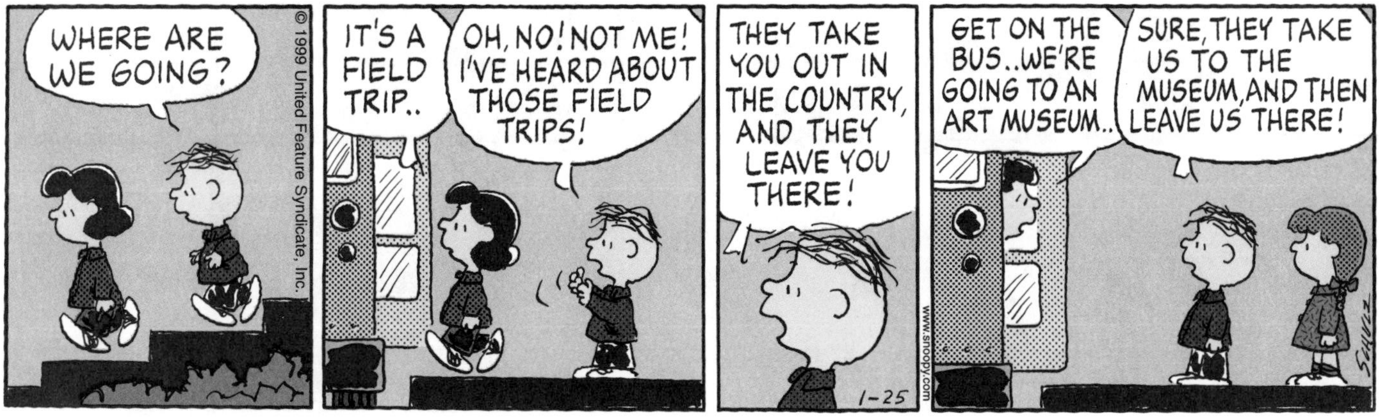
WHERE ARE WE GOING?
© 1999 United Feature Syndicate, Inc.
IT'S A FIELD TRIP..
OH, NO! NOT ME! I'VE HEARD ABOUT THOSE FIELD TRIPS!
THEY TAKE YOU OUT IN THE COUNTRY, AND THEY LEAVE YOU THERE!
1-25
www.snoopy.com
GET ON THE BUS..WE'RE GOING TO AN ART MUSEUM..
SURE, THEY TAKE US TO THE MUSEUM, AND THEN LEAVE US THERE!
SCHULZ

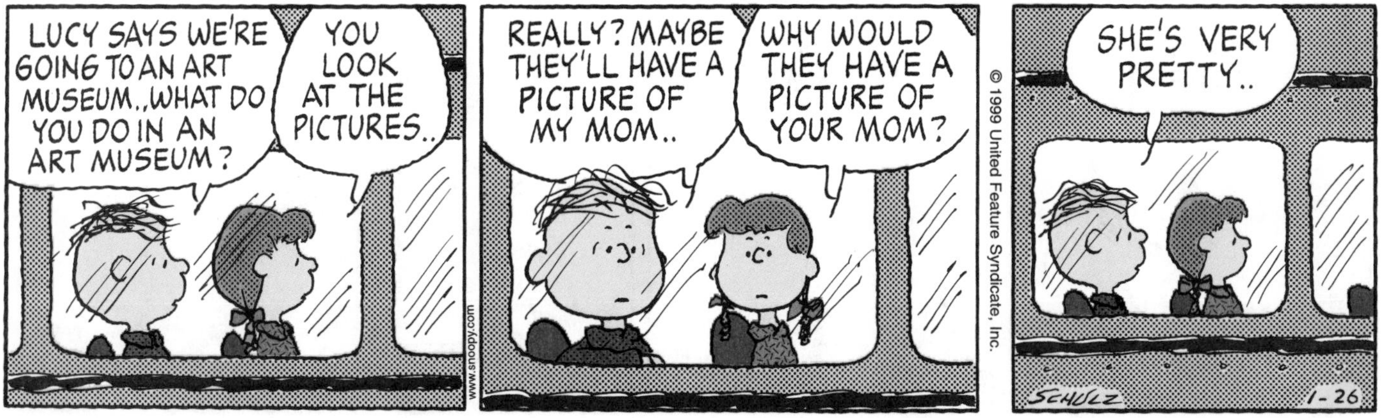
LUCY SAYS WE'RE GOING TO AN ART MUSEUM..WHAT DO YOU DO IN AN ART MUSEUM?
YOU LOOK AT THE PICTURES..
www.snoopy.com
REALLY? MAYBE THEY'LL HAVE A PICTURE OF MY MOM..
WHY WOULD THEY HAVE A PICTURE OF YOUR MOM?
© 1999 United Feature Syndicate, Inc.
SHE'S VERY PRETTY..
SCHULZ
1-26

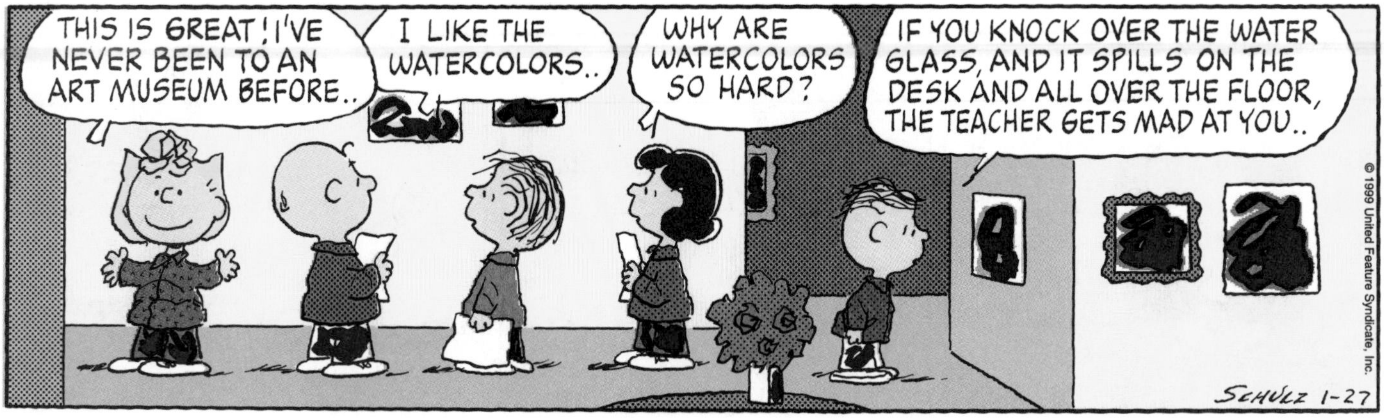
THIS IS GREAT! I'VE NEVER BEEN TO AN ART MUSEUM BEFORE..
I LIKE THE WATERCOLORS..
WHY ARE WATERCOLORS SO HARD?
IF YOU KNOCK OVER THE WATER GLASS, AND IT SPILLS ON THE DESK AND ALL OVER THE FLOOR, THE TEACHER GETS MAD AT YOU..
© 1999 United Feature Syndicate, Inc.
SCHULZ 1-27

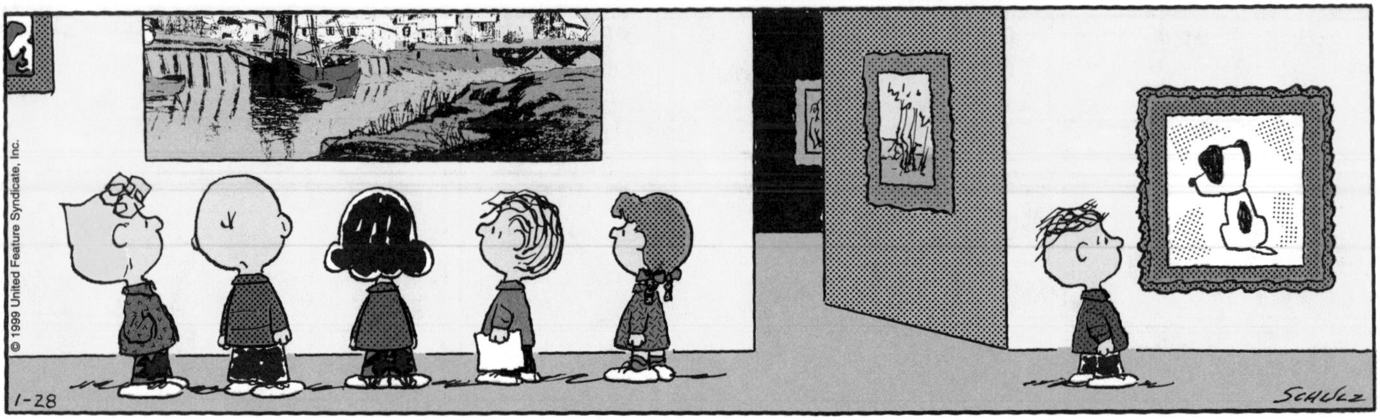
© 1999 United Feature Syndicate, Inc.
1-28
SCHULZ

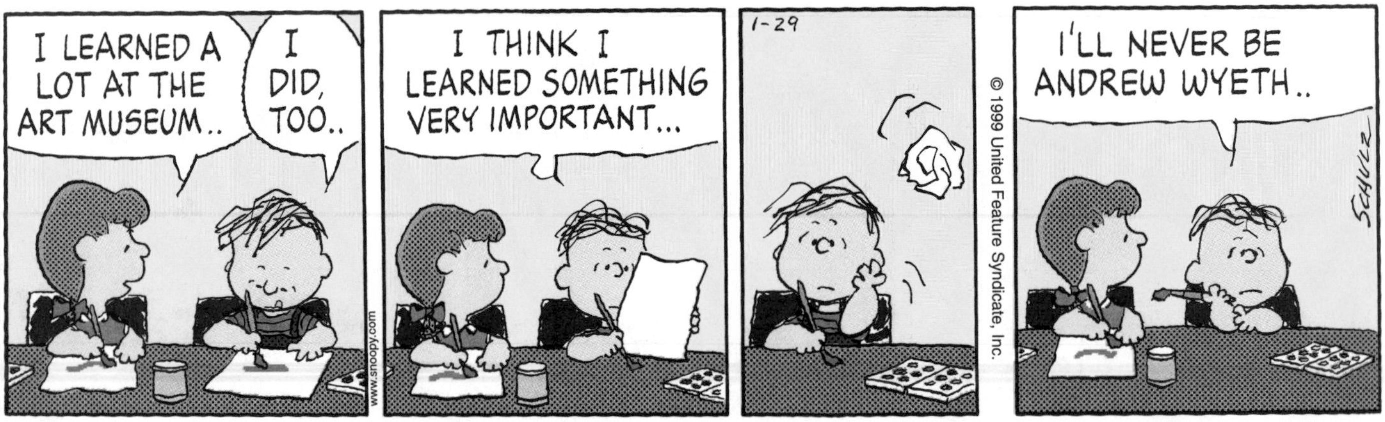
I LEARNED A LOT AT THE ART MUSEUM..
I DID, TOO..
www.snoopy.com
I THINK I LEARNED SOMETHING VERY IMPORTANT...
1-29
© 1999 United Feature Syndicate, Inc.
I'LL NEVER BE ANDREW WYETH..
SCHULZ

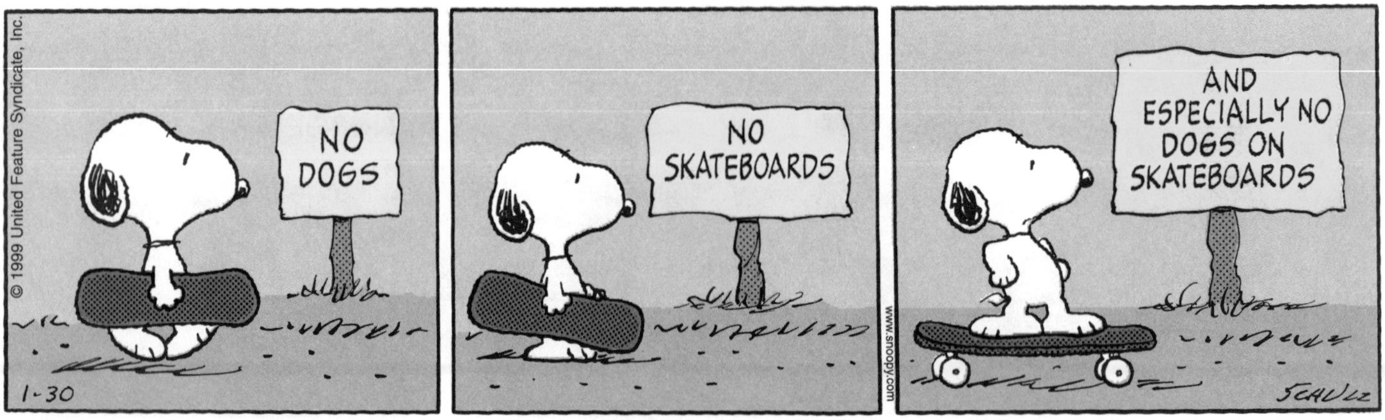
© 1999 United Feature Syndicate, Inc.
NO DOGS
1-30
NO SKATEBOARDS
www.snoopy.com
AND ESPECIALLY NO DOGS ON SKATEBOARDS
SCHULZ

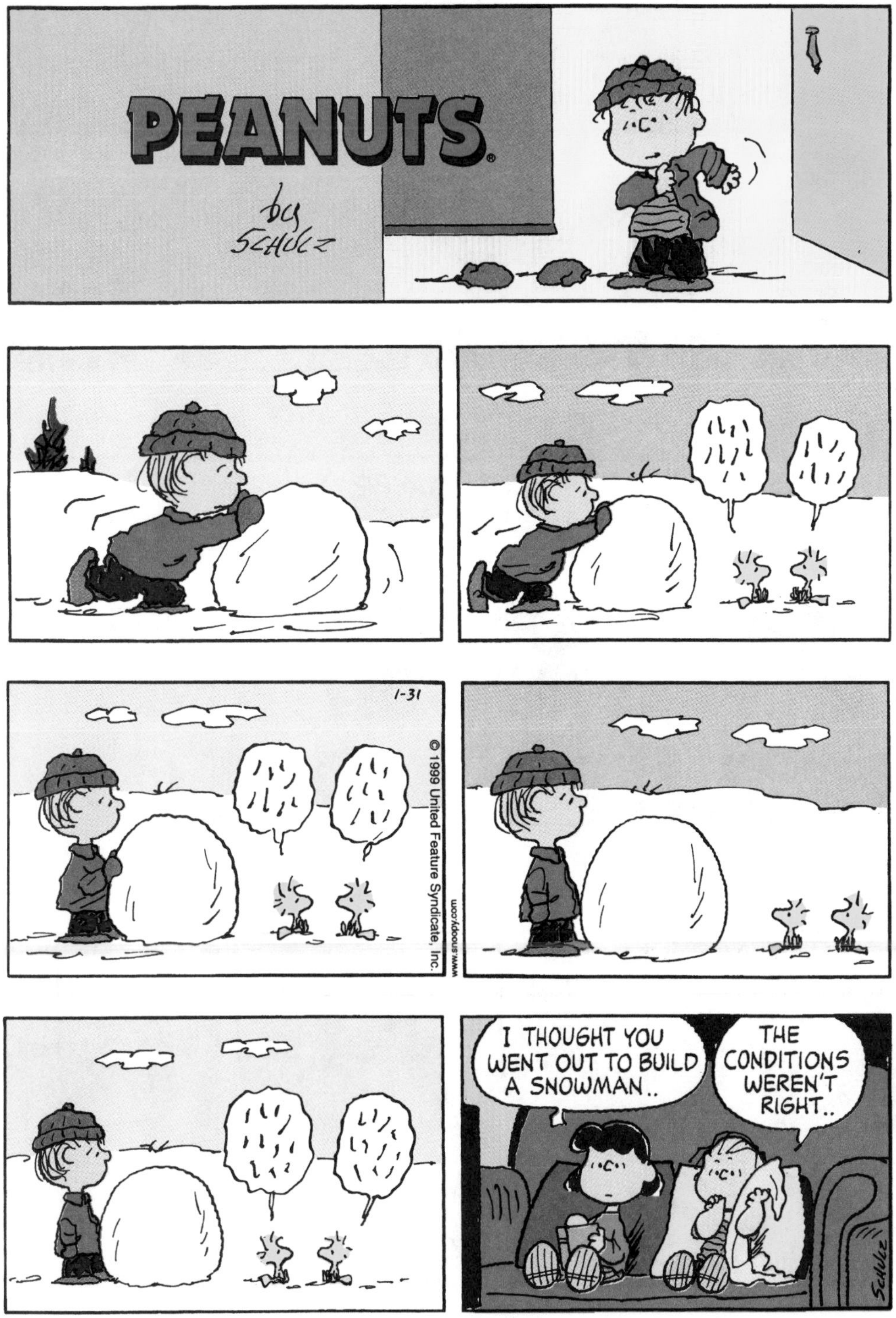
PEANUTS
by SCHULZ
1-31
© 1999 United Feature Syndicate, Inc.
www.snoopy.com
I THOUGHT YOU WENT OUT TO BUILD A SNOWMAN..
THE CONDITIONS WEREN'T RIGHT..
SCHULZ

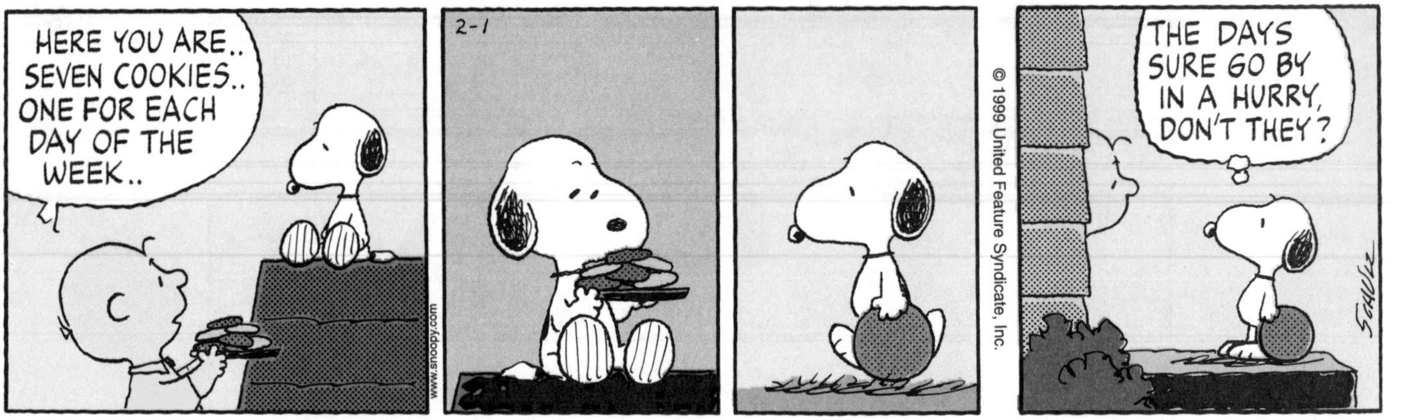
HERE YOU ARE.. SEVEN COOKIES.. ONE FOR EACH DAY OF THE WEEK..
2-1
www.snoopy.com
THE DAYS SURE GO BY IN A HURRY, DON'T THEY?
© 1999 United Feature Syndicate, Inc.
SCHULZ

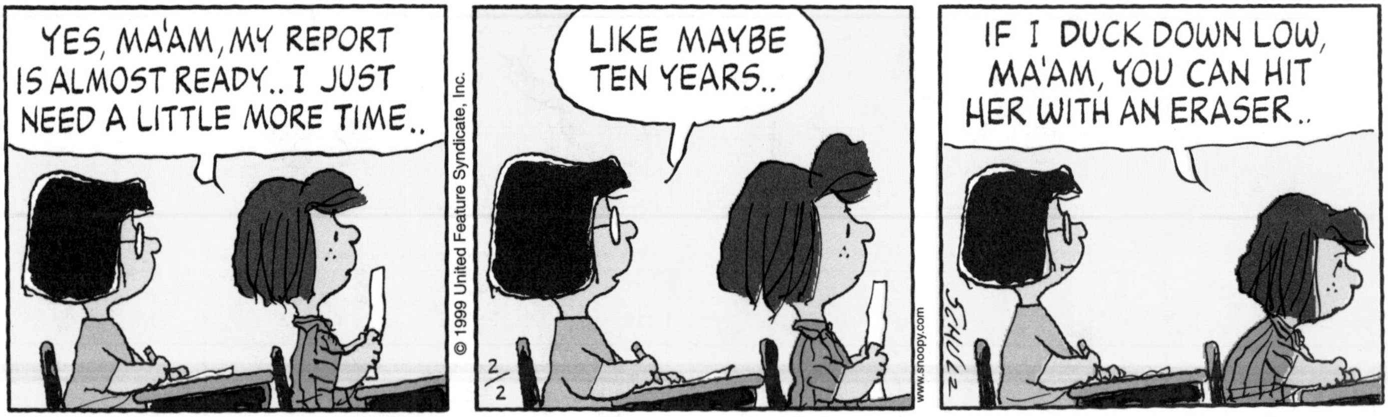
YES, MA'AM, MY REPORT IS ALMOST READY.. I JUST NEED A LITTLE MORE TIME..
© 1999 United Feature Syndicate, Inc.
LIKE MAYBE TEN YEARS..
2/2
www.snoopy.com
IF I DUCK DOWN LOW, MA'AM, YOU CAN HIT HER WITH AN ERASER..
SCHULZ

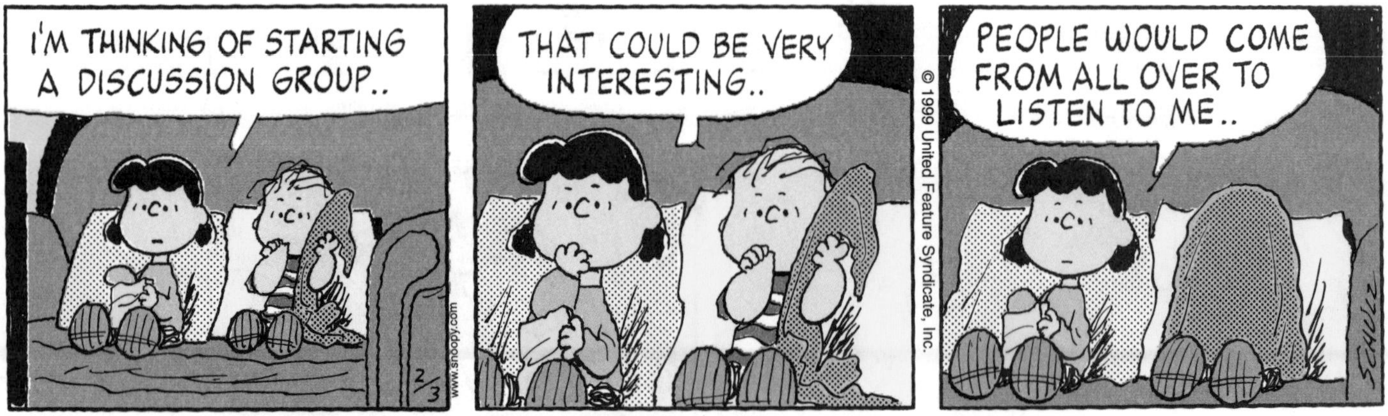
I'M THINKING OF STARTING A DISCUSSION GROUP..
2/3
www.snoopy.com
THAT COULD BE VERY INTERESTING..
© 1999 United Feature Syndicate, Inc.
PEOPLE WOULD COME FROM ALL OVER TO LISTEN TO ME..
SCHULZ

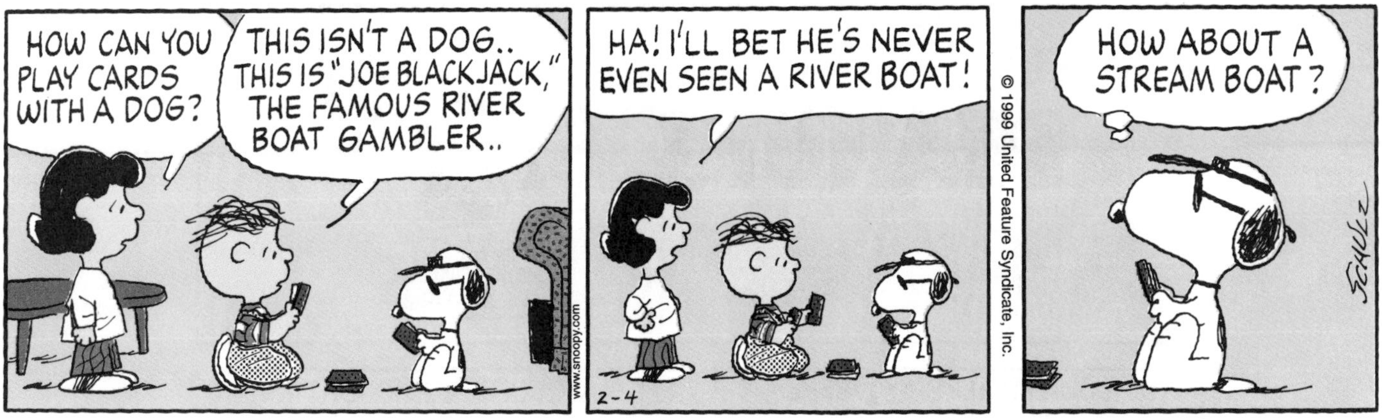
HOW CAN YOU PLAY CARDS WITH A DOG?
THIS ISN'T A DOG.. THIS IS "JOE BLACKJACK," THE FAMOUS RIVER BOAT GAMBLER..
www.snoopy.com
HA! I'LL BET HE'S NEVER EVEN SEEN A RIVER BOAT!
2-4
© 1999 United Feature Syndicate, Inc.
HOW ABOUT A STREAM BOAT?
SCHULZ

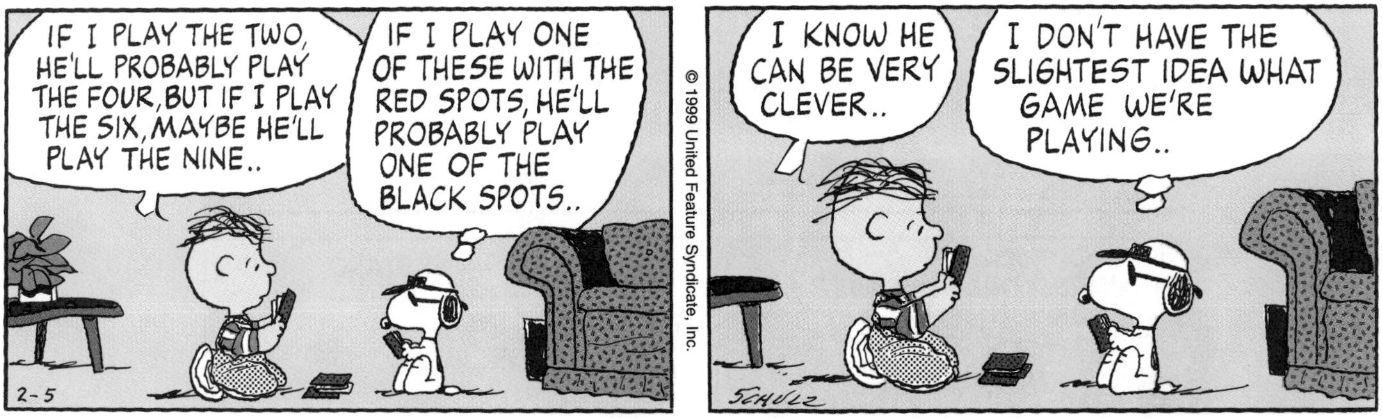
IF I PLAY THE TWO, HE'LL PROBABLY PLAY THE FOUR, BUT IF I PLAY THE SIX, MAYBE HE'LL PLAY THE NINE..
IF I PLAY ONE OF THESE WITH THE RED SPOTS, HE'LL PROBABLY PLAY ONE OF THE BLACK SPOTS..
2-5
© 1999 United Feature Syndicate, Inc.
I KNOW HE CAN BE VERY CLEVER..
I DON'T HAVE THE SLIGHTEST IDEA WHAT GAME WE'RE PLAYING..
SCHULZ

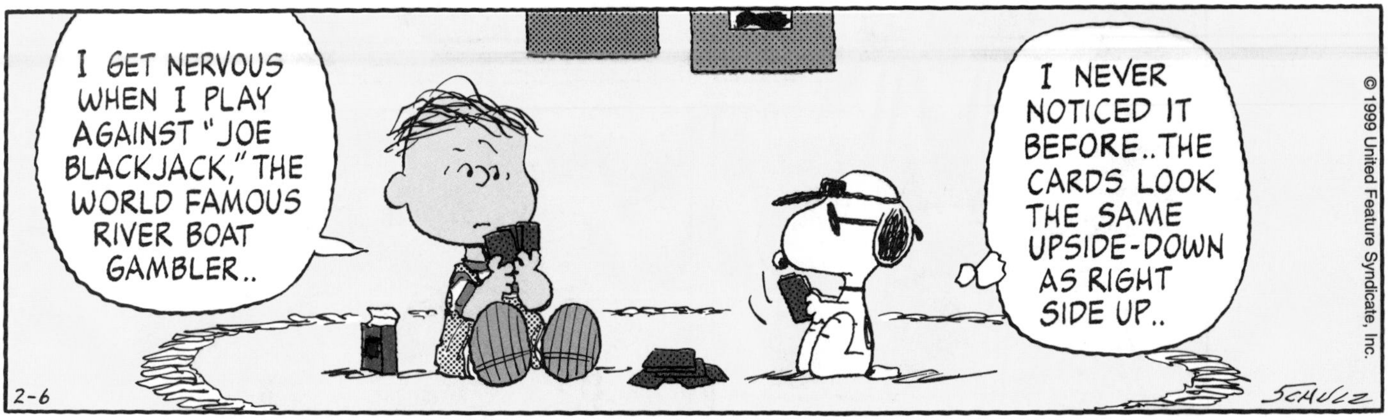
I GET NERVOUS WHEN I PLAY AGAINST "JOE BLACKJACK," THE WORLD FAMOUS RIVER BOAT GAMBLER..
I NEVER NOTICED IT BEFORE..THE CARDS LOOK THE SAME UPSIDE-DOWN AS RIGHT SIDE UP..
2-6
SCHULZ
© 1999 United Feature Syndicate, Inc.

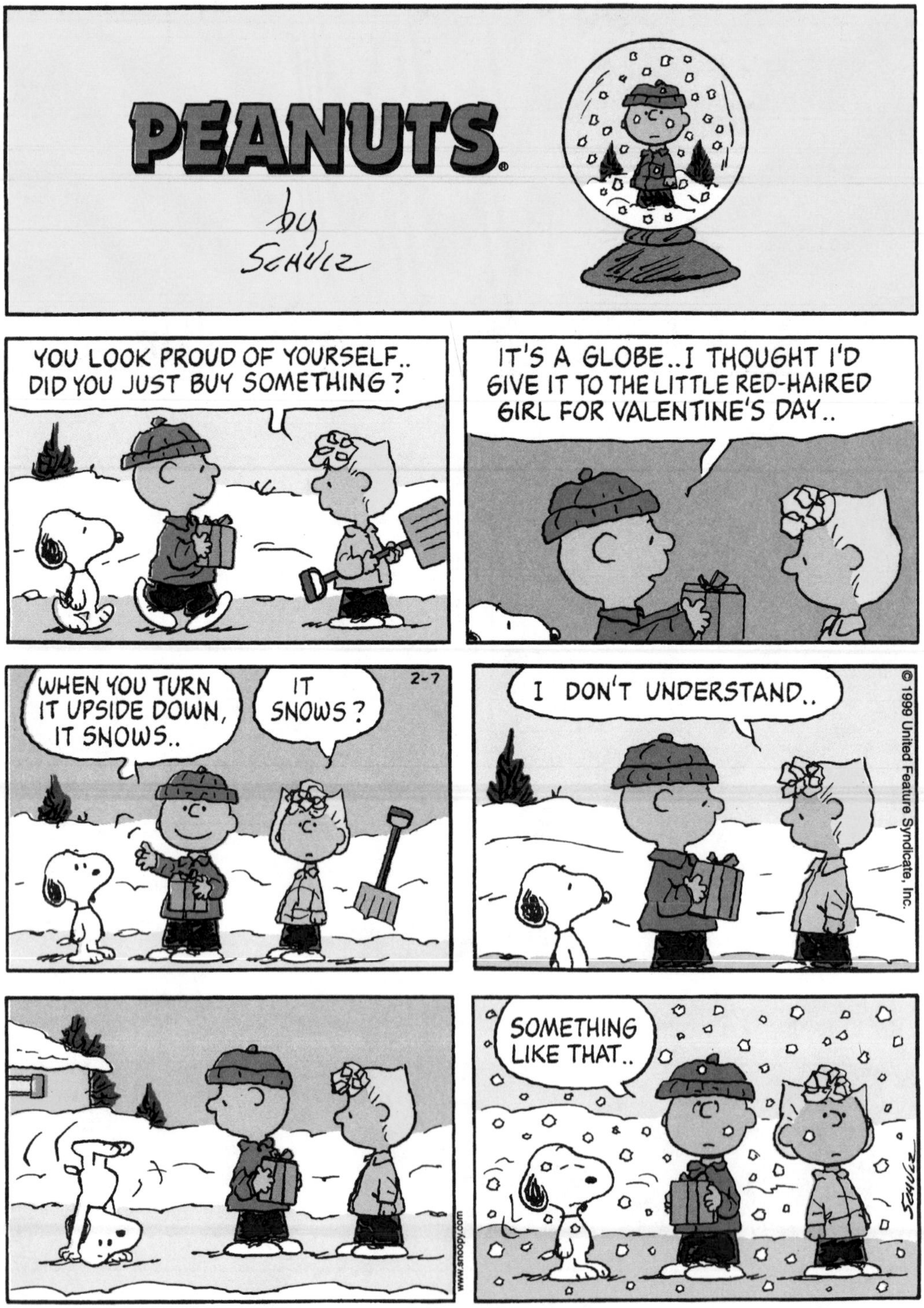
PEANUTS
by SCHULZ
YOU LOOK PROUD OF YOURSELF.. DID YOU JUST BUY SOMETHING?
IT'S A GLOBE..I THOUGHT I'D GIVE IT TO THE LITTLE RED-HAIRED GIRL FOR VALENTINE'S DAY..
2-7
WHEN YOU TURN IT UPSIDE DOWN, IT SNOWS..
IT SNOWS?
I DON'T UNDERSTAND..
© 1999 United Feature Syndicate, Inc.
www.snoopy.com
SOMETHING LIKE THAT..
SCHULZ

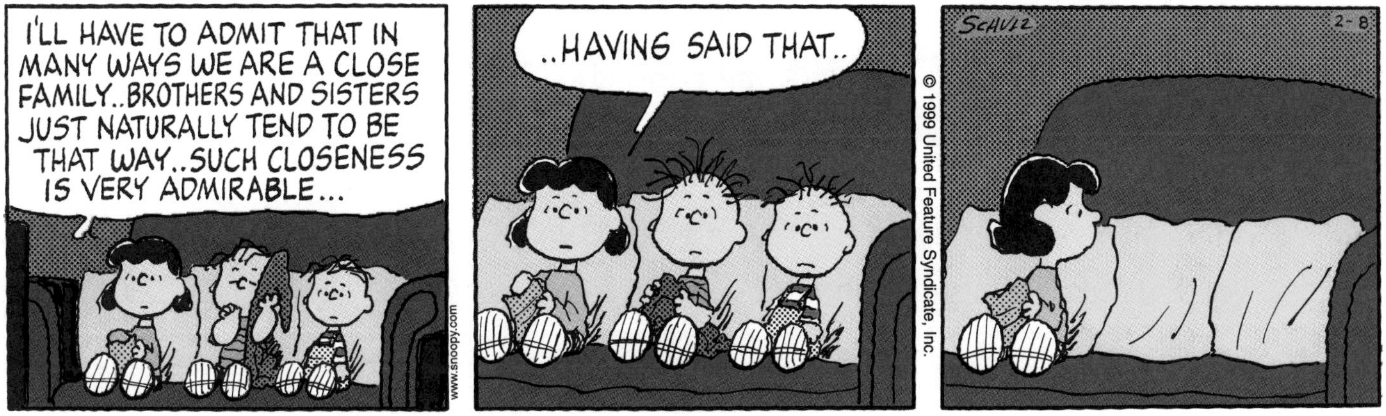
I'LL HAVE TO ADMIT THAT IN MANY WAYS WE ARE A CLOSE FAMILY..BROTHERS AND SISTERS JUST NATURALLY TEND TO BE THAT WAY..SUCH CLOSENESS IS VERY ADMIRABLE...
www.snoopy.com
..HAVING SAID THAT..
© 1999 United Feature Syndicate, Inc.
SCHULZ
2-8

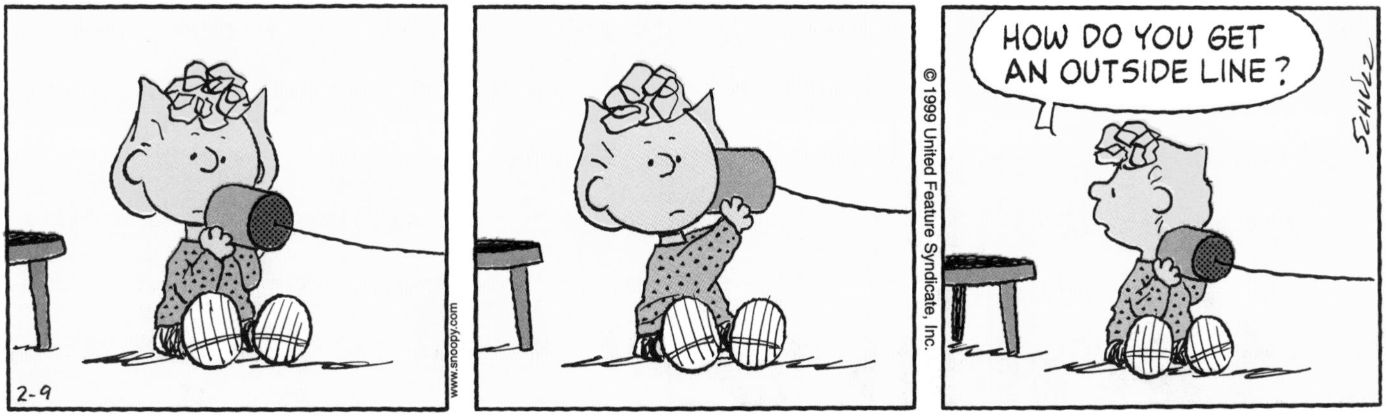
2-9
www.snoopy.com
© 1999 United Feature Syndicate, Inc.
HOW DO YOU GET AN OUTSIDE LINE?
SCHULZ

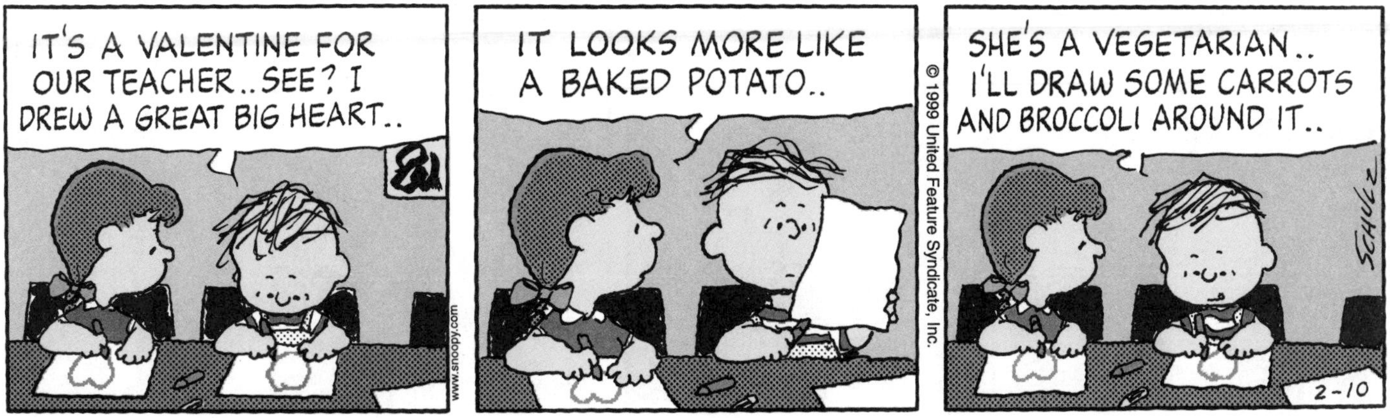
IT'S A VALENTINE FOR OUR TEACHER..SEE? I DREW A GREAT BIG HEART..
www.snoopy.com
IT LOOKS MORE LIKE A BAKED POTATO..
© 1999 United Feature Syndicate, Inc.
SHE'S A VEGETARIAN.. I'LL DRAW SOME CARROTS AND BROCCOLI AROUND IT..
SCHULZ
2-10

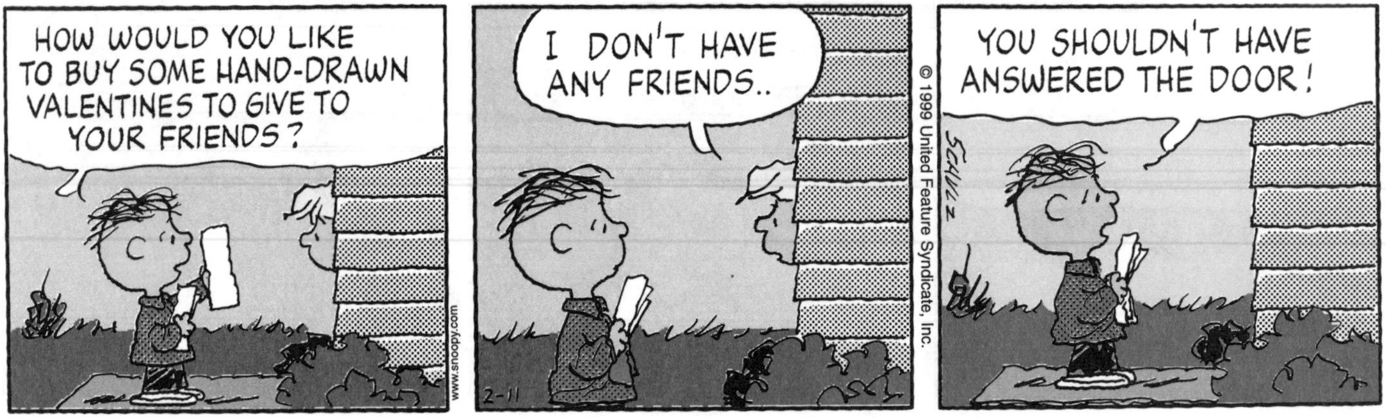
HOW WOULD YOU LIKE TO BUY SOME HAND-DRAWN VALENTINES TO GIVE TO YOUR FRIENDS?
www.snoopy.com
2-11
I DON'T HAVE ANY FRIENDS..
© 1999 United Feature Syndicate, Inc.
SCHULZ
YOU SHOULDN'T HAVE ANSWERED THE DOOR!

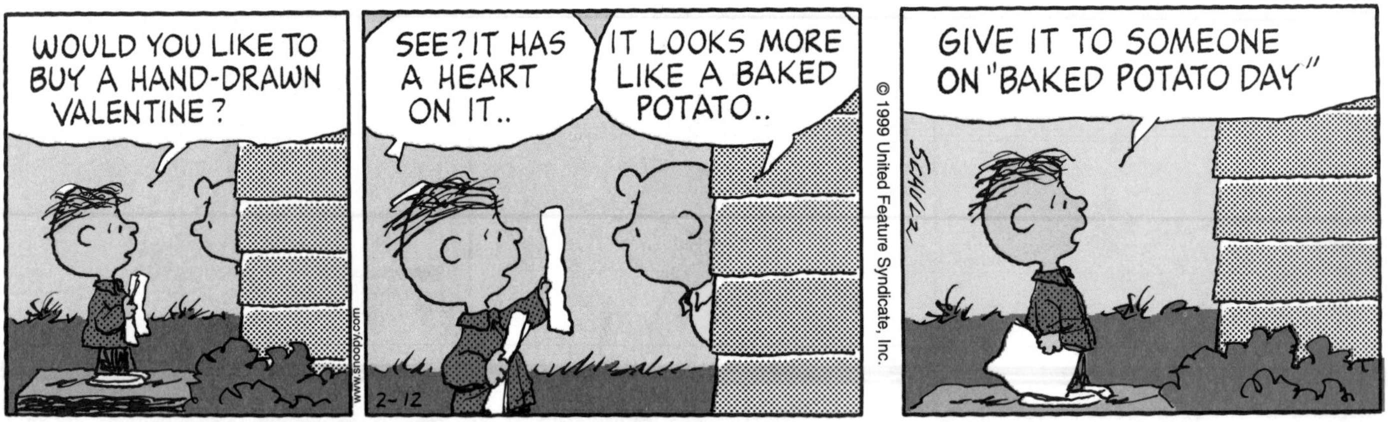
WOULD YOU LIKE TO BUY A HAND-DRAWN VALENTINE?
www.snoopy.com
2-12
SEE? IT HAS A HEART ON IT..
IT LOOKS MORE LIKE A BAKED POTATO..
© 1999 United Feature Syndicate, Inc.
SCHULZ
GIVE IT TO SOMEONE ON "BAKED POTATO DAY"

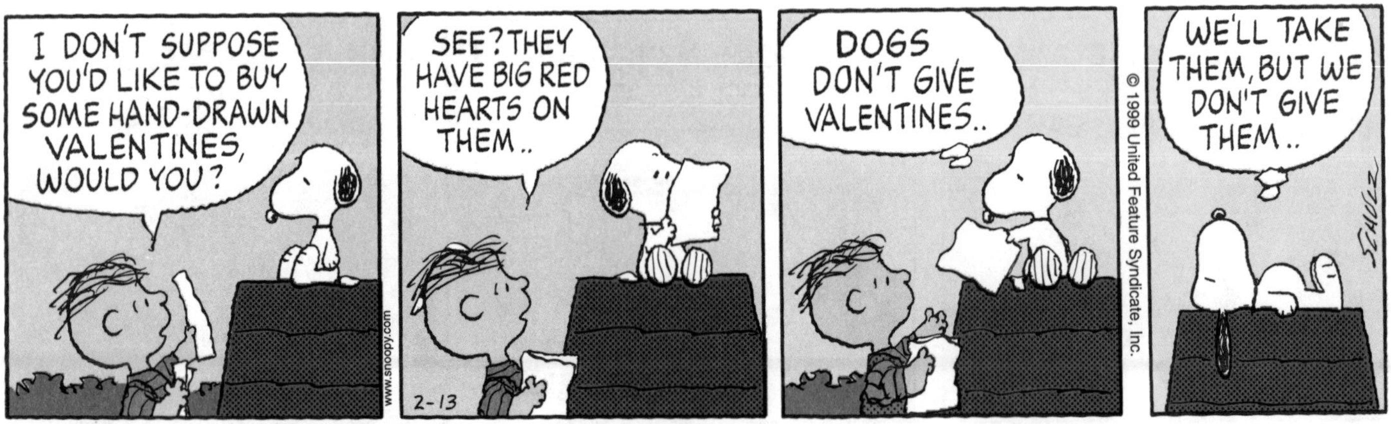
I DON'T SUPPOSE YOU'D LIKE TO BUY SOME HAND-DRAWN VALENTINES, WOULD YOU?
www.snoopy.com
2-13
SEE? THEY HAVE BIG RED HEARTS ON THEM..
DOGS DON'T GIVE VALENTINES..
© 1999 United Feature Syndicate, Inc.
WE'LL TAKE THEM, BUT WE DON'T GIVE THEM..
SCHULZ

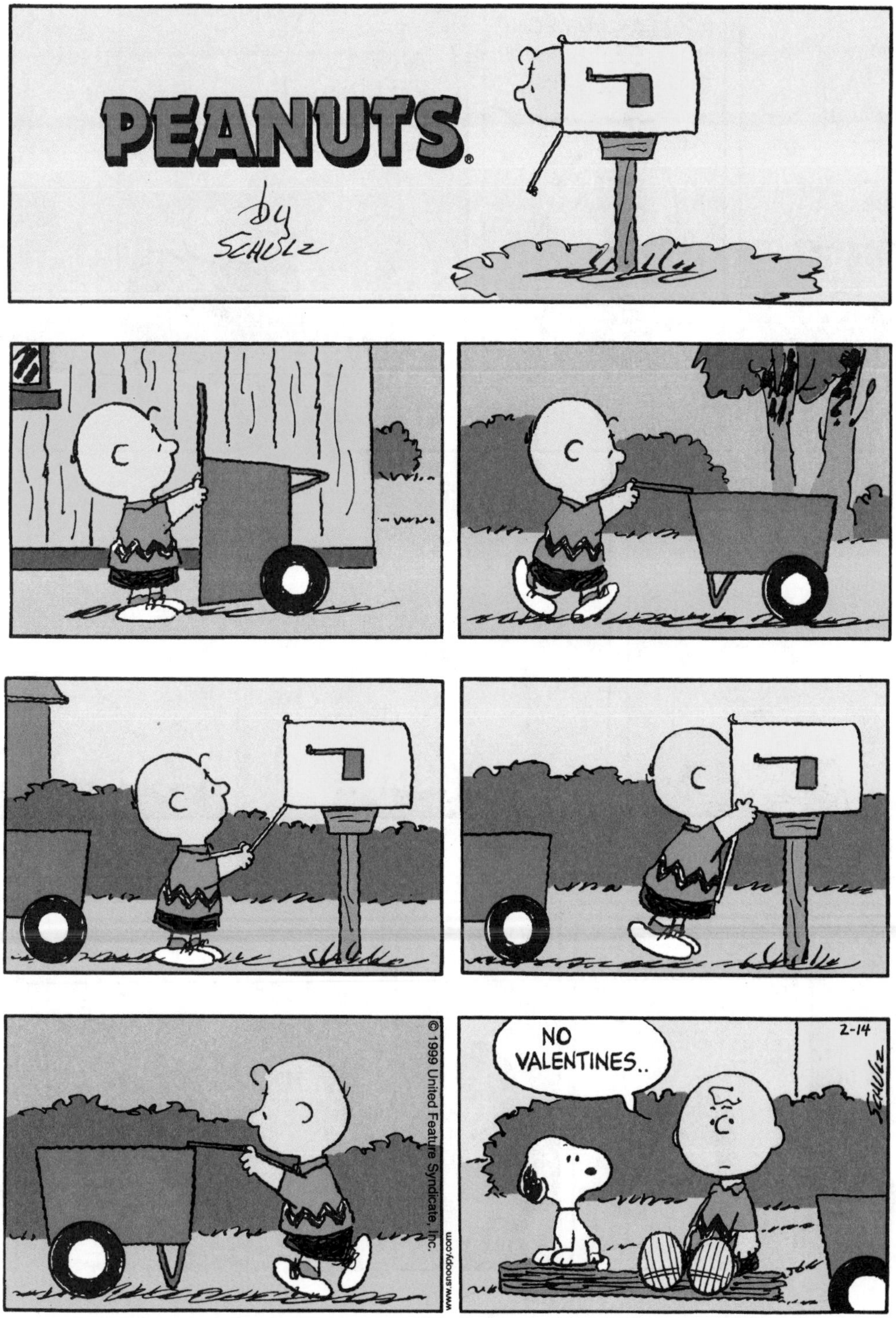
PEANUTS®
by SCHULZ
© 1999 United Feature Syndicate, Inc.
www.snoopy.com
NO VALENTINES..
2-14
SCHULZ

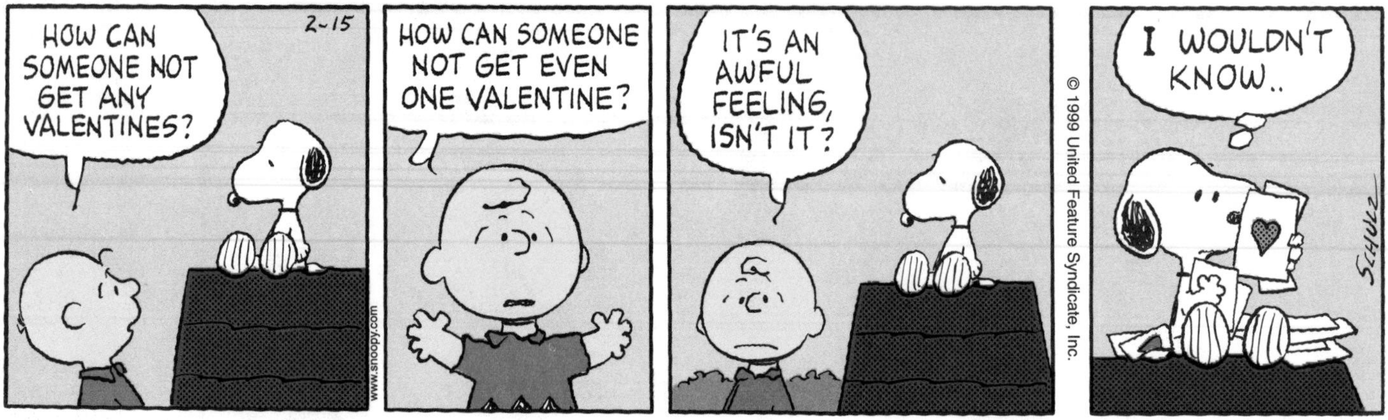
2-15
HOW CAN SOMEONE NOT GET ANY VALENTINES?
HOW CAN SOMEONE NOT GET EVEN ONE VALENTINE?
IT'S AN AWFUL FEELING, ISN'T IT?
I WOULDN'T KNOW..
www.snoopy.com
© 1999 United Feature Syndicate, Inc.
SCHULZ

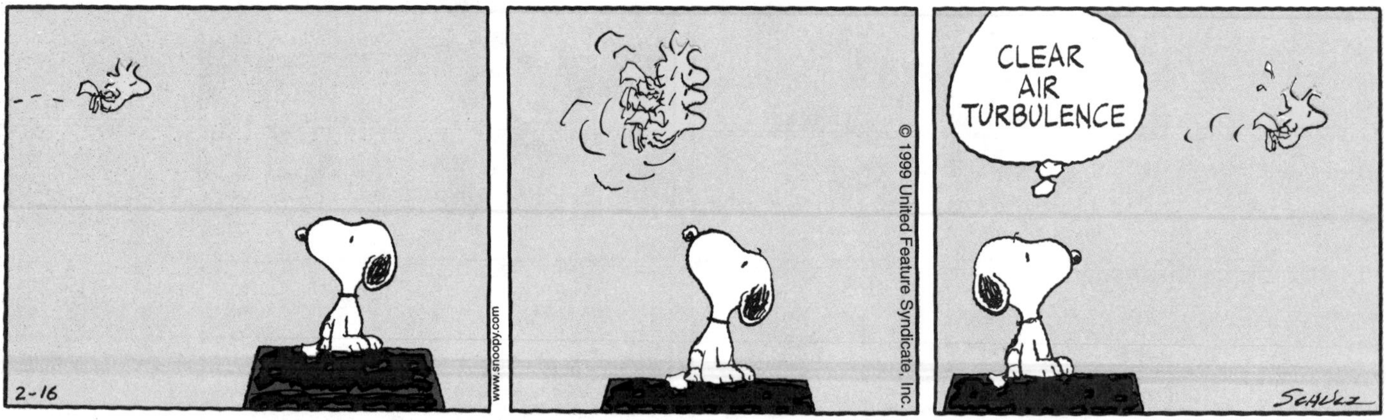
2-16
CLEAR AIR TURBULENCE
www.snoopy.com
© 1999 United Feature Syndicate, Inc.
SCHULZ

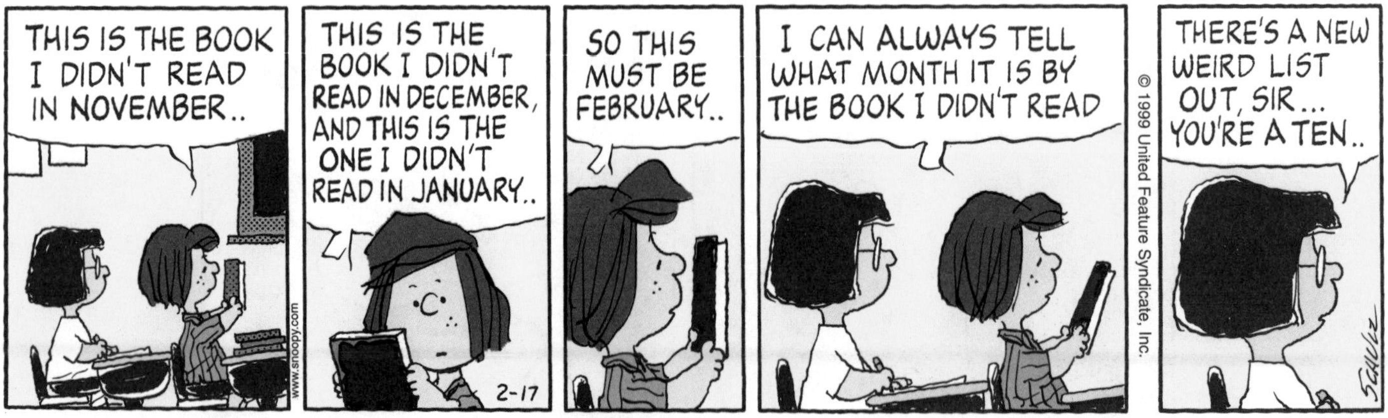
THIS IS THE BOOK I DIDN'T READ IN NOVEMBER..
THIS IS THE BOOK I DIDN'T READ IN DECEMBER, AND THIS IS THE ONE I DIDN'T READ IN JANUARY..
2-17
SO THIS MUST BE FEBRUARY..
I CAN ALWAYS TELL WHAT MONTH IT IS BY THE BOOK I DIDN'T READ
THERE'S A NEW WEIRD LIST OUT, SIR... YOU'RE A TEN..
www.snoopy.com
© 1999 United Feature Syndicate, Inc.
SCHULZ

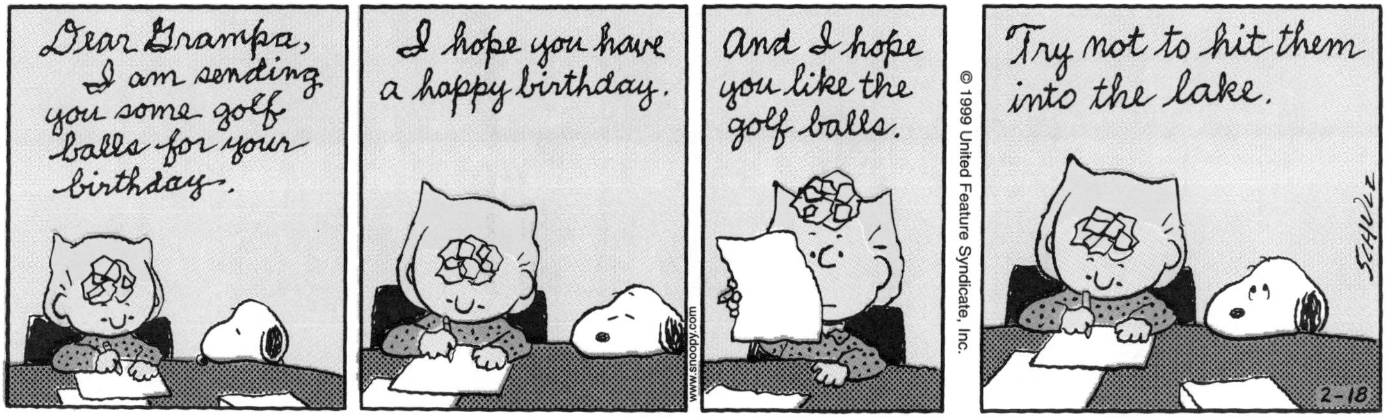
Dear Grampa,
I am sending you some golf balls for your birthday.
I hope you have a happy birthday.
And I hope you like the golf balls.
© 1999 United Feature Syndicate, Inc.
www.snoopy.com
Try not to hit them into the lake.
SCHULZ
2-18

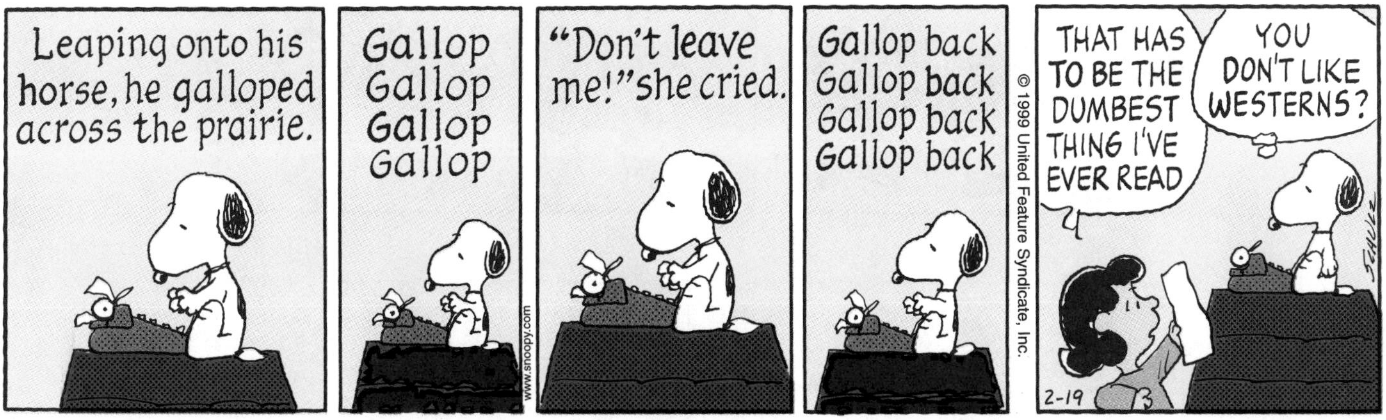
Leaping onto his horse, he galloped across the prairie.
Gallop Gallop Gallop Gallop
www.snoopy.com
"Don't leave me!" she cried.
Gallop back Gallop back Gallop back Gallop back
© 1999 United Feature Syndicate, Inc.
THAT HAS TO BE THE DUMBEST THING I'VE EVER READ
YOU DON'T LIKE WESTERNS?
SCHULZ
2-19

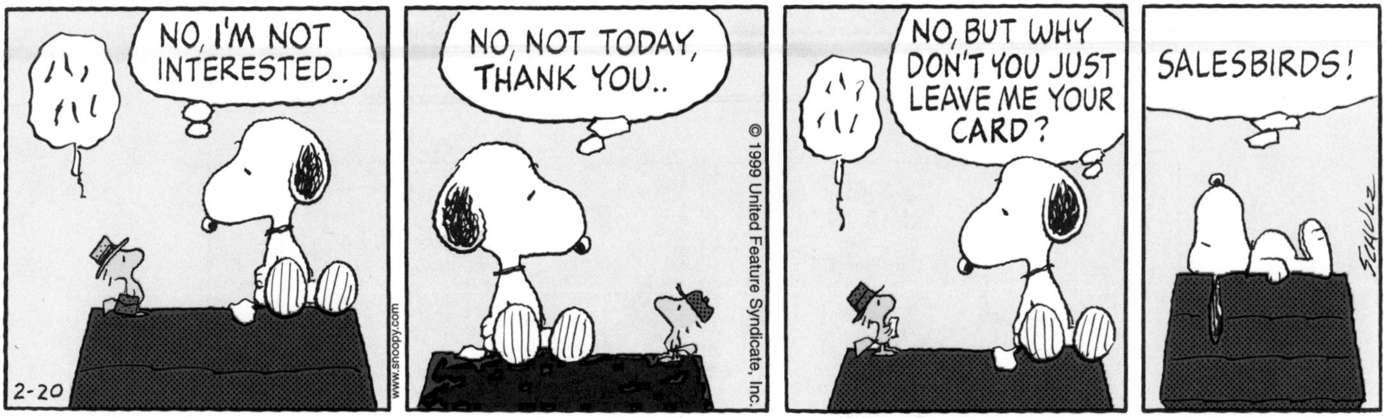
NO, I'M NOT INTERESTED..
2-20
www.snoopy.com
NO, NOT TODAY, THANK YOU..
© 1999 United Feature Syndicate, Inc.
NO, BUT WHY DON'T YOU JUST LEAVE ME YOUR CARD?
SALESBIRDS!
SCHULZ

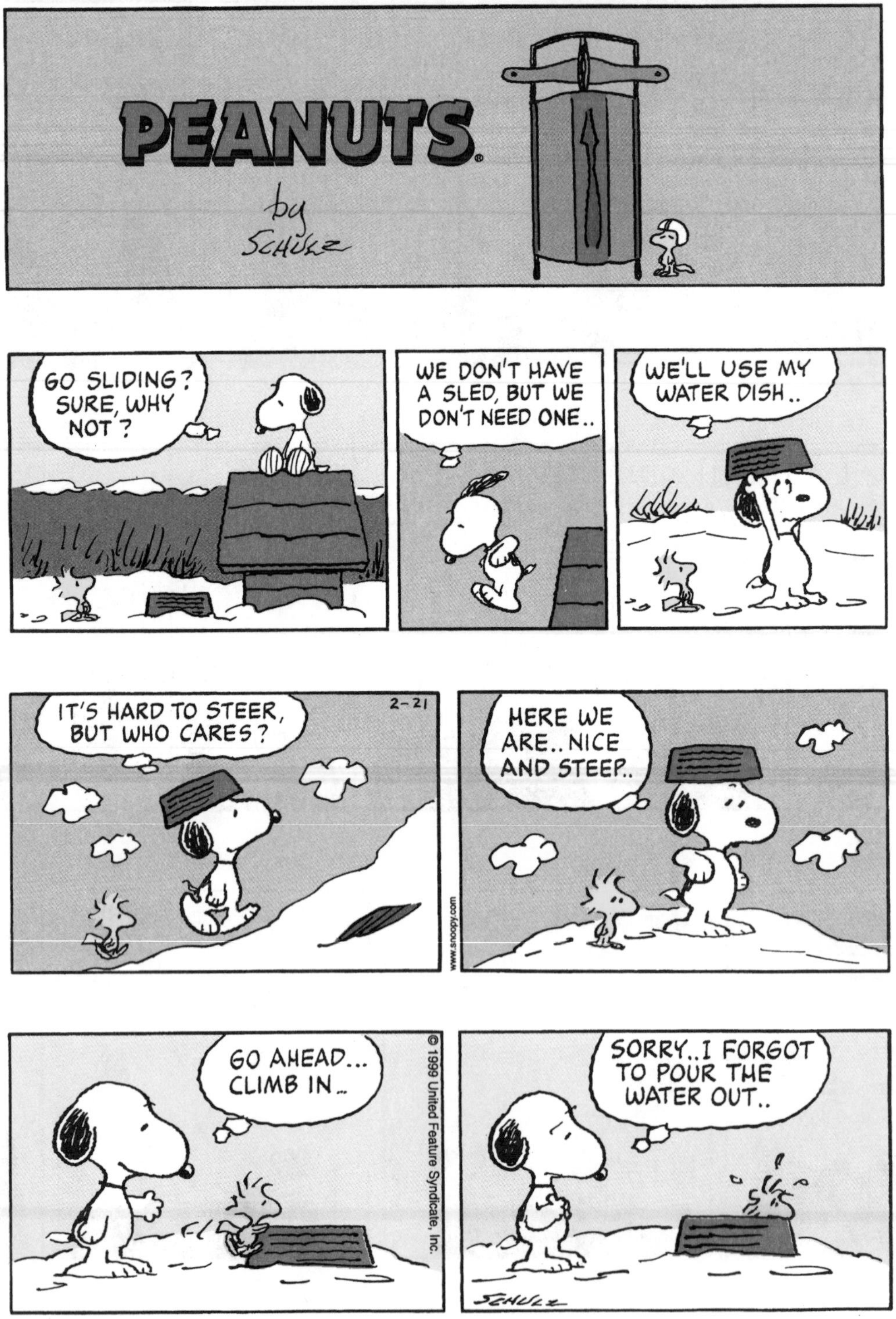
PEANUTS
by SCHULZ
GO SLIDING? SURE, WHY NOT?
WE DON'T HAVE A SLED, BUT WE DON'T NEED ONE..
WE'LL USE MY WATER DISH..
IT'S HARD TO STEER, BUT WHO CARES?
2-21
HERE WE ARE.. NICE AND STEEP..
www.snoopy.com
GO AHEAD... CLIMB IN...
© 1999 United Feature Syndicate, Inc.
SORRY..I FORGOT TO POUR THE WATER OUT..
SCHULZ

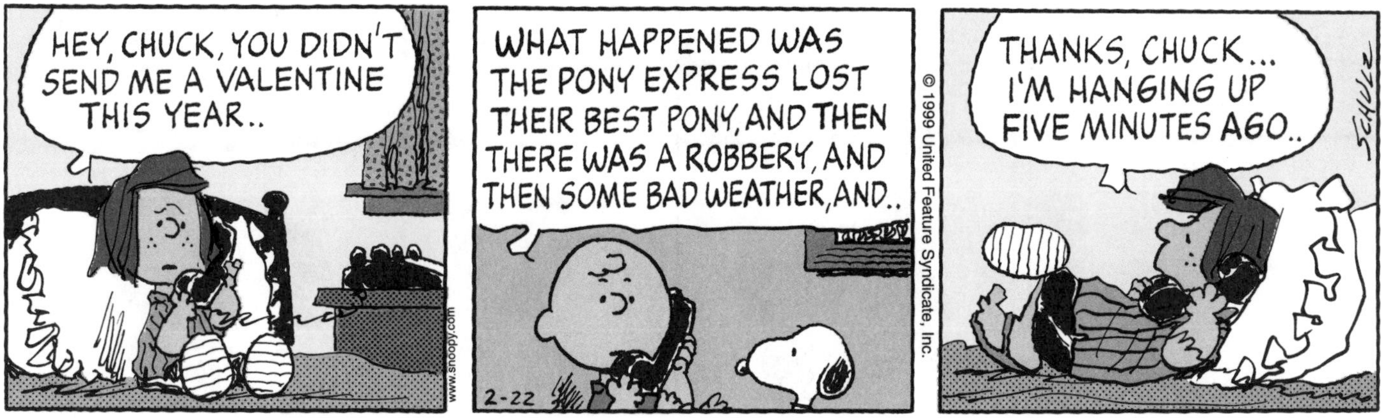
HEY, CHUCK, YOU DIDN'T SEND ME A VALENTINE THIS YEAR..
WHAT HAPPENED WAS THE PONY EXPRESS LOST THEIR BEST PONY, AND THEN THERE WAS A ROBBERY, AND THEN SOME BAD WEATHER, AND..
THANKS, CHUCK... I'M HANGING UP FIVE MINUTES AGO..
www.snoopy.com
2-22
© 1999 United Feature Syndicate, Inc.
SCHULZ

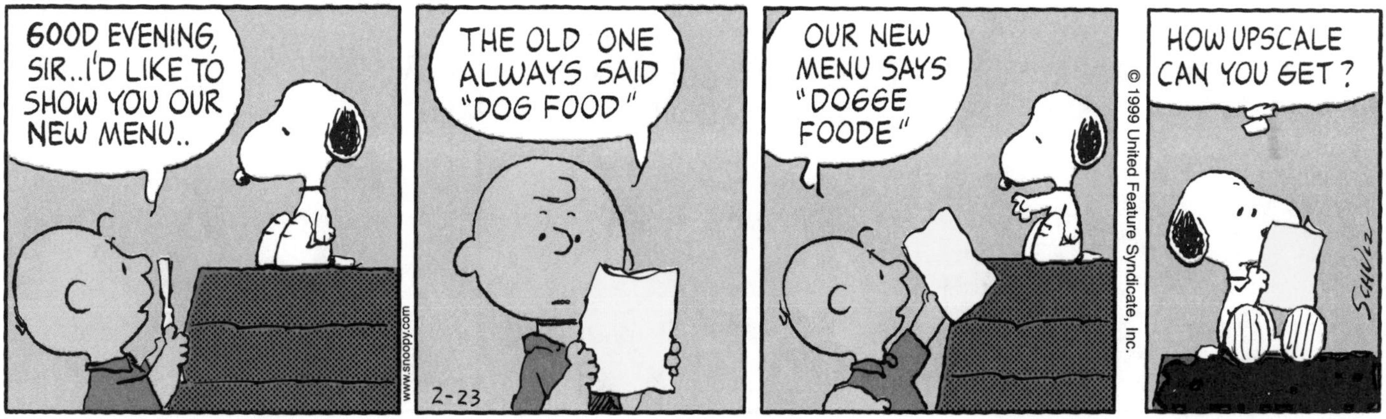
GOOD EVENING, SIR..I'D LIKE TO SHOW YOU OUR NEW MENU..
THE OLD ONE ALWAYS SAID "DOG FOOD"
OUR NEW MENU SAYS "DOGGE FOODE"
HOW UPSCALE CAN YOU GET?
www.snoopy.com
2-23
© 1999 United Feature Syndicate, Inc.
SCHULZ

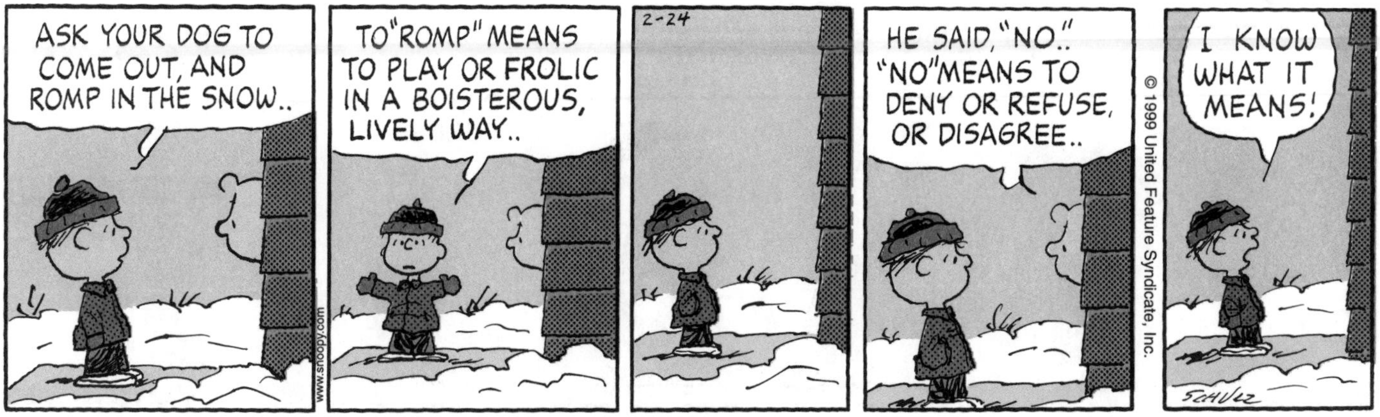
ASK YOUR DOG TO COME OUT, AND ROMP IN THE SNOW..
TO "ROMP" MEANS TO PLAY OR FROLIC IN A BOISTEROUS, LIVELY WAY..
2-24
HE SAID, "NO." "NO" MEANS TO DENY OR REFUSE, OR DISAGREE..
I KNOW WHAT IT MEANS!
www.snoopy.com
© 1999 United Feature Syndicate, Inc.
SCHULZ

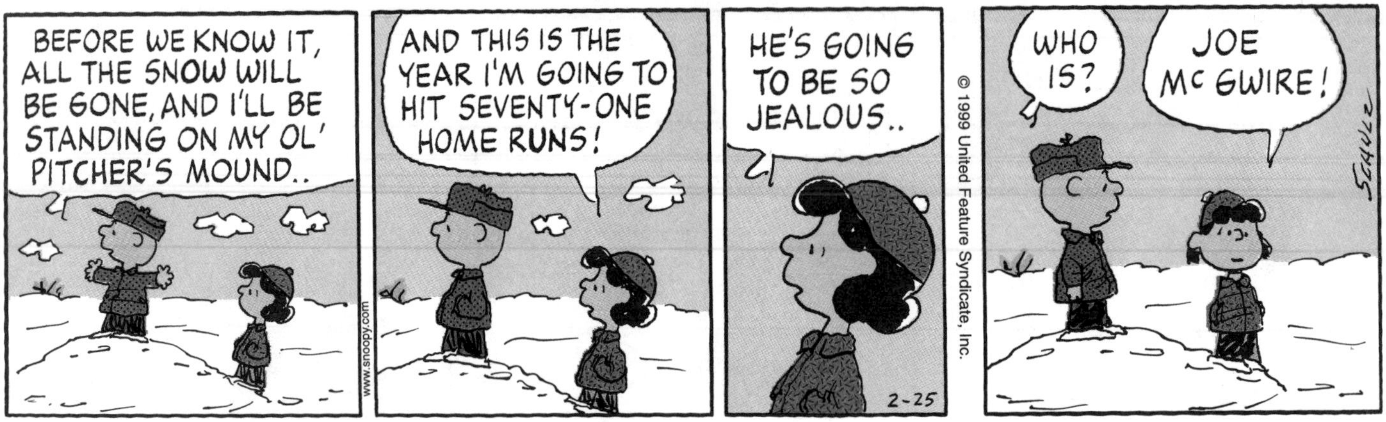
BEFORE WE KNOW IT, ALL THE SNOW WILL BE GONE, AND I'LL BE STANDING ON MY OL' PITCHER'S MOUND..
www.snoopy.com
AND THIS IS THE YEAR I'M GOING TO HIT SEVENTY-ONE HOME RUNS!
HE'S GOING TO BE SO JEALOUS..
© 1999 United Feature Syndicate, Inc.
2-25
WHO IS?
JOE McGWIRE!
SCHULZ

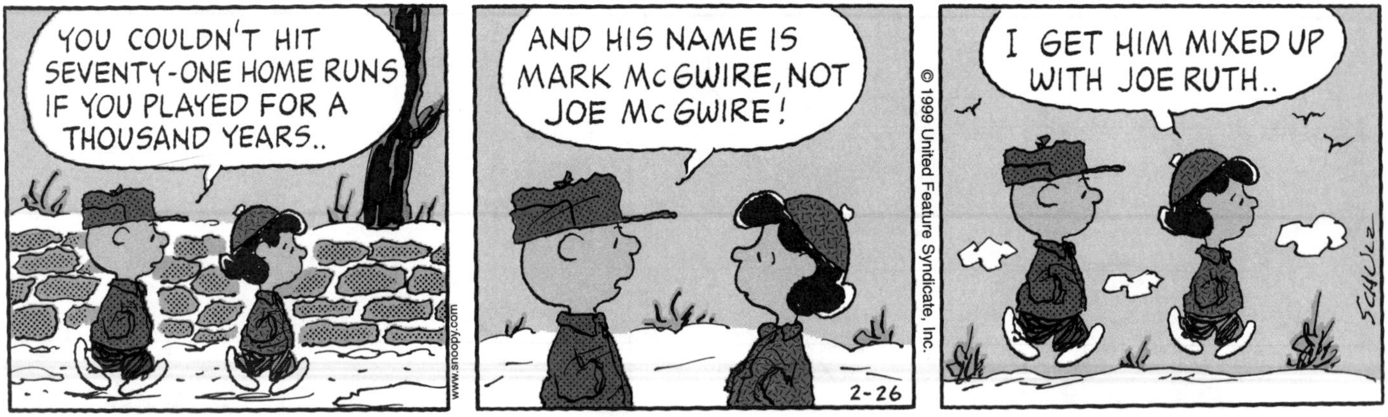
YOU COULDN'T HIT SEVENTY-ONE HOME RUNS IF YOU PLAYED FOR A THOUSAND YEARS..
www.snoopy.com
AND HIS NAME IS MARK McGWIRE, NOT JOE McGWIRE!
© 1999 United Feature Syndicate, Inc.
2-26
I GET HIM MIXED UP WITH JOE RUTH..
SCHULZ

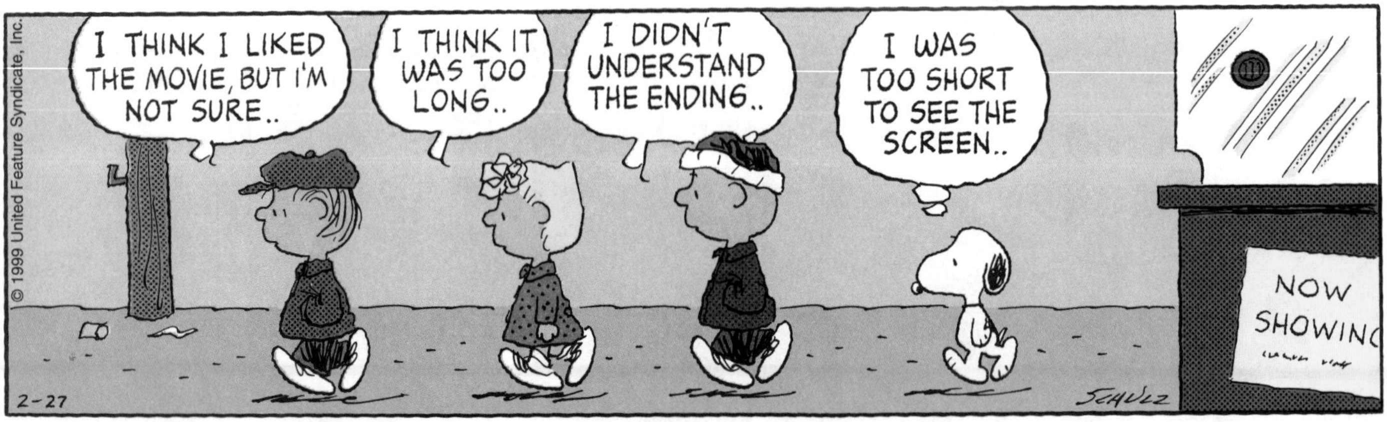
© 1999 United Feature Syndicate, Inc.
I THINK I LIKED THE MOVIE, BUT I'M NOT SURE..
I THINK IT WAS TOO LONG..
I DIDN'T UNDERSTAND THE ENDING..
I WAS TOO SHORT TO SEE THE SCREEN..
NOW SHOWING
2-27
SCHULZ

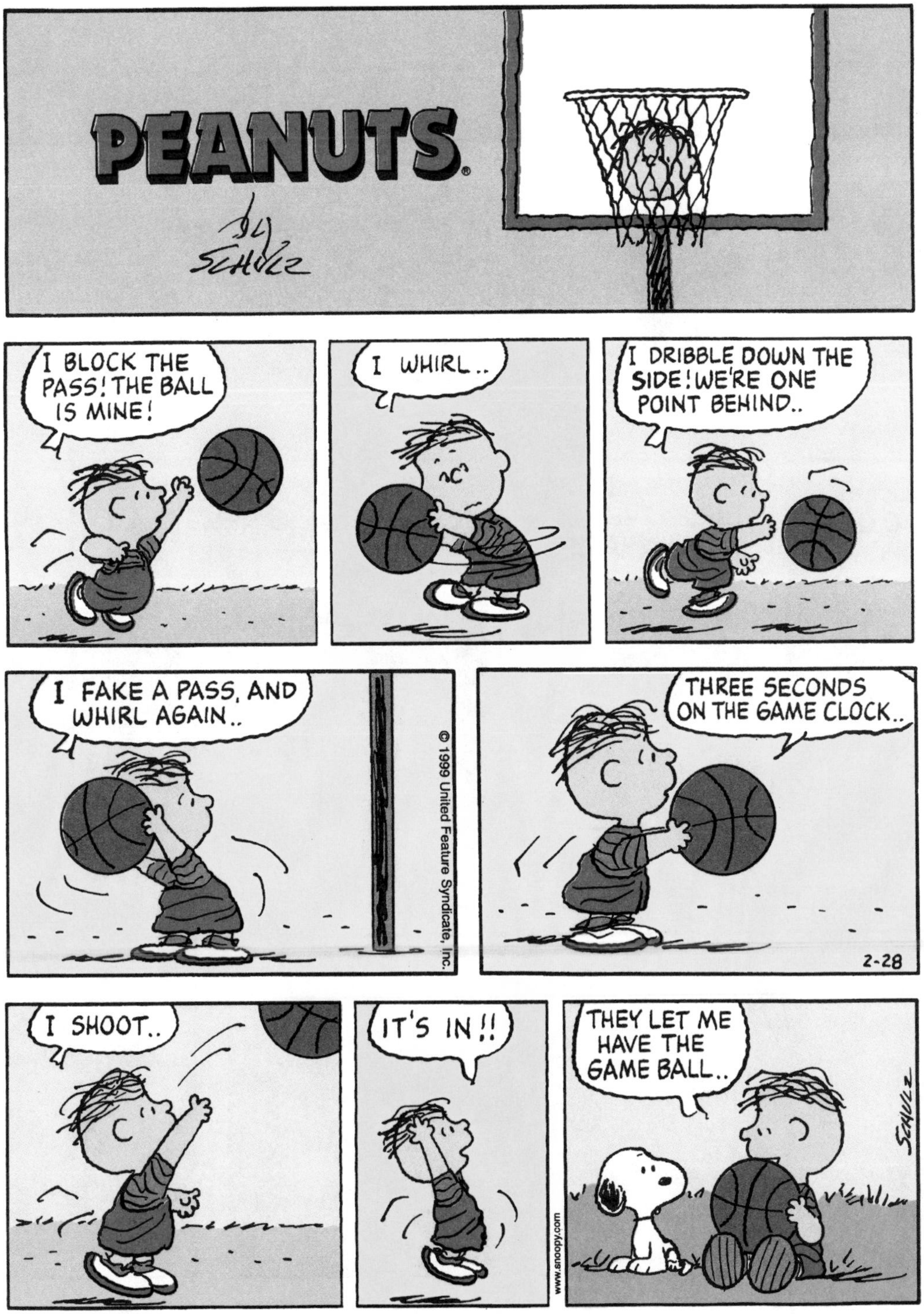
PEANUTS
SCHULZ
I BLOCK THE PASS! THE BALL IS MINE!
I WHIRL..
I DRIBBLE DOWN THE SIDE! WE'RE ONE POINT BEHIND..
I FAKE A PASS, AND WHIRL AGAIN..
© 1999 United Feature Syndicate, Inc.
THREE SECONDS ON THE GAME CLOCK..
2-28
I SHOOT..
IT'S IN!!
www.snoopy.com
THEY LET ME HAVE THE GAME BALL..
SCHULZ

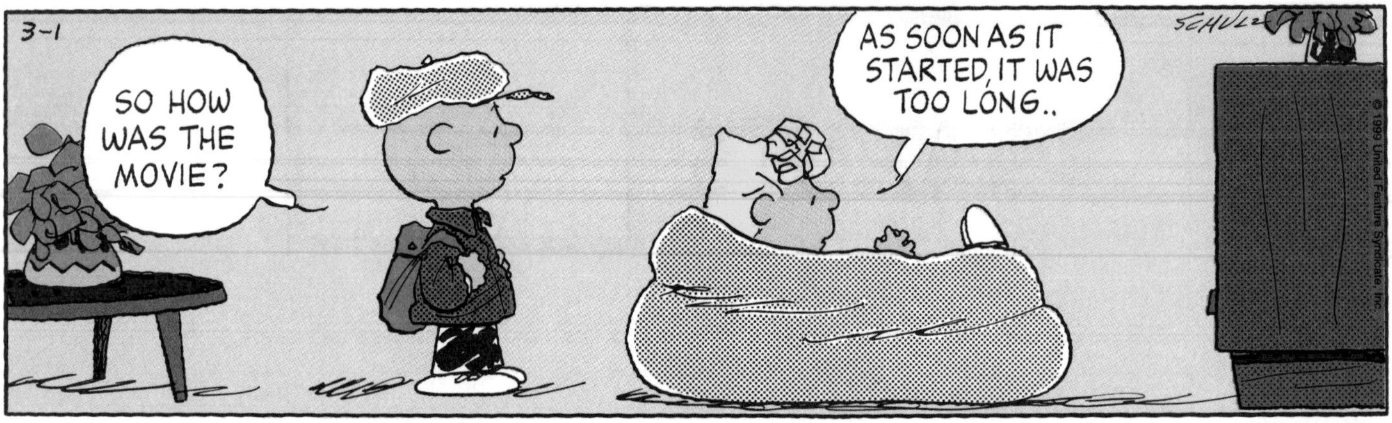
3-1
SO HOW WAS THE MOVIE?
AS SOON AS IT STARTED, IT WAS TOO LONG..
SCHULZ
© 1999 United Feature Syndicate, Inc.

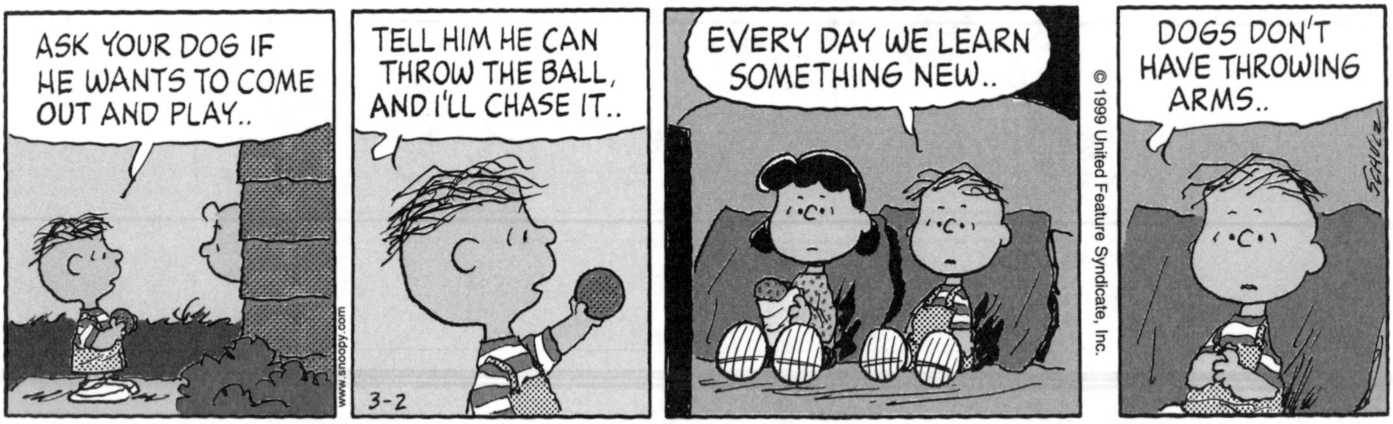
ASK YOUR DOG IF HE WANTS TO COME OUT AND PLAY..
www.snoopy.com
TELL HIM HE CAN THROW THE BALL, AND I'LL CHASE IT..
3-2
EVERY DAY WE LEARN SOMETHING NEW..
© 1999 United Feature Syndicate, Inc.
DOGS DON'T HAVE THROWING ARMS..
SCHULZ

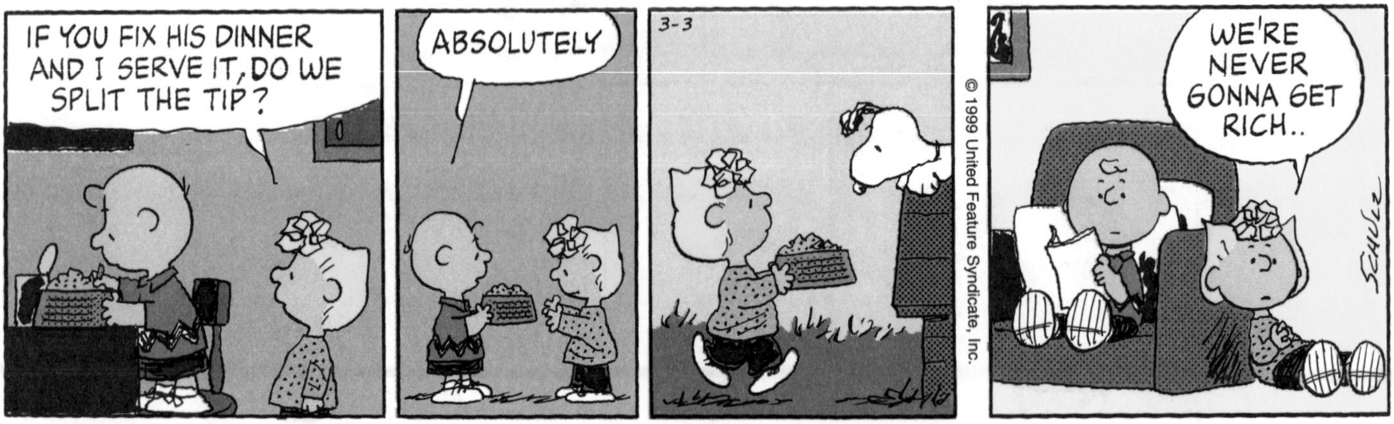
IF YOU FIX HIS DINNER AND I SERVE IT, DO WE SPLIT THE TIP?
ABSOLUTELY
3-3
© 1999 United Feature Syndicate, Inc.
WE'RE NEVER GONNA GET RICH..
SCHULZ

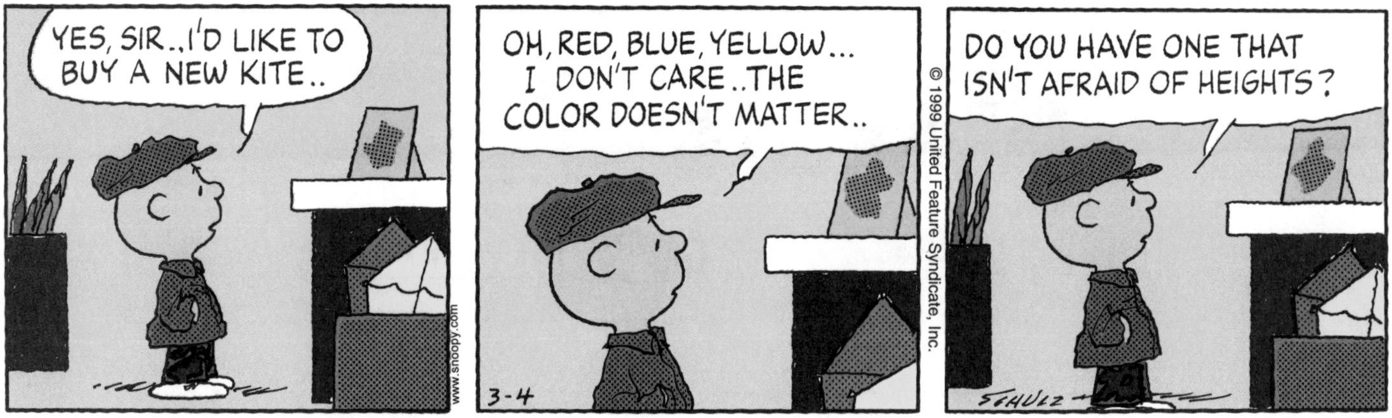
YES, SIR..I'D LIKE TO BUY A NEW KITE..
OH, RED, BLUE, YELLOW... I DON'T CARE..THE COLOR DOESN'T MATTER..
DO YOU HAVE ONE THAT ISN'T AFRAID OF HEIGHTS?
www.snoopy.com
3-4
© 1999 United Feature Syndicate, Inc.
SCHULZ

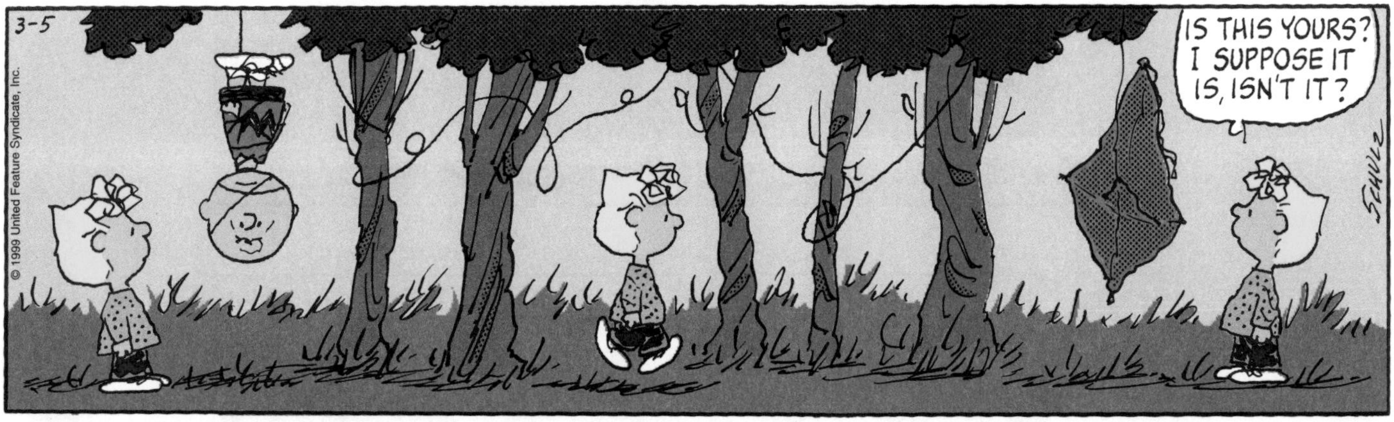
3-5
© 1999 United Feature Syndicate, Inc.
IS THIS YOURS? I SUPPOSE IT IS, ISN'T IT?
SCHULZ

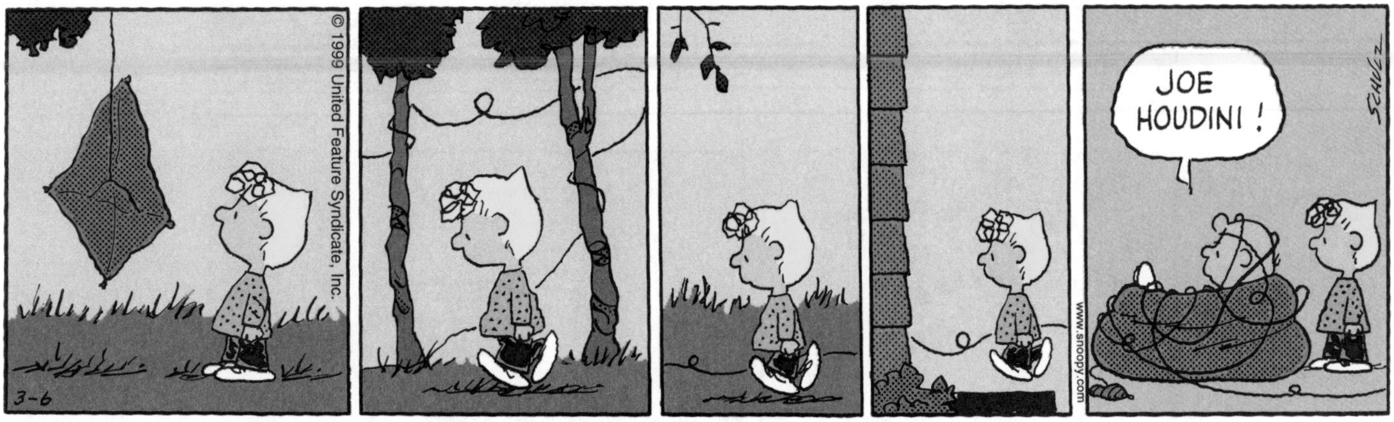
3-6
© 1999 United Feature Syndicate, Inc.
www.snoopy.com
JOE HOUDINI!
SCHULZ

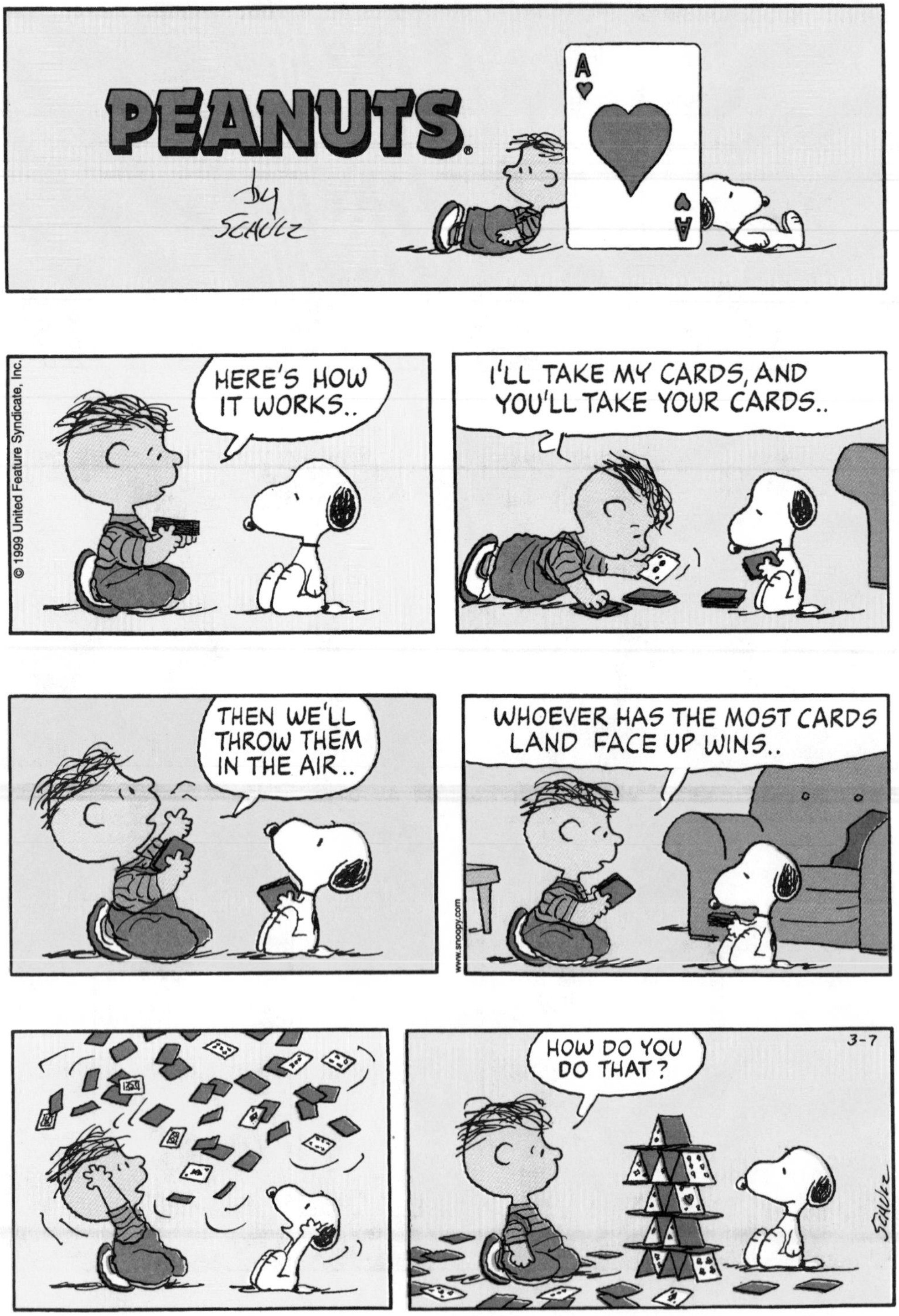
PEANUTS
by SCHULZ
© 1999 United Feature Syndicate, Inc.
HERE'S HOW IT WORKS..
I'LL TAKE MY CARDS, AND YOU'LL TAKE YOUR CARDS..
THEN WE'LL THROW THEM IN THE AIR..
WHOEVER HAS THE MOST CARDS LAND FACE UP WINS..
www.snoopy.com
3-7
HOW DO YOU DO THAT?
SCHULZ

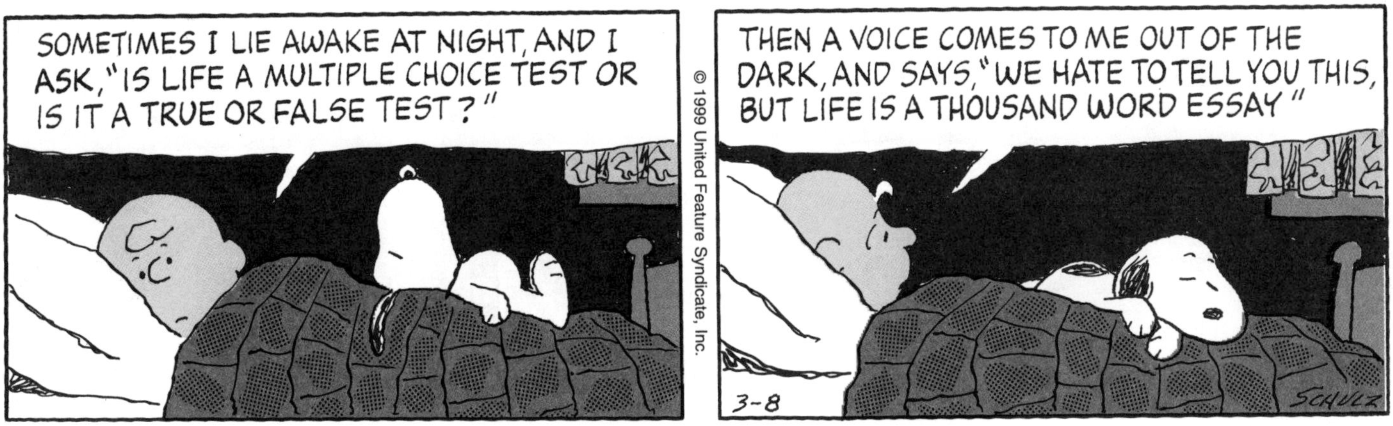
SOMETIMES I LIE AWAKE AT NIGHT, AND I ASK, "IS LIFE A MULTIPLE CHOICE TEST OR IS IT A TRUE OR FALSE TEST?"
THEN A VOICE COMES TO ME OUT OF THE DARK, AND SAYS, "WE HATE TO TELL YOU THIS, BUT LIFE IS A THOUSAND WORD ESSAY"
3-8
SCHULZ
© 1999 United Feature Syndicate, Inc.

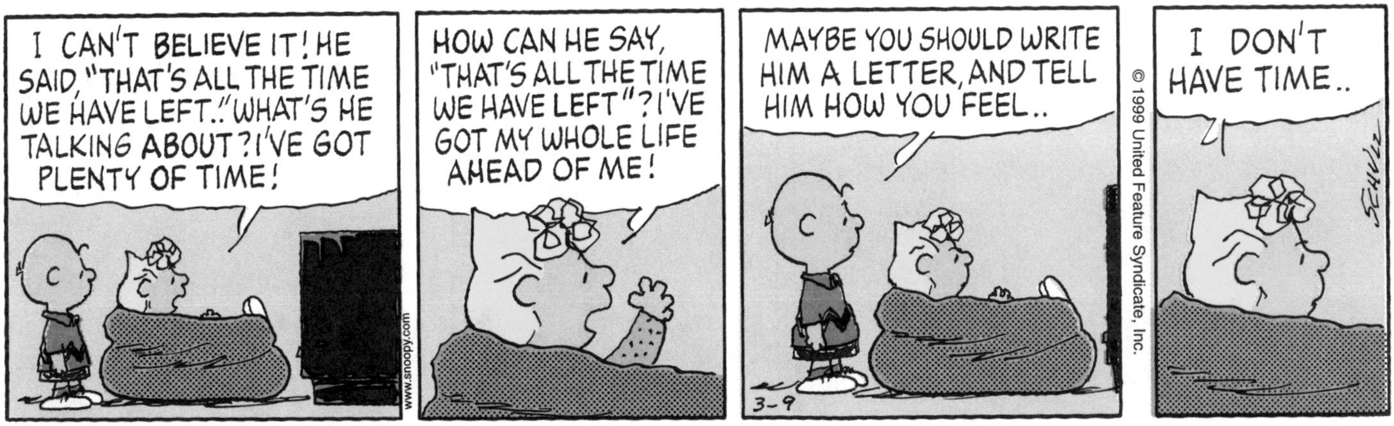
I CAN'T BELIEVE IT! HE SAID, "THAT'S ALL THE TIME WE HAVE LEFT.." WHAT'S HE TALKING ABOUT? I'VE GOT PLENTY OF TIME!
www.snoopy.com
HOW CAN HE SAY, "THAT'S ALL THE TIME WE HAVE LEFT"? I'VE GOT MY WHOLE LIFE AHEAD OF ME!
MAYBE YOU SHOULD WRITE HIM A LETTER, AND TELL HIM HOW YOU FEEL..
3-9
© 1999 United Feature Syndicate, Inc.
I DON'T HAVE TIME..
SCHULZ

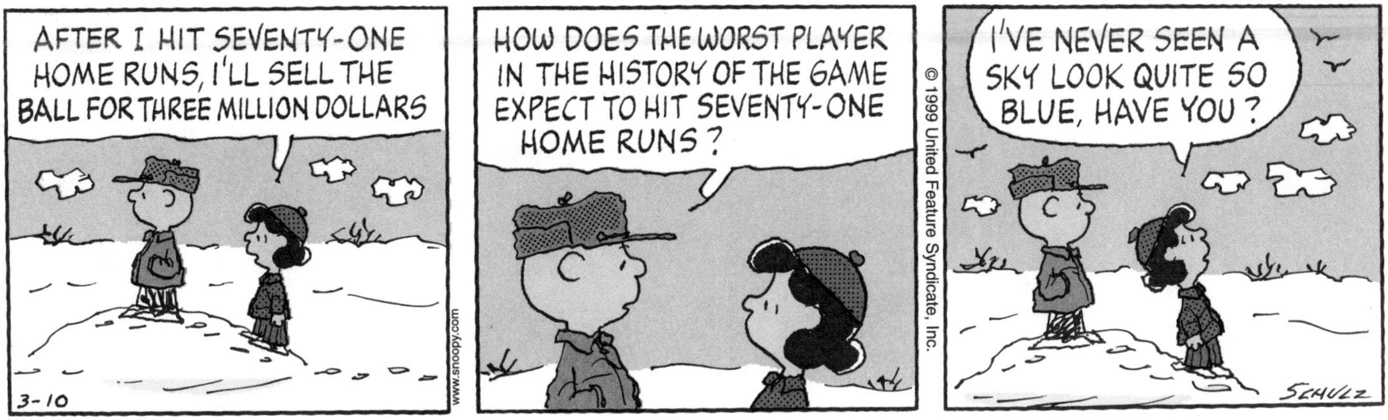
AFTER I HIT SEVENTY-ONE HOME RUNS, I'LL SELL THE BALL FOR THREE MILLION DOLLARS
3-10
www.snoopy.com
HOW DOES THE WORST PLAYER IN THE HISTORY OF THE GAME EXPECT TO HIT SEVENTY-ONE HOME RUNS?
© 1999 United Feature Syndicate, Inc.
I'VE NEVER SEEN A SKY LOOK QUITE SO BLUE, HAVE YOU?
SCHULZ

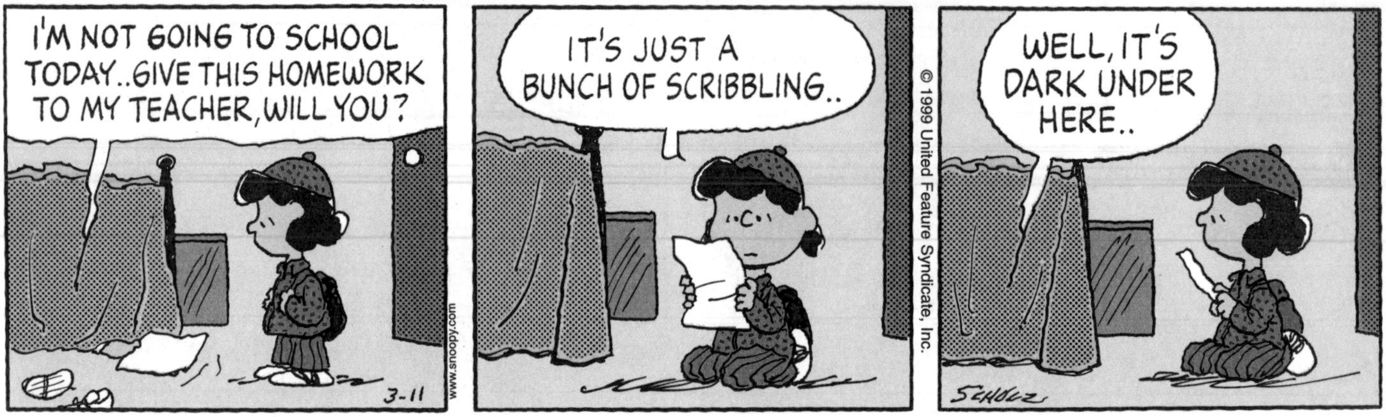
I'M NOT GOING TO SCHOOL TODAY..GIVE THIS HOMEWORK TO MY TEACHER, WILL YOU?
IT'S JUST A BUNCH OF SCRIBBLING..
WELL, IT'S DARK UNDER HERE..
3-11
www.snoopy.com
© 1999 United Feature Syndicate, Inc.
SCHULZ

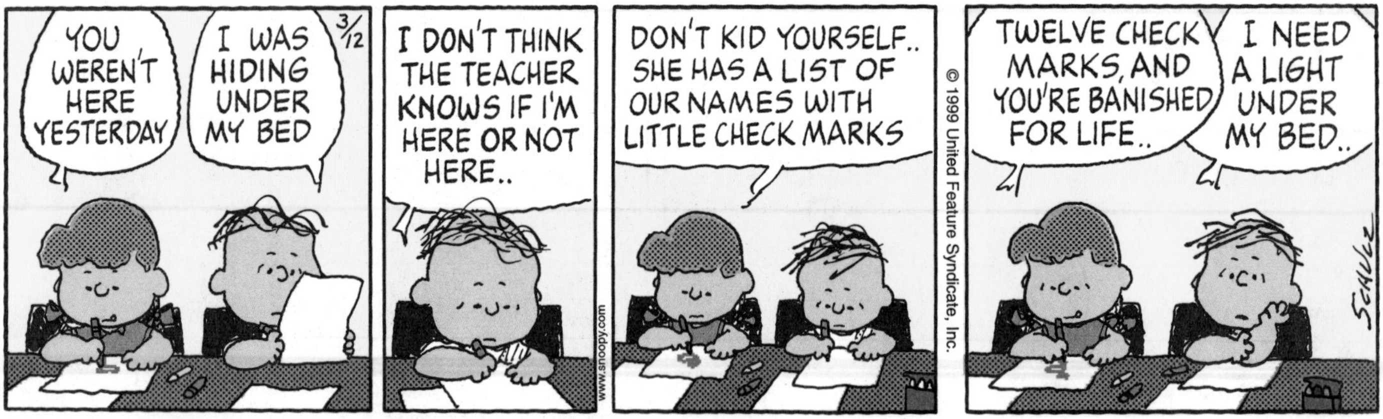
YOU WEREN'T HERE YESTERDAY
I WAS HIDING UNDER MY BED
3/12
I DON'T THINK THE TEACHER KNOWS IF I'M HERE OR NOT HERE..
DON'T KID YOURSELF.. SHE HAS A LIST OF OUR NAMES WITH LITTLE CHECK MARKS
TWELVE CHECK MARKS, AND YOU'RE BANISHED FOR LIFE..
I NEED A LIGHT UNDER MY BED..
www.snoopy.com
© 1999 United Feature Syndicate, Inc.
SCHULZ

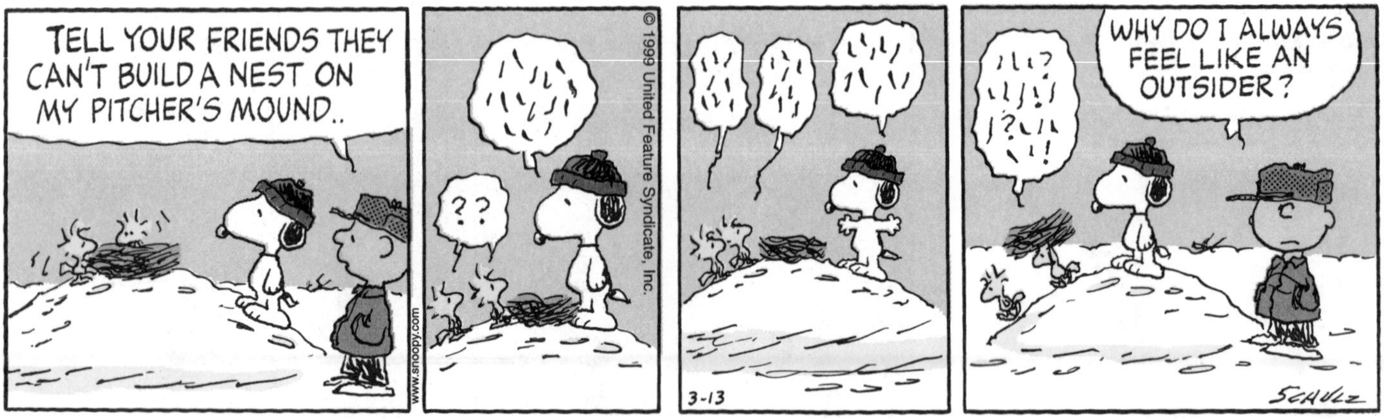
TELL YOUR FRIENDS THEY CAN'T BUILD A NEST ON MY PITCHER'S MOUND..
? ?
WHY DO I ALWAYS FEEL LIKE AN OUTSIDER?
3-13
www.snoopy.com
© 1999 United Feature Syndicate, Inc.
SCHULZ

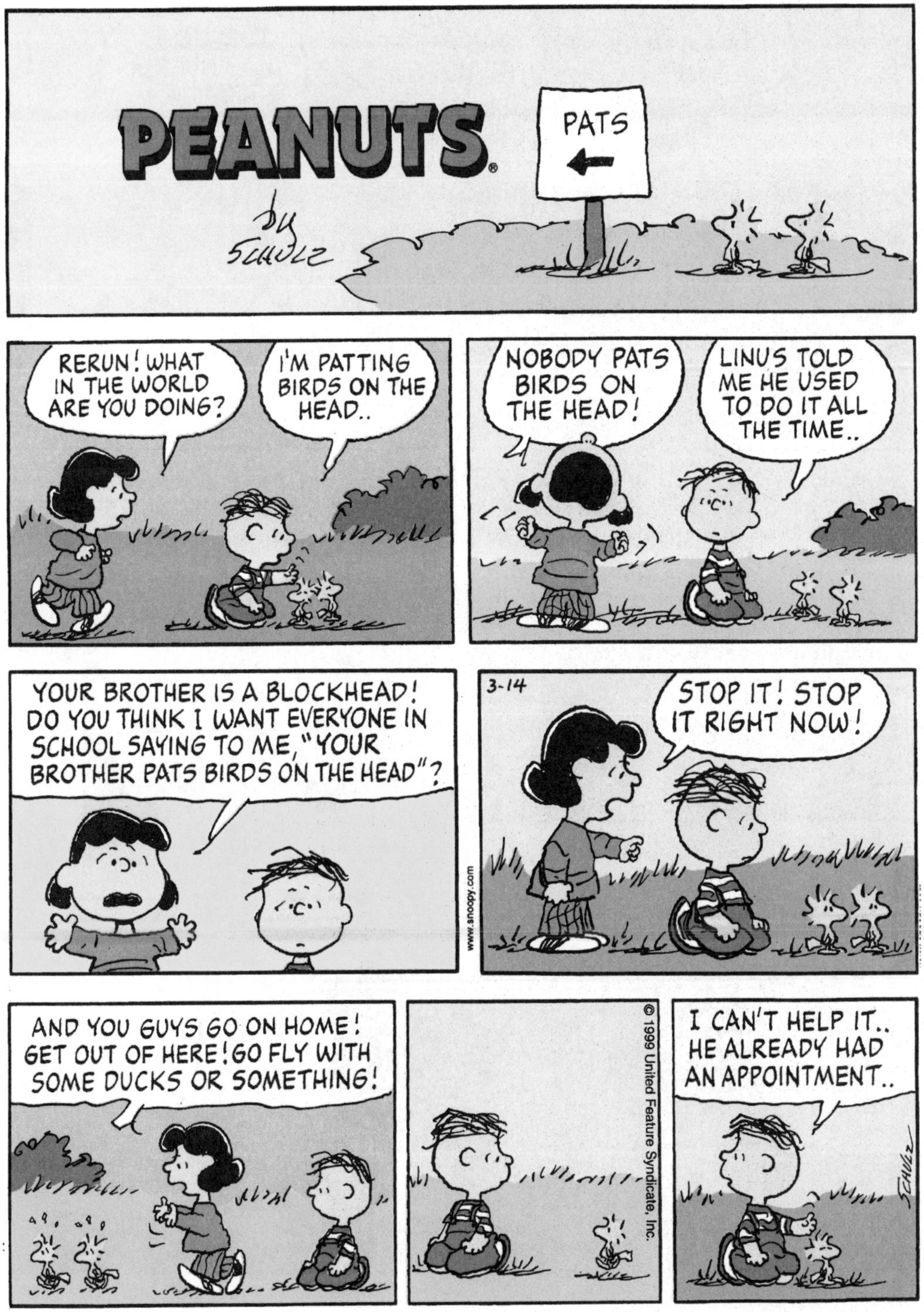
PEANUTS
by SCHULZ
PATS
RERUN! WHAT IN THE WORLD ARE YOU DOING?
I'M PATTING BIRDS ON THE HEAD..
NOBODY PATS BIRDS ON THE HEAD!
LINUS TOLD ME HE USED TO DO IT ALL THE TIME..
YOUR BROTHER IS A BLOCKHEAD! DO YOU THINK I WANT EVERYONE IN SCHOOL SAYING TO ME, "YOUR BROTHER PATS BIRDS ON THE HEAD"?
www.snoopy.com
3-14
STOP IT! STOP IT RIGHT NOW!
AND YOU GUYS GO ON HOME! GET OUT OF HERE! GO FLY WITH SOME DUCKS OR SOMETHING!
© 1999 United Feature Syndicate, Inc.
I CAN'T HELP IT.. HE ALREADY HAD AN APPOINTMENT..
SCHULZ

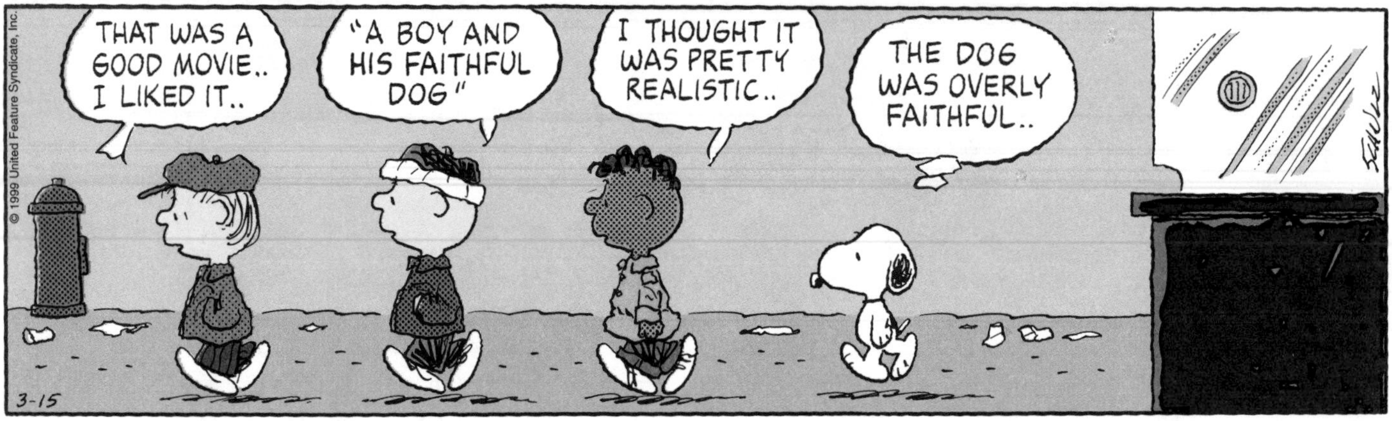
© 1999 United Feature Syndicate, Inc.
THAT WAS A GOOD MOVIE.. I LIKED IT..
"A BOY AND HIS FAITHFUL DOG"
I THOUGHT IT WAS PRETTY REALISTIC..
THE DOG WAS OVERLY FAITHFUL..
111
SCHULZ
3-15

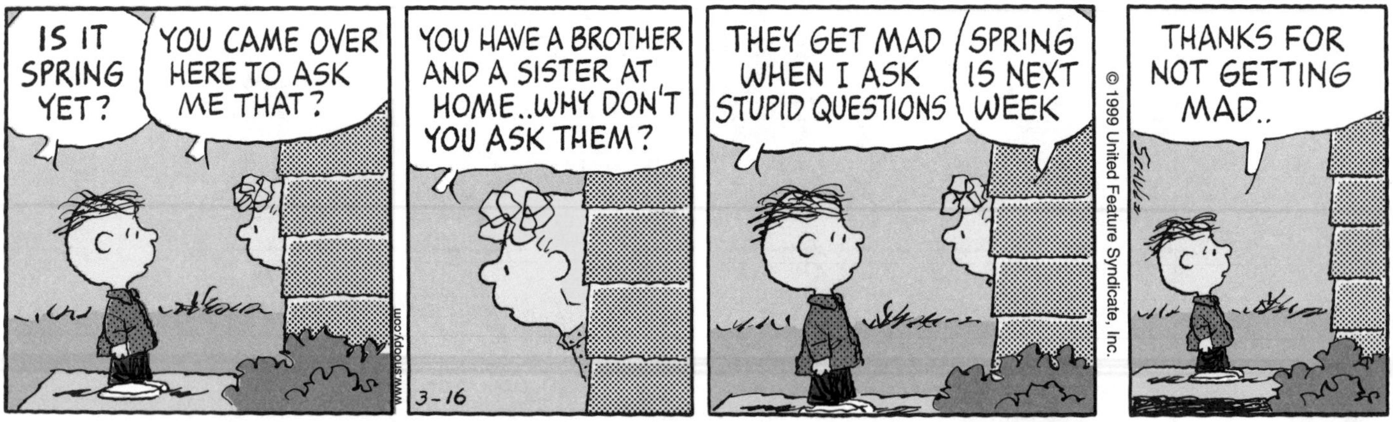
IS IT SPRING YET?
YOU CAME OVER HERE TO ASK ME THAT?
YOU HAVE A BROTHER AND A SISTER AT HOME..WHY DON'T YOU ASK THEM?
www.snoopy.com
3-16
THEY GET MAD WHEN I ASK STUPID QUESTIONS
SPRING IS NEXT WEEK
© 1999 United Feature Syndicate, Inc.
SCHULZ
THANKS FOR NOT GETTING MAD..

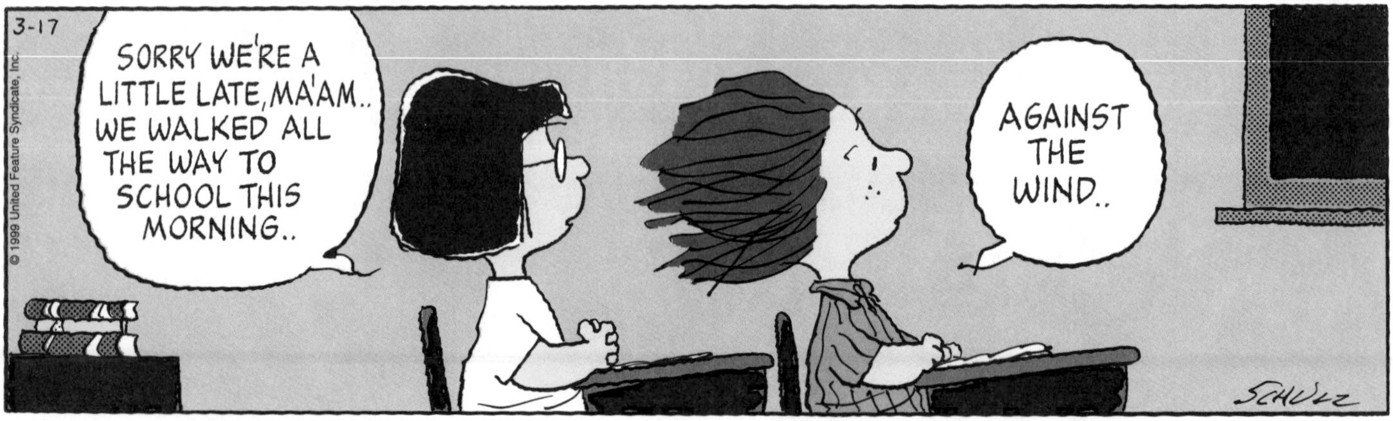
3-17
© 1999 United Feature Syndicate, Inc.
SORRY WE'RE A LITTLE LATE, MA'AM.. WE WALKED ALL THE WAY TO SCHOOL THIS MORNING..
AGAINST THE WIND..
SCHULZ

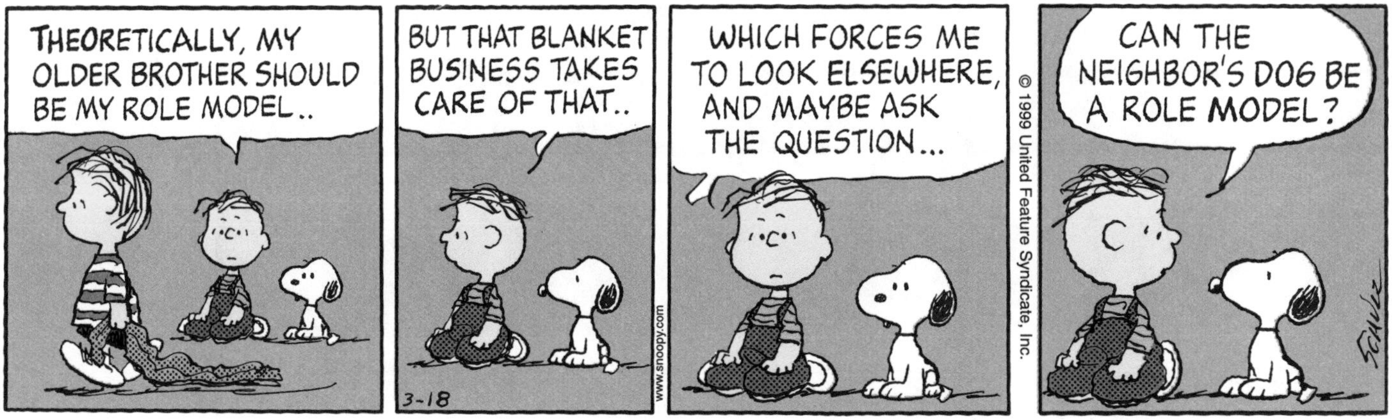
THEORETICALLY, MY OLDER BROTHER SHOULD BE MY ROLE MODEL..
BUT THAT BLANKET BUSINESS TAKES CARE OF THAT..
3-18
www.snoopy.com
WHICH FORCES ME TO LOOK ELSEWHERE, AND MAYBE ASK THE QUESTION...
© 1999 United Feature Syndicate, Inc.
CAN THE NEIGHBOR'S DOG BE A ROLE MODEL?
SCHULZ

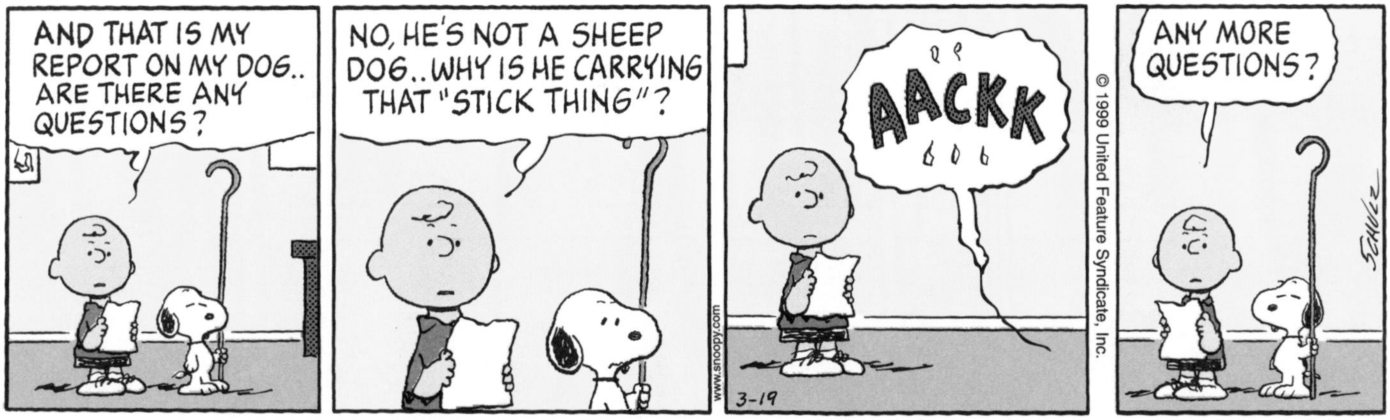
AND THAT IS MY REPORT ON MY DOG.. ARE THERE ANY QUESTIONS?
NO, HE'S NOT A SHEEP DOG..WHY IS HE CARRYING THAT "STICK THING"?
www.snoopy.com
AACKK
3-19
© 1999 United Feature Syndicate, Inc.
ANY MORE QUESTIONS?
SCHULZ

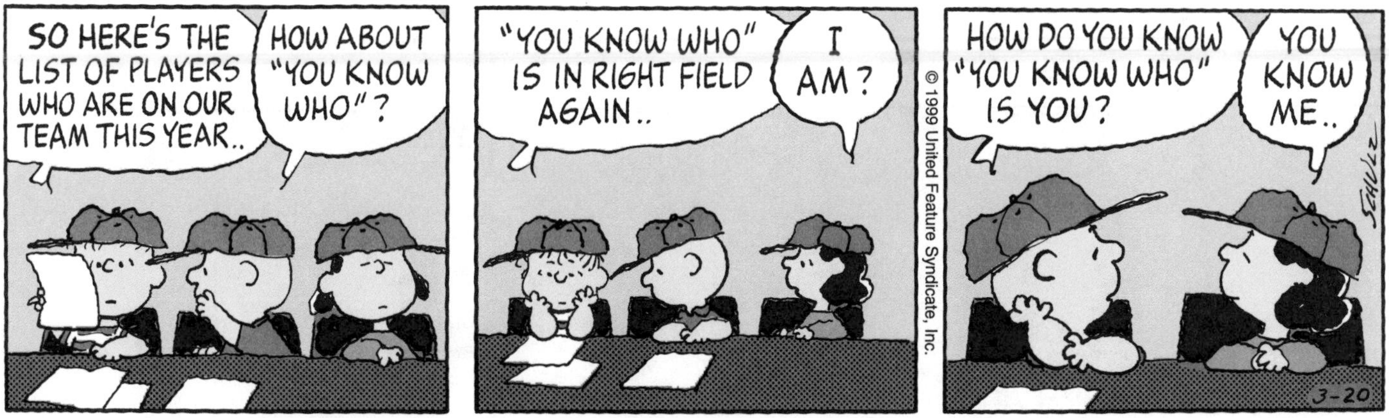
SO HERE'S THE LIST OF PLAYERS WHO ARE ON OUR TEAM THIS YEAR..
HOW ABOUT "YOU KNOW WHO"?
"YOU KNOW WHO" IS IN RIGHT FIELD AGAIN..
I AM?
© 1999 United Feature Syndicate, Inc.
HOW DO YOU KNOW "YOU KNOW WHO" IS YOU?
YOU KNOW ME..
SCHULZ
3-20

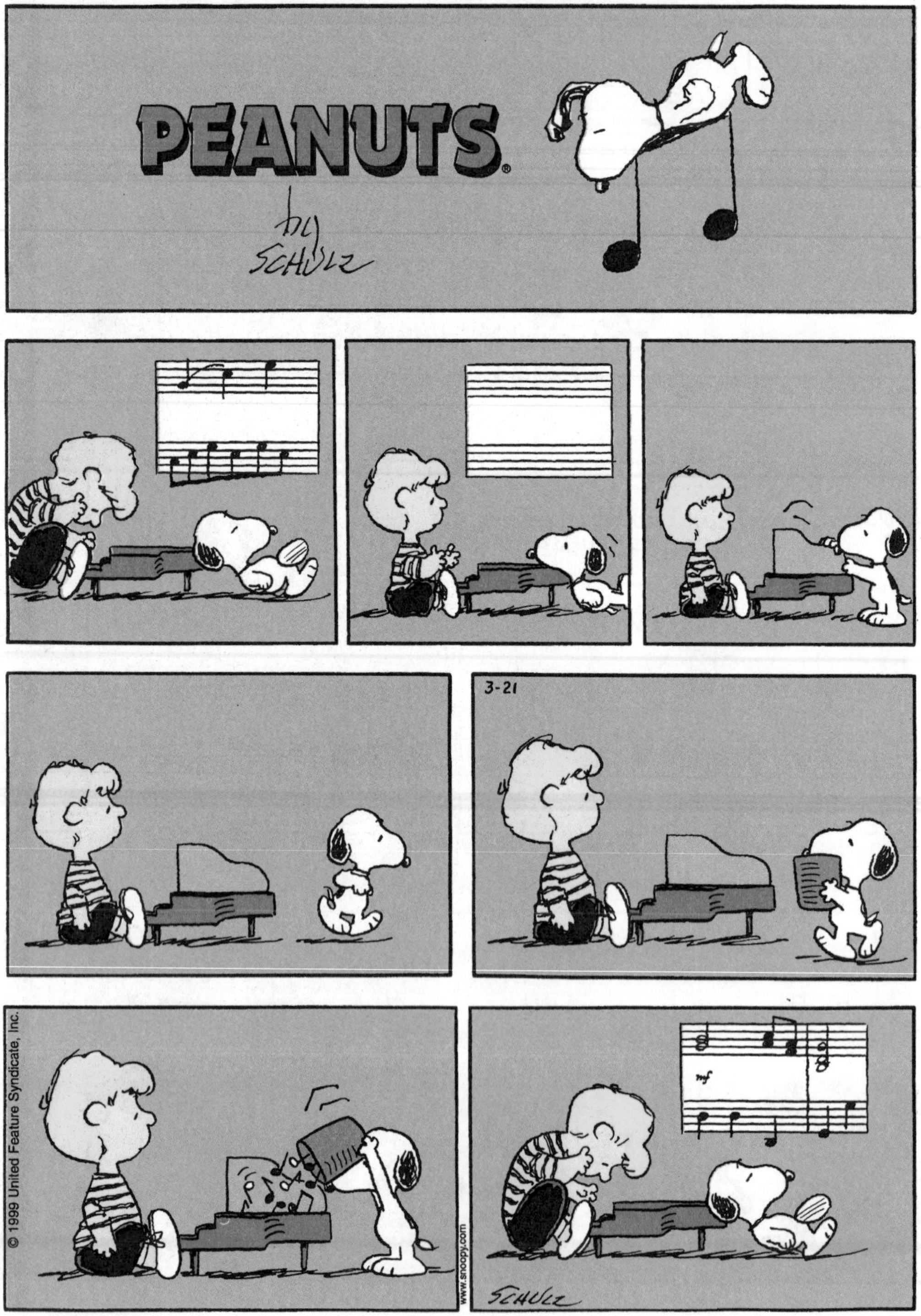
PEANUTS
by SCHULZ
3-21
© 1999 United Feature Syndicate, Inc.
www.snoopy.com
SCHULZ

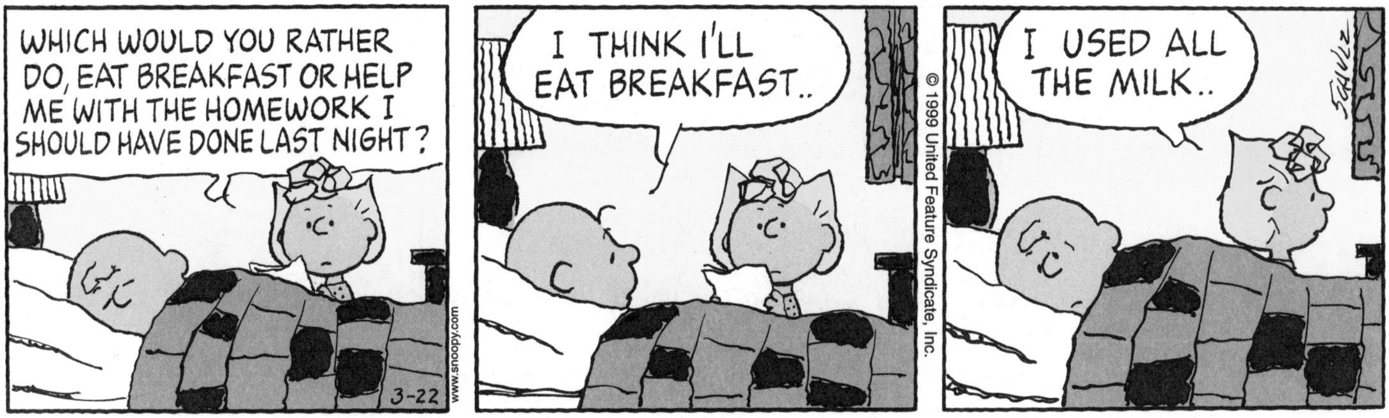
WHICH WOULD YOU RATHER DO, EAT BREAKFAST OR HELP ME WITH THE HOMEWORK I SHOULD HAVE DONE LAST NIGHT?
I THINK I'LL EAT BREAKFAST..
I USED ALL THE MILK..
3-22
www.snoopy.com
© 1999 United Feature Syndicate, Inc.
SCHULZ

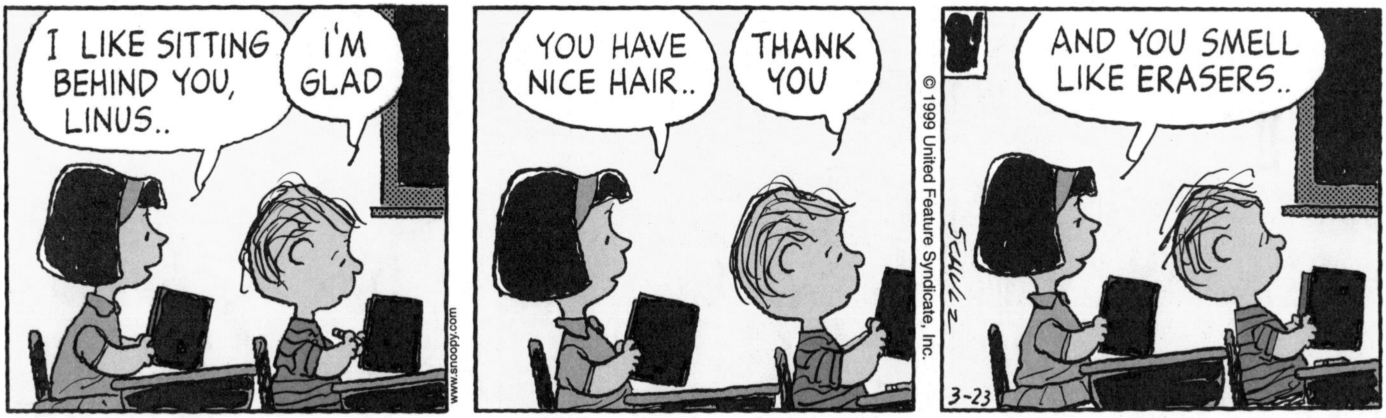
I LIKE SITTING BEHIND YOU, LINUS..
I'M GLAD
YOU HAVE NICE HAIR..
THANK YOU
AND YOU SMELL LIKE ERASERS..
3-23
www.snoopy.com
© 1999 United Feature Syndicate, Inc.
SCHULZ

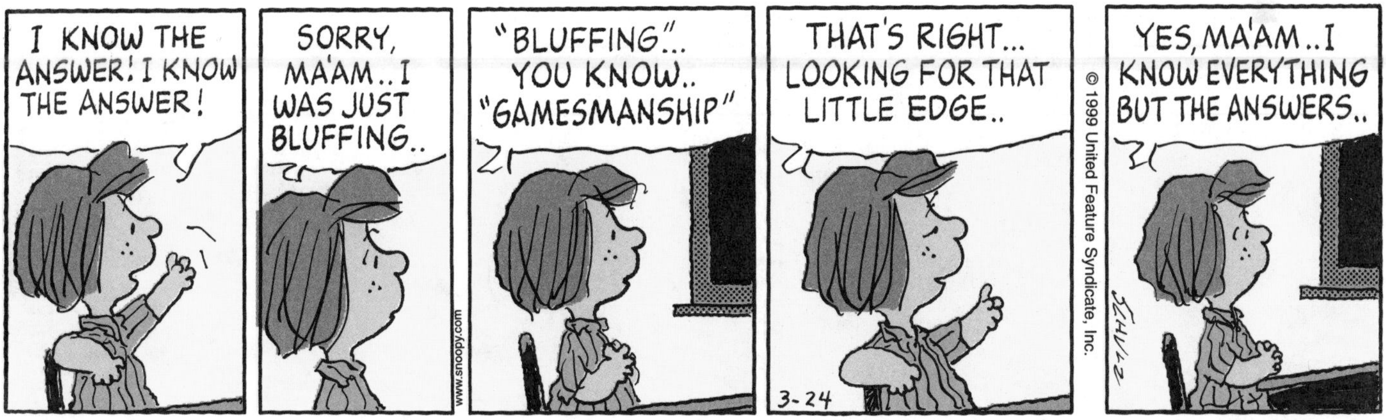
I KNOW THE ANSWER! I KNOW THE ANSWER!
SORRY, MA'AM.. I WAS JUST BLUFFING..
"BLUFFING"... YOU KNOW.. "GAMESMANSHIP"
THAT'S RIGHT... LOOKING FOR THAT LITTLE EDGE..
YES, MA'AM.. I KNOW EVERYTHING BUT THE ANSWERS..
3-24
www.snoopy.com
© 1999 United Feature Syndicate, Inc.
SCHULZ

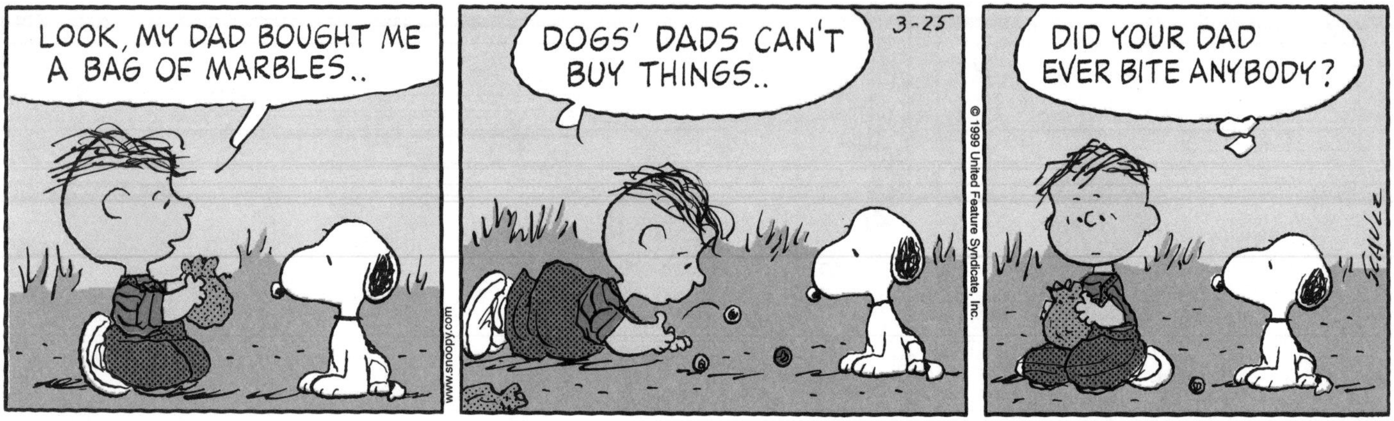
LOOK, MY DAD BOUGHT ME A BAG OF MARBLES..
www.snoopy.com
3-25
DOGS' DADS CAN'T BUY THINGS..
© 1999 United Feature Syndicate, Inc.
DID YOUR DAD EVER BITE ANYBODY?
SCHULZ

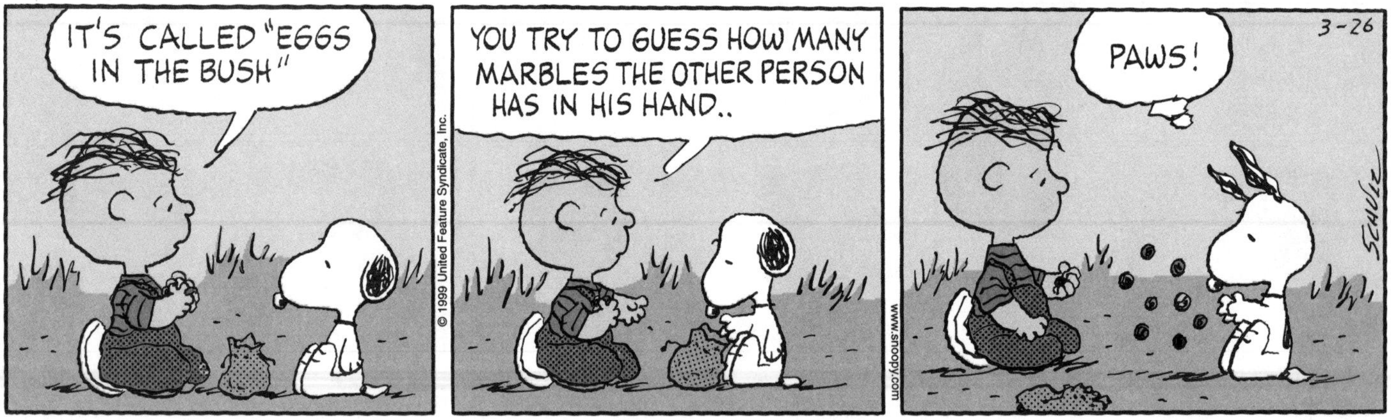
IT'S CALLED "EGGS IN THE BUSH"
© 1999 United Feature Syndicate, Inc.
YOU TRY TO GUESS HOW MANY MARBLES THE OTHER PERSON HAS IN HIS HAND..
www.snoopy.com
3-26
PAWS!
SCHULZ

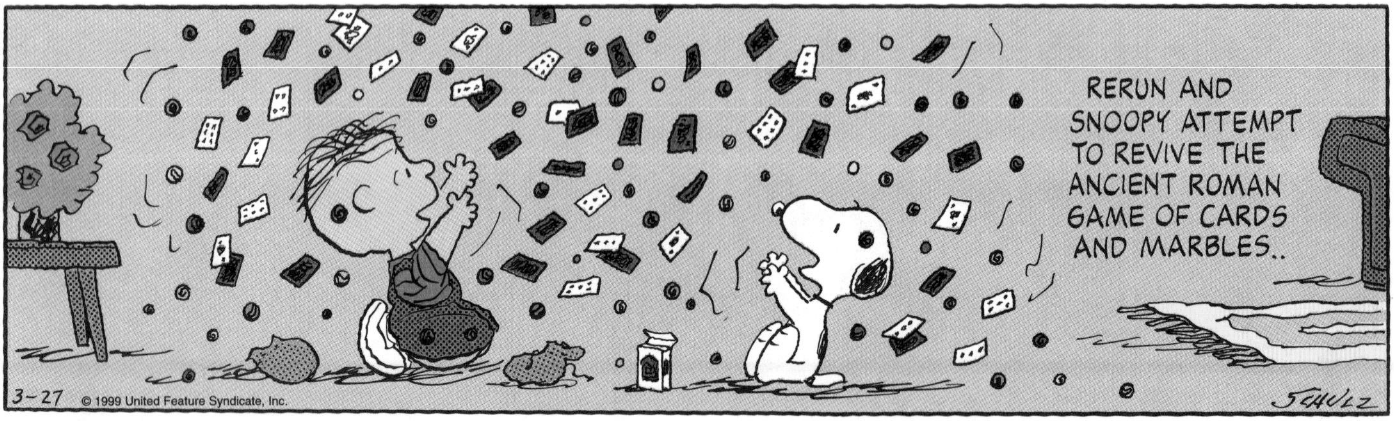
RERUN AND SNOOPY ATTEMPT TO REVIVE THE ANCIENT ROMAN GAME OF CARDS AND MARBLES..
3-27
© 1999 United Feature Syndicate, Inc.
SCHULZ

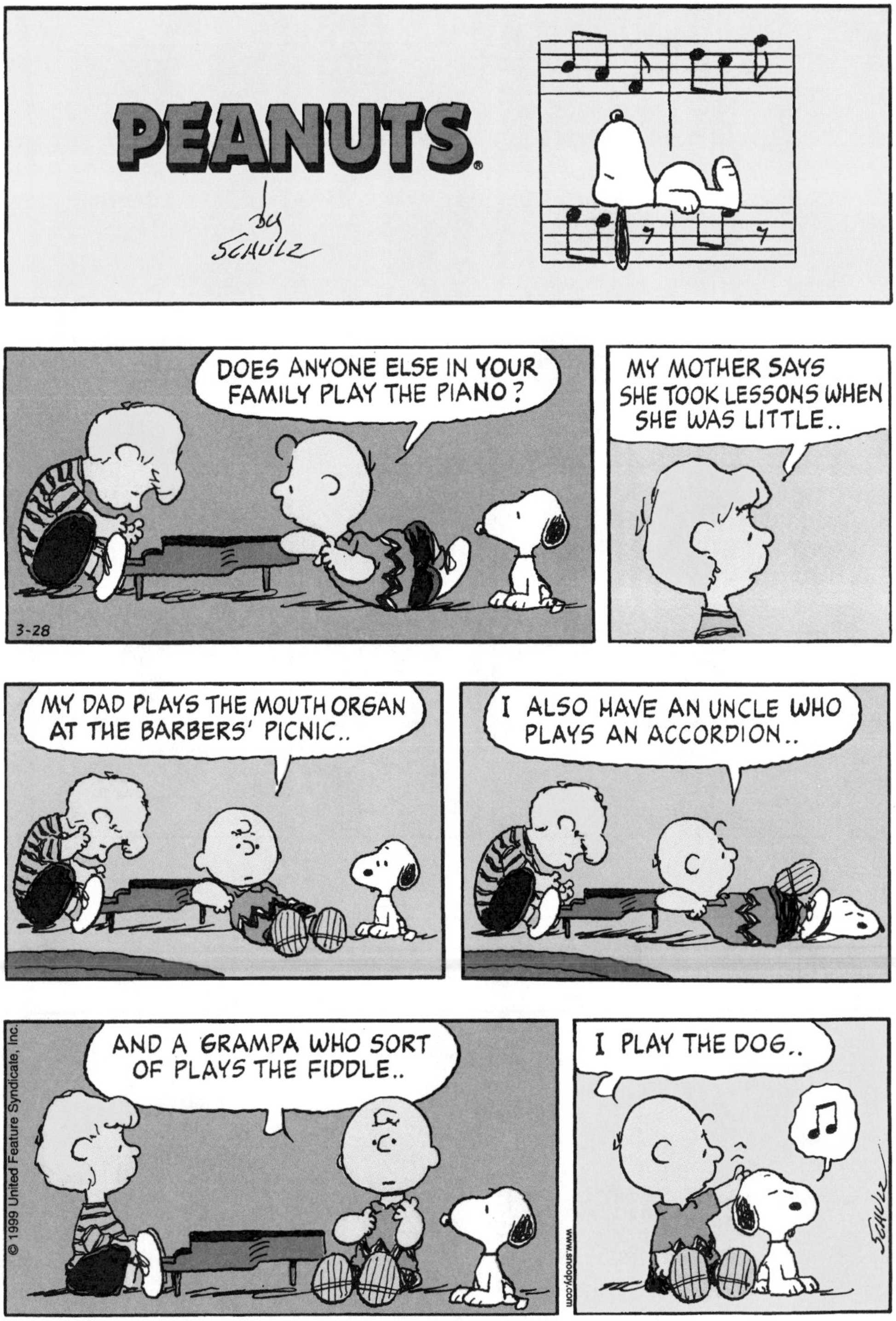
PEANUTS
by SCHULZ
DOES ANYONE ELSE IN YOUR FAMILY PLAY THE PIANO?
3-28
MY MOTHER SAYS SHE TOOK LESSONS WHEN SHE WAS LITTLE..
MY DAD PLAYS THE MOUTH ORGAN AT THE BARBERS' PICNIC..
I ALSO HAVE AN UNCLE WHO PLAYS AN ACCORDION..
© 1999 United Feature Syndicate, Inc.
AND A GRAMPA WHO SORT OF PLAYS THE FIDDLE..
www.snoopy.com
I PLAY THE DOG..
SCHULZ

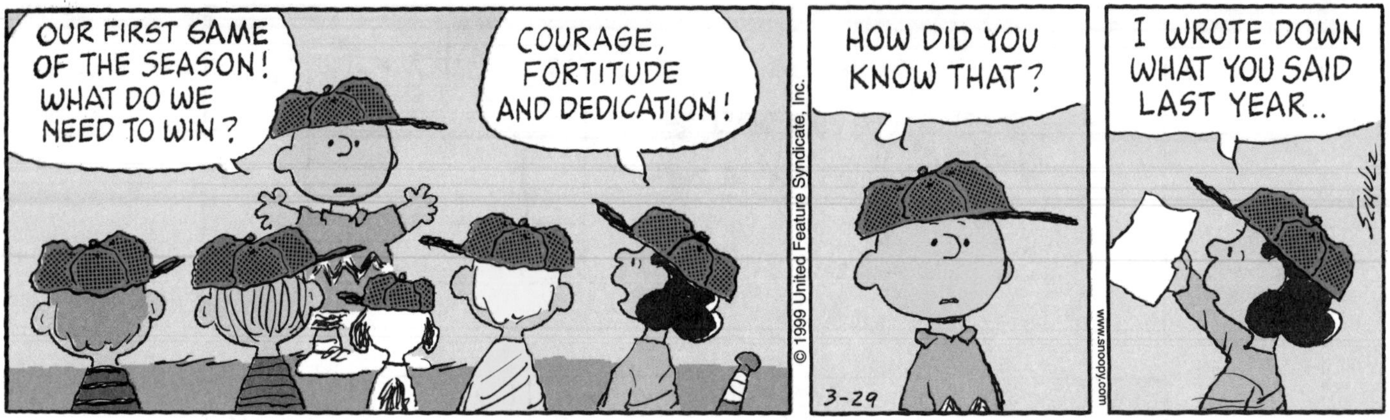
OUR FIRST GAME OF THE SEASON! WHAT DO WE NEED TO WIN?
COURAGE, FORTITUDE AND DEDICATION!
© 1999 United Feature Syndicate, Inc.
HOW DID YOU KNOW THAT?
3-29
www.snoopy.com
I WROTE DOWN WHAT YOU SAID LAST YEAR..
SCHULZ

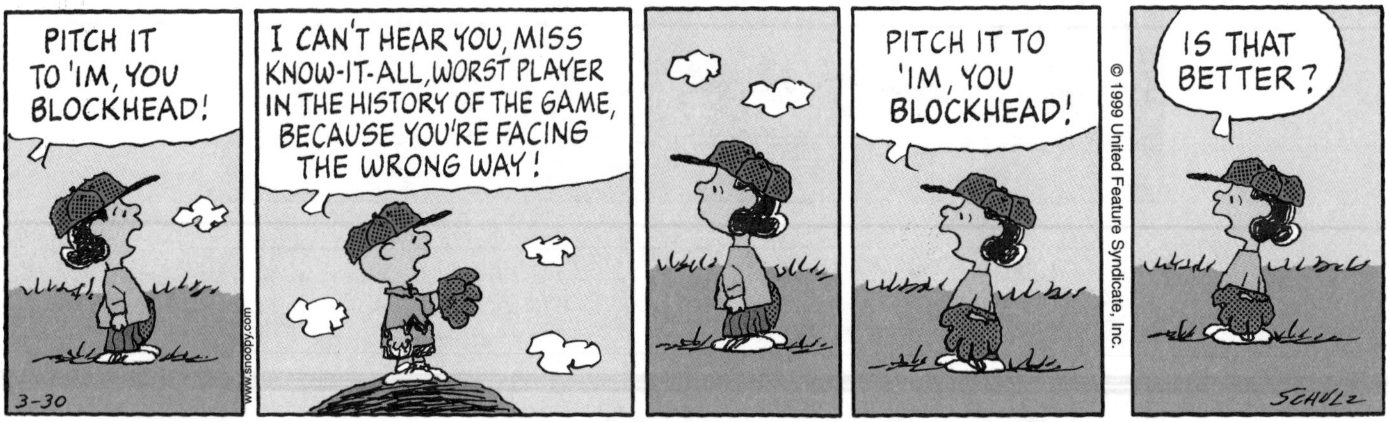
PITCH IT TO 'IM, YOU BLOCKHEAD!
3-30
www.snoopy.com
I CAN'T HEAR YOU, MISS KNOW-IT-ALL, WORST PLAYER IN THE HISTORY OF THE GAME, BECAUSE YOU'RE FACING THE WRONG WAY!
PITCH IT TO 'IM, YOU BLOCKHEAD!
© 1999 United Feature Syndicate, Inc.
IS THAT BETTER?
SCHULZ

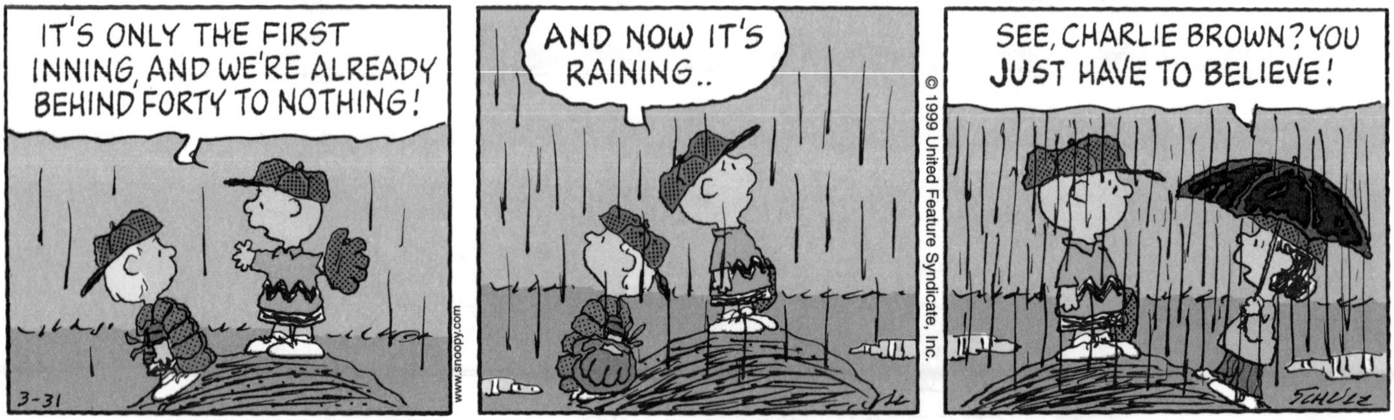
IT'S ONLY THE FIRST INNING, AND WE'RE ALREADY BEHIND FORTY TO NOTHING!
3-31
www.snoopy.com
AND NOW IT'S RAINING..
© 1999 United Feature Syndicate, Inc.
SEE, CHARLIE BROWN? YOU JUST HAVE TO BELIEVE!
SCHULZ

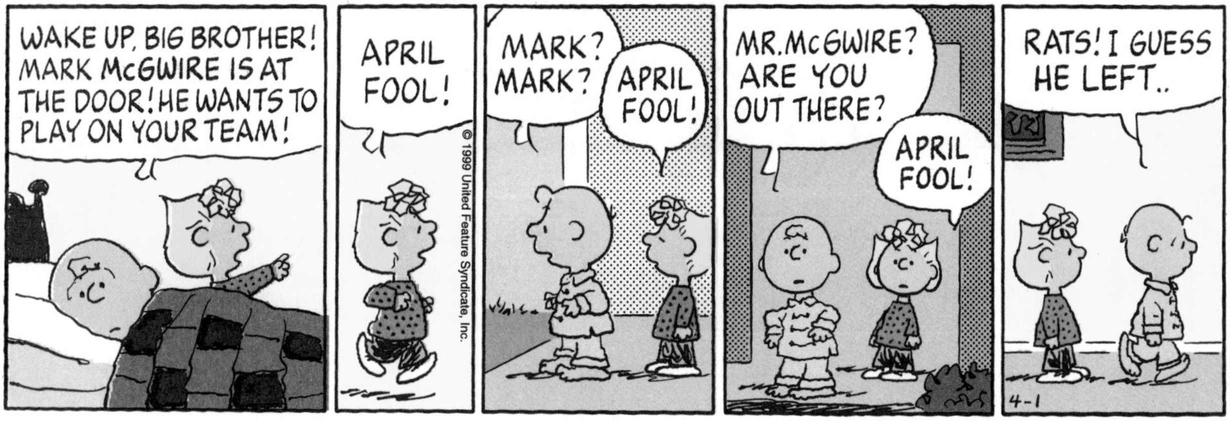
WAKE UP, BIG BROTHER! MARK McGWIRE IS AT THE DOOR! HE WANTS TO PLAY ON YOUR TEAM!
APRIL FOOL!
© 1999 United Feature Syndicate, Inc.
MARK? MARK?
APRIL FOOL!
MR. McGWIRE? ARE YOU OUT THERE?
APRIL FOOL!
RATS! I GUESS HE LEFT..
4-1
THERE'S A SPIDER ON YOUR BACK! APRIL FOOL!
SCHULZ

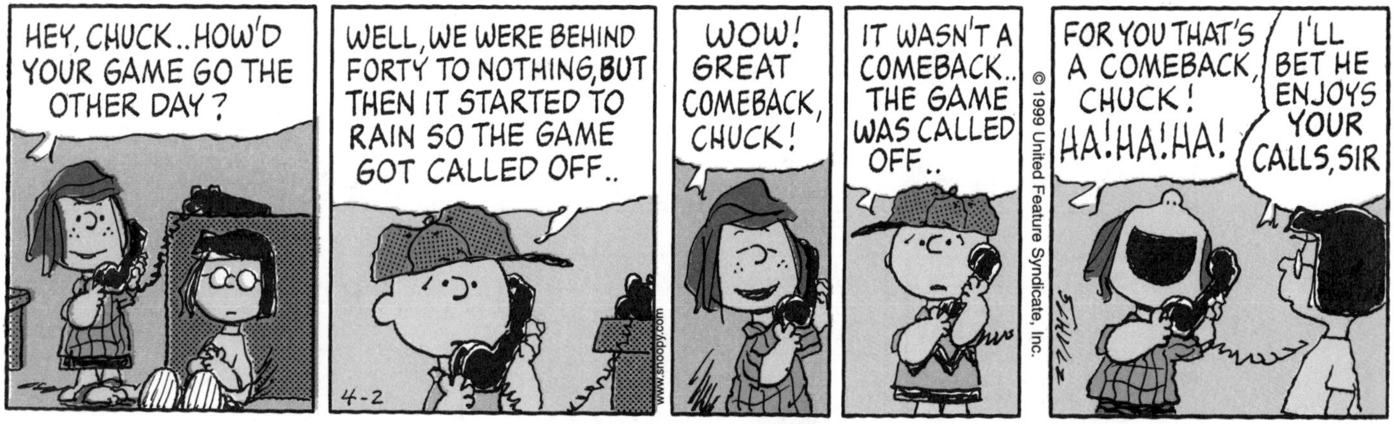
HEY, CHUCK..HOW'D YOUR GAME GO THE OTHER DAY?
WELL, WE WERE BEHIND FORTY TO NOTHING, BUT THEN IT STARTED TO RAIN SO THE GAME GOT CALLED OFF..
4-2
www.snoopy.com
WOW! GREAT COMEBACK, CHUCK!
IT WASN'T A COMEBACK.. THE GAME WAS CALLED OFF..
© 1999 United Feature Syndicate, Inc.
FOR YOU THAT'S A COMEBACK, CHUCK! HA! HA! HA!
I'LL BET HE ENJOYS YOUR CALLS, SIR
SCHULZ

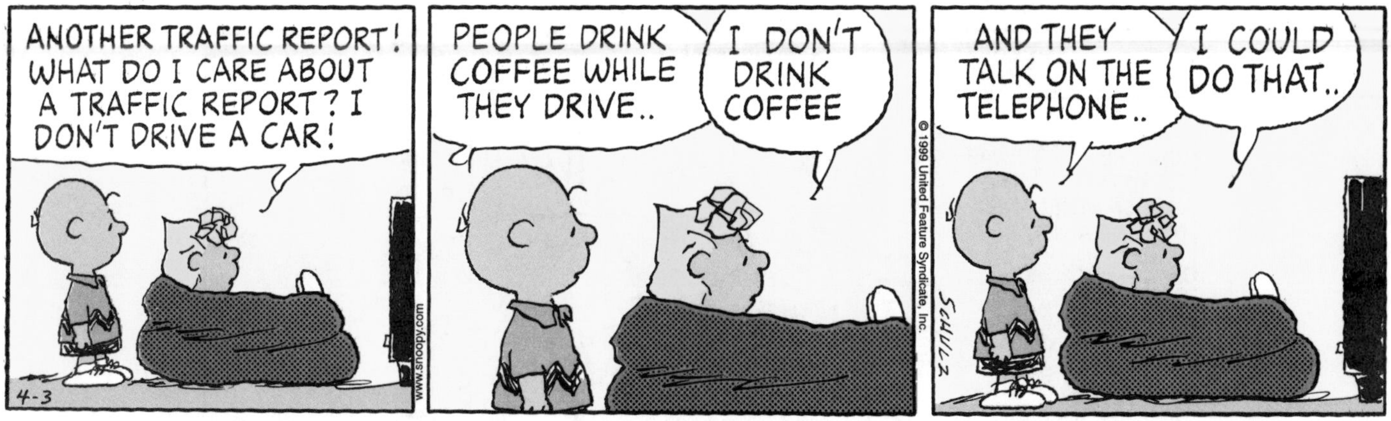
ANOTHER TRAFFIC REPORT! WHAT DO I CARE ABOUT A TRAFFIC REPORT? I DON'T DRIVE A CAR!
4-3
www.snoopy.com
PEOPLE DRINK COFFEE WHILE THEY DRIVE..
I DON'T DRINK COFFEE
© 1999 United Feature Syndicate, Inc.
AND THEY TALK ON THE TELEPHONE..
I COULD DO THAT..
SCHULZ

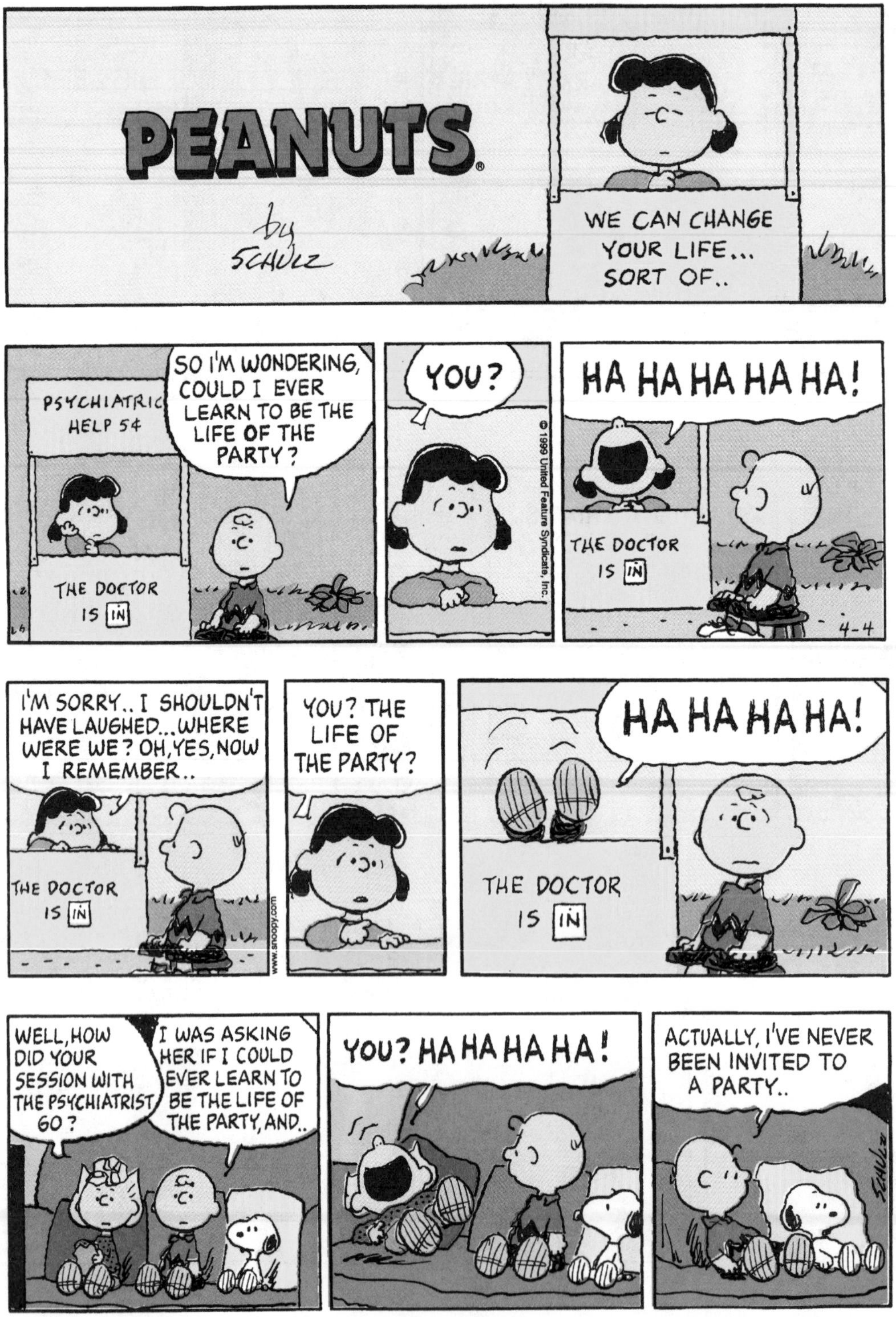
PEANUTS
by SCHULZ
WE CAN CHANGE YOUR LIFE... SORT OF..
PSYCHIATRIC HELP 5¢
THE DOCTOR IS IN
SO I'M WONDERING, COULD I EVER LEARN TO BE THE LIFE OF THE PARTY?
YOU?
© 1999 United Feature Syndicate, Inc.
HA HA HA HA HA!
THE DOCTOR IS IN
4-4
I'M SORRY.. I SHOULDN'T HAVE LAUGHED...WHERE WERE WE? OH, YES, NOW I REMEMBER..
THE DOCTOR IS IN
www.snoopy.com
YOU? THE LIFE OF THE PARTY?
HA HA HA HA!
THE DOCTOR IS IN
WELL, HOW DID YOUR SESSION WITH THE PSYCHIATRIST GO?
I WAS ASKING HER IF I COULD EVER LEARN TO BE THE LIFE OF THE PARTY, AND..
YOU? HA HA HA HA HA!
ACTUALLY, I'VE NEVER BEEN INVITED TO A PARTY..
SCHULZ

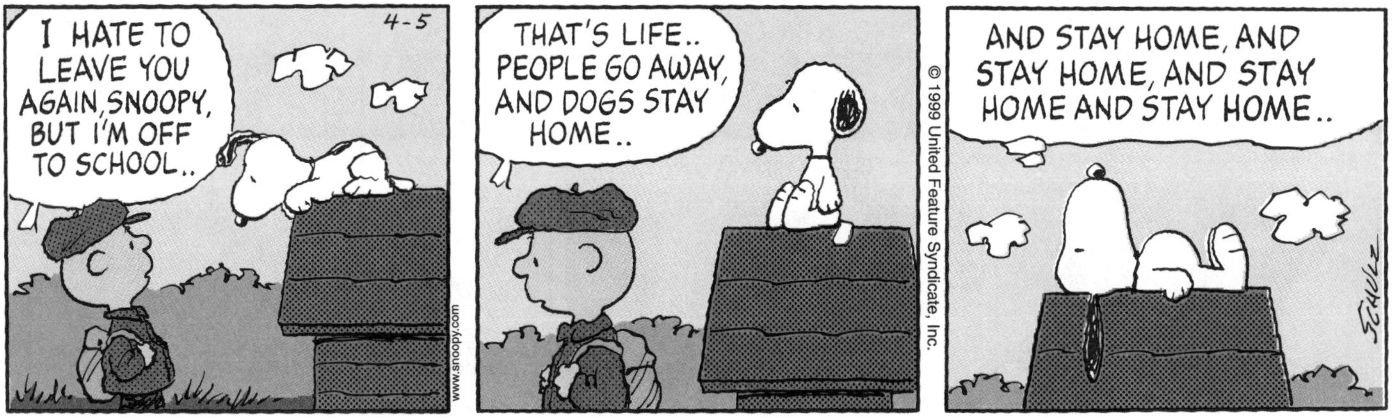
4-5
I HATE TO LEAVE YOU AGAIN, SNOOPY, BUT I'M OFF TO SCHOOL..
www.snoopy.com
THAT'S LIFE.. PEOPLE GO AWAY, AND DOGS STAY HOME..
© 1999 United Feature Syndicate, Inc.
AND STAY HOME, AND STAY HOME, AND STAY HOME AND STAY HOME..
SCHULZ

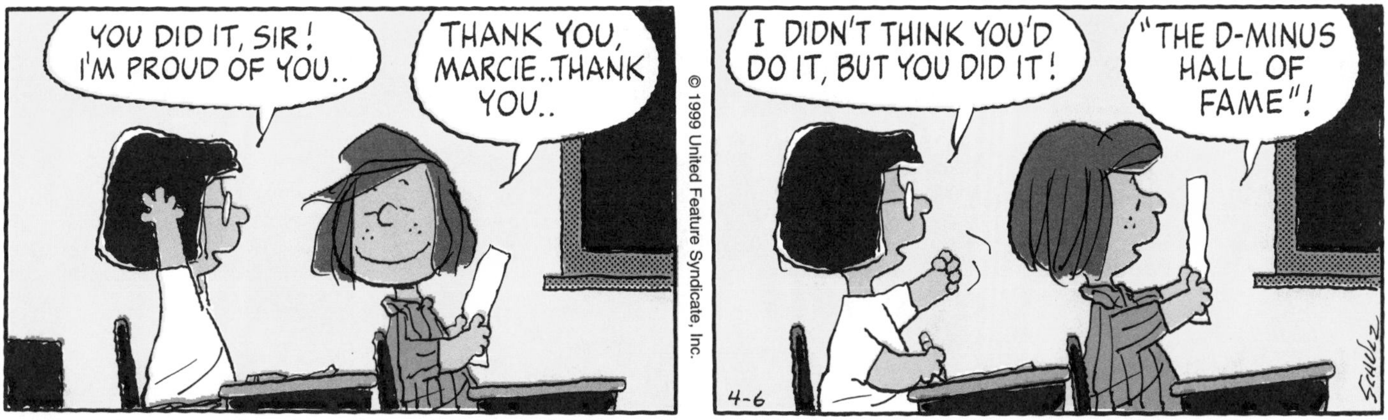
YOU DID IT, SIR! I'M PROUD OF YOU..
THANK YOU, MARCIE..THANK YOU..
© 1999 United Feature Syndicate, Inc.
I DIDN'T THINK YOU'D DO IT, BUT YOU DID IT!
"THE D-MINUS HALL OF FAME"!
4-6
SCHULZ

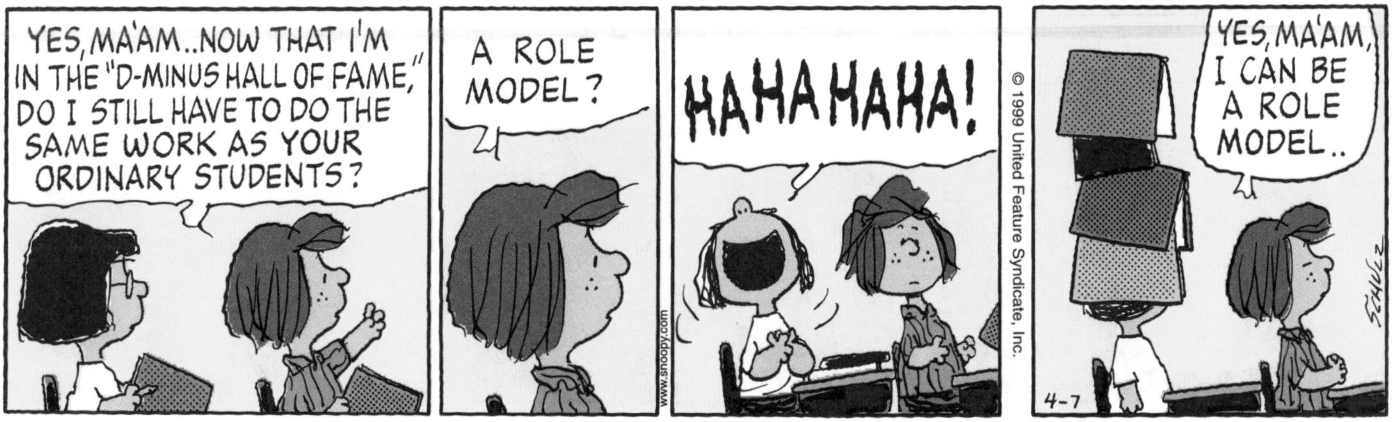
YES, MA'AM..NOW THAT I'M IN THE "D-MINUS HALL OF FAME," DO I STILL HAVE TO DO THE SAME WORK AS YOUR ORDINARY STUDENTS?
A ROLE MODEL?
www.snoopy.com
HAHAHAHA!
© 1999 United Feature Syndicate, Inc.
YES, MA'AM, I CAN BE A ROLE MODEL..
4-7
SCHULZ

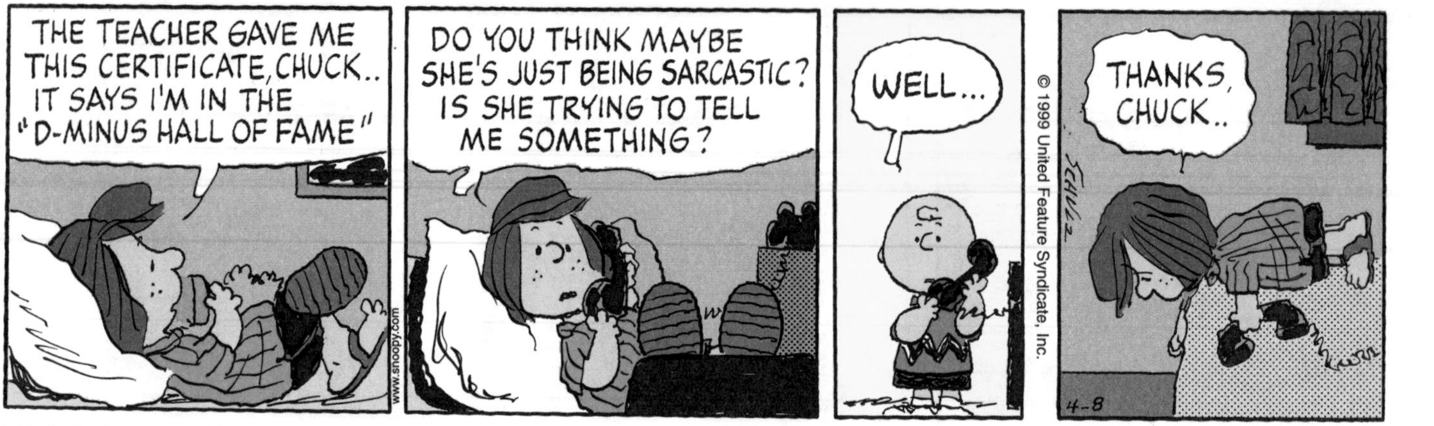
THE TEACHER GAVE ME THIS CERTIFICATE, CHUCK.. IT SAYS I'M IN THE "D-MINUS HALL OF FAME"
DO YOU THINK MAYBE SHE'S JUST BEING SARCASTIC? IS SHE TRYING TO TELL ME SOMETHING?
WELL...
THANKS, CHUCK..
www.snoopy.com
© 1999 United Feature Syndicate, Inc.
SCHULZ
4-8

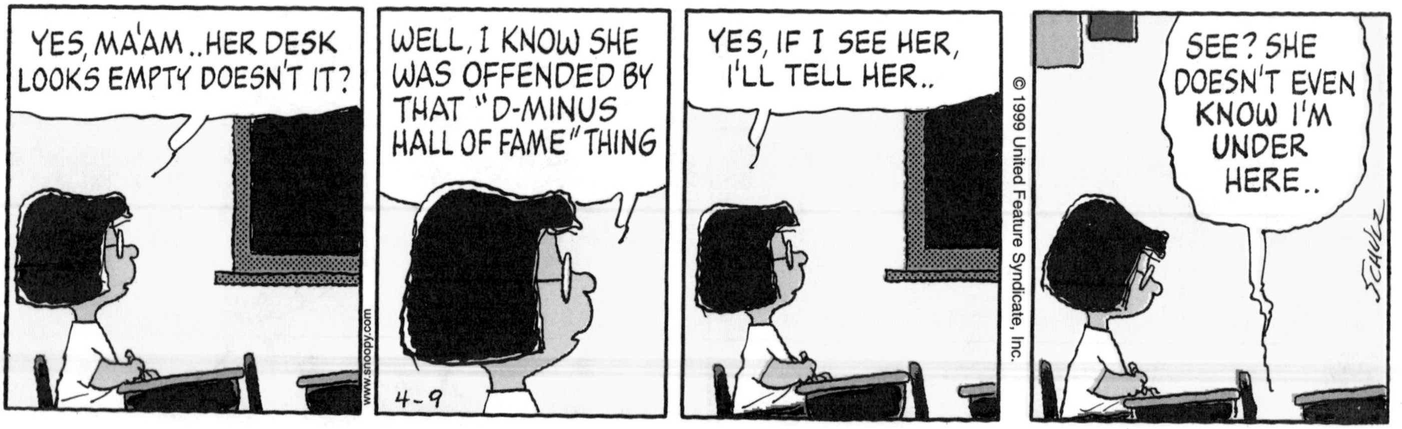
YES, MA'AM..HER DESK LOOKS EMPTY DOESN'T IT?
WELL, I KNOW SHE WAS OFFENDED BY THAT "D-MINUS HALL OF FAME" THING
YES, IF I SEE HER, I'LL TELL HER..
SEE? SHE DOESN'T EVEN KNOW I'M UNDER HERE..
www.snoopy.com
4-9
© 1999 United Feature Syndicate, Inc.
SCHULZ

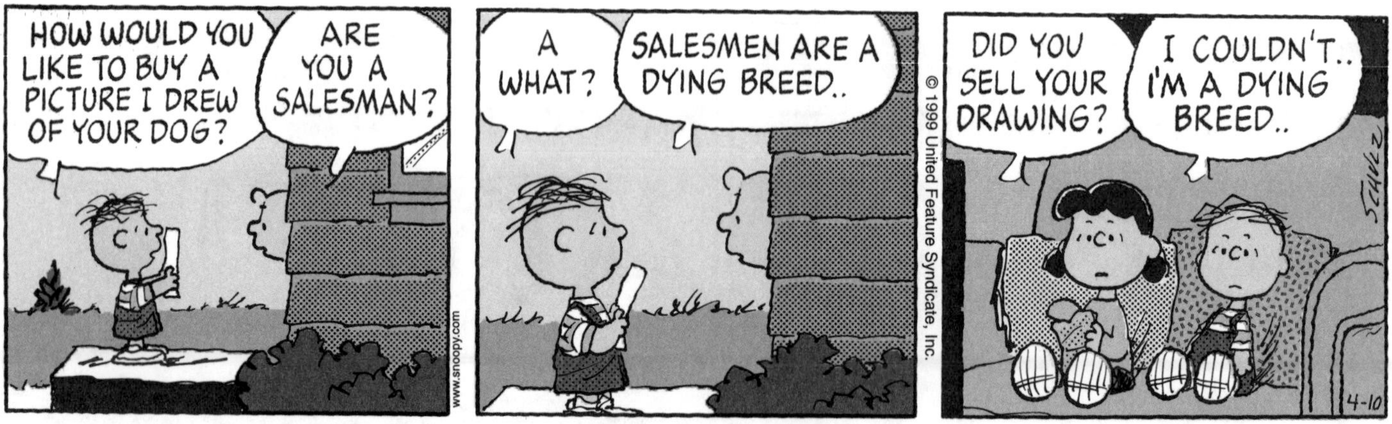
HOW WOULD YOU LIKE TO BUY A PICTURE I DREW OF YOUR DOG?
ARE YOU A SALESMAN?
A WHAT?
SALESMEN ARE A DYING BREED..
DID YOU SELL YOUR DRAWING?
I COULDN'T.. I'M A DYING BREED..
www.snoopy.com
© 1999 United Feature Syndicate, Inc.
SCHULZ
4-10

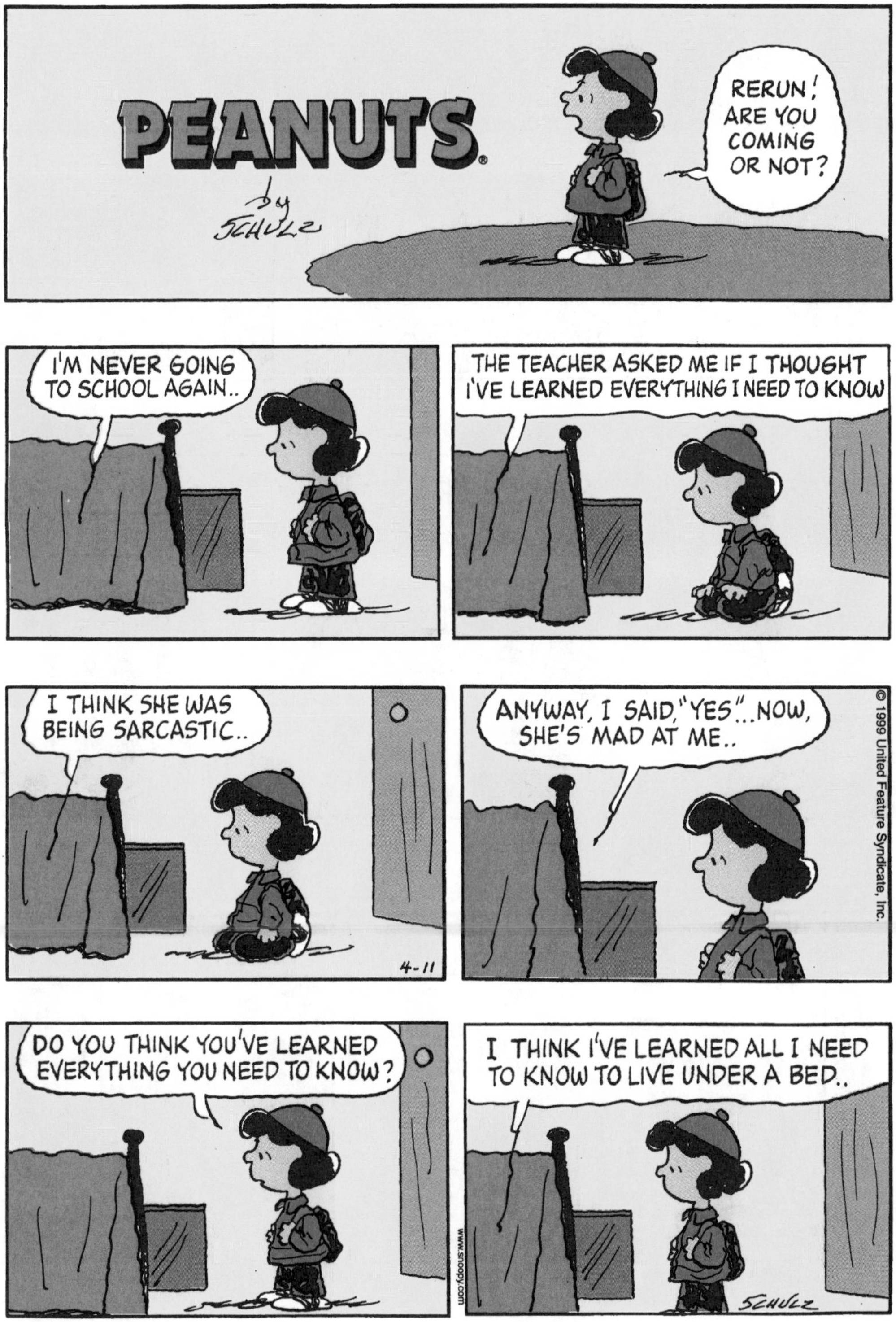
PEANUTS
by SCHULZ
RERUN! ARE YOU COMING OR NOT?
I'M NEVER GOING TO SCHOOL AGAIN..
THE TEACHER ASKED ME IF I THOUGHT I'VE LEARNED EVERYTHING I NEED TO KNOW
I THINK SHE WAS BEING SARCASTIC..
4-11
ANYWAY, I SAID, "YES"...NOW, SHE'S MAD AT ME..
DO YOU THINK YOU'VE LEARNED EVERYTHING YOU NEED TO KNOW?
I THINK I'VE LEARNED ALL I NEED TO KNOW TO LIVE UNDER A BED..
www.snoopy.com
SCHULZ

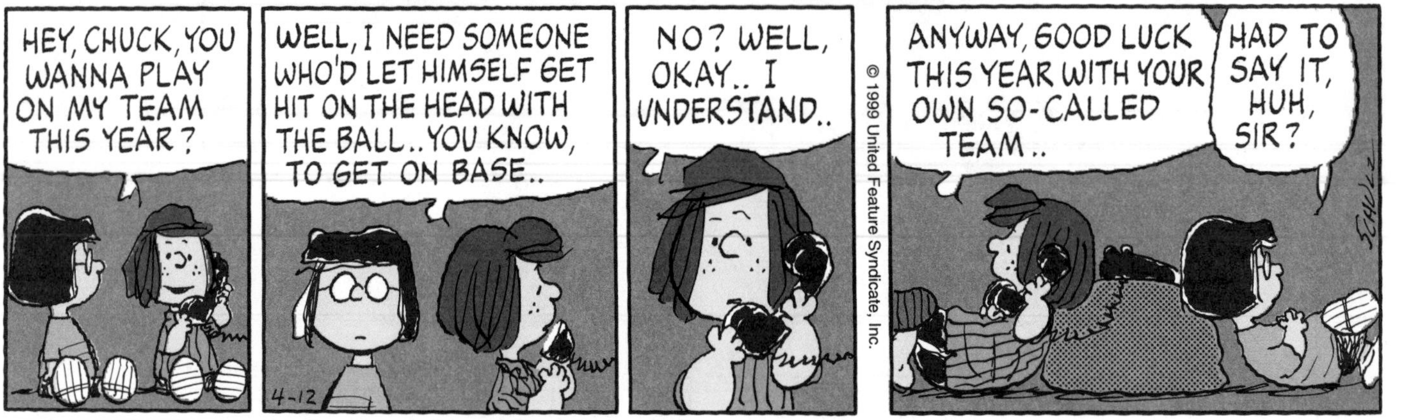
HEY, CHUCK, YOU WANNA PLAY ON MY TEAM THIS YEAR?
WELL, I NEED SOMEONE WHO'D LET HIMSELF GET HIT ON THE HEAD WITH THE BALL..YOU KNOW, TO GET ON BASE..
4-12
NO? WELL, OKAY.. I UNDERSTAND..
© 1999 United Feature Syndicate, Inc.
ANYWAY, GOOD LUCK THIS YEAR WITH YOUR OWN SO-CALLED TEAM..
HAD TO SAY IT, HUH, SIR?
SCHULZ

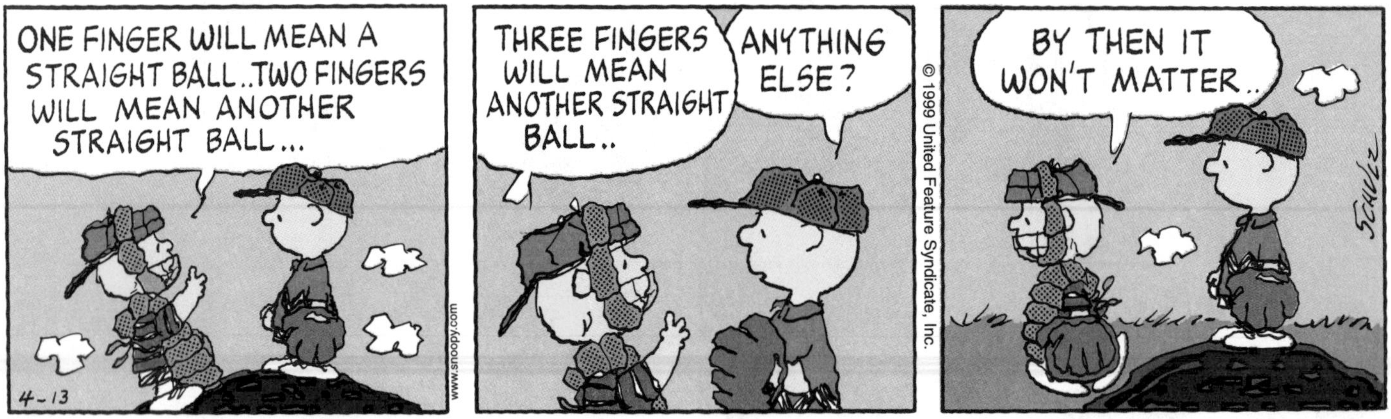
ONE FINGER WILL MEAN A STRAIGHT BALL..TWO FINGERS WILL MEAN ANOTHER STRAIGHT BALL...
4-13
www.snoopy.com
THREE FINGERS WILL MEAN ANOTHER STRAIGHT BALL..
ANYTHING ELSE?
© 1999 United Feature Syndicate, Inc.
BY THEN IT WON'T MATTER..
SCHULZ

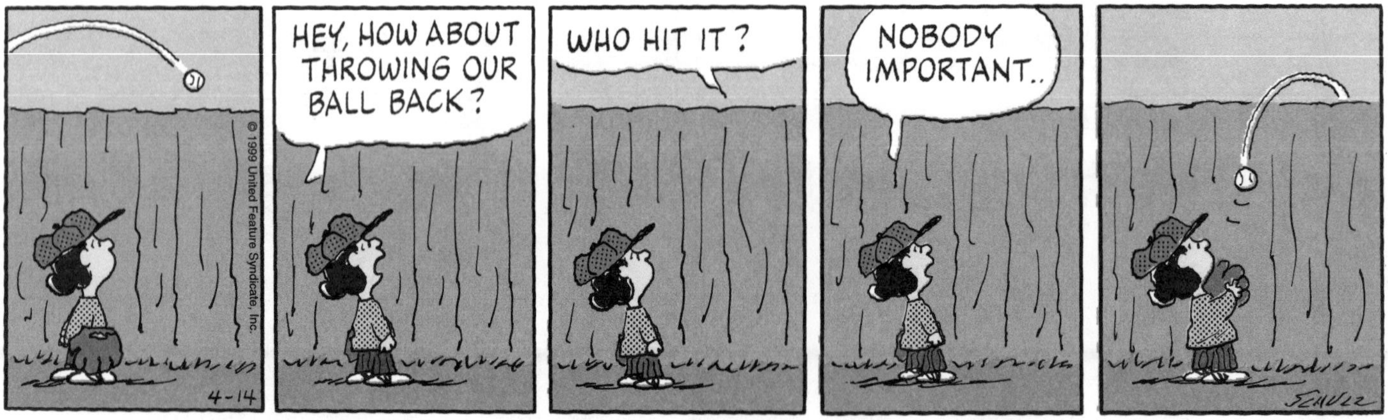
© 1999 United Feature Syndicate, Inc.
4-14
HEY, HOW ABOUT THROWING OUR BALL BACK?
WHO HIT IT?
NOBODY IMPORTANT..
SCHULZ

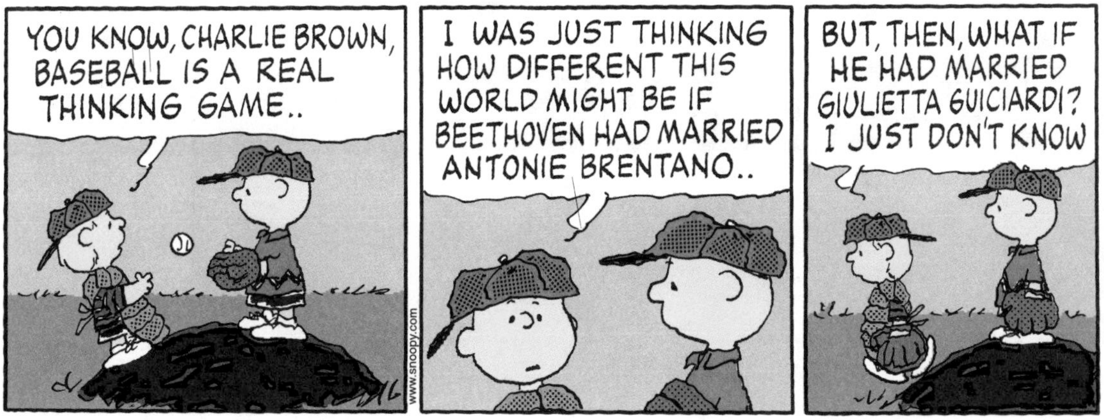
YOU KNOW, CHARLIE BROWN, BASEBALL IS A REAL THINKING GAME..
I WAS JUST THINKING HOW DIFFERENT THIS WORLD MIGHT BE IF BEETHOVEN HAD MARRIED ANTONIE BRENTANO..
BUT, THEN, WHAT IF HE HAD MARRIED GIULIETTA GUICIARDI? I JUST DON'T KNOW
CATCHERS HAVE TOO MUCH TIME TO THINK..
SCHULZ
4-15
www.snoopy.com
© 1999 United Feature Syndicate, Inc.

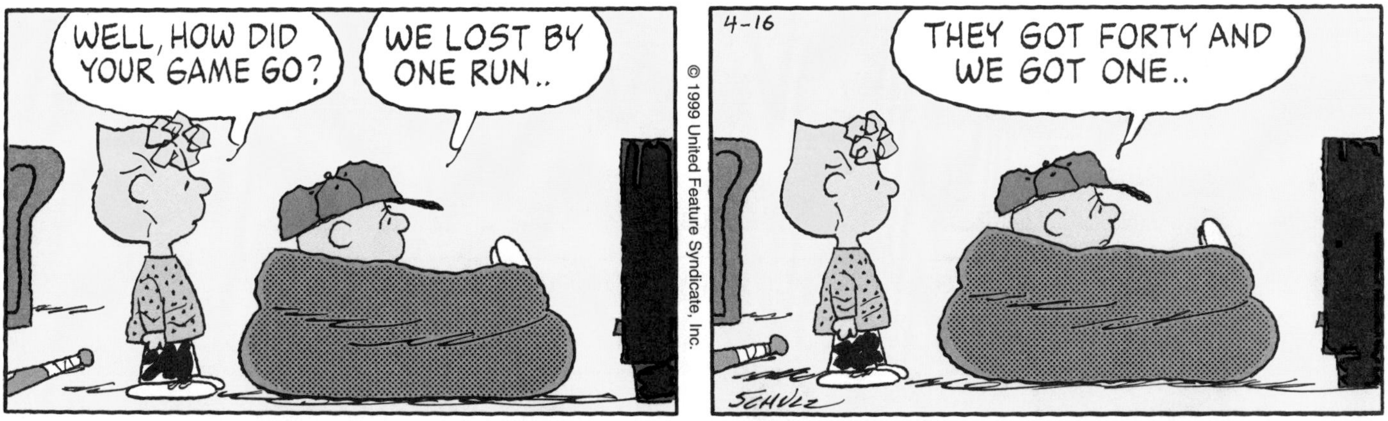
WELL, HOW DID YOUR GAME GO?
WE LOST BY ONE RUN..
THEY GOT FORTY AND WE GOT ONE..
4-16
SCHULZ
© 1999 United Feature Syndicate, Inc.

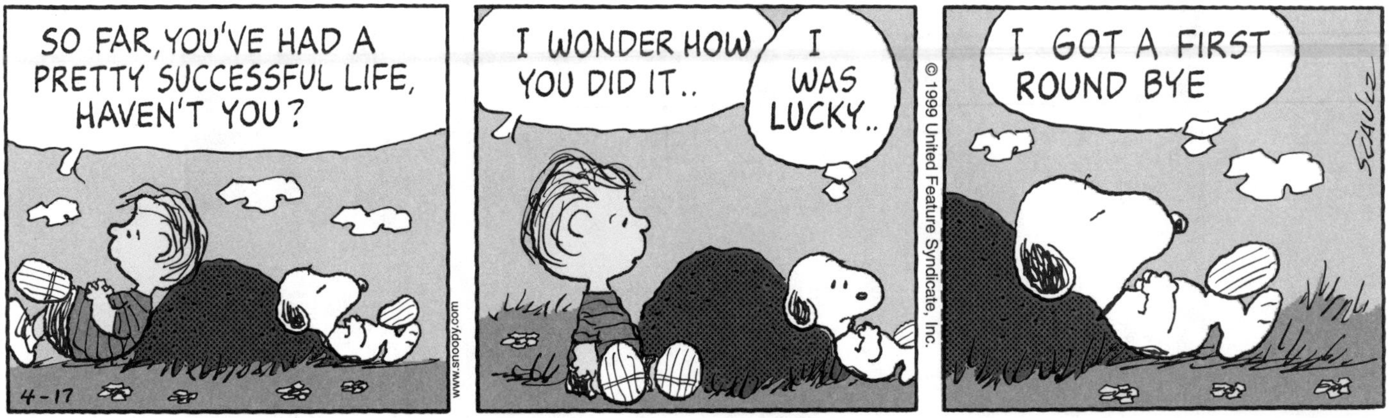
SO FAR, YOU'VE HAD A PRETTY SUCCESSFUL LIFE, HAVEN'T YOU?
I WONDER HOW YOU DID IT..
I WAS LUCKY..
I GOT A FIRST ROUND BYE
4-17
SCHULZ
www.snoopy.com
© 1999 United Feature Syndicate, Inc.

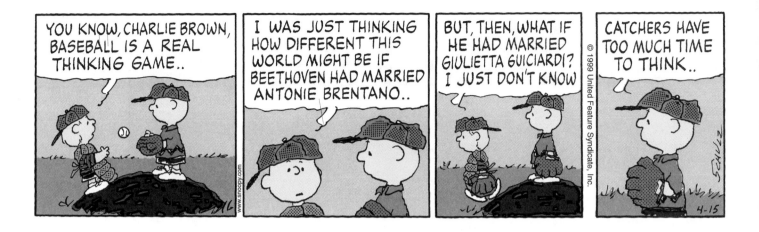

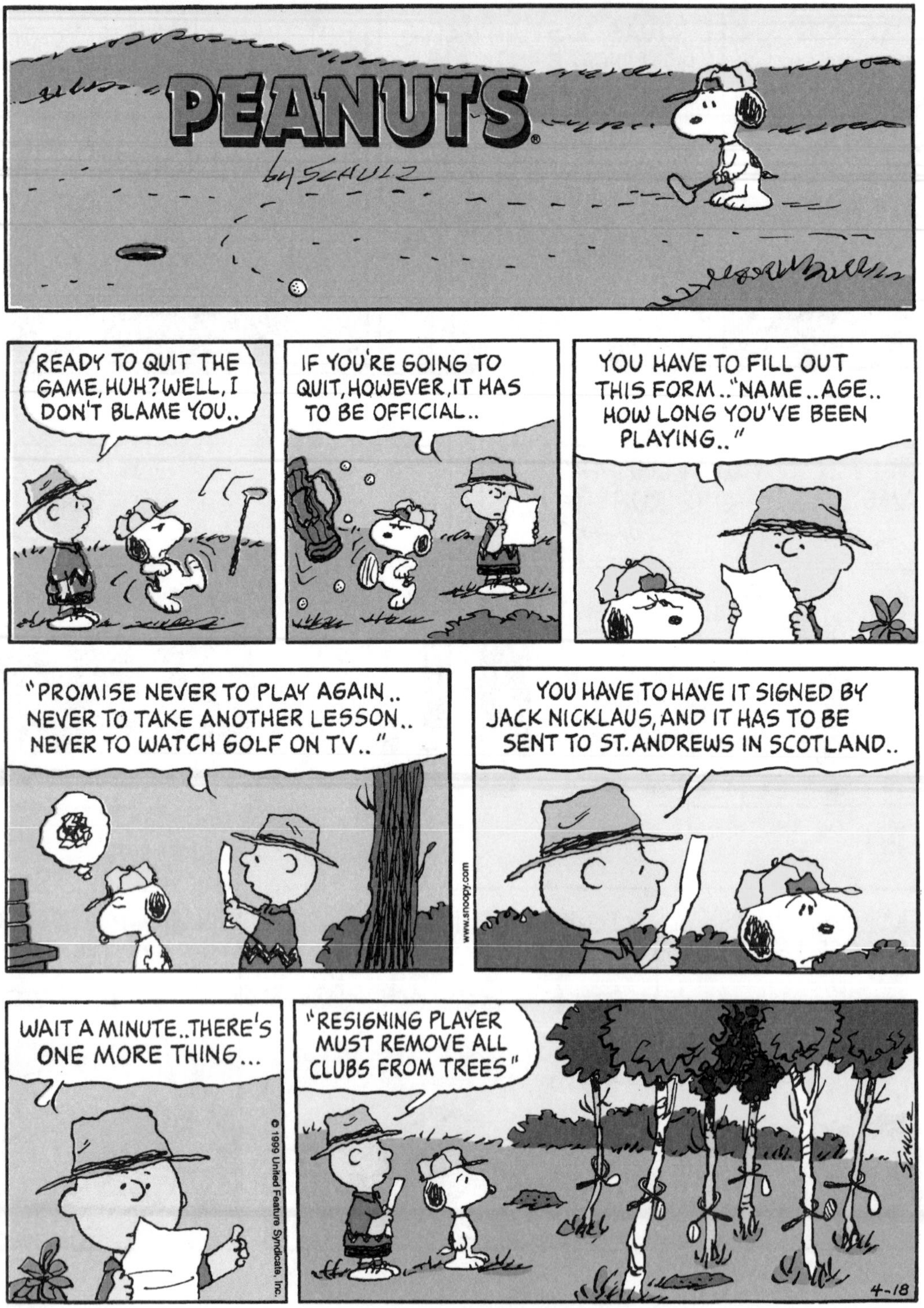
PEANUTS
by SCHULZ
READY TO QUIT THE GAME, HUH? WELL, I DON'T BLAME YOU..
IF YOU'RE GOING TO QUIT, HOWEVER, IT HAS TO BE OFFICIAL..
YOU HAVE TO FILL OUT THIS FORM.."NAME..AGE.. HOW LONG YOU'VE BEEN PLAYING.."
"PROMISE NEVER TO PLAY AGAIN.. NEVER TO TAKE ANOTHER LESSON.. NEVER TO WATCH GOLF ON TV.."
www.snoopy.com
YOU HAVE TO HAVE IT SIGNED BY JACK NICKLAUS, AND IT HAS TO BE SENT TO ST. ANDREWS IN SCOTLAND..
WAIT A MINUTE..THERE'S ONE MORE THING...
© 1999 United Feature Syndicate, Inc.
"RESIGNING PLAYER MUST REMOVE ALL CLUBS FROM TREES"
SCHULZ
4-18

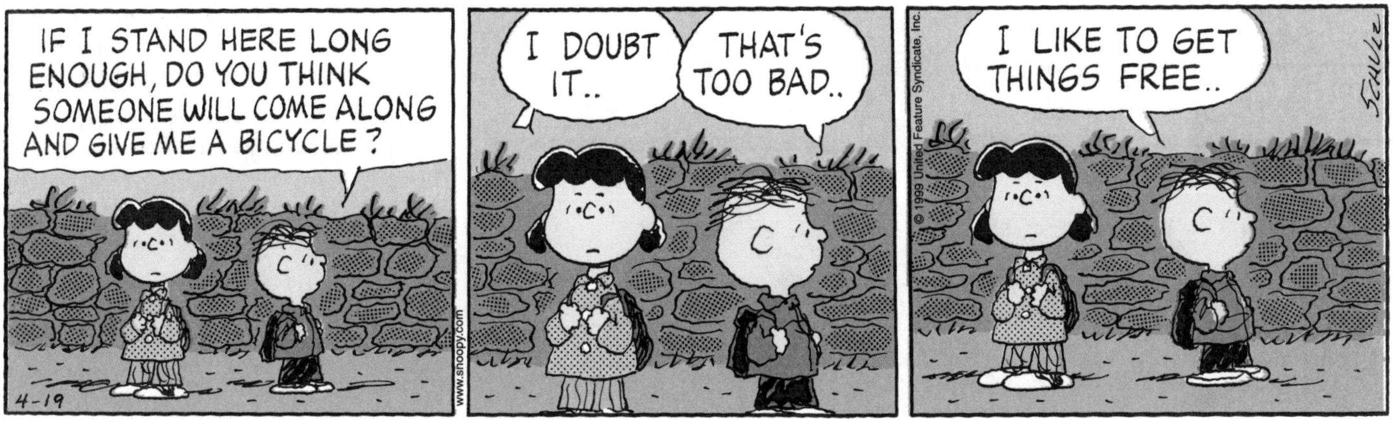
IF I STAND HERE LONG ENOUGH, DO YOU THINK SOMEONE WILL COME ALONG AND GIVE ME A BICYCLE?
4-19
www.snoopy.com
I DOUBT IT..
THAT'S TOO BAD..
© 1999 United Feature Syndicate, Inc.
I LIKE TO GET THINGS FREE..
SCHULZ

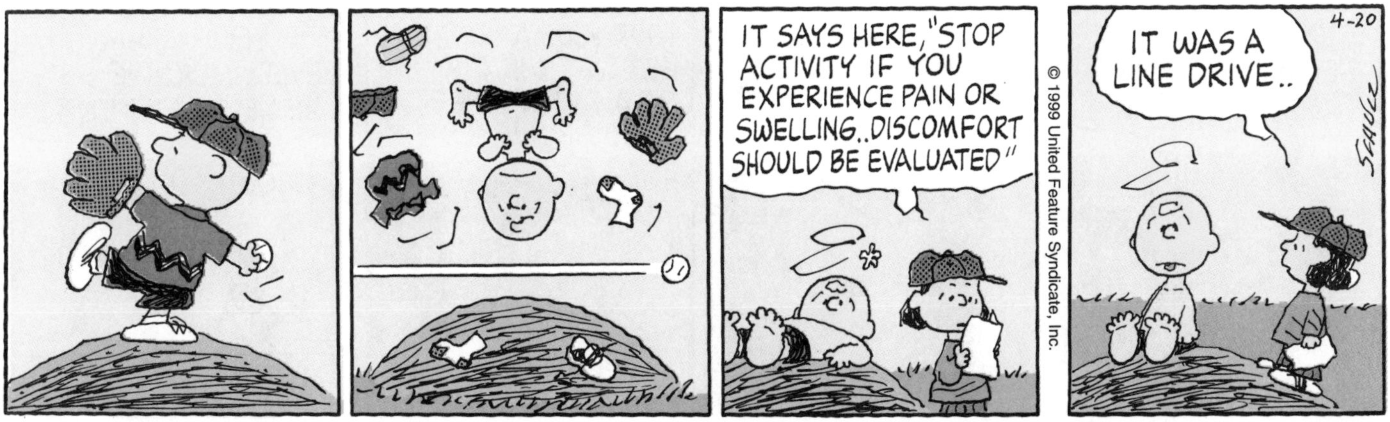
IT SAYS HERE, "STOP ACTIVITY IF YOU EXPERIENCE PAIN OR SWELLING..DISCOMFORT SHOULD BE EVALUATED"
© 1999 United Feature Syndicate, Inc.
4-20
IT WAS A LINE DRIVE..
SCHULZ

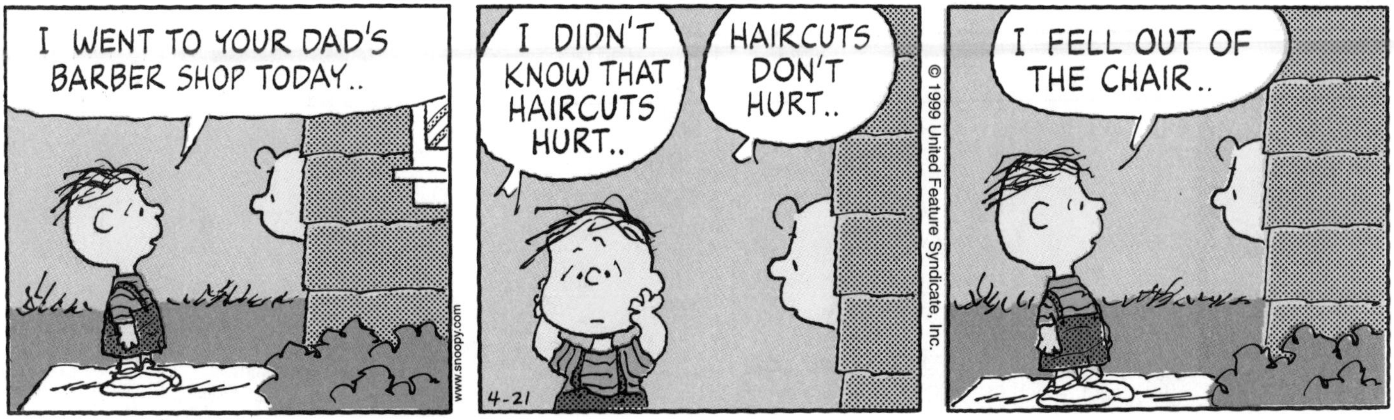
I WENT TO YOUR DAD'S BARBER SHOP TODAY..
www.snoopy.com
I DIDN'T KNOW THAT HAIRCUTS HURT..
HAIRCUTS DON'T HURT..
4-21
© 1999 United Feature Syndicate, Inc.
I FELL OUT OF THE CHAIR..

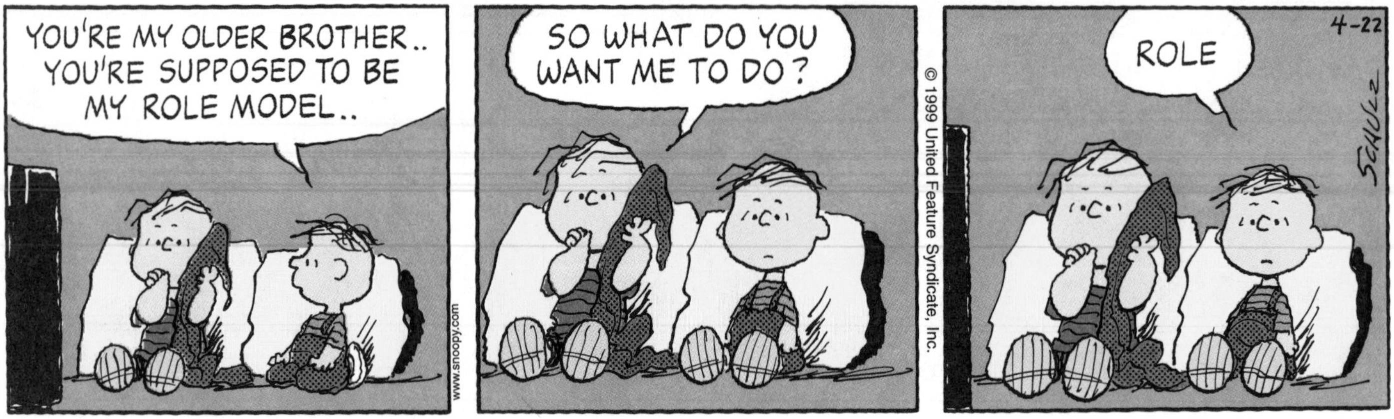
YOU'RE MY OLDER BROTHER.. YOU'RE SUPPOSED TO BE MY ROLE MODEL..
SO WHAT DO YOU WANT ME TO DO?
ROLE
4-22
www.snoopy.com
© 1999 United Feature Syndicate, Inc.
SCHULZ

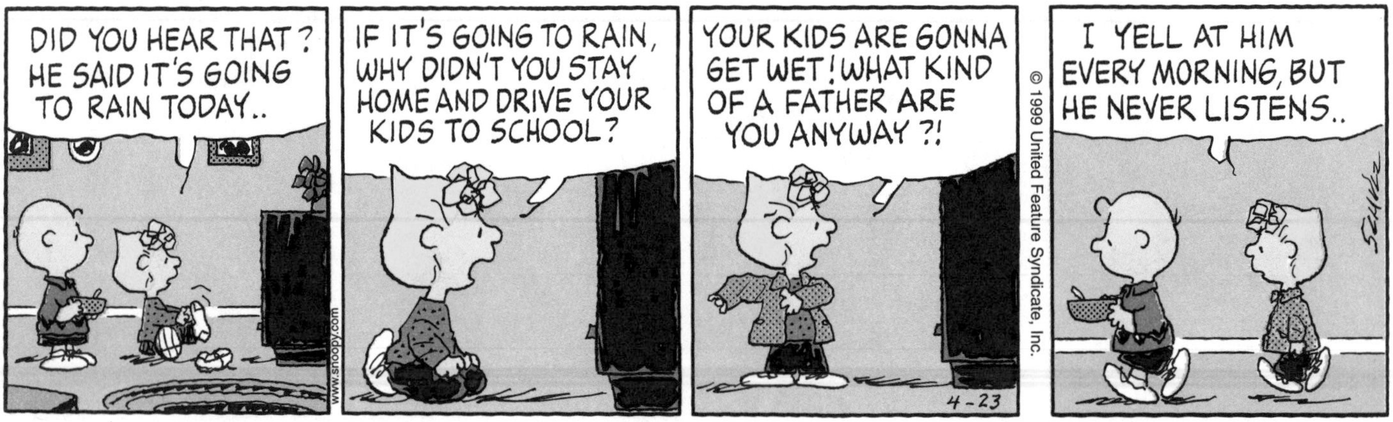
DID YOU HEAR THAT? HE SAID IT'S GOING TO RAIN TODAY..
IF IT'S GOING TO RAIN, WHY DIDN'T YOU STAY HOME AND DRIVE YOUR KIDS TO SCHOOL?
YOUR KIDS ARE GONNA GET WET! WHAT KIND OF A FATHER ARE YOU ANYWAY?!
I YELL AT HIM EVERY MORNING, BUT HE NEVER LISTENS..
4-23
www.snoopy.com
© 1999 United Feature Syndicate, Inc.
SCHULZ

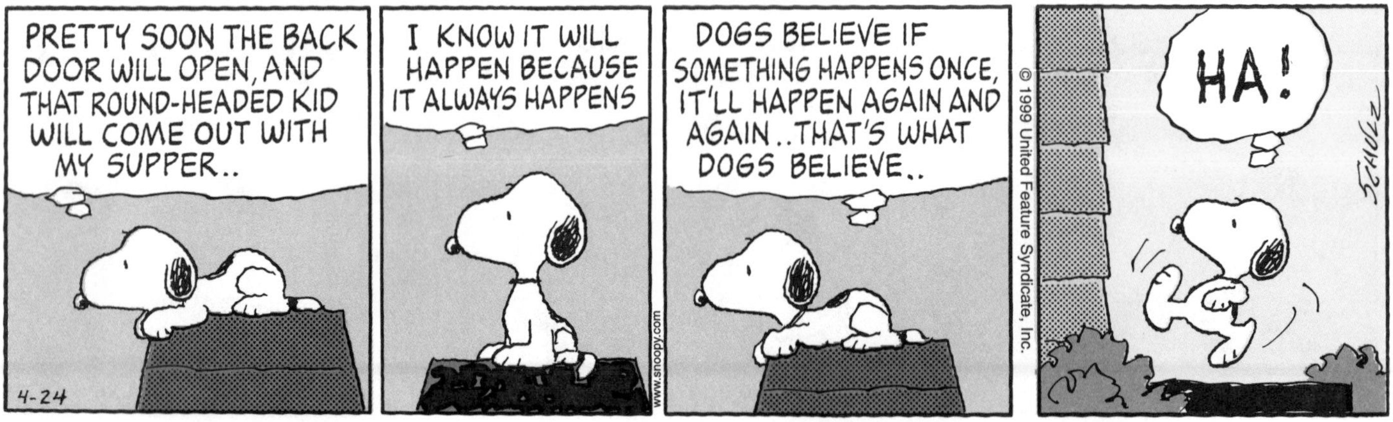
PRETTY SOON THE BACK DOOR WILL OPEN, AND THAT ROUND-HEADED KID WILL COME OUT WITH MY SUPPER..
I KNOW IT WILL HAPPEN BECAUSE IT ALWAYS HAPPENS
DOGS BELIEVE IF SOMETHING HAPPENS ONCE, IT'LL HAPPEN AGAIN AND AGAIN..THAT'S WHAT DOGS BELIEVE..
HA!
4-24
www.snoopy.com
© 1999 United Feature Syndicate, Inc.
SCHULZ

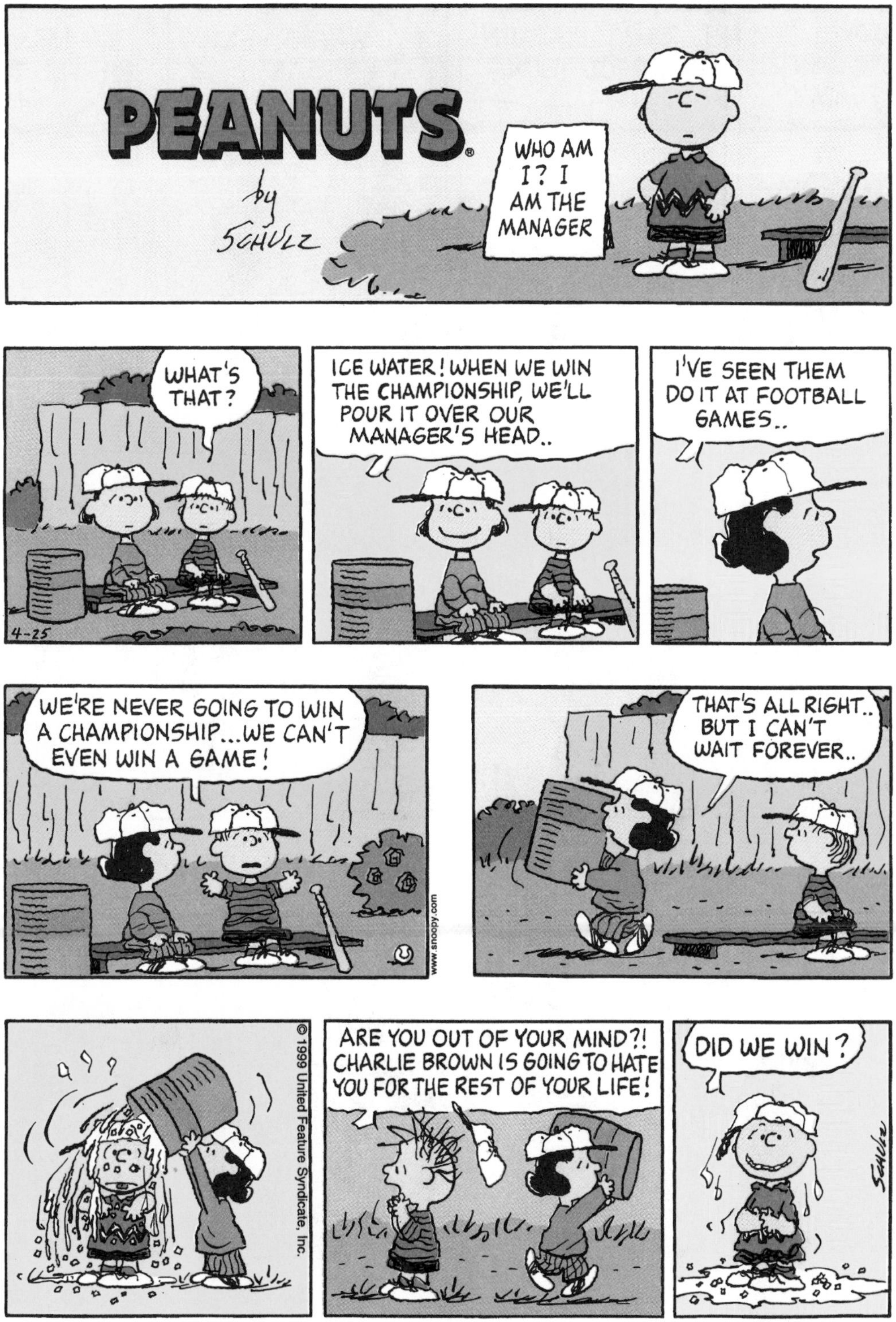
PEANUTS
by SCHULZ
WHO AM I? I AM THE MANAGER
4-25
WHAT'S THAT?
ICE WATER! WHEN WE WIN THE CHAMPIONSHIP, WE'LL POUR IT OVER OUR MANAGER'S HEAD..
I'VE SEEN THEM DO IT AT FOOTBALL GAMES..
WE'RE NEVER GOING TO WIN A CHAMPIONSHIP...WE CAN'T EVEN WIN A GAME!
www.snoopy.com
THAT'S ALL RIGHT.. BUT I CAN'T WAIT FOREVER..
© 1999 United Feature Syndicate, Inc.
ARE YOU OUT OF YOUR MIND?! CHARLIE BROWN IS GOING TO HATE YOU FOR THE REST OF YOUR LIFE!
DID WE WIN?
SCHULZ

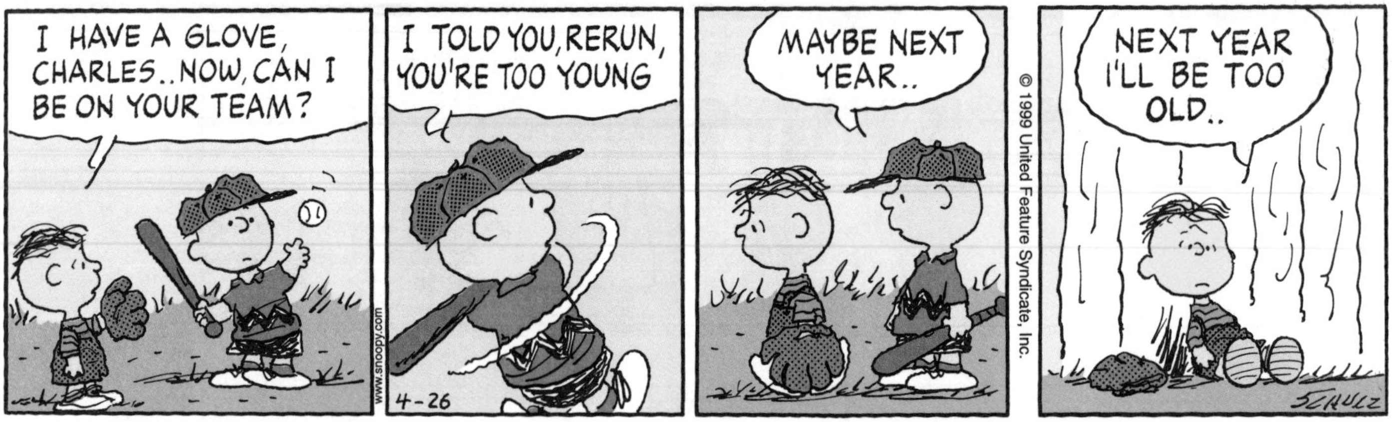
I HAVE A GLOVE, CHARLES..NOW, CAN I BE ON YOUR TEAM?
I TOLD YOU, RERUN, YOU'RE TOO YOUNG
MAYBE NEXT YEAR..
NEXT YEAR I'LL BE TOO OLD..
4-26
www.snoopy.com
© 1999 United Feature Syndicate, Inc.
SCHULZ

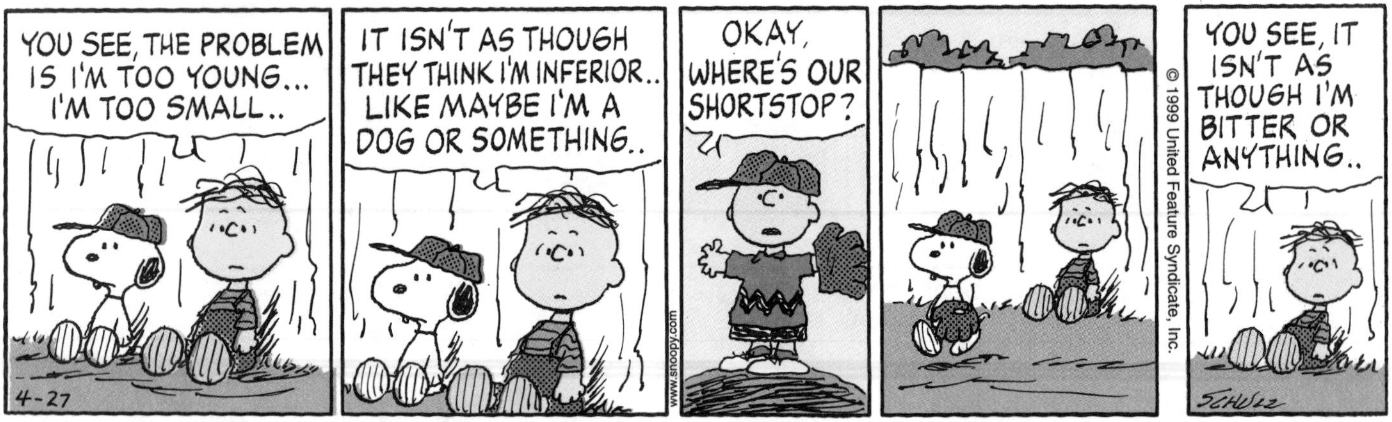
YOU SEE, THE PROBLEM IS I'M TOO YOUNG... I'M TOO SMALL..
IT ISN'T AS THOUGH THEY THINK I'M INFERIOR.. LIKE MAYBE I'M A DOG OR SOMETHING..
OKAY, WHERE'S OUR SHORTSTOP?
YOU SEE, IT ISN'T AS THOUGH I'M BITTER OR ANYTHING..
4-27
www.snoopy.com
© 1999 United Feature Syndicate, Inc.
SCHULZ

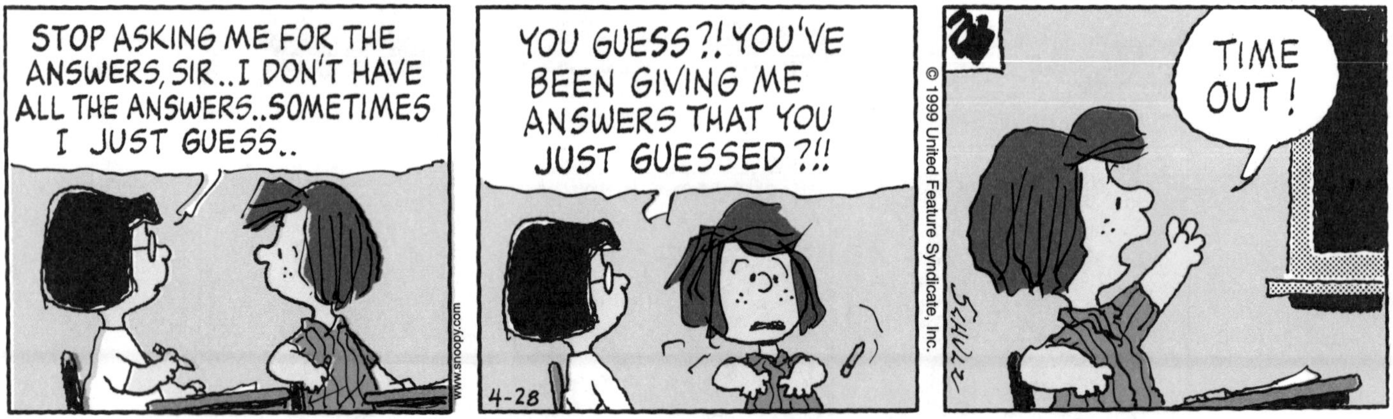
STOP ASKING ME FOR THE ANSWERS, SIR..I DON'T HAVE ALL THE ANSWERS..SOMETIMES I JUST GUESS..
YOU GUESS?! YOU'VE BEEN GIVING ME ANSWERS THAT YOU JUST GUESSED?!!
TIME OUT!
4-28
www.snoopy.com
© 1999 United Feature Syndicate, Inc.
SCHULZ

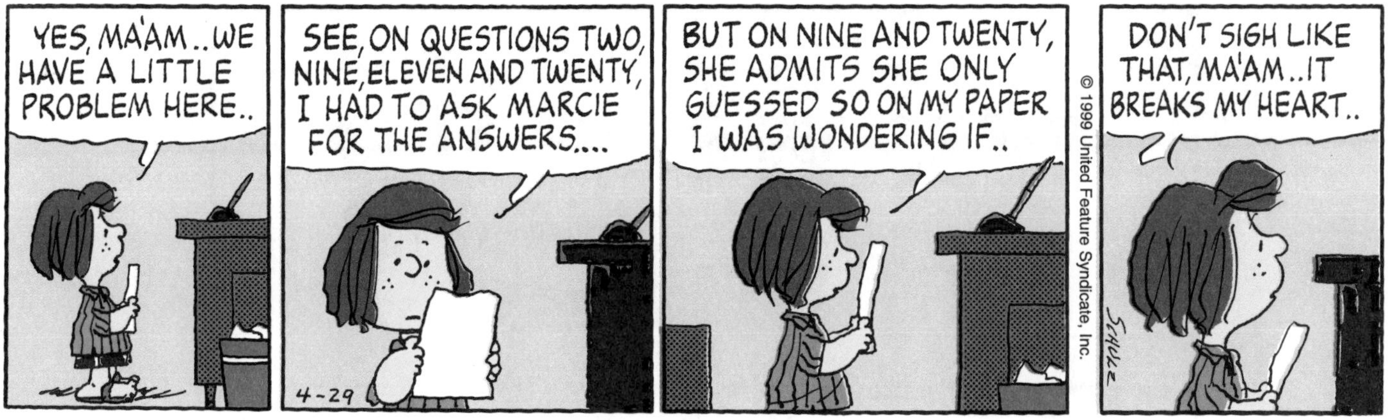
YES, MA'AM..WE HAVE A LITTLE PROBLEM HERE..
SEE, ON QUESTIONS TWO, NINE, ELEVEN AND TWENTY, I HAD TO ASK MARCIE FOR THE ANSWERS....
4-29
BUT ON NINE AND TWENTY, SHE ADMITS SHE ONLY GUESSED SO ON MY PAPER I WAS WONDERING IF..
© 1999 United Feature Syndicate, Inc.
DON'T SIGH LIKE THAT, MA'AM..IT BREAKS MY HEART..
SCHULZ

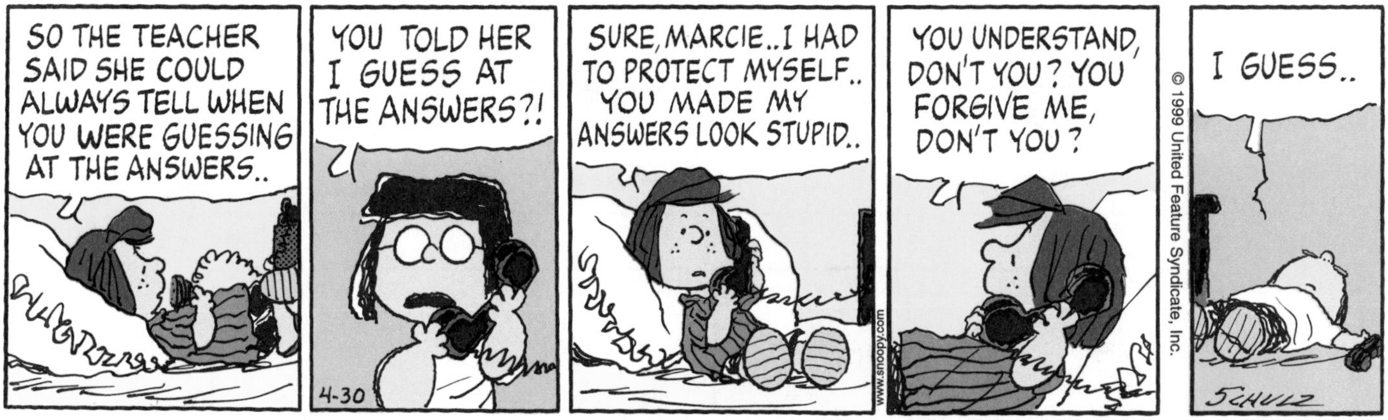
SO THE TEACHER SAID SHE COULD ALWAYS TELL WHEN YOU WERE GUESSING AT THE ANSWERS..
YOU TOLD HER I GUESS AT THE ANSWERS?!
4-30
SURE, MARCIE..I HAD TO PROTECT MYSELF.. YOU MADE MY ANSWERS LOOK STUPID..
www.snoopy.com
YOU UNDERSTAND, DON'T YOU? YOU FORGIVE ME, DON'T YOU?
© 1999 United Feature Syndicate, Inc.
I GUESS..
SCHULZ

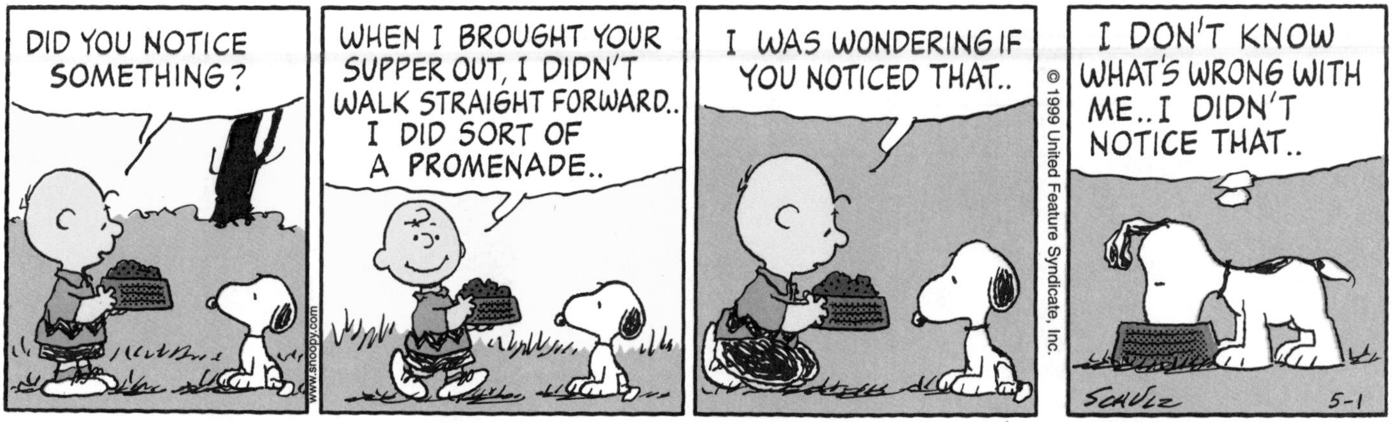
DID YOU NOTICE SOMETHING?
www.snoopy.com
WHEN I BROUGHT YOUR SUPPER OUT, I DIDN'T WALK STRAIGHT FORWARD.. I DID SORT OF A PROMENADE..
I WAS WONDERING IF YOU NOTICED THAT..
© 1999 United Feature Syndicate, Inc.
I DON'T KNOW WHAT'S WRONG WITH ME..I DIDN'T NOTICE THAT..
SCHULZ
5-1

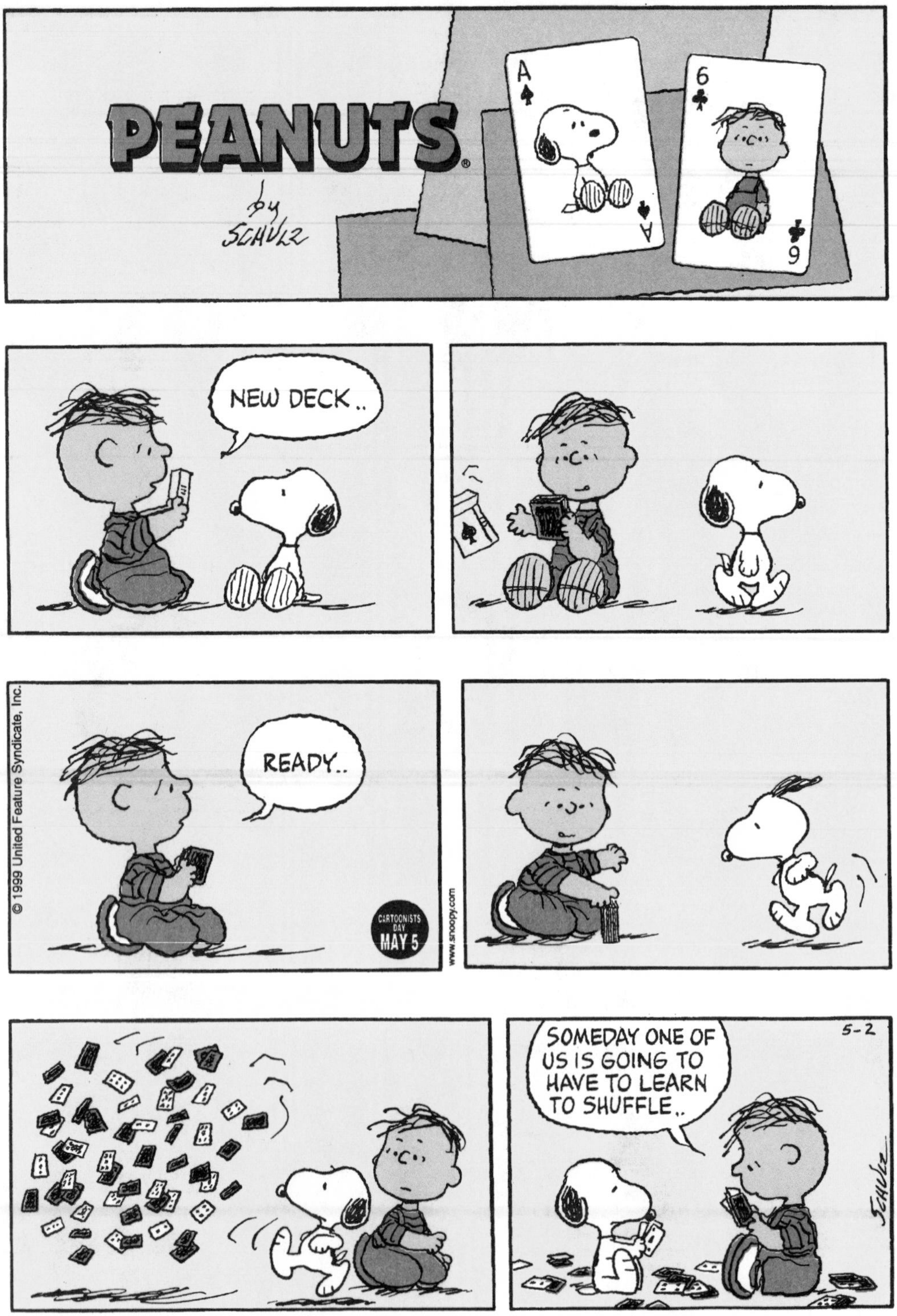
PEANUTS®
by SCHULZ
NEW DECK..
© 1999 United Feature Syndicate, Inc.
READY..
CARTOONISTS DAY MAY 5
www.snoopy.com
5-2
SOMEDAY ONE OF US IS GOING TO HAVE TO LEARN TO SHUFFLE..
SCHULZ

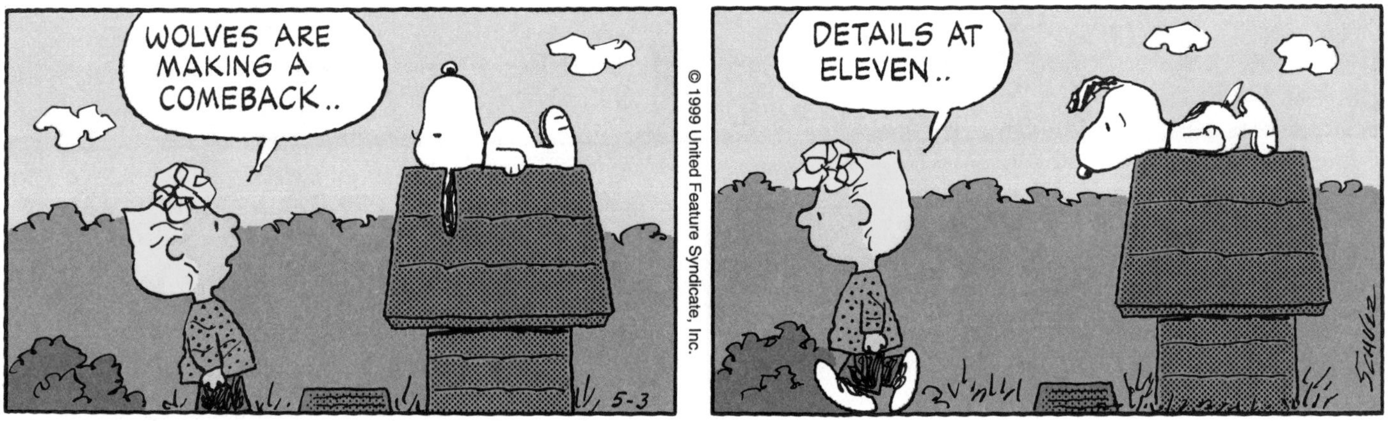
WOLVES ARE MAKING A COMEBACK..
5-3
© 1999 United Feature Syndicate, Inc.
DETAILS AT ELEVEN..
SCHULZ

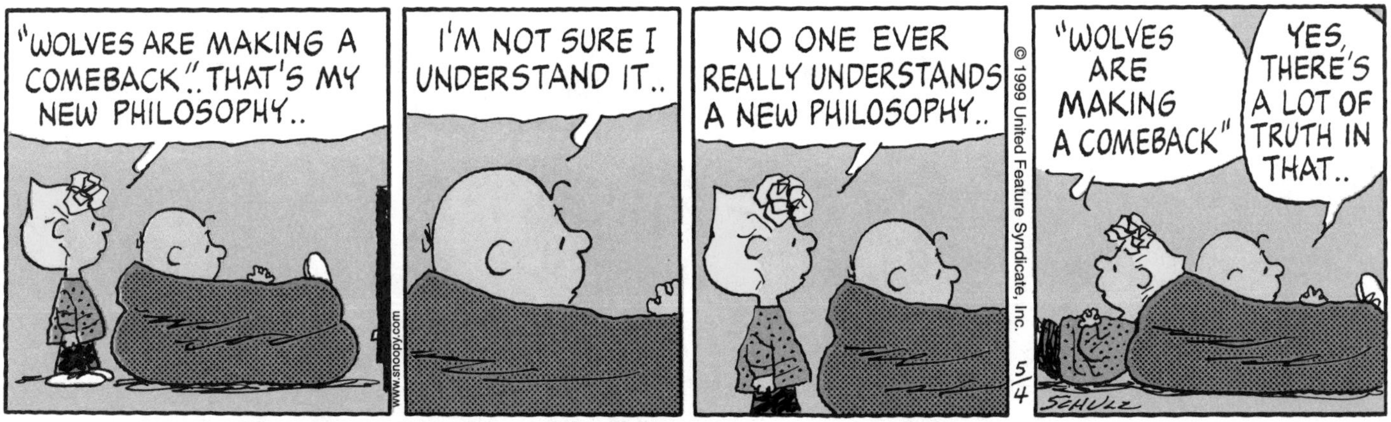
"WOLVES ARE MAKING A COMEBACK".. THAT'S MY NEW PHILOSOPHY..
www.snoopy.com
I'M NOT SURE I UNDERSTAND IT..
NO ONE EVER REALLY UNDERSTANDS A NEW PHILOSOPHY..
© 1999 United Feature Syndicate, Inc.
5/4
"WOLVES ARE MAKING A COMEBACK"
YES, THERE'S A LOT OF TRUTH IN THAT..
SCHULZ

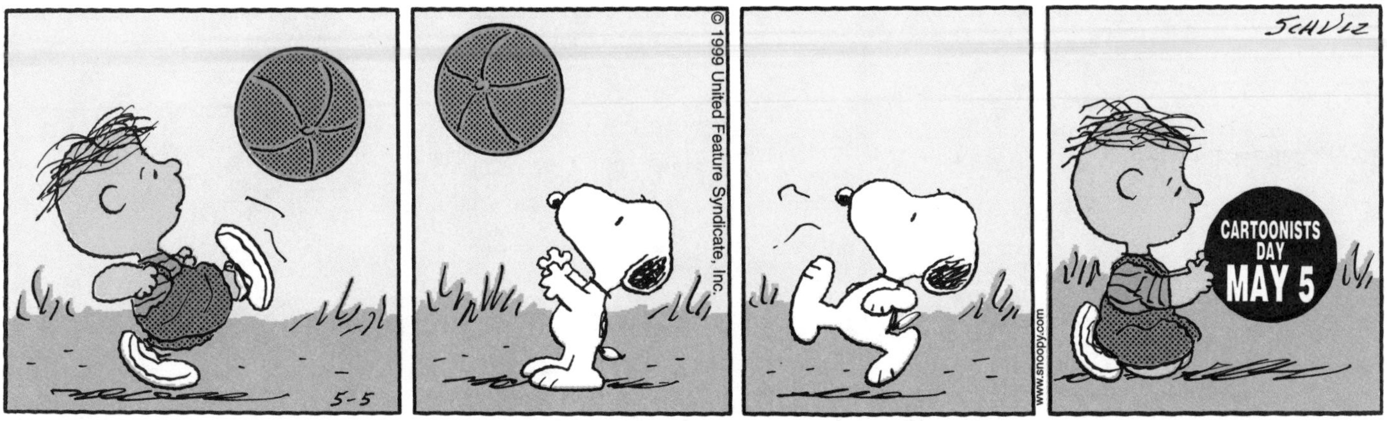
5-5
© 1999 United Feature Syndicate, Inc.
www.snoopy.com
SCHULZ
CARTOONISTS DAY MAY 5

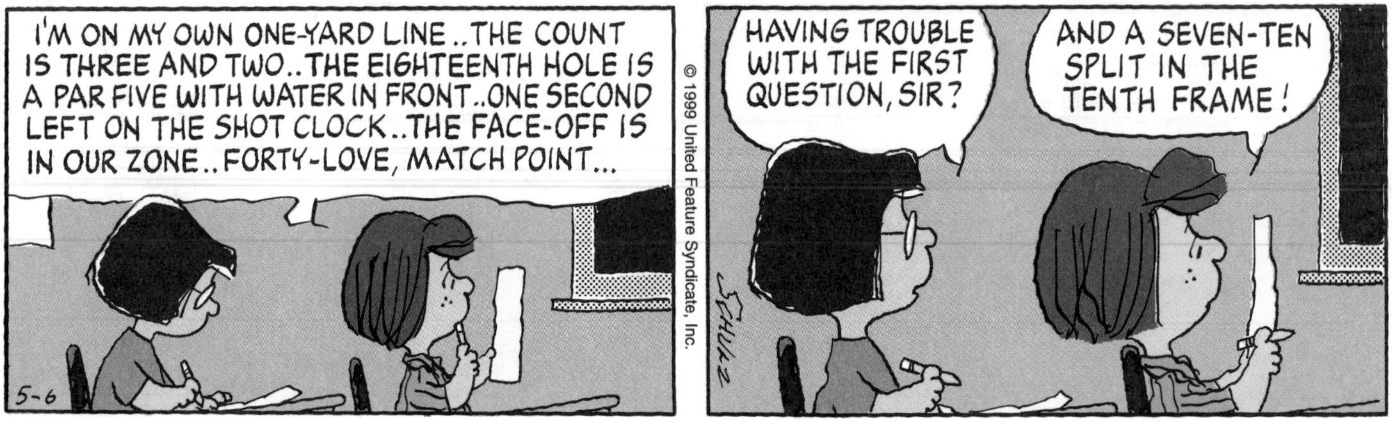
I'M ON MY OWN ONE-YARD LINE..THE COUNT IS THREE AND TWO..THE EIGHTEENTH HOLE IS A PAR FIVE WITH WATER IN FRONT..ONE SECOND LEFT ON THE SHOT CLOCK..THE FACE-OFF IS IN OUR ZONE..FORTY-LOVE, MATCH POINT...
HAVING TROUBLE WITH THE FIRST QUESTION, SIR?
AND A SEVEN-TEN SPLIT IN THE TENTH FRAME!
5-6
© 1999 United Feature Syndicate, Inc.
SCHULZ

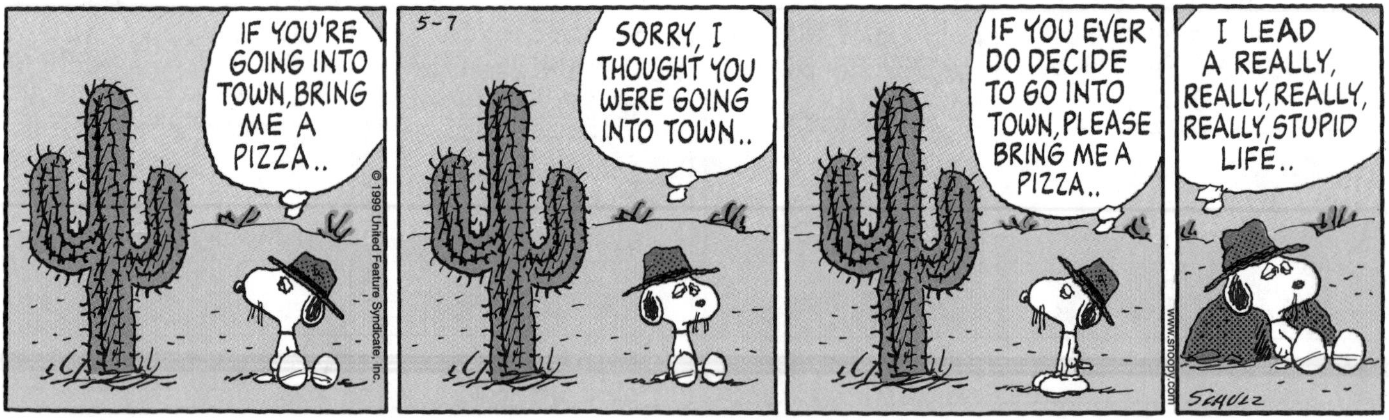
IF YOU'RE GOING INTO TOWN, BRING ME A PIZZA..
5-7
SORRY, I THOUGHT YOU WERE GOING INTO TOWN..
IF YOU EVER DO DECIDE TO GO INTO TOWN, PLEASE BRING ME A PIZZA..
I LEAD A REALLY, REALLY, REALLY, REALLY, STUPID LIFE..
© 1999 United Feature Syndicate, Inc.
www.snoopy.com
SCHULZ

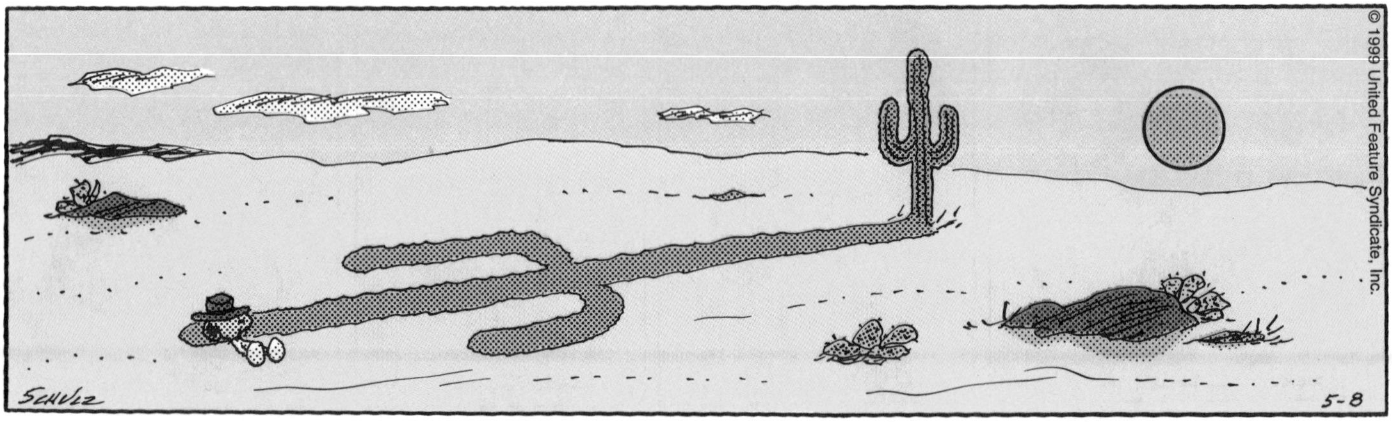
© 1999 United Feature Syndicate, Inc.
SCHULZ
5-8

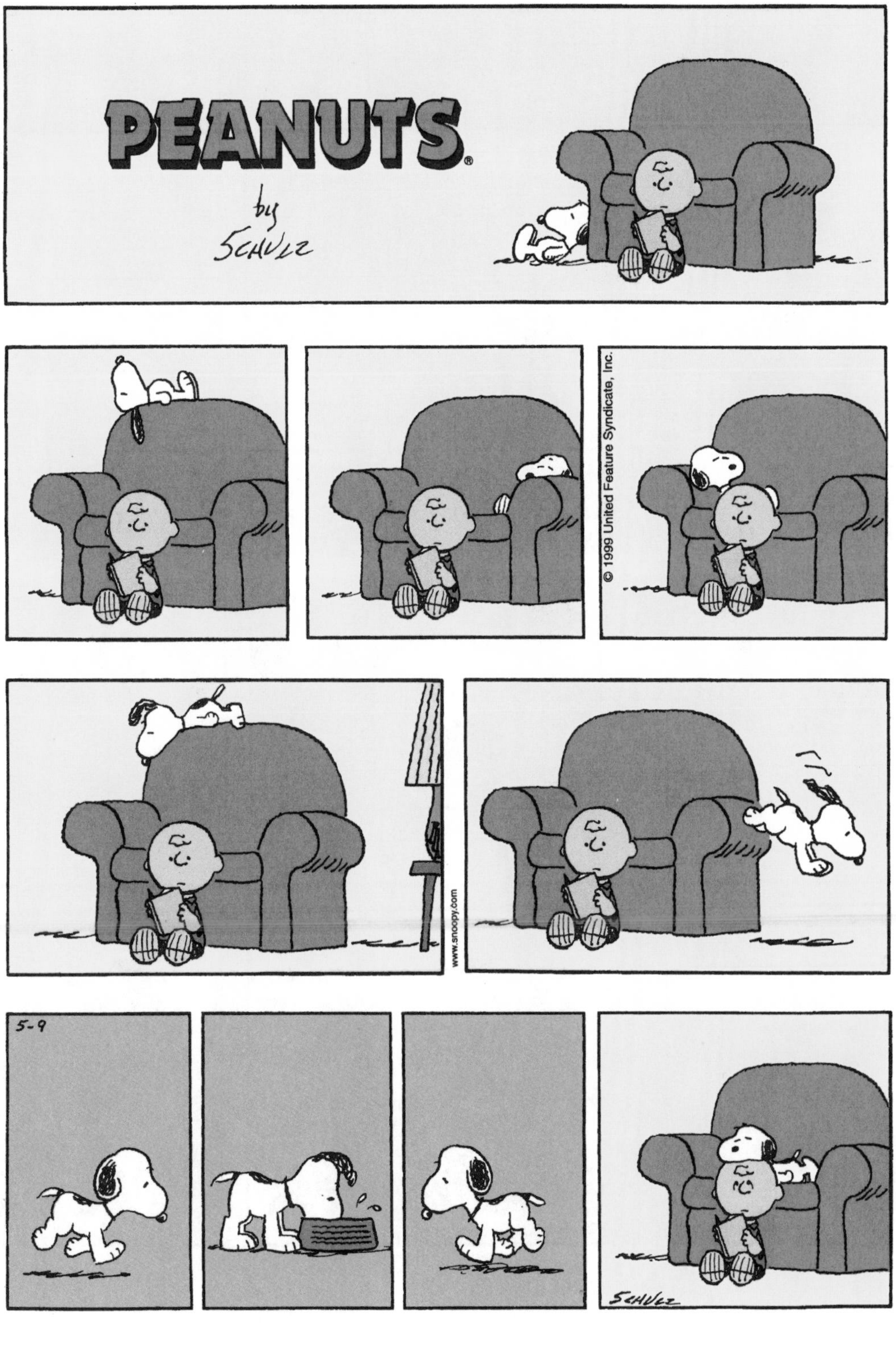
PEANUTS®
by SCHULZ
© 1999 United Feature Syndicate, Inc.
www.snoopy.com
5-9
SCHULZ

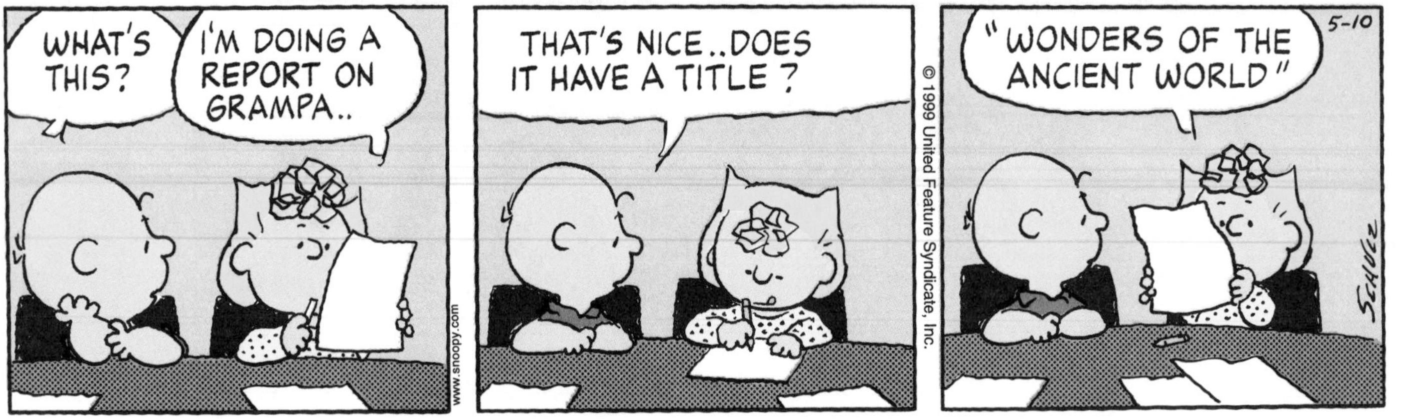
WHAT'S THIS?
I'M DOING A REPORT ON GRAMPA..
THAT'S NICE..DOES IT HAVE A TITLE ?
"WONDERS OF THE ANCIENT WORLD"
5-10
www.snoopy.com
© 1999 United Feature Syndicate, Inc.
SCHULZ

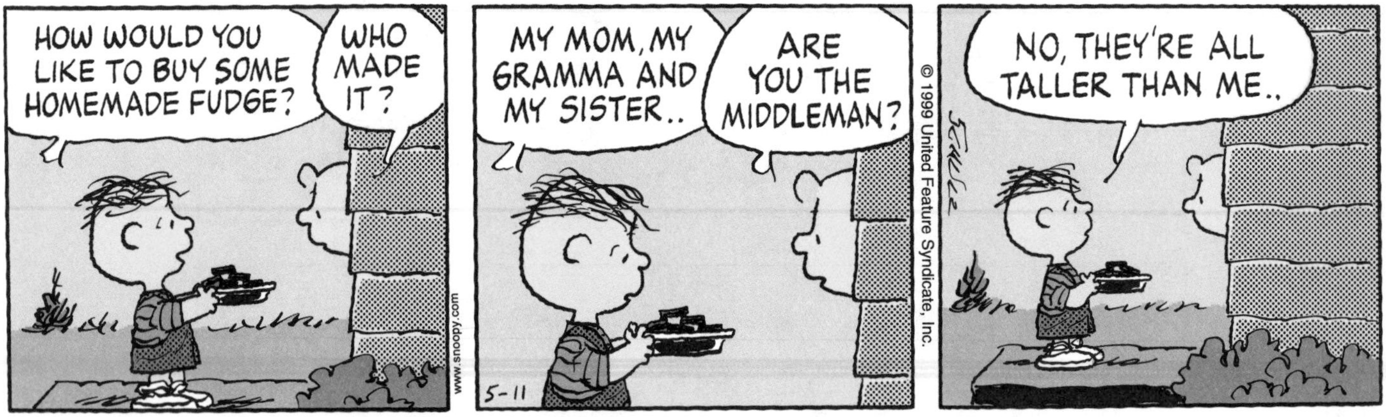
HOW WOULD YOU LIKE TO BUY SOME HOMEMADE FUDGE?
WHO MADE IT ?
MY MOM, MY GRAMMA AND MY SISTER..
ARE YOU THE MIDDLEMAN?
NO, THEY'RE ALL TALLER THAN ME..
5-11
www.snoopy.com
© 1999 United Feature Syndicate, Inc.
SCHULZ

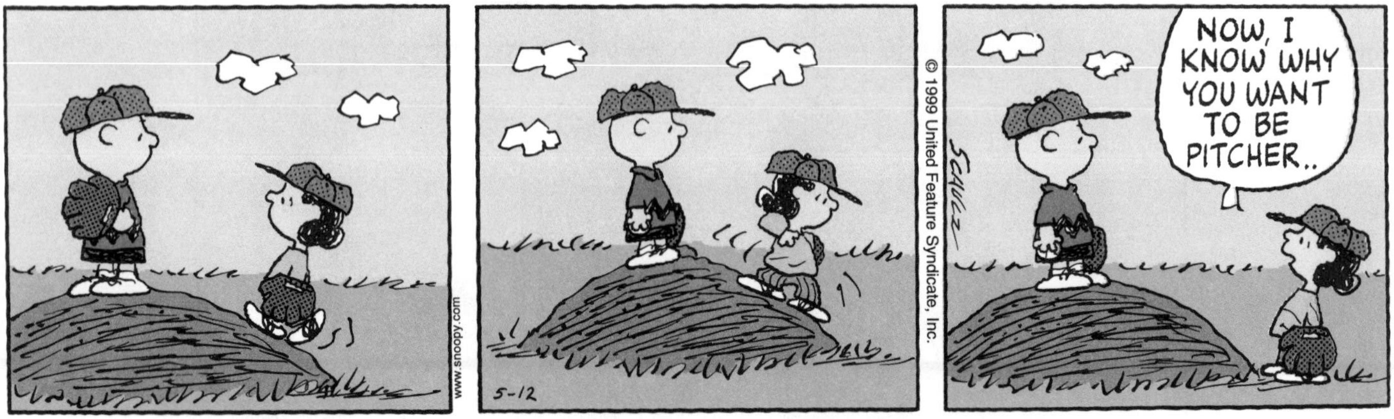
NOW, I KNOW WHY YOU WANT TO BE PITCHER..
5-12
www.snoopy.com
© 1999 United Feature Syndicate, Inc.
SCHULZ

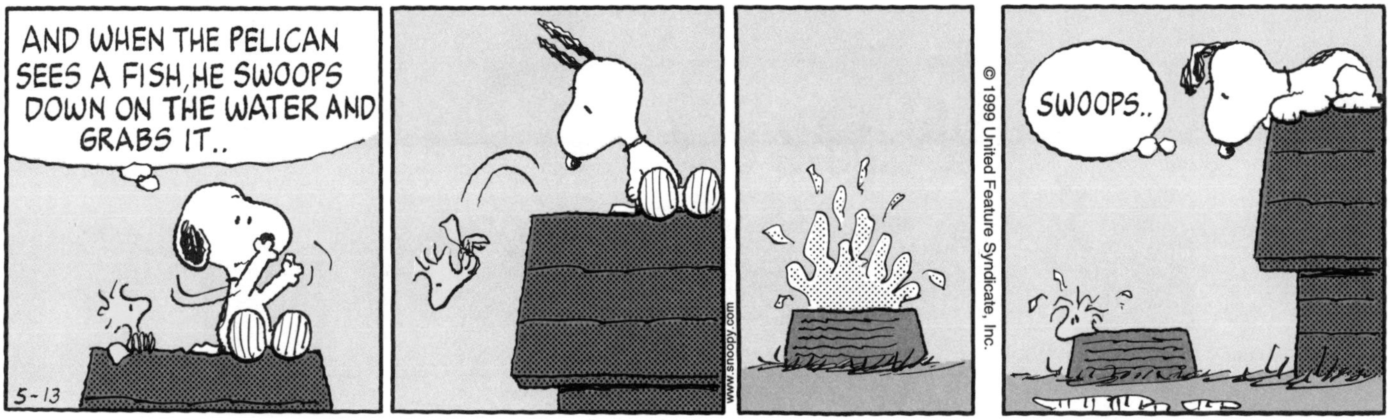
AND WHEN THE PELICAN SEES A FISH, HE SWOOPS DOWN ON THE WATER AND GRABS IT..
5-13
www.snoopy.com
© 1999 United Feature Syndicate, Inc.
SWOOPS..

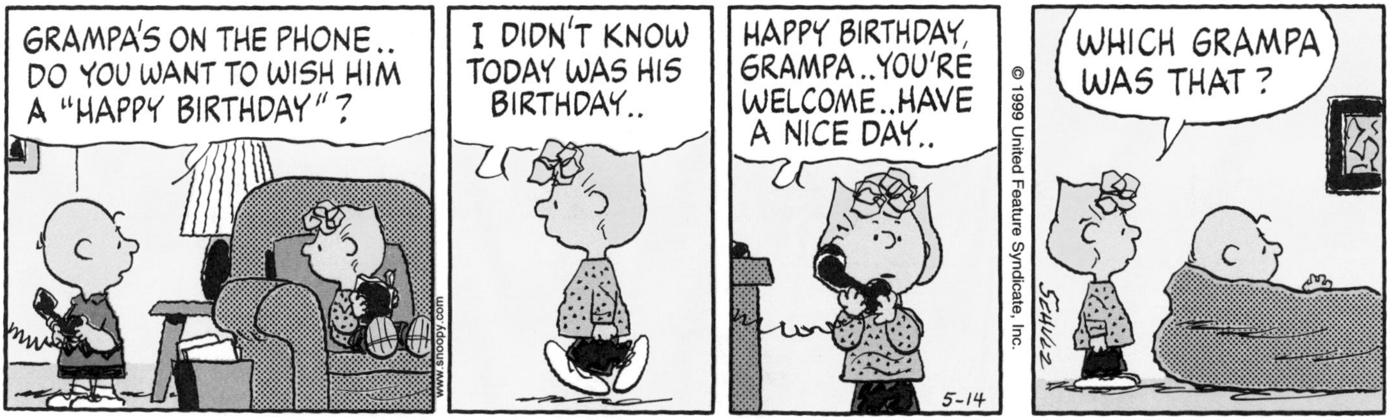
GRAMPA'S ON THE PHONE.. DO YOU WANT TO WISH HIM A "HAPPY BIRTHDAY"?
www.snoopy.com
I DIDN'T KNOW TODAY WAS HIS BIRTHDAY..
HAPPY BIRTHDAY, GRAMPA..YOU'RE WELCOME..HAVE A NICE DAY..
5-14
© 1999 United Feature Syndicate, Inc.
WHICH GRAMPA WAS THAT?
SCHULZ

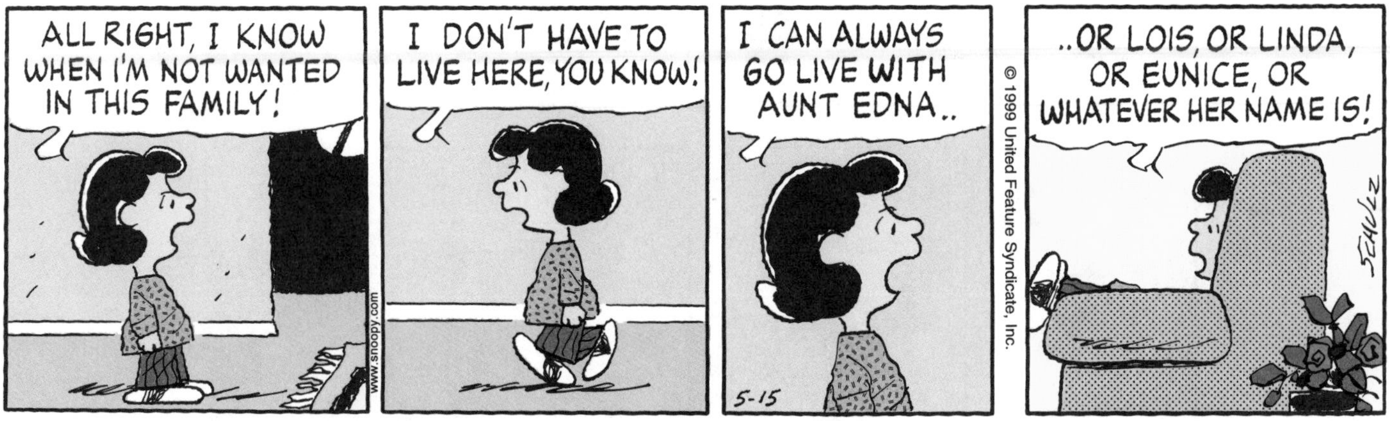
ALL RIGHT, I KNOW WHEN I'M NOT WANTED IN THIS FAMILY!
www.snoopy.com
I DON'T HAVE TO LIVE HERE, YOU KNOW!
I CAN ALWAYS GO LIVE WITH AUNT EDNA..
5-15
© 1999 United Feature Syndicate, Inc.
..OR LOIS, OR LINDA, OR EUNICE, OR WHATEVER HER NAME IS!
SCHULZ

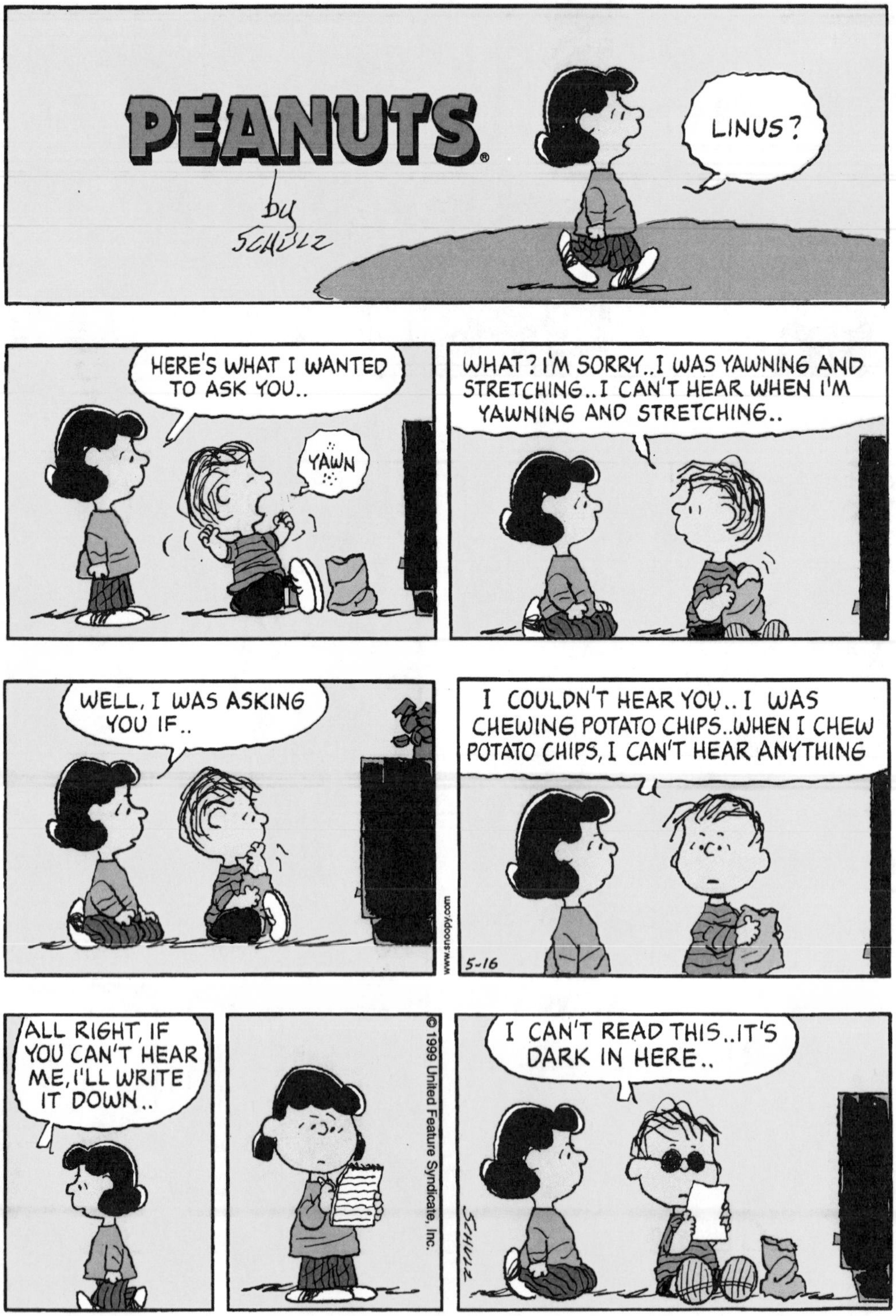
PEANUTS®
by SCHULZ
LINUS?
HERE'S WHAT I WANTED TO ASK YOU..
YAWN
WHAT? I'M SORRY..I WAS YAWNING AND STRETCHING..I CAN'T HEAR WHEN I'M YAWNING AND STRETCHING..
WELL, I WAS ASKING YOU IF..
www.snoopy.com
I COULDN'T HEAR YOU..I WAS CHEWING POTATO CHIPS..WHEN I CHEW POTATO CHIPS, I CAN'T HEAR ANYTHING
5-16
ALL RIGHT, IF YOU CAN'T HEAR ME, I'LL WRITE IT DOWN..
© 1999 United Feature Syndicate, Inc.
I CAN'T READ THIS..IT'S DARK IN HERE..
SCHULZ

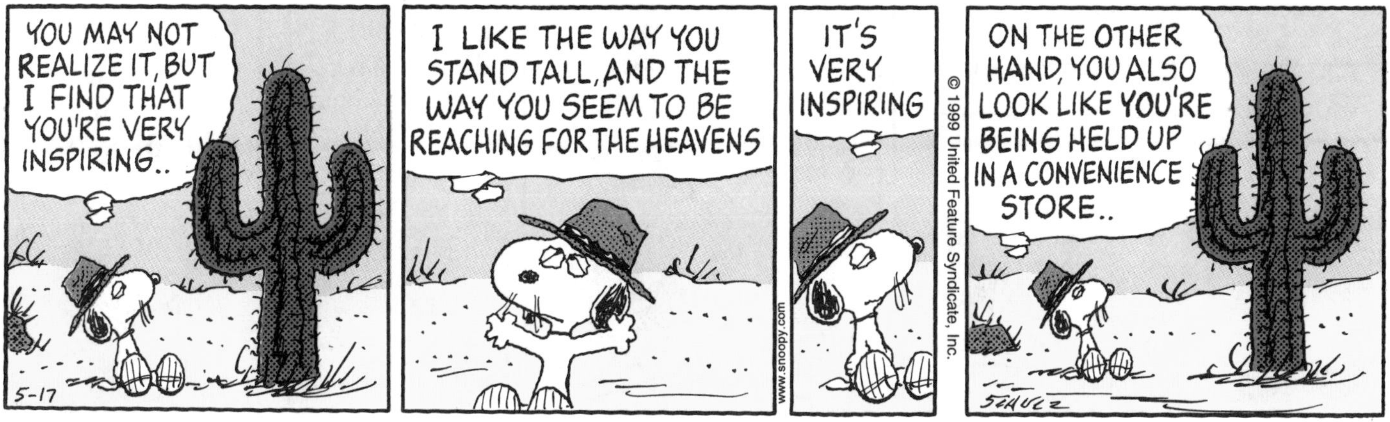

5-17
YOU MAY NOT REALIZE IT, BUT I FIND THAT YOU'RE VERY INSPIRING..
I LIKE THE WAY YOU STAND TALL, AND THE WAY YOU SEEM TO BE REACHING FOR THE HEAVENS
IT'S VERY INSPIRING
ON THE OTHER HAND, YOU ALSO LOOK LIKE YOU'RE BEING HELD UP IN A CONVENIENCE STORE..
www.snoopy.com
© 1999 United Feature Syndicate, Inc.

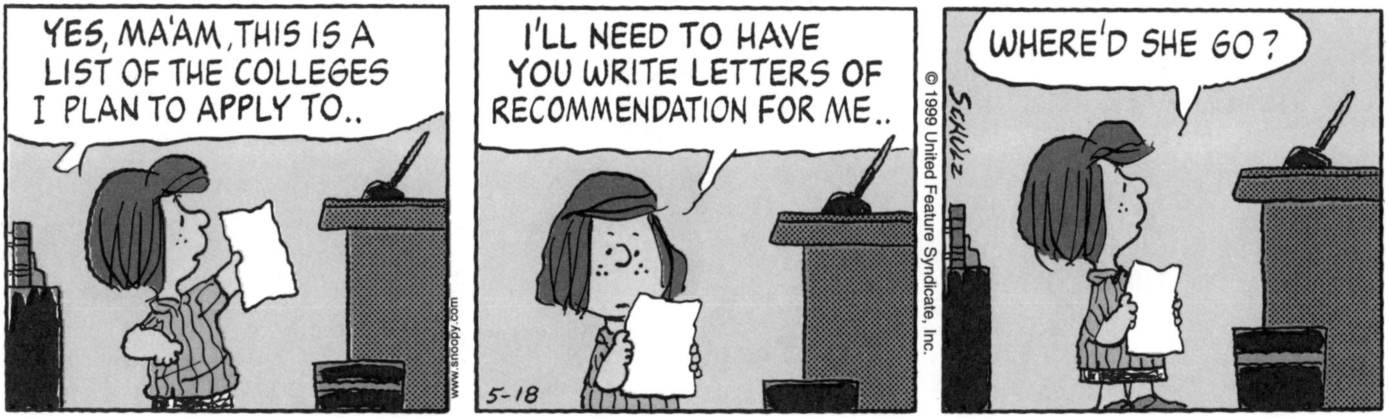

YES, MA'AM, THIS IS A LIST OF THE COLLEGES I PLAN TO APPLY TO..
I'LL NEED TO HAVE YOU WRITE LETTERS OF RECOMMENDATION FOR ME..
WHERE'D SHE GO?
5-18
www.snoopy.com
© 1999 United Feature Syndicate, Inc.

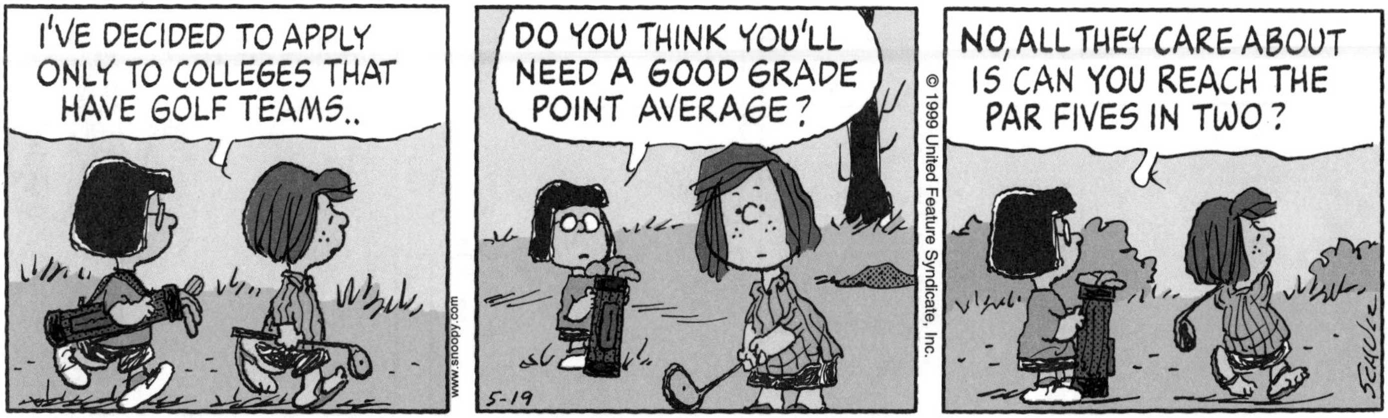

I'VE DECIDED TO APPLY ONLY TO COLLEGES THAT HAVE GOLF TEAMS..
DO YOU THINK YOU'LL NEED A GOOD GRADE POINT AVERAGE?
NO, ALL THEY CARE ABOUT IS CAN YOU REACH THE PAR FIVES IN TWO?
5-19
www.snoopy.com
© 1999 United Feature Syndicate, Inc.

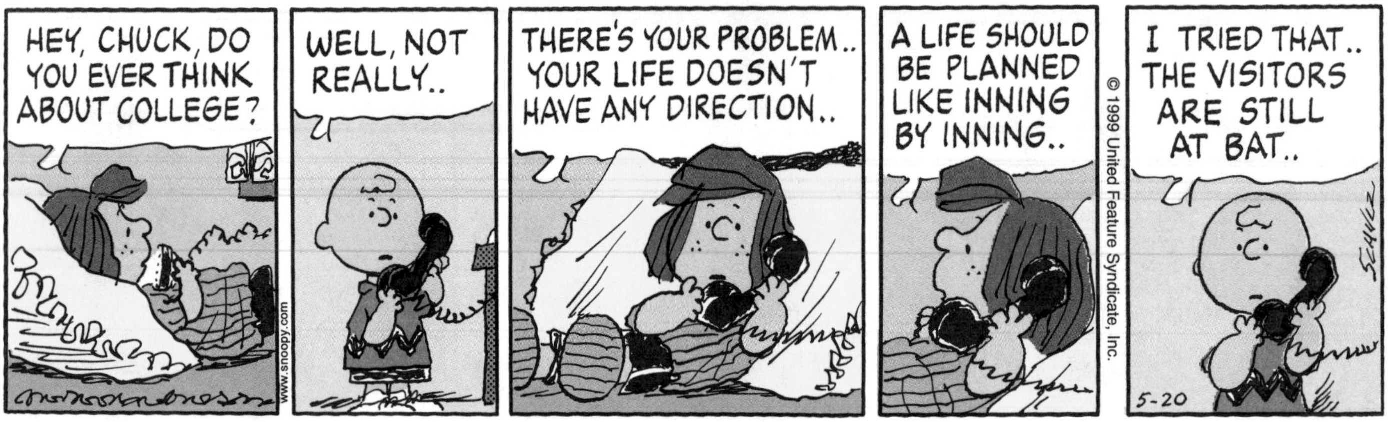
HEY, CHUCK, DO YOU EVER THINK ABOUT COLLEGE?
WELL, NOT REALLY..
THERE'S YOUR PROBLEM.. YOUR LIFE DOESN'T HAVE ANY DIRECTION..
A LIFE SHOULD BE PLANNED LIKE INNING BY INNING..
I TRIED THAT.. THE VISITORS ARE STILL AT BAT..
5-20
www.snoopy.com
© 1999 United Feature Syndicate, Inc.

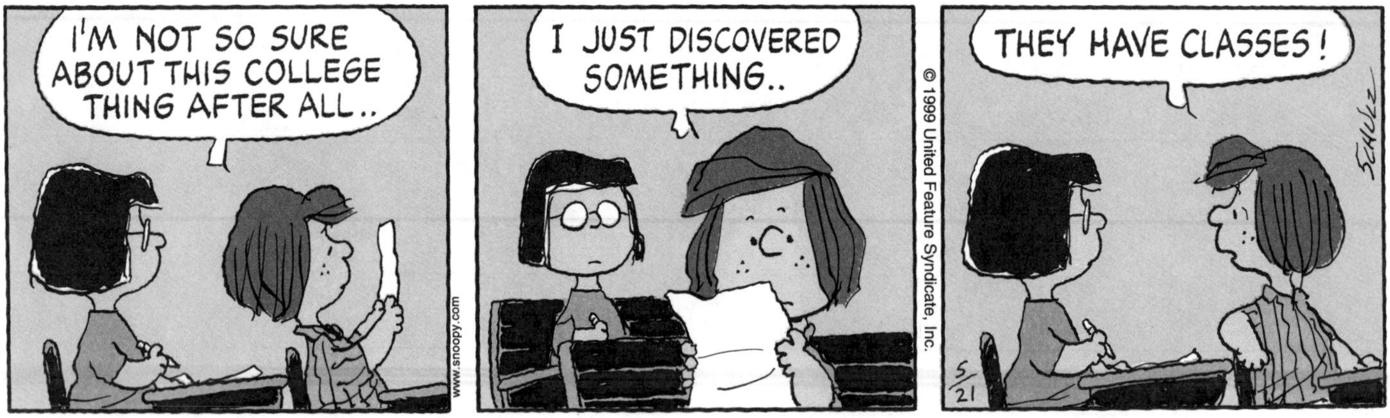
I'M NOT SO SURE ABOUT THIS COLLEGE THING AFTER ALL..
I JUST DISCOVERED SOMETHING..
THEY HAVE CLASSES!
5/21
www.snoopy.com
© 1999 United Feature Syndicate, Inc.

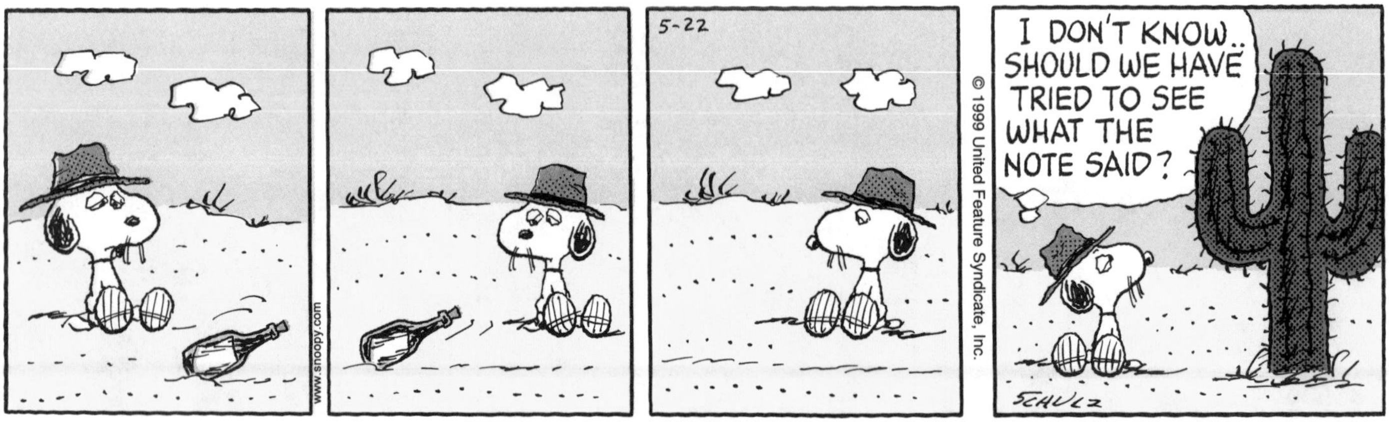
5-22
I DON'T KNOW.. SHOULD WE HAVE TRIED TO SEE WHAT THE NOTE SAID?
www.snoopy.com
© 1999 United Feature Syndicate, Inc.

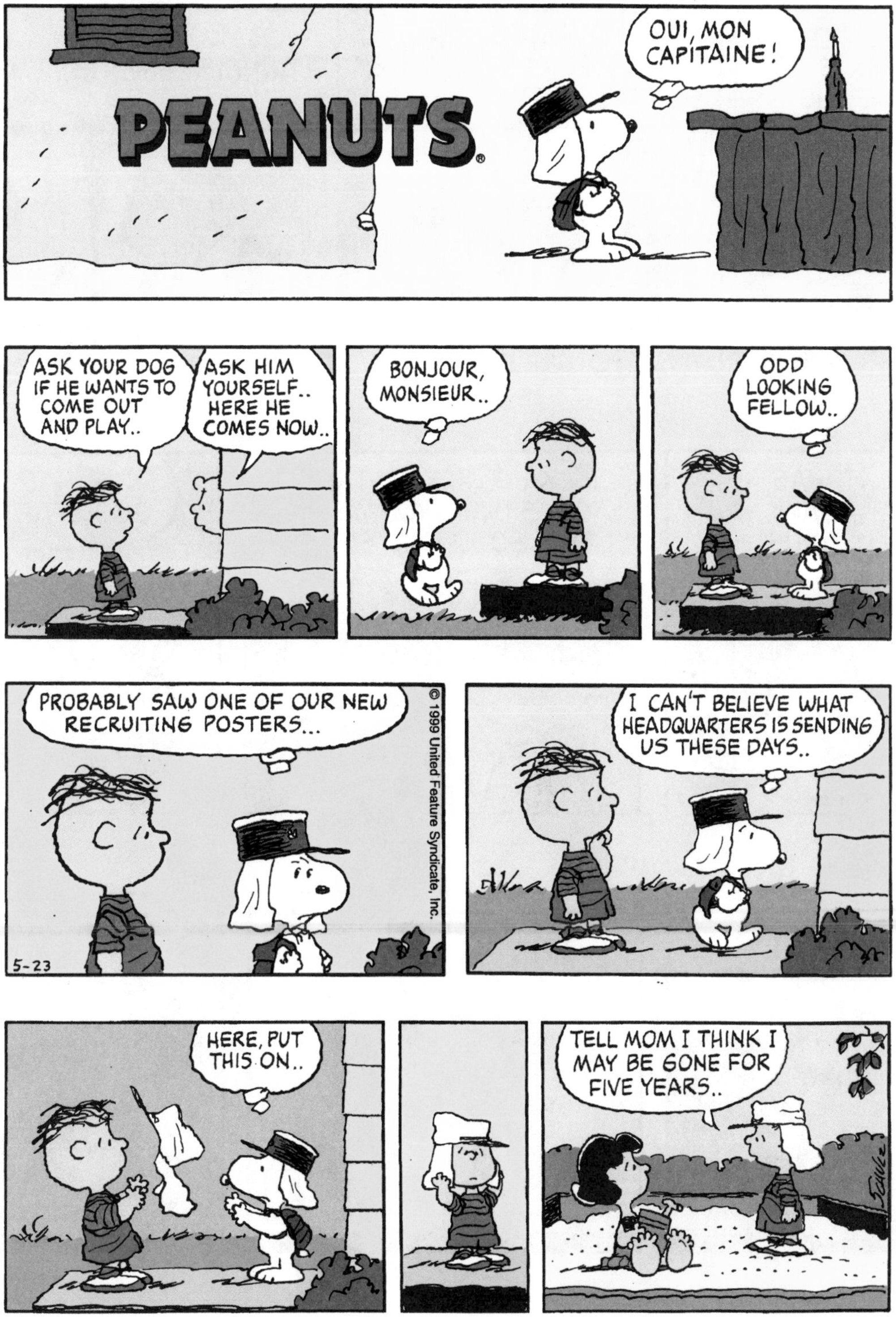
PEANUTS
OUI, MON CAPITAINE!
ASK YOUR DOG IF HE WANTS TO COME OUT AND PLAY..
ASK HIM YOURSELF.. HERE HE COMES NOW..
BONJOUR, MONSIEUR..
ODD LOOKING FELLOW..
PROBABLY SAW ONE OF OUR NEW RECRUITING POSTERS...
© 1999 United Feature Syndicate, Inc.
5-23
I CAN'T BELIEVE WHAT HEADQUARTERS IS SENDING US THESE DAYS..
HERE, PUT THIS ON..
TELL MOM I THINK I MAY BE GONE FOR FIVE YEARS..
SCHULZ

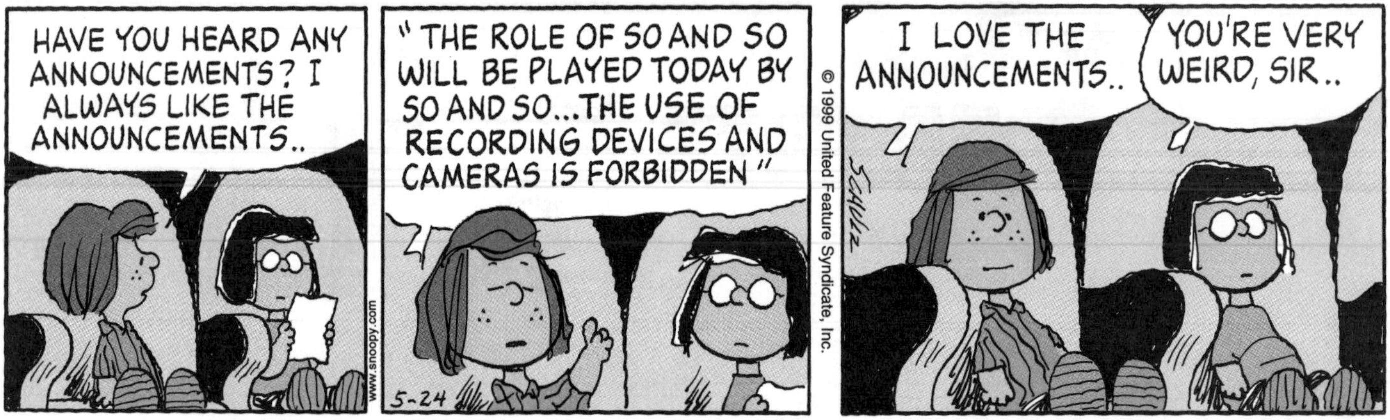
HAVE YOU HEARD ANY ANNOUNCEMENTS? I ALWAYS LIKE THE ANNOUNCEMENTS..
www.snoopy.com
5-24
" THE ROLE OF SO AND SO WILL BE PLAYED TODAY BY SO AND SO...THE USE OF RECORDING DEVICES AND CAMERAS IS FORBIDDEN "
© 1999 United Feature Syndicate, Inc.
I LOVE THE ANNOUNCEMENTS..
YOU'RE VERY WEIRD, SIR..
SCHULZ

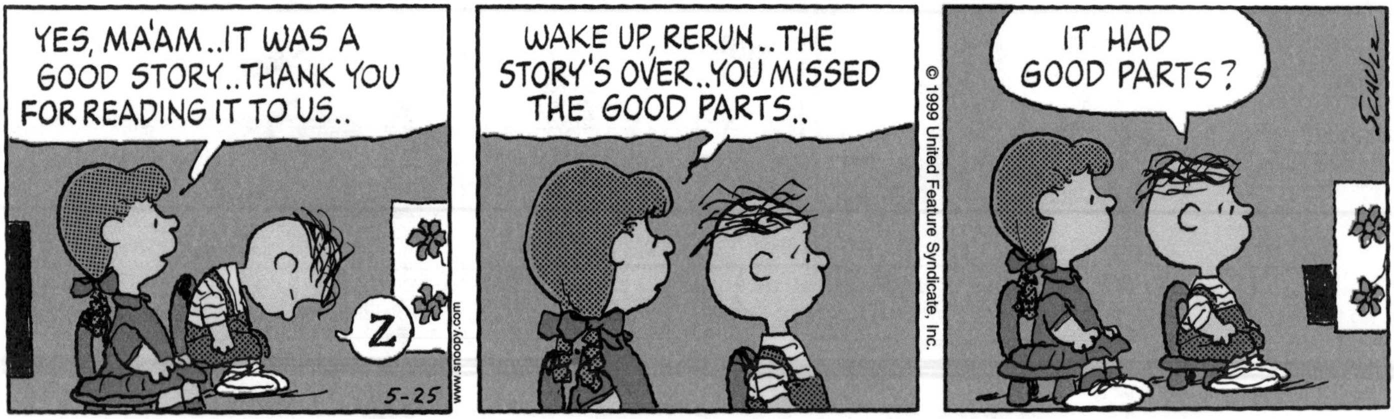
YES, MA'AM..IT WAS A GOOD STORY..THANK YOU FOR READING IT TO US..
Z
5-25
www.snoopy.com
WAKE UP, RERUN..THE STORY'S OVER..YOU MISSED THE GOOD PARTS..
© 1999 United Feature Syndicate, Inc.
IT HAD GOOD PARTS?
SCHULZ

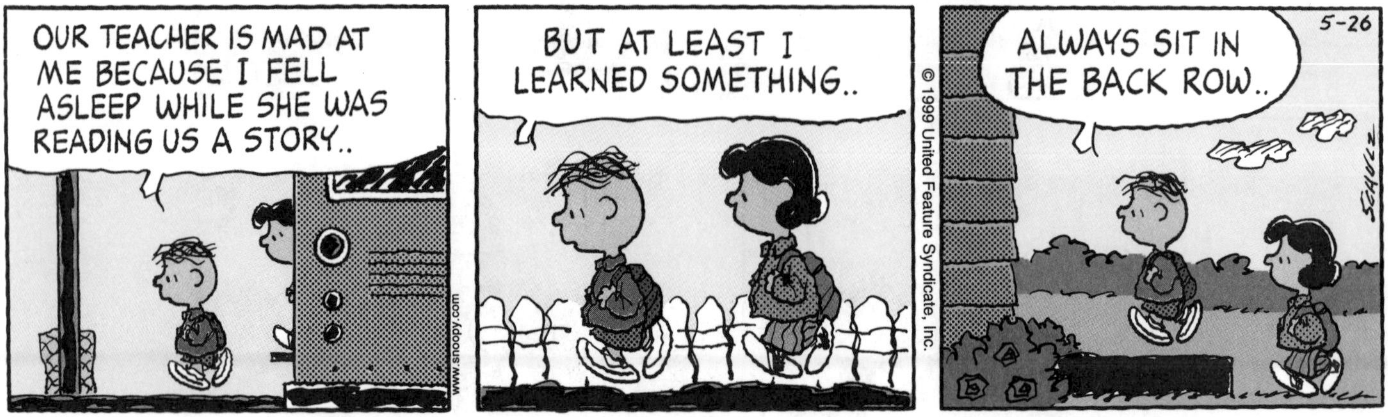
OUR TEACHER IS MAD AT ME BECAUSE I FELL ASLEEP WHILE SHE WAS READING US A STORY..
www.snoopy.com
BUT AT LEAST I LEARNED SOMETHING..
© 1999 United Feature Syndicate, Inc.
5-26
ALWAYS SIT IN THE BACK ROW..
SCHULZ

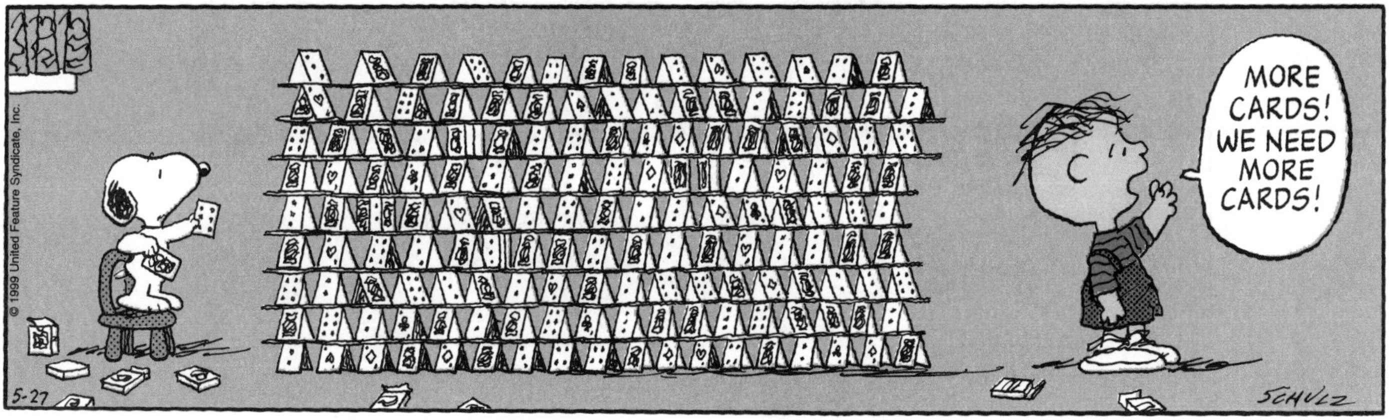
© 1999 United Feature Syndicate, Inc.
MORE CARDS! WE NEED MORE CARDS!
5-27
SCHULZ

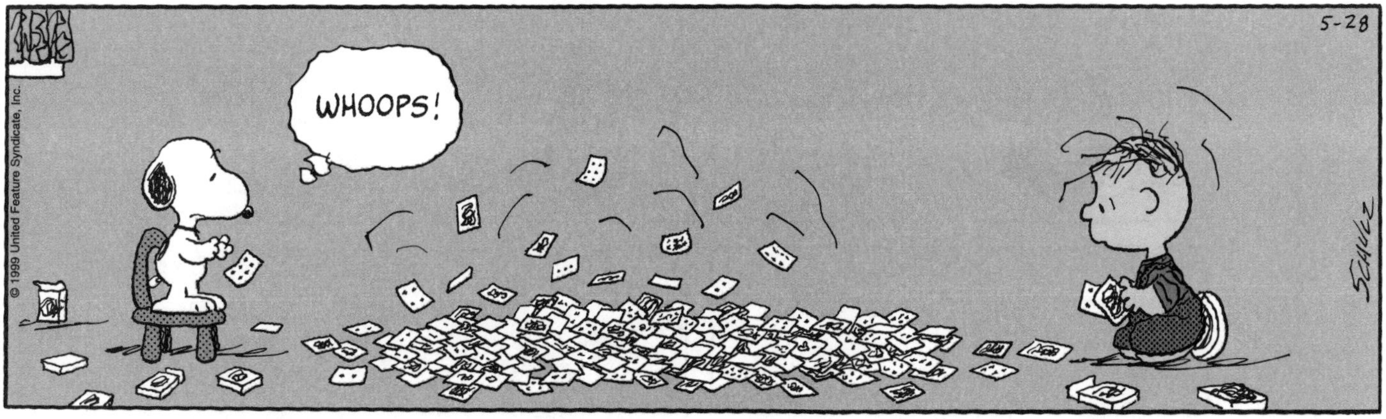
© 1999 United Feature Syndicate, Inc.
5-28
WHOOPS!
SCHULZ

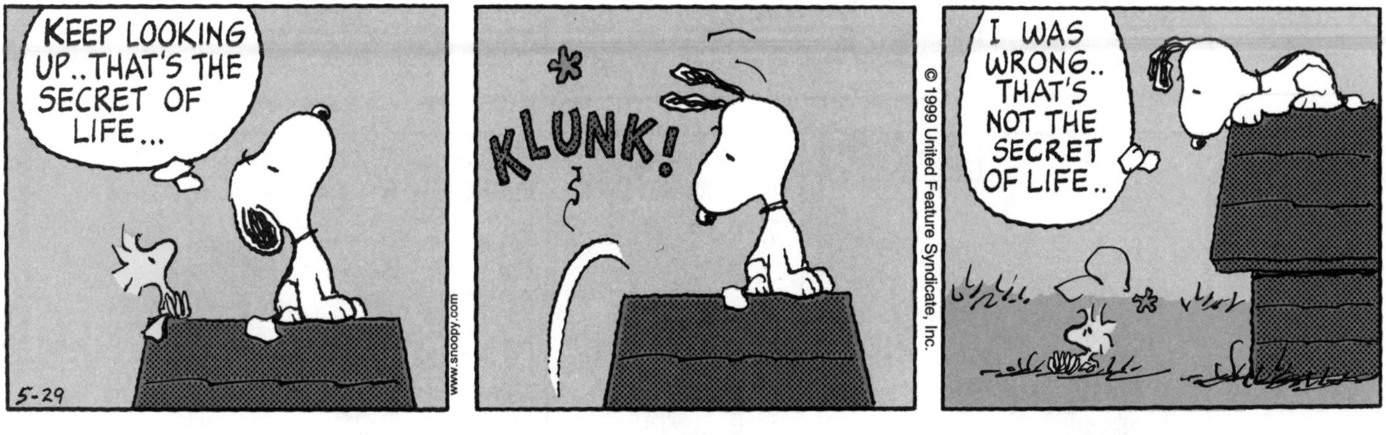
KEEP LOOKING UP..THAT'S THE SECRET OF LIFE...
5-29
www.snoopy.com
KLUNK!
© 1999 United Feature Syndicate, Inc.
I WAS WRONG.. THAT'S NOT THE SECRET OF LIFE..
SCHULZ

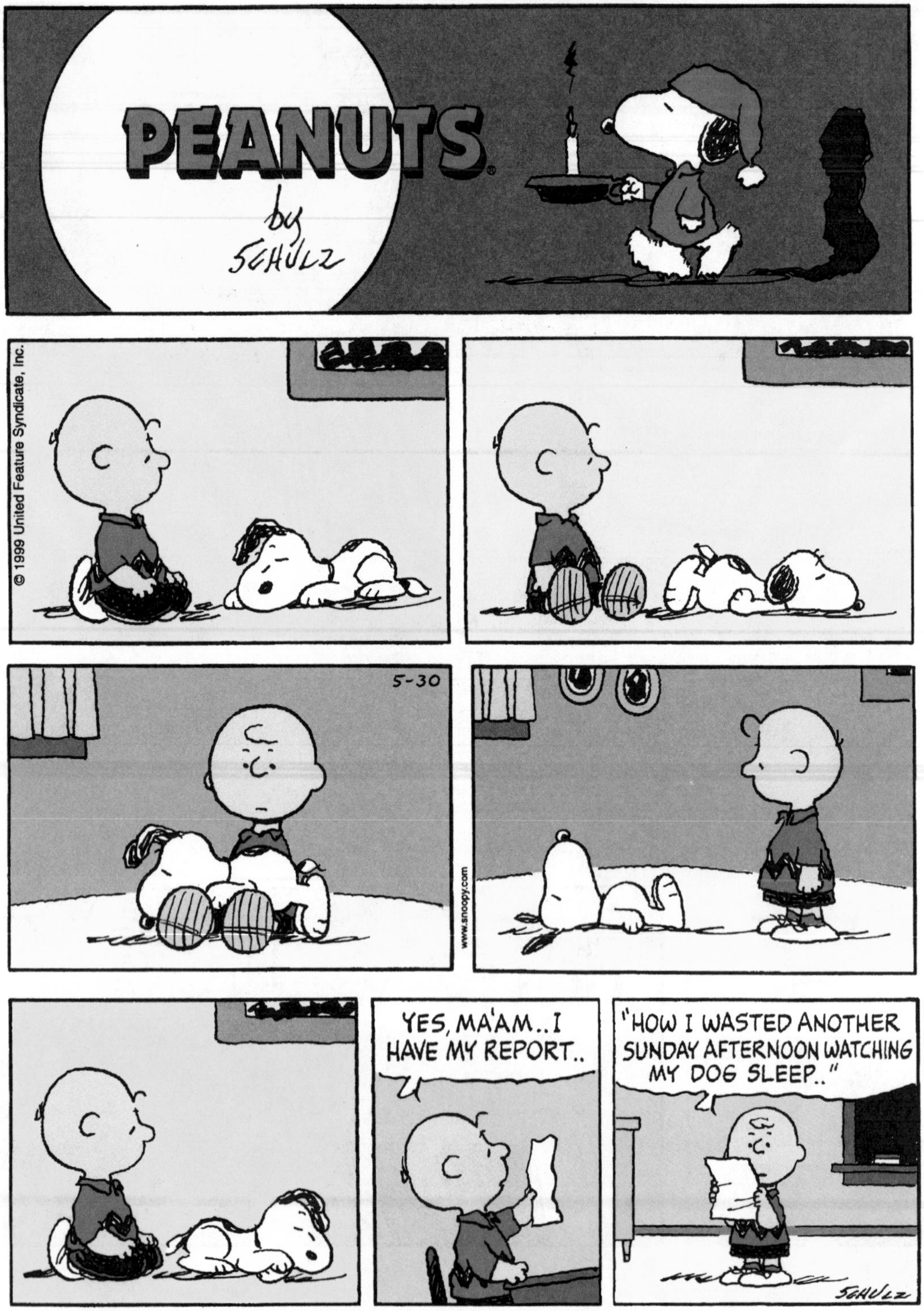
PEANUTS
by SCHULZ
© 1999 United Feature Syndicate, Inc.
5-30
www.snoopy.com
YES, MA'AM.. I HAVE MY REPORT..
"HOW I WASTED ANOTHER SUNDAY AFTERNOON WATCHING MY DOG SLEEP.."
SCHULZ

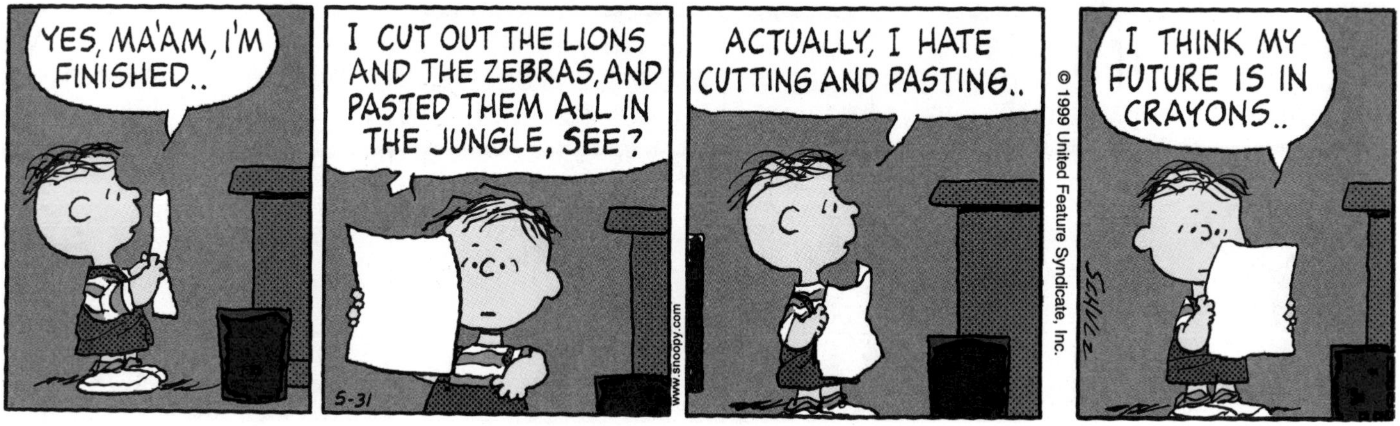
YES, MA'AM, I'M FINISHED..
I CUT OUT THE LIONS AND THE ZEBRAS, AND PASTED THEM ALL IN THE JUNGLE, SEE?
5-31
www.snoopy.com
ACTUALLY, I HATE CUTTING AND PASTING..
© 1999 United Feature Syndicate, Inc.
I THINK MY FUTURE IS IN CRAYONS..
SCHULZ

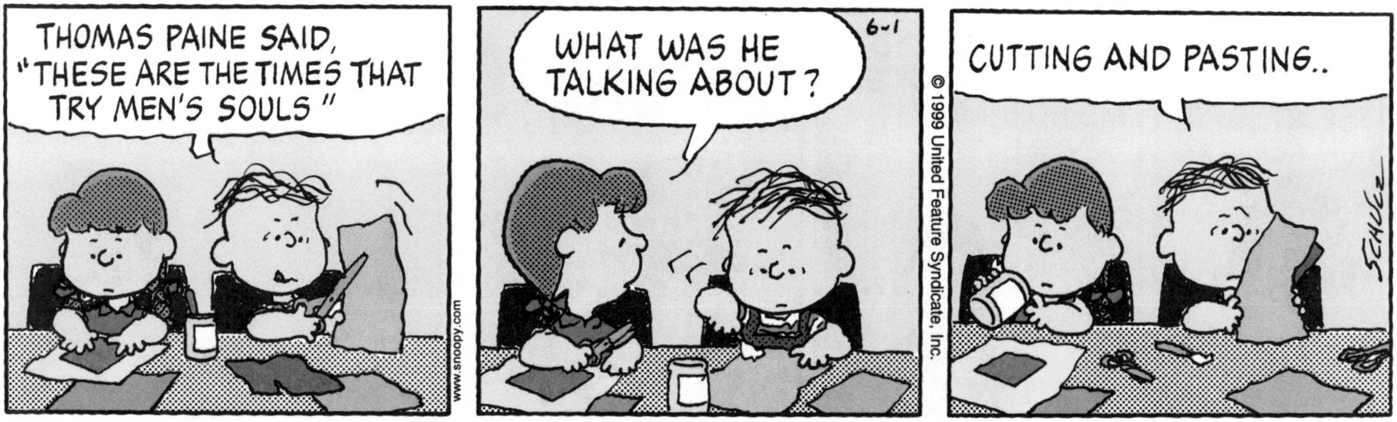
THOMAS PAINE SAID, "THESE ARE THE TIMES THAT TRY MEN'S SOULS"
www.snoopy.com
6-1
WHAT WAS HE TALKING ABOUT?
© 1999 United Feature Syndicate, Inc.
CUTTING AND PASTING..
SCHULZ

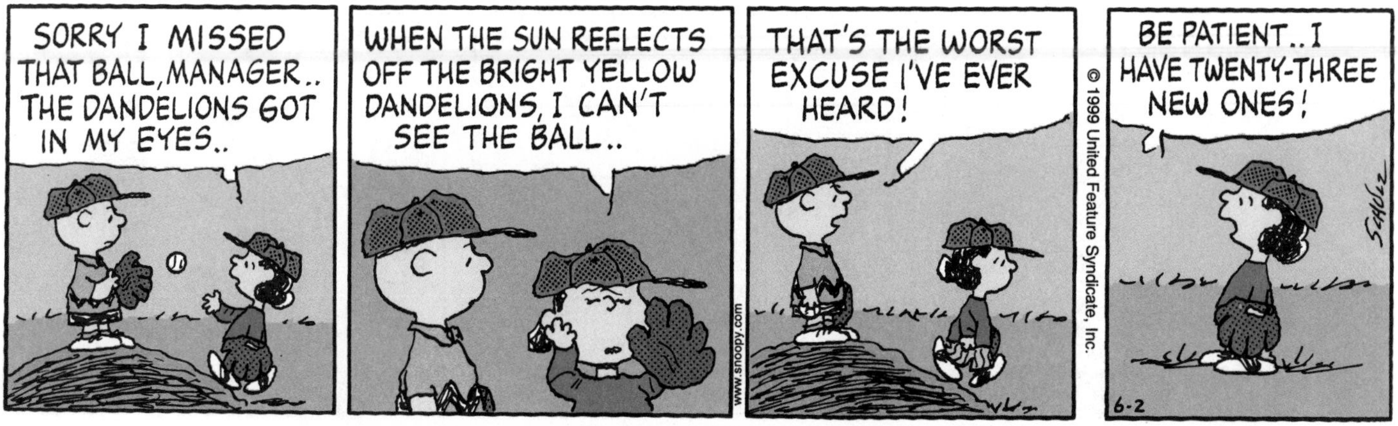
SORRY I MISSED THAT BALL, MANAGER.. THE DANDELIONS GOT IN MY EYES..
WHEN THE SUN REFLECTS OFF THE BRIGHT YELLOW DANDELIONS, I CAN'T SEE THE BALL..
www.snoopy.com
THAT'S THE WORST EXCUSE I'VE EVER HEARD!
© 1999 United Feature Syndicate, Inc.
BE PATIENT.. I HAVE TWENTY-THREE NEW ONES!
SCHULZ
6-2

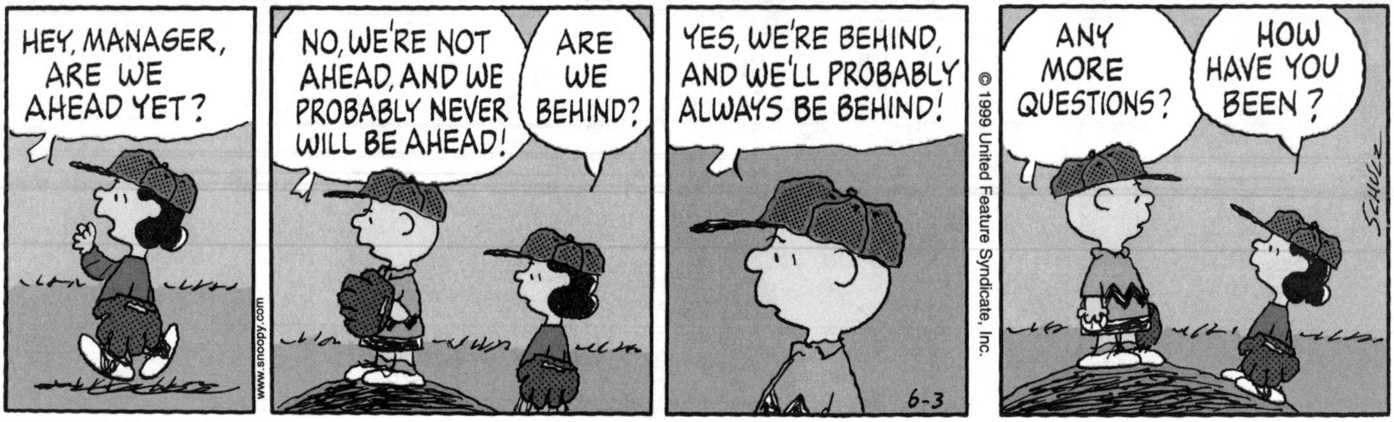
HEY, MANAGER, ARE WE AHEAD YET?
www.snoopy.com
NO, WE'RE NOT AHEAD, AND WE PROBABLY NEVER WILL BE AHEAD!
ARE WE BEHIND?
YES, WE'RE BEHIND, AND WE'LL PROBABLY ALWAYS BE BEHIND!
6-3
© 1999 United Feature Syndicate, Inc.
ANY MORE QUESTIONS?
HOW HAVE YOU BEEN?
SCHULZ

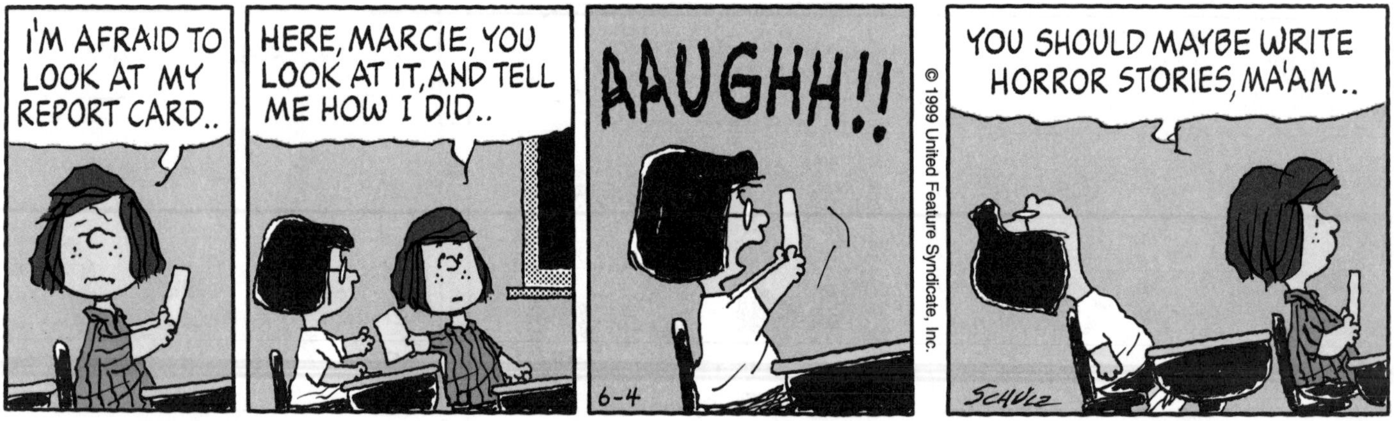
I'M AFRAID TO LOOK AT MY REPORT CARD..
HERE, MARCIE, YOU LOOK AT IT, AND TELL ME HOW I DID..
AAUGHH!!
6-4
© 1999 United Feature Syndicate, Inc.
YOU SHOULD MAYBE WRITE HORROR STORIES, MA'AM..
SCHULZ

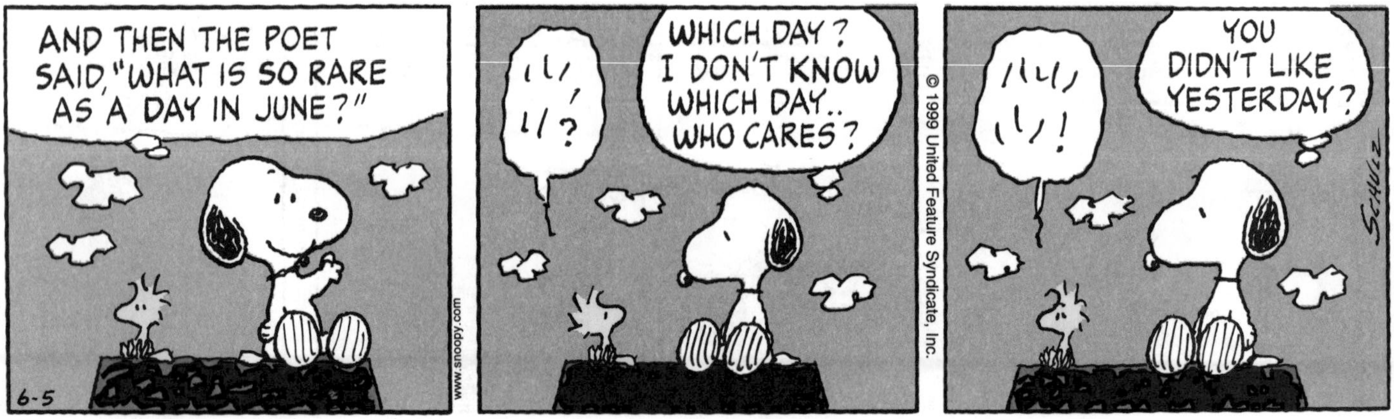
AND THEN THE POET SAID, "WHAT IS SO RARE AS A DAY IN JUNE?"
6-5
www.snoopy.com
WHICH DAY? I DON'T KNOW WHICH DAY.. WHO CARES?
© 1999 United Feature Syndicate, Inc.
YOU DIDN'T LIKE YESTERDAY?
SCHULZ

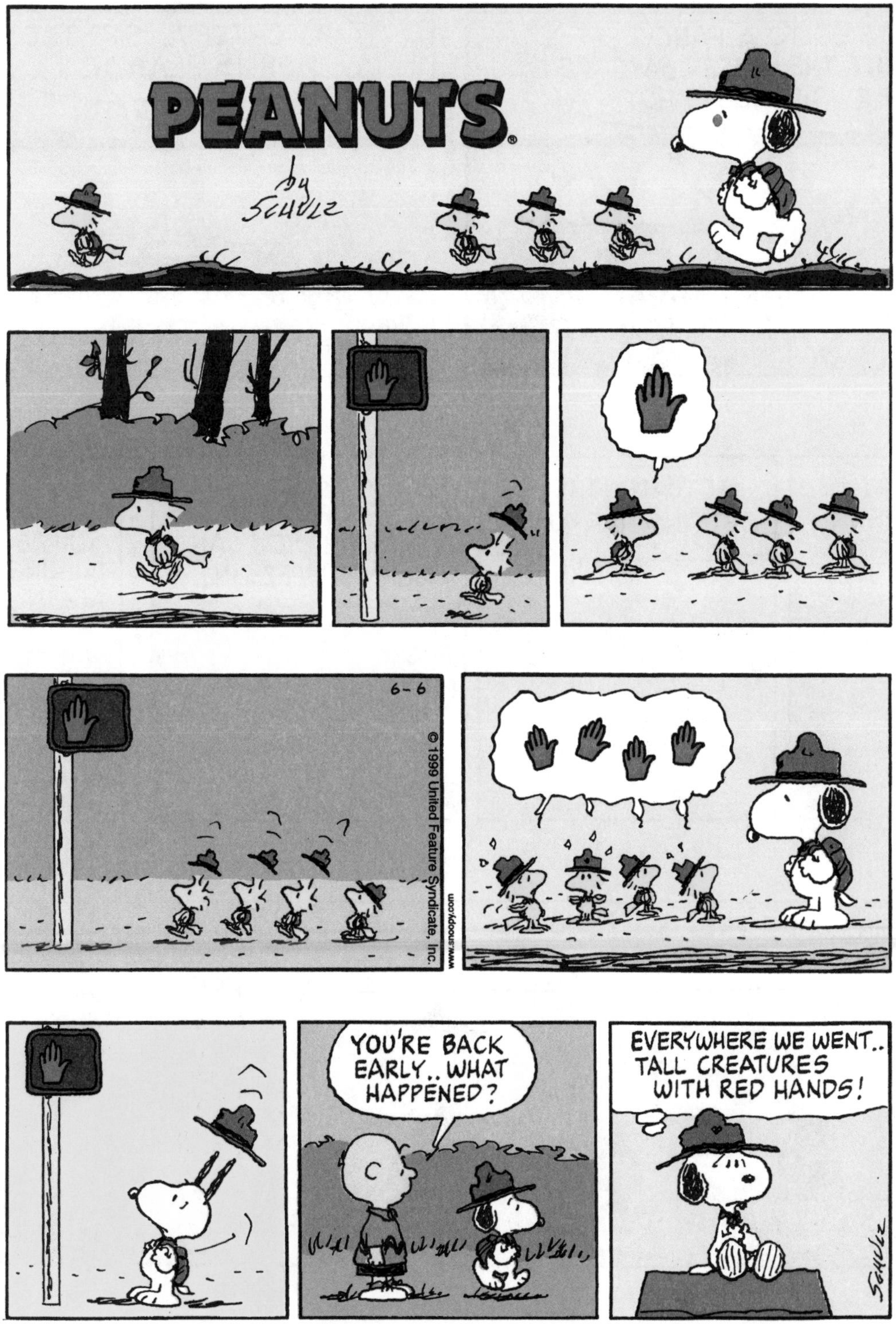
PEANUTS
by SCHULZ
6-6
© 1999 United Feature Syndicate, Inc.
www.snoopy.com
YOU'RE BACK EARLY.. WHAT HAPPENED?
EVERYWHERE WE WENT.. TALL CREATURES WITH RED HANDS!
SCHULZ

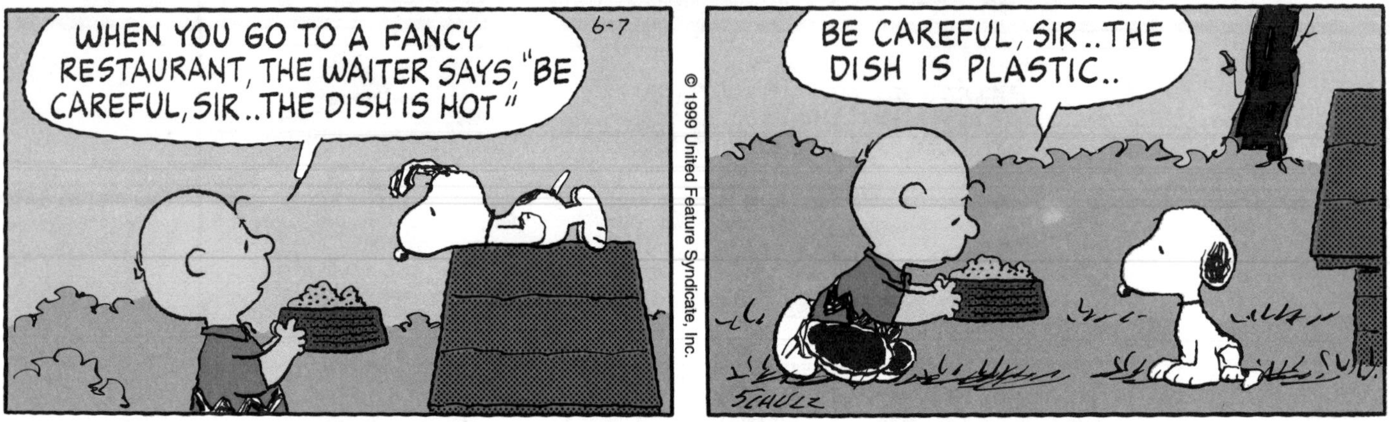
WHEN YOU GO TO A FANCY RESTAURANT, THE WAITER SAYS, "BE CAREFUL, SIR..THE DISH IS HOT"
6-7
© 1999 United Feature Syndicate, Inc.
BE CAREFUL, SIR..THE DISH IS PLASTIC..
SCHULZ

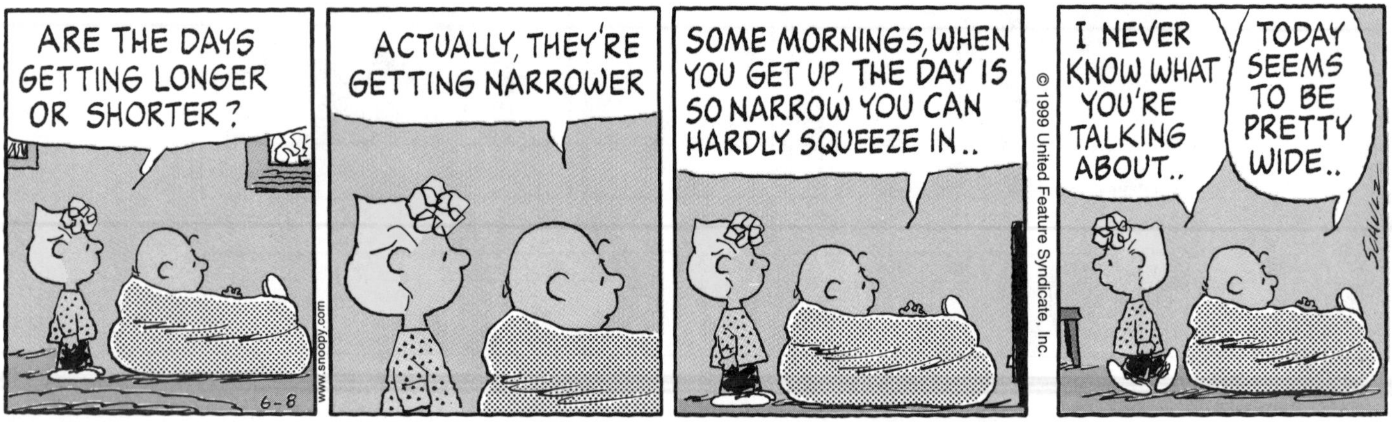
ARE THE DAYS GETTING LONGER OR SHORTER?
6-8
www.snoopy.com
ACTUALLY, THEY'RE GETTING NARROWER
SOME MORNINGS, WHEN YOU GET UP, THE DAY IS SO NARROW YOU CAN HARDLY SQUEEZE IN..
© 1999 United Feature Syndicate, Inc.
I NEVER KNOW WHAT YOU'RE TALKING ABOUT..
TODAY SEEMS TO BE PRETTY WIDE..
SCHULZ

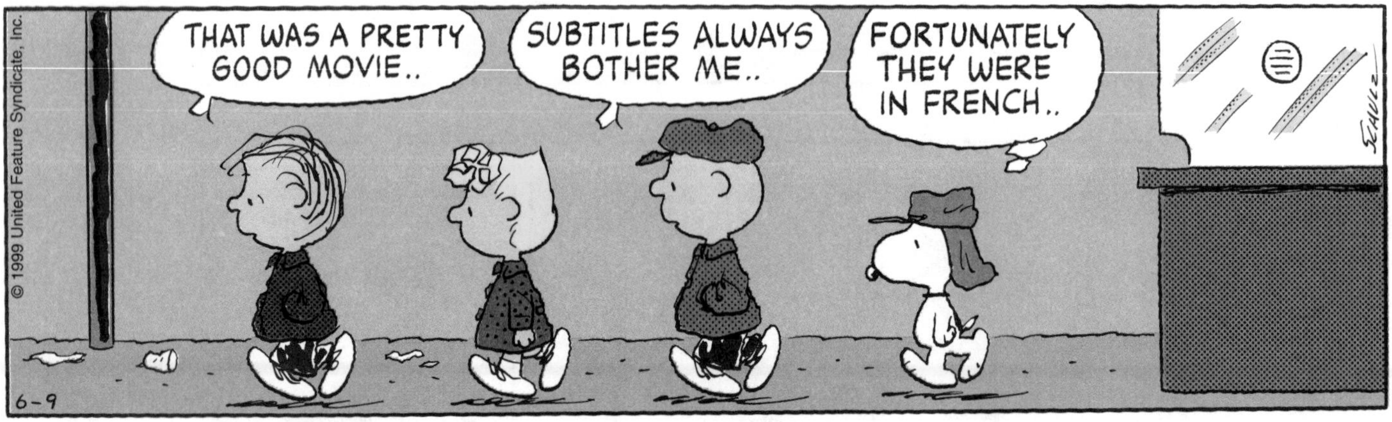
© 1999 United Feature Syndicate, Inc.
THAT WAS A PRETTY GOOD MOVIE..
SUBTITLES ALWAYS BOTHER ME..
FORTUNATELY THEY WERE IN FRENCH..
SCHULZ
6-9

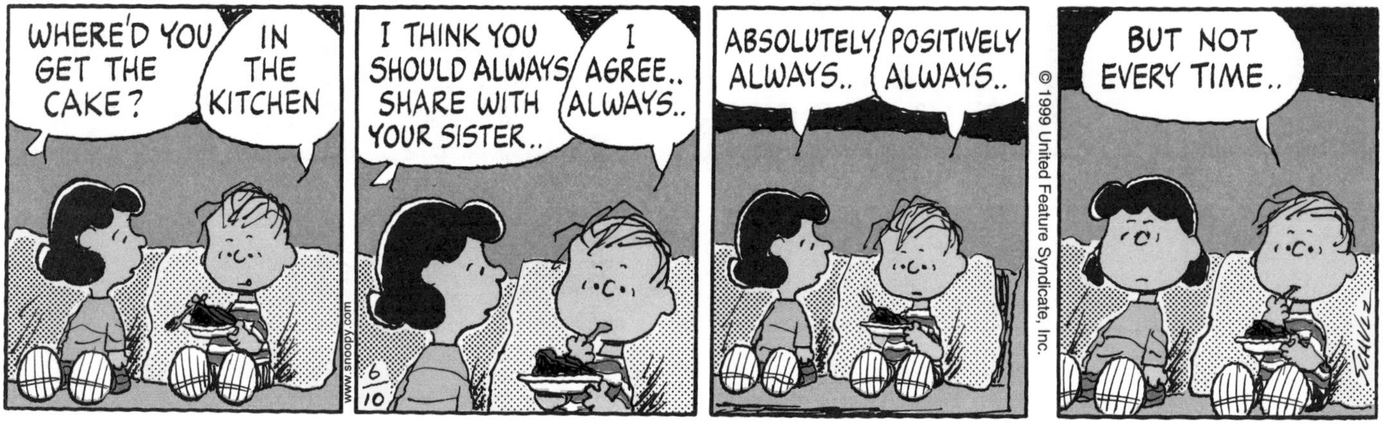
WHERE'D YOU GET THE CAKE?
IN THE KITCHEN
I THINK YOU SHOULD ALWAYS SHARE WITH YOUR SISTER..
I AGREE.. ALWAYS..
ABSOLUTELY ALWAYS..
POSITIVELY ALWAYS..
BUT NOT EVERY TIME..
6/10
www.snoopy.com
© 1999 United Feature Syndicate, Inc.
SCHULZ

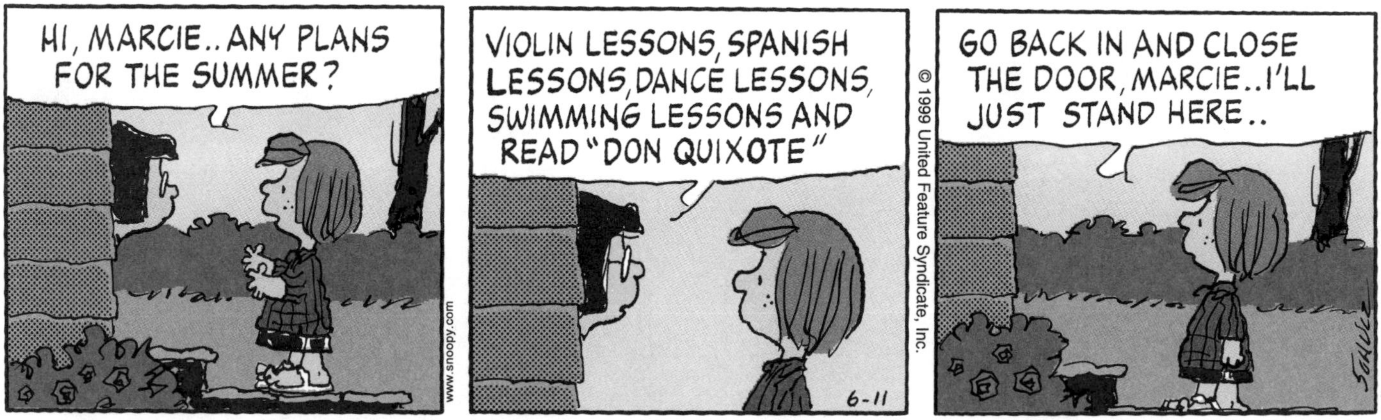
HI, MARCIE.. ANY PLANS FOR THE SUMMER?
VIOLIN LESSONS, SPANISH LESSONS, DANCE LESSONS, SWIMMING LESSONS AND READ "DON QUIXOTE"
GO BACK IN AND CLOSE THE DOOR, MARCIE.. I'LL JUST STAND HERE..
6-11
www.snoopy.com
© 1999 United Feature Syndicate, Inc.
SCHULZ

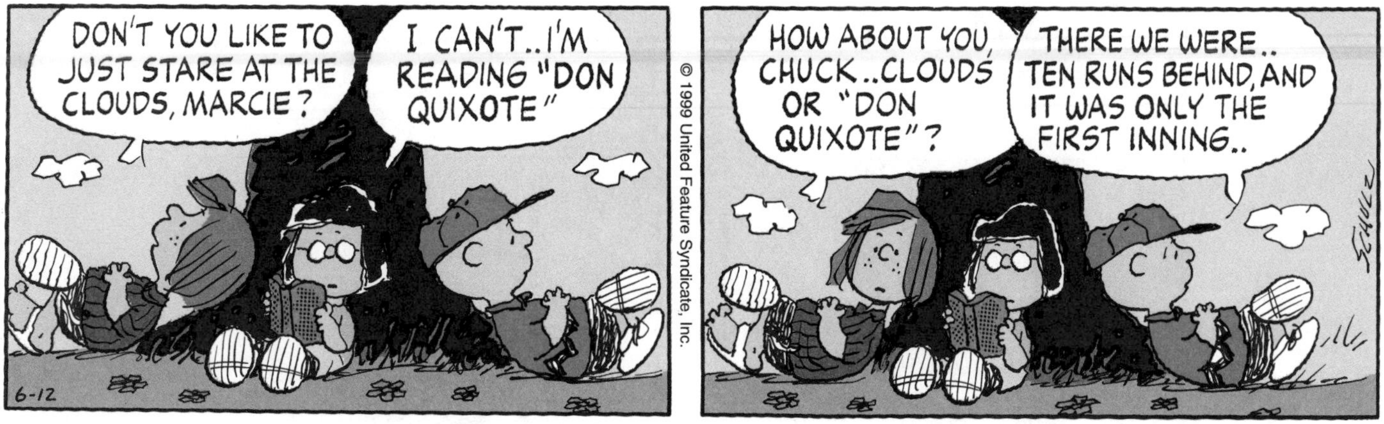
DON'T YOU LIKE TO JUST STARE AT THE CLOUDS, MARCIE?
I CAN'T.. I'M READING "DON QUIXOTE"
HOW ABOUT YOU, CHUCK.. CLOUDS OR "DON QUIXOTE"?
THERE WE WERE.. TEN RUNS BEHIND, AND IT WAS ONLY THE FIRST INNING..
6-12
© 1999 United Feature Syndicate, Inc.
SCHULZ

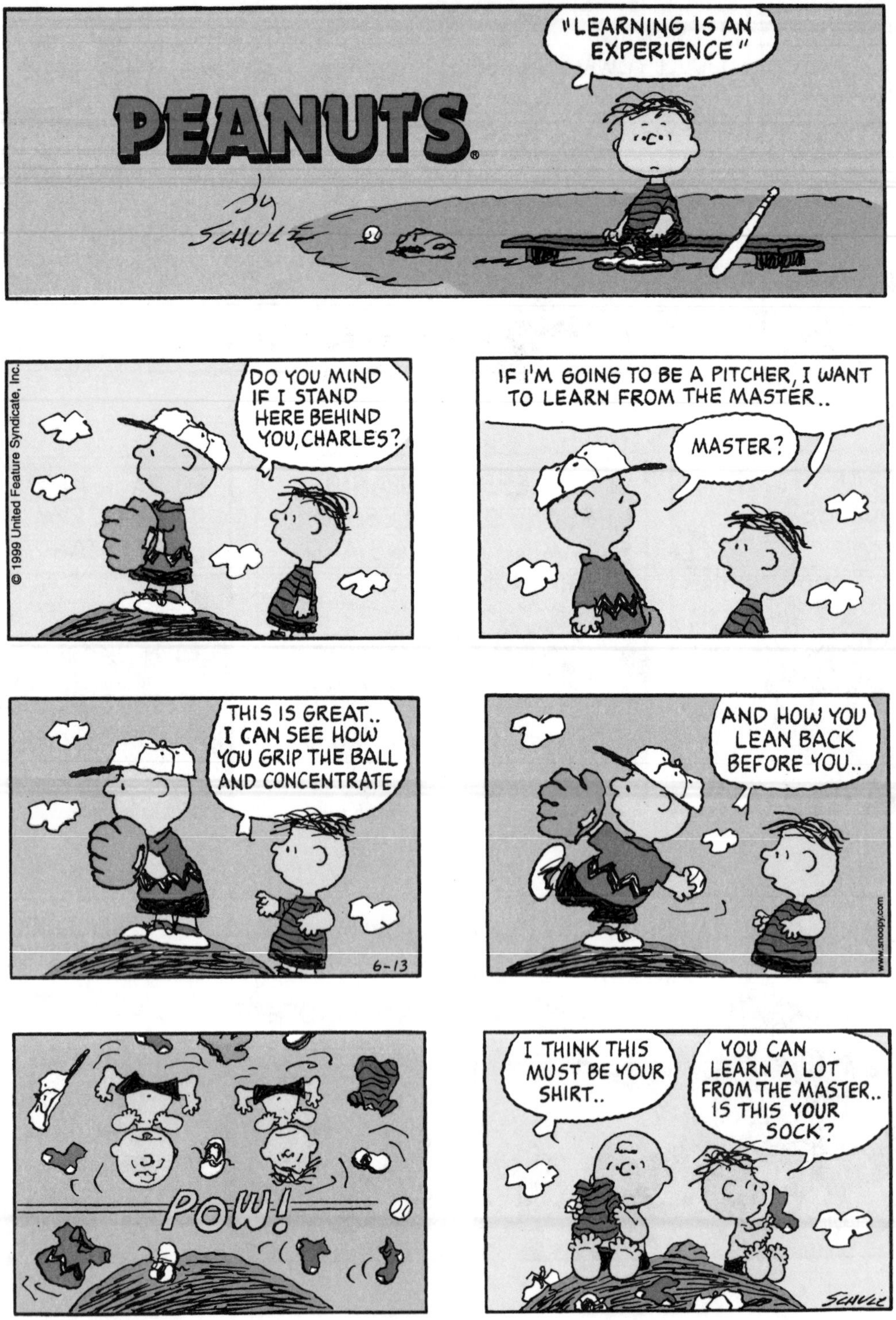
"LEARNING IS AN EXPERIENCE"
PEANUTS®
SCHULZ
© 1999 United Feature Syndicate, Inc.
DO YOU MIND IF I STAND HERE BEHIND YOU, CHARLES?
IF I'M GOING TO BE A PITCHER, I WANT TO LEARN FROM THE MASTER..
MASTER?
THIS IS GREAT.. I CAN SEE HOW YOU GRIP THE BALL AND CONCENTRATE
6-13
AND HOW YOU LEAN BACK BEFORE YOU..
www.snoopy.com
POW!
I THINK THIS MUST BE YOUR SHIRT..
YOU CAN LEARN A LOT FROM THE MASTER.. IS THIS YOUR SOCK?
SCHULZ

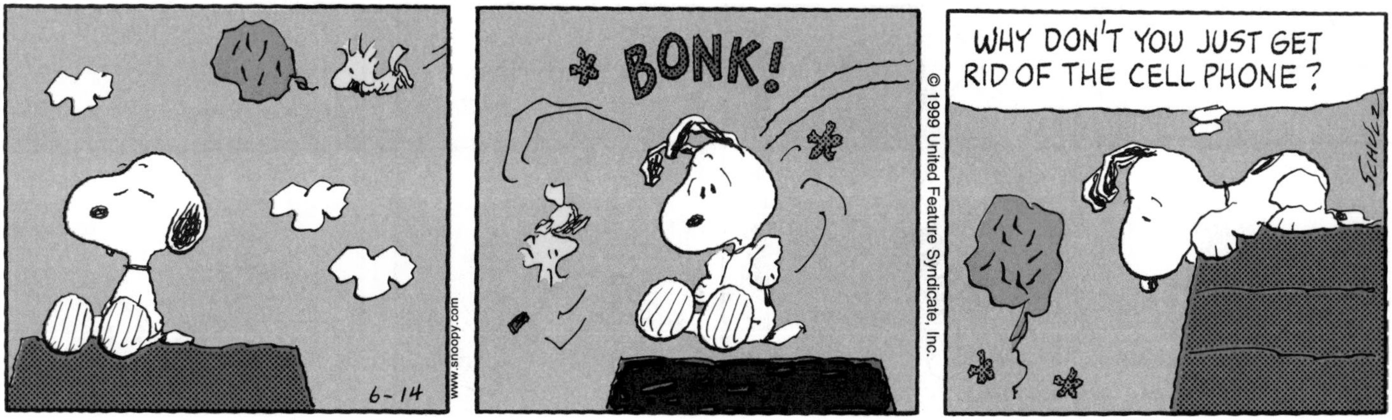
6-14
www.snoopy.com
* BONK!
© 1999 United Feature Syndicate, Inc.
WHY DON'T YOU JUST GET RID OF THE CELL PHONE?
SCHULZ

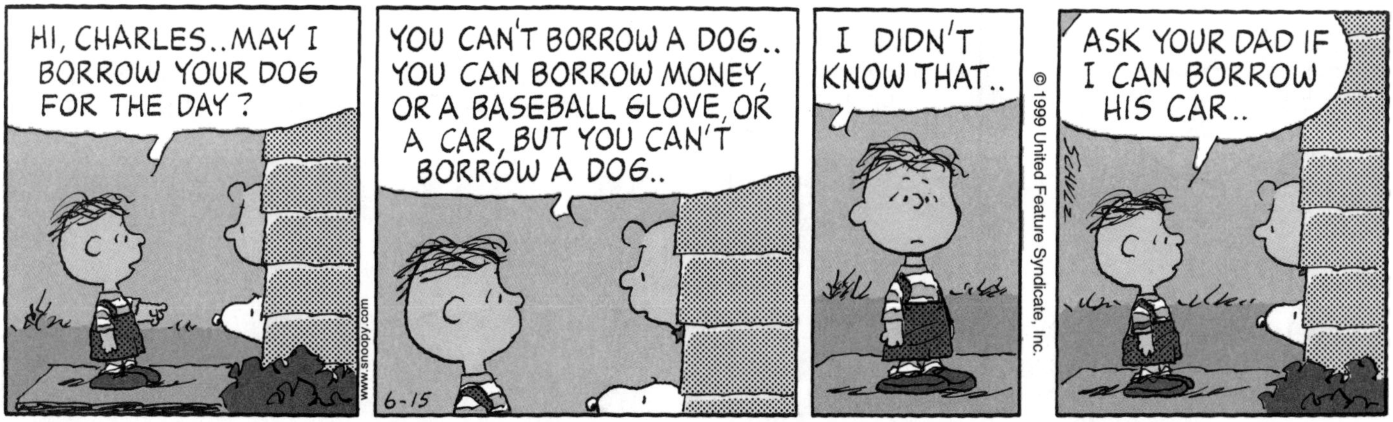
HI, CHARLES..MAY I BORROW YOUR DOG FOR THE DAY?
www.snoopy.com
YOU CAN'T BORROW A DOG.. YOU CAN BORROW MONEY, OR A BASEBALL GLOVE, OR A CAR, BUT YOU CAN'T BORROW A DOG..
6-15
I DIDN'T KNOW THAT..
© 1999 United Feature Syndicate, Inc.
SCHULZ
ASK YOUR DAD IF I CAN BORROW HIS CAR..

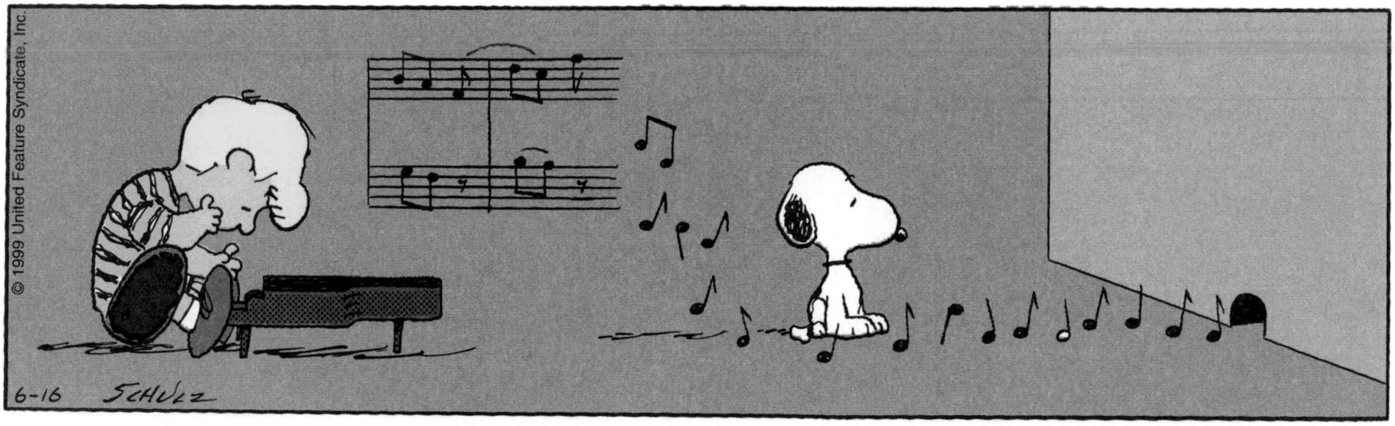
© 1999 United Feature Syndicate, Inc.
6-16
SCHULZ

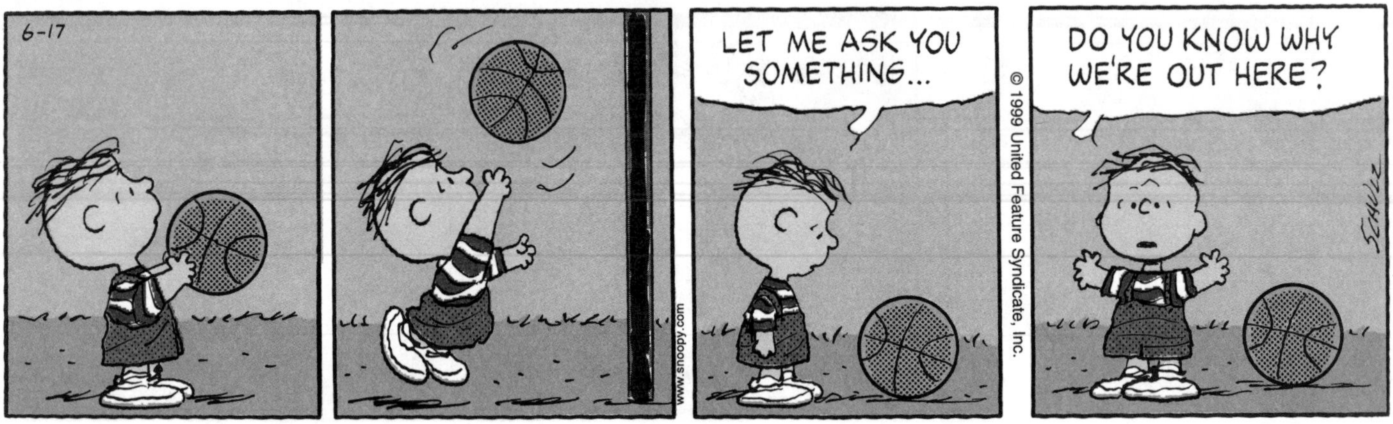
6-17
LET ME ASK YOU SOMETHING...
DO YOU KNOW WHY WE'RE OUT HERE?
SCHULZ

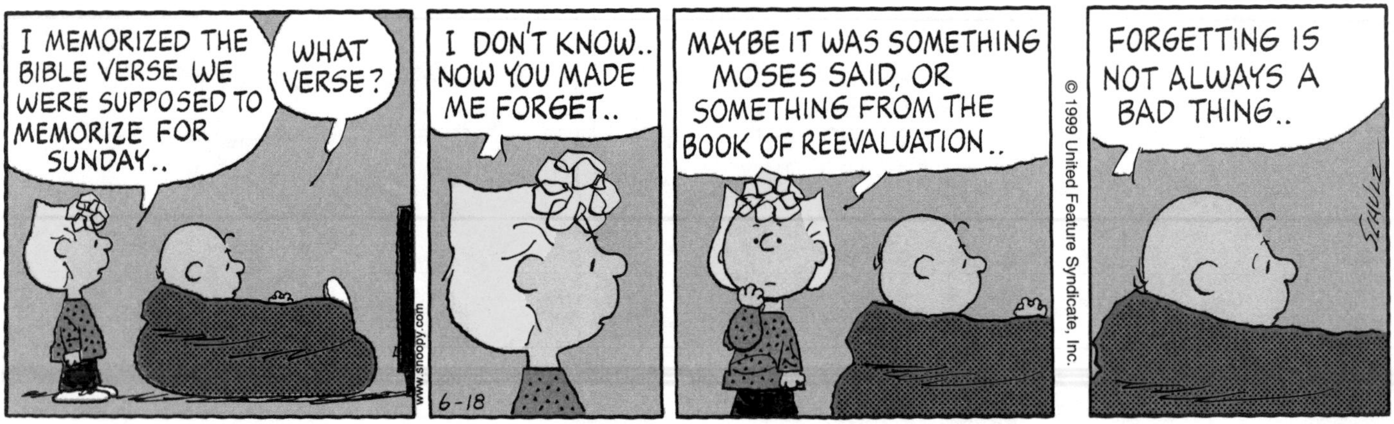
I MEMORIZED THE BIBLE VERSE WE WERE SUPPOSED TO MEMORIZE FOR SUNDAY..
WHAT VERSE?
6-18
I DON'T KNOW.. NOW YOU MADE ME FORGET..
MAYBE IT WAS SOMETHING MOSES SAID, OR SOMETHING FROM THE BOOK OF REEVALUATION..
FORGETTING IS NOT ALWAYS A BAD THING..
SCHULZ

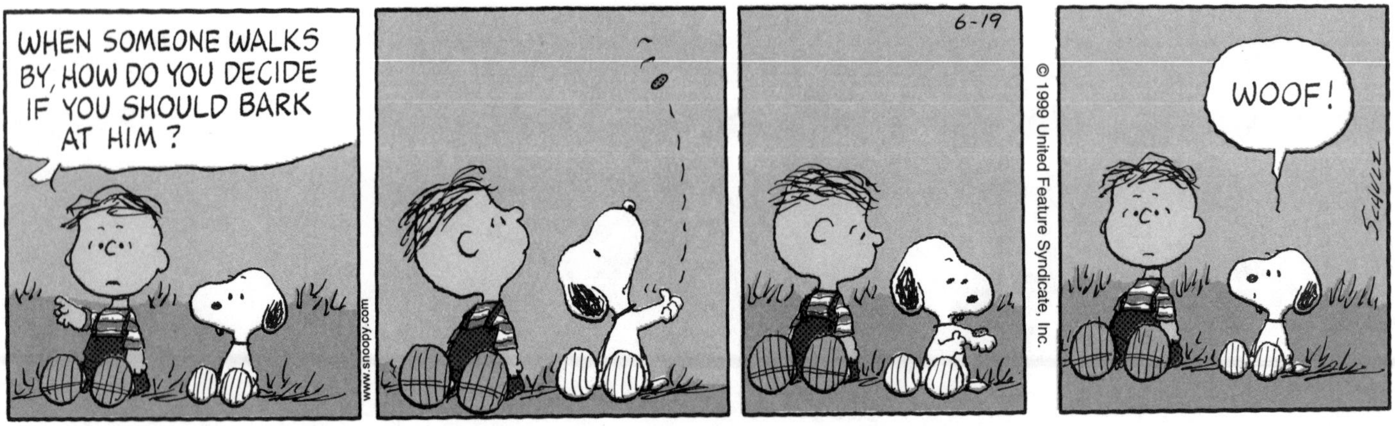
WHEN SOMEONE WALKS BY, HOW DO YOU DECIDE IF YOU SHOULD BARK AT HIM?
6-19
WOOF!
SCHULZ

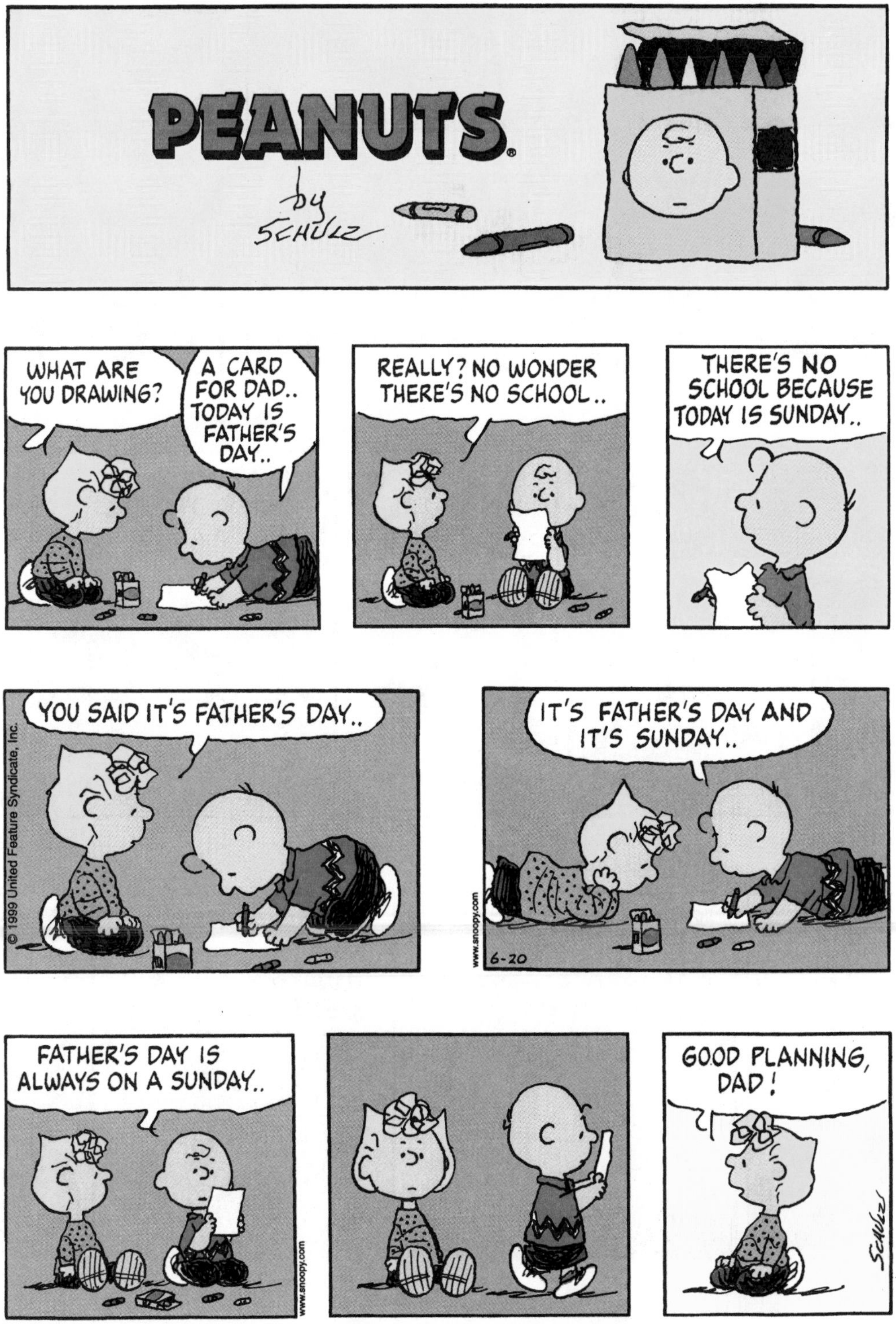
PEANUTS
by SCHULZ
WHAT ARE YOU DRAWING?
A CARD FOR DAD.. TODAY IS FATHER'S DAY..
REALLY? NO WONDER THERE'S NO SCHOOL..
THERE'S NO SCHOOL BECAUSE TODAY IS SUNDAY..
YOU SAID IT'S FATHER'S DAY..
© 1999 United Feature Syndicate, Inc.
IT'S FATHER'S DAY AND IT'S SUNDAY..
www.snoopy.com
6-20
FATHER'S DAY IS ALWAYS ON A SUNDAY..
www.snoopy.com
GOOD PLANNING, DAD!
SCHULZ

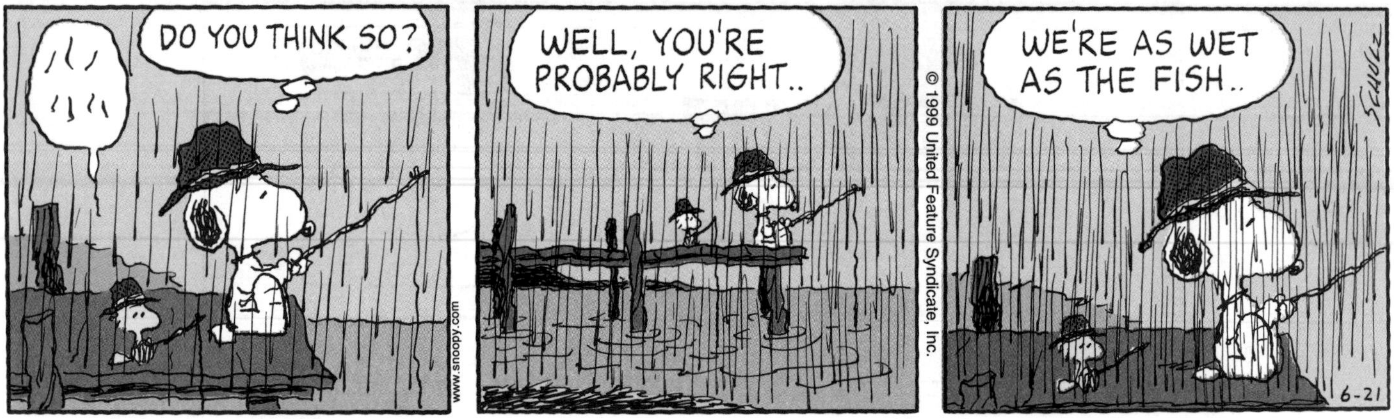
DO YOU THINK SO?
WELL, YOU'RE PROBABLY RIGHT..
WE'RE AS WET AS THE FISH..
SCHULZ
6-21
www.snoopy.com
© 1999 United Feature Syndicate, Inc.

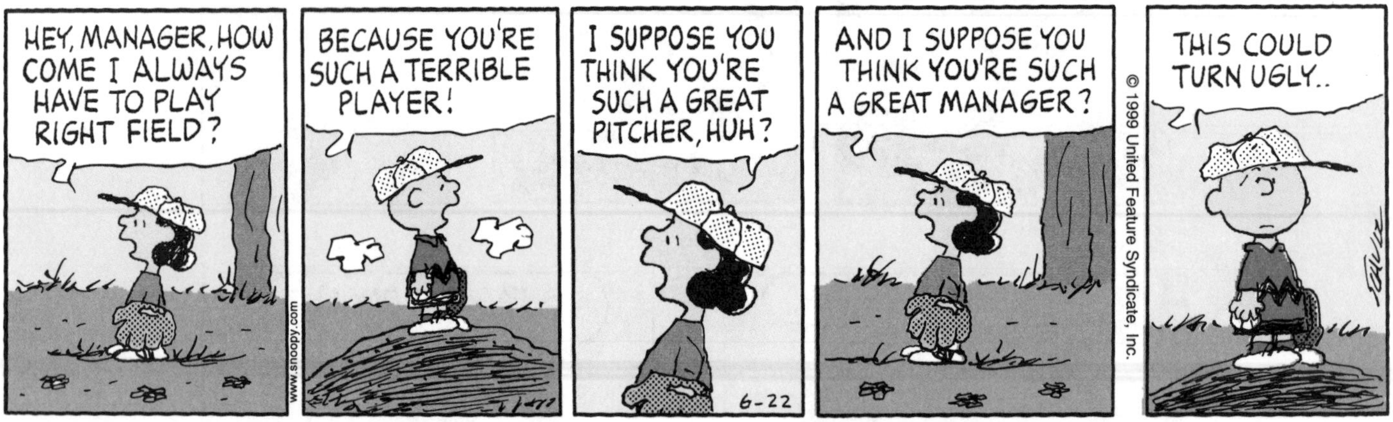
HEY, MANAGER, HOW COME I ALWAYS HAVE TO PLAY RIGHT FIELD?
BECAUSE YOU'RE SUCH A TERRIBLE PLAYER!
I SUPPOSE YOU THINK YOU'RE SUCH A GREAT PITCHER, HUH?
AND I SUPPOSE YOU THINK YOU'RE SUCH A GREAT MANAGER?
THIS COULD TURN UGLY..
SCHULZ
6-22
www.snoopy.com
© 1999 United Feature Syndicate, Inc.

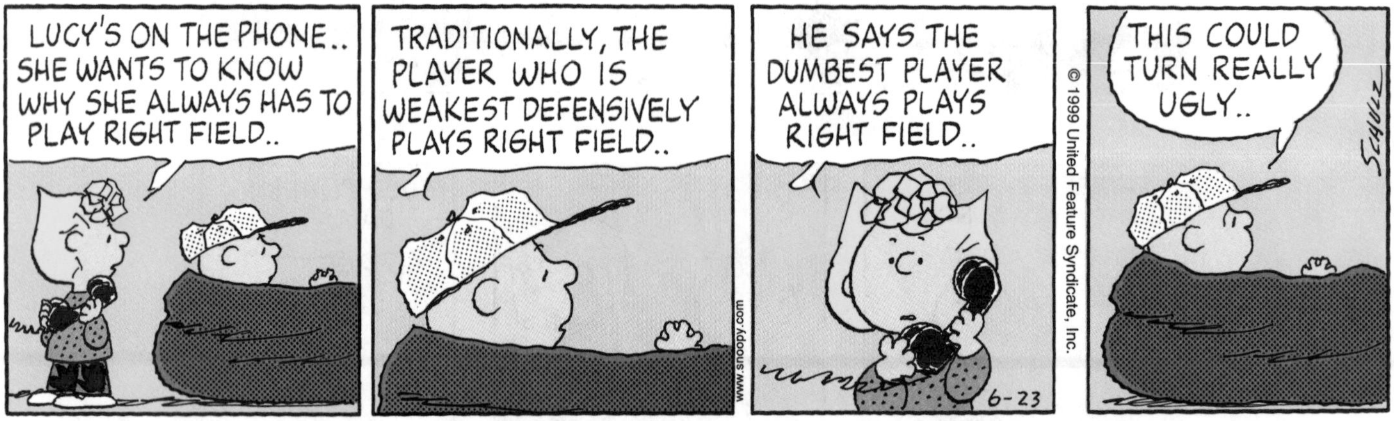
LUCY'S ON THE PHONE.. SHE WANTS TO KNOW WHY SHE ALWAYS HAS TO PLAY RIGHT FIELD..
TRADITIONALLY, THE PLAYER WHO IS WEAKEST DEFENSIVELY PLAYS RIGHT FIELD..
HE SAYS THE DUMBEST PLAYER ALWAYS PLAYS RIGHT FIELD..
THIS COULD TURN REALLY UGLY..
SCHULZ
6-23
www.snoopy.com
© 1999 United Feature Syndicate, Inc.

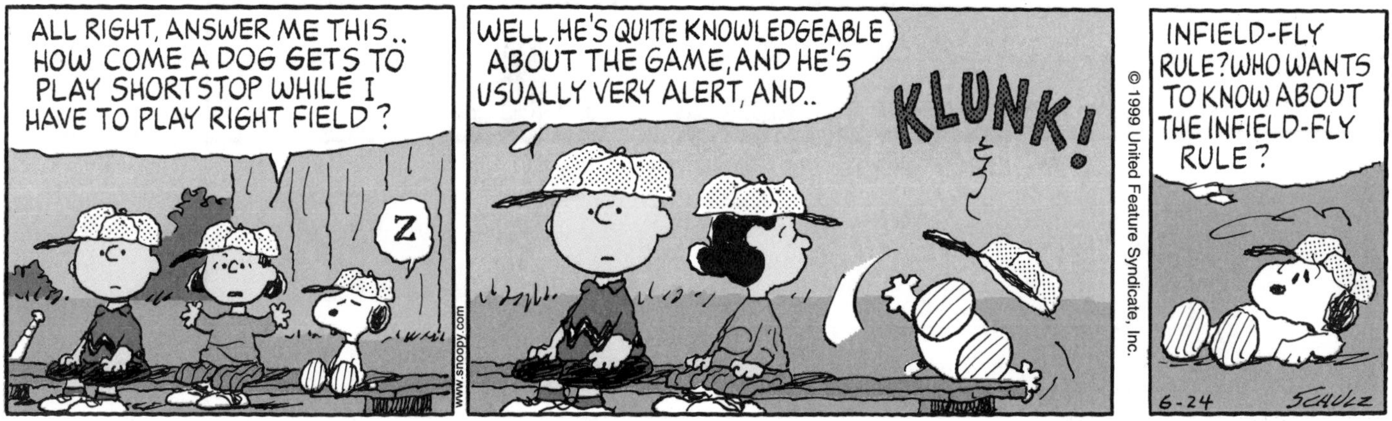
ALL RIGHT, ANSWER ME THIS.. HOW COME A DOG GETS TO PLAY SHORTSTOP WHILE I HAVE TO PLAY RIGHT FIELD ?
Z
www.snoopy.com
WELL, HE'S QUITE KNOWLEDGEABLE ABOUT THE GAME, AND HE'S USUALLY VERY ALERT, AND..
KLUNK!
© 1999 United Feature Syndicate, Inc.
INFIELD-FLY RULE? WHO WANTS TO KNOW ABOUT THE INFIELD-FLY RULE ?
6-24
SCHULZ

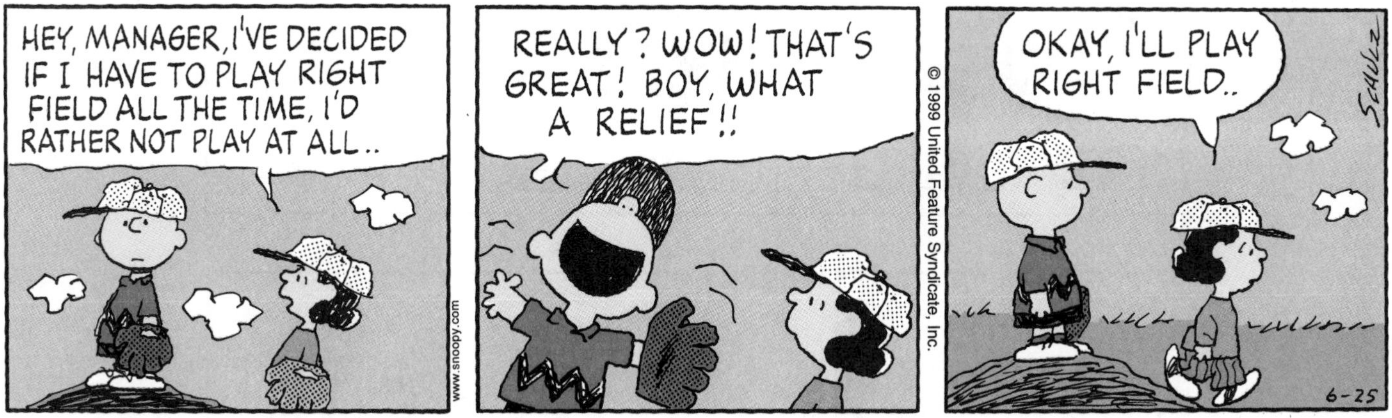
HEY, MANAGER, I'VE DECIDED IF I HAVE TO PLAY RIGHT FIELD ALL THE TIME, I'D RATHER NOT PLAY AT ALL..
www.snoopy.com
REALLY ? WOW! THAT'S GREAT! BOY, WHAT A RELIEF !!
© 1999 United Feature Syndicate, Inc.
OKAY, I'LL PLAY RIGHT FIELD..
SCHULZ
6-25

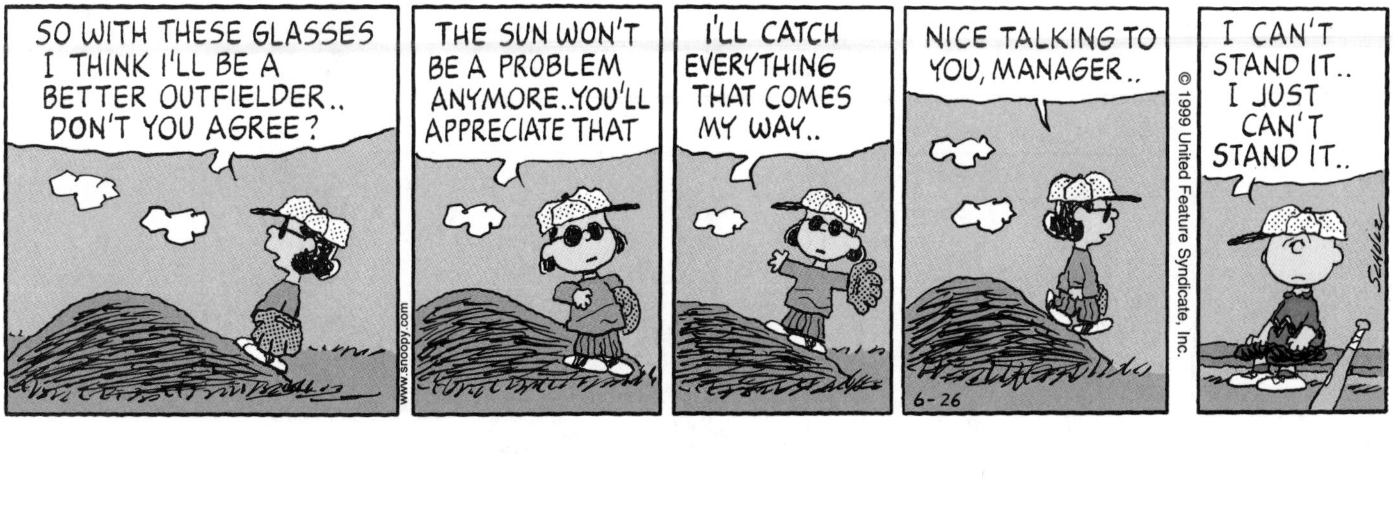
SO WITH THESE GLASSES I THINK I'LL BE A BETTER OUTFIELDER.. DON'T YOU AGREE?
www.snoopy.com
THE SUN WON'T BE A PROBLEM ANYMORE..YOU'LL APPRECIATE THAT
I'LL CATCH EVERYTHING THAT COMES MY WAY..
NICE TALKING TO YOU, MANAGER..
6-26
© 1999 United Feature Syndicate, Inc.
I CAN'T STAND IT.. I JUST CAN'T STAND IT..
SCHULZ

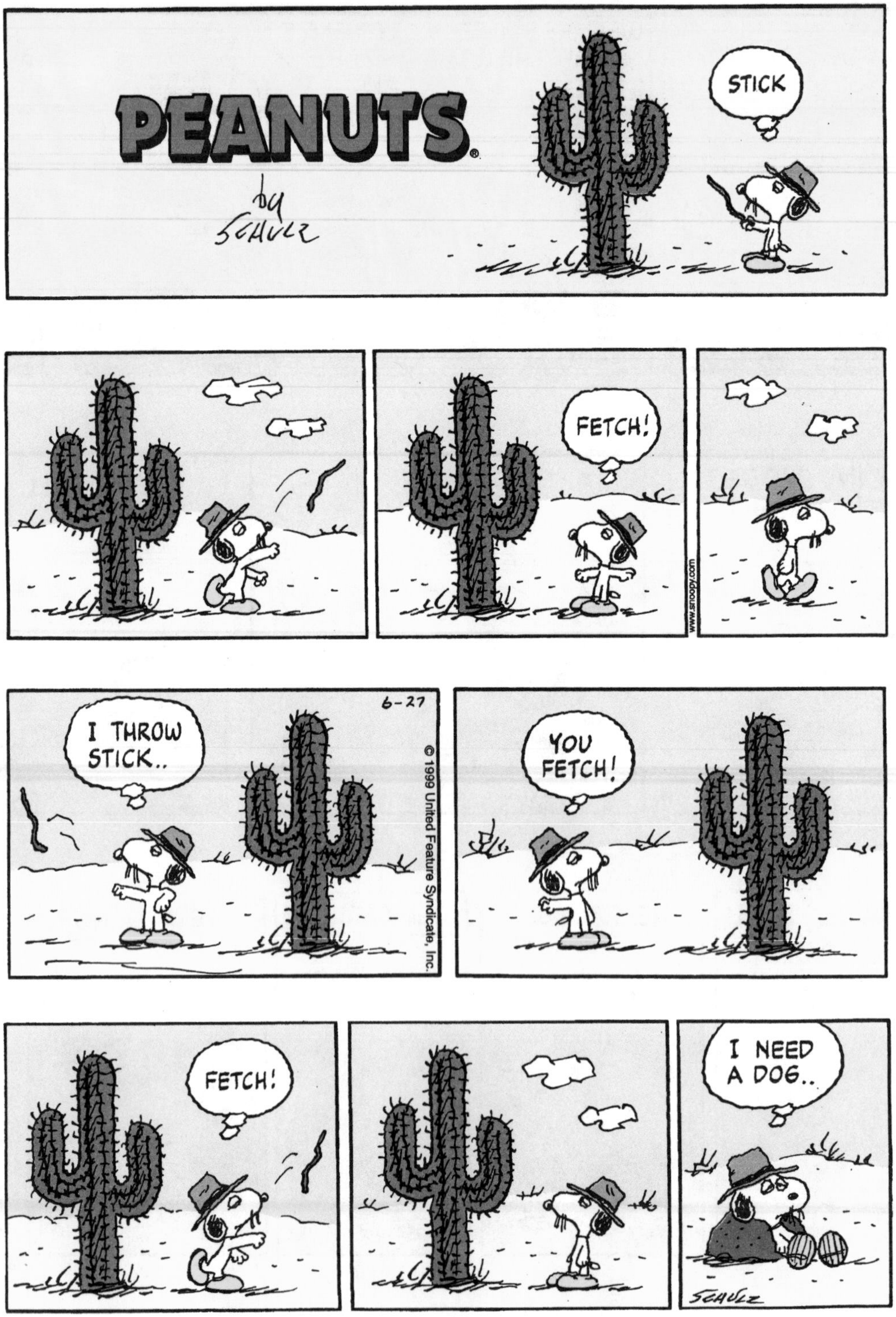
PEANUTS
by SCHULZ
STICK
FETCH!
www.snoopy.com
6-27
I THROW STICK..
© 1999 United Feature Syndicate, Inc.
YOU FETCH!
FETCH!
I NEED A DOG..
SCHULZ

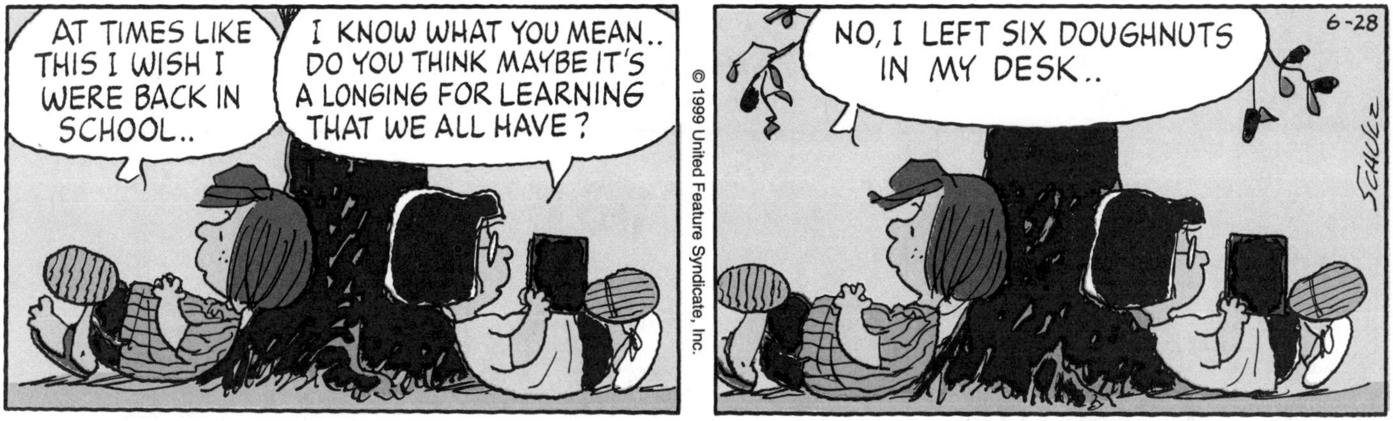
AT TIMES LIKE THIS I WISH I WERE BACK IN SCHOOL..
I KNOW WHAT YOU MEAN.. DO YOU THINK MAYBE IT'S A LONGING FOR LEARNING THAT WE ALL HAVE?
© 1999 United Feature Syndicate, Inc.
6-28
NO, I LEFT SIX DOUGHNUTS IN MY DESK..
SCHULZ

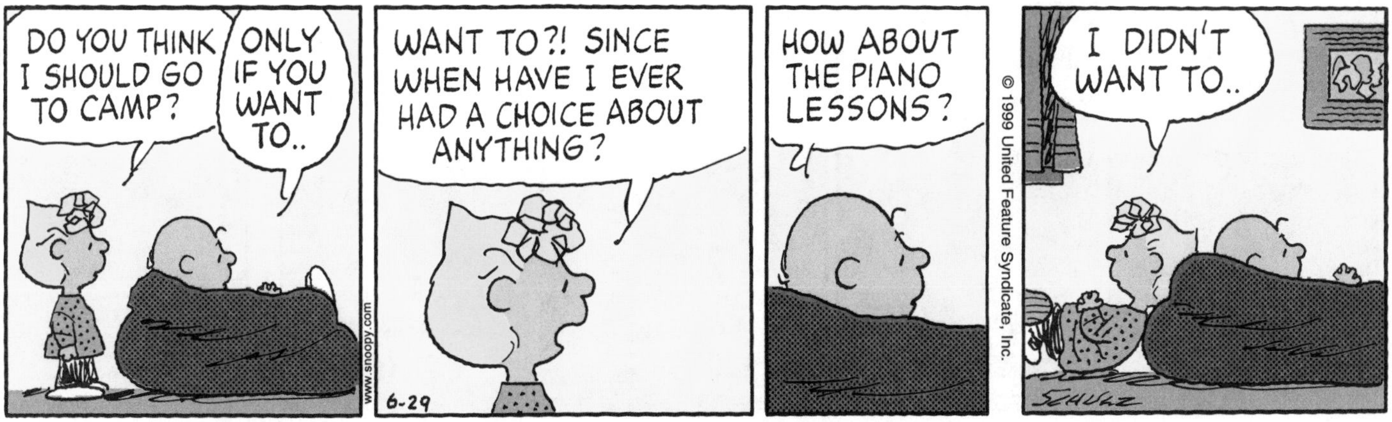
DO YOU THINK I SHOULD GO TO CAMP?
ONLY IF YOU WANT TO..
www.snoopy.com
6-29
WANT TO?! SINCE WHEN HAVE I EVER HAD A CHOICE ABOUT ANYTHING?
HOW ABOUT THE PIANO LESSONS?
© 1999 United Feature Syndicate, Inc.
I DIDN'T WANT TO..
SCHULZ

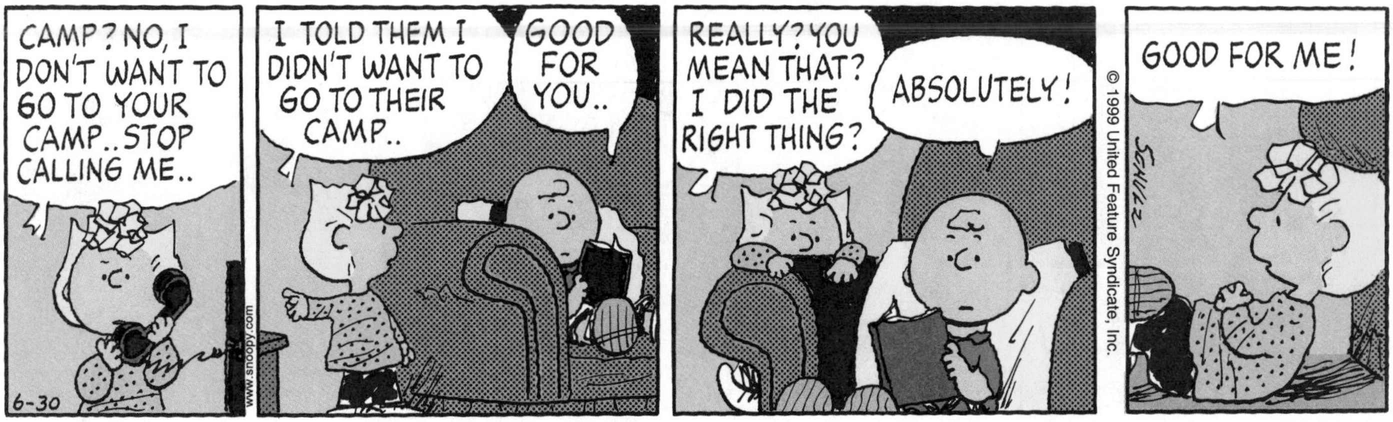
CAMP? NO, I DON'T WANT TO GO TO YOUR CAMP..STOP CALLING ME..
6-30
www.snoopy.com
I TOLD THEM I DIDN'T WANT TO GO TO THEIR CAMP..
GOOD FOR YOU..
REALLY? YOU MEAN THAT? I DID THE RIGHT THING?
ABSOLUTELY!
© 1999 United Feature Syndicate, Inc.
SCHULZ
GOOD FOR ME!

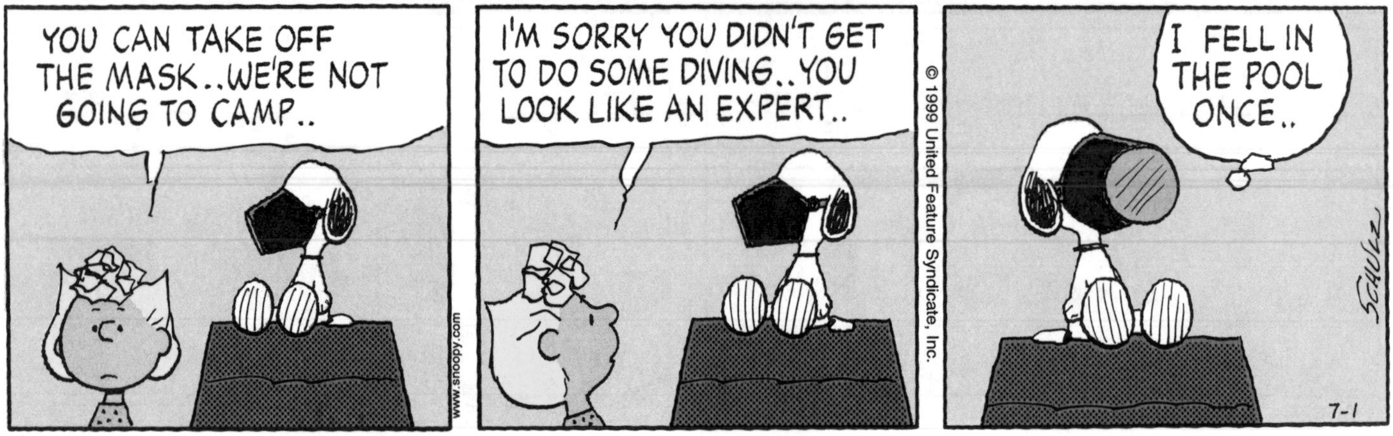
YOU CAN TAKE OFF THE MASK..WE'RE NOT GOING TO CAMP..
www.snoopy.com
I'M SORRY YOU DIDN'T GET TO DO SOME DIVING..YOU LOOK LIKE AN EXPERT..
© 1999 United Feature Syndicate, Inc.
I FELL IN THE POOL ONCE..
SCHULZ
7-1

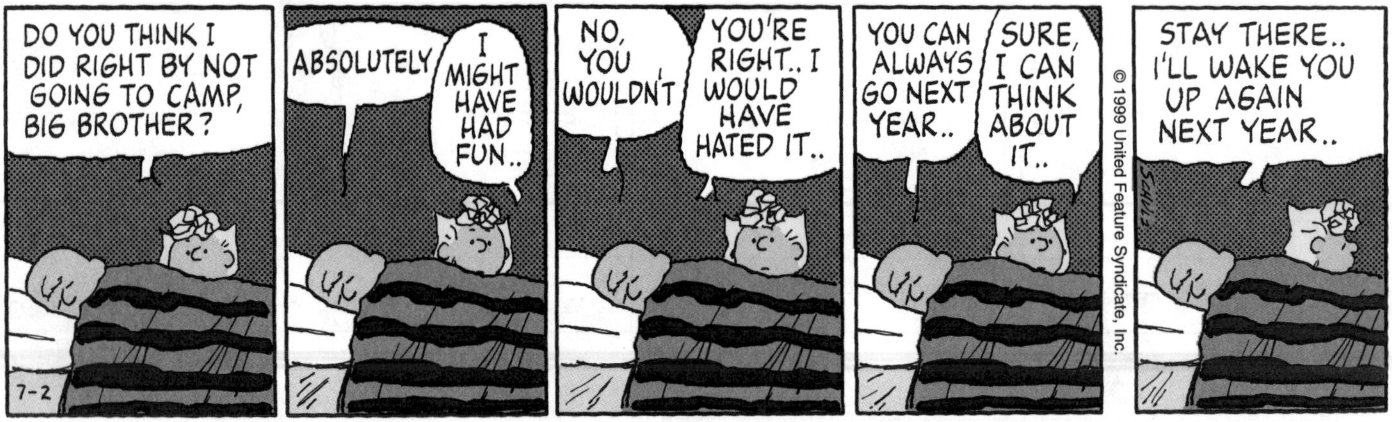
DO YOU THINK I DID RIGHT BY NOT GOING TO CAMP, BIG BROTHER?
7-2
ABSOLUTELY
I MIGHT HAVE HAD FUN..
NO, YOU WOULDN'T
YOU'RE RIGHT.. I WOULD HAVE HATED IT..
YOU CAN ALWAYS GO NEXT YEAR..
SURE, I CAN THINK ABOUT IT..
SCHULZ
© 1999 United Feature Syndicate, Inc.
STAY THERE.. I'LL WAKE YOU UP AGAIN NEXT YEAR..

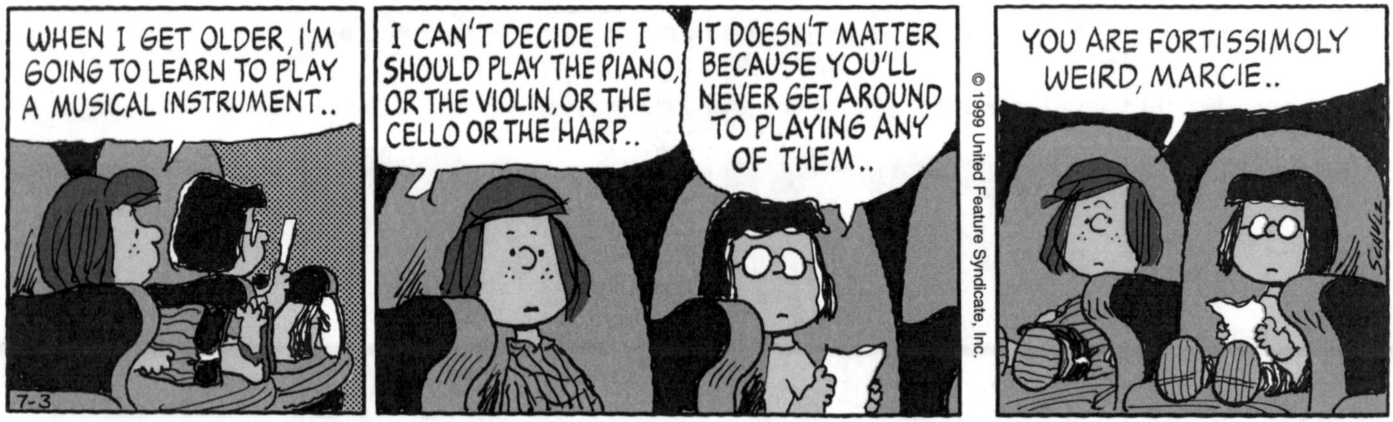
WHEN I GET OLDER, I'M GOING TO LEARN TO PLAY A MUSICAL INSTRUMENT..
7-3
I CAN'T DECIDE IF I SHOULD PLAY THE PIANO, OR THE VIOLIN, OR THE CELLO OR THE HARP..
IT DOESN'T MATTER BECAUSE YOU'LL NEVER GET AROUND TO PLAYING ANY OF THEM..
© 1999 United Feature Syndicate, Inc.
YOU ARE FORTISSIMOLY WEIRD, MARCIE..
SCHULZ

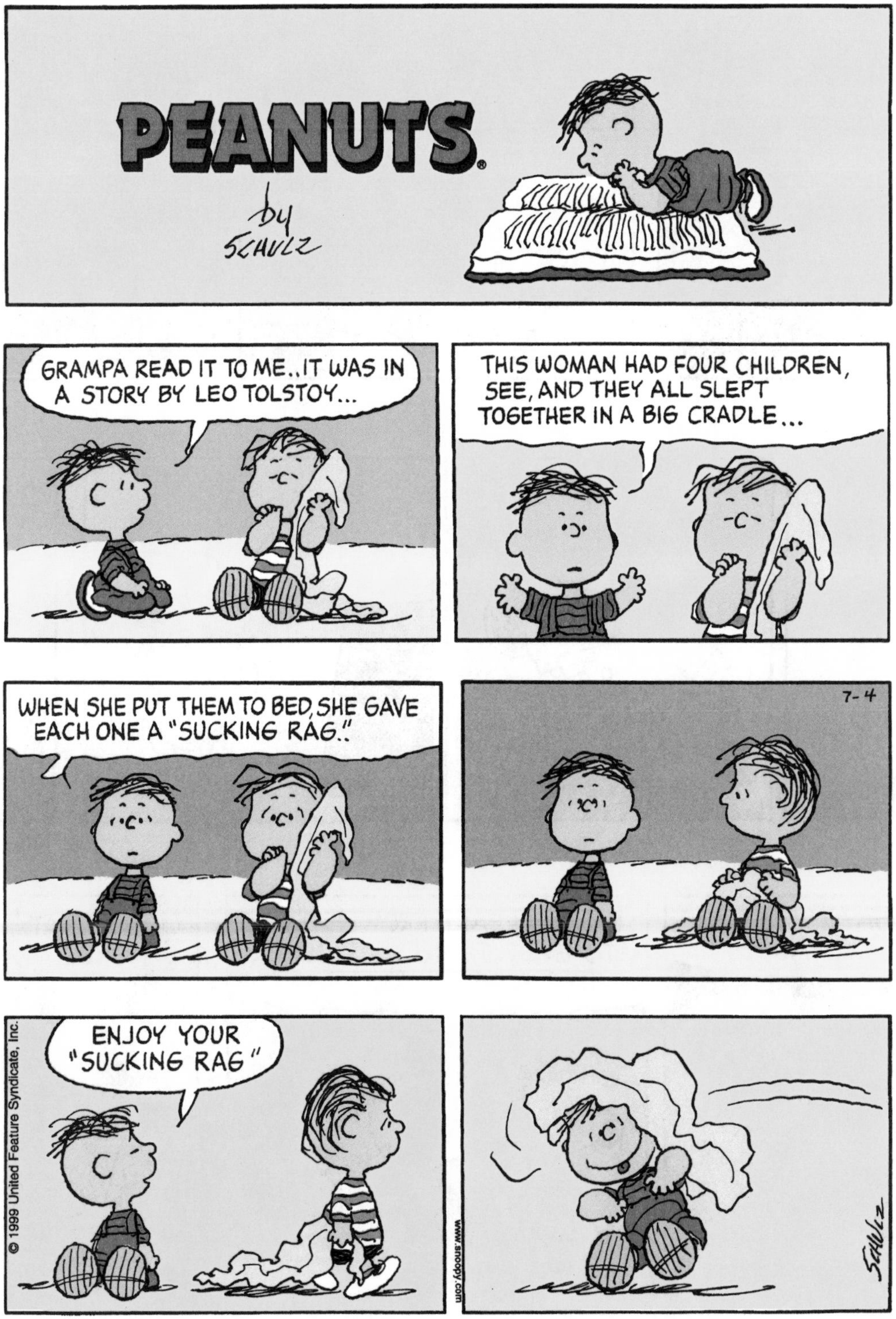
PEANUTS®
by SCHULZ
GRAMPA READ IT TO ME..IT WAS IN A STORY BY LEO TOLSTOY...
THIS WOMAN HAD FOUR CHILDREN, SEE, AND THEY ALL SLEPT TOGETHER IN A BIG CRADLE...
WHEN SHE PUT THEM TO BED, SHE GAVE EACH ONE A "SUCKING RAG."
7-4
ENJOY YOUR "SUCKING RAG"
© 1999 United Feature Syndicate, Inc.
www.snoopy.com
SCHULZ

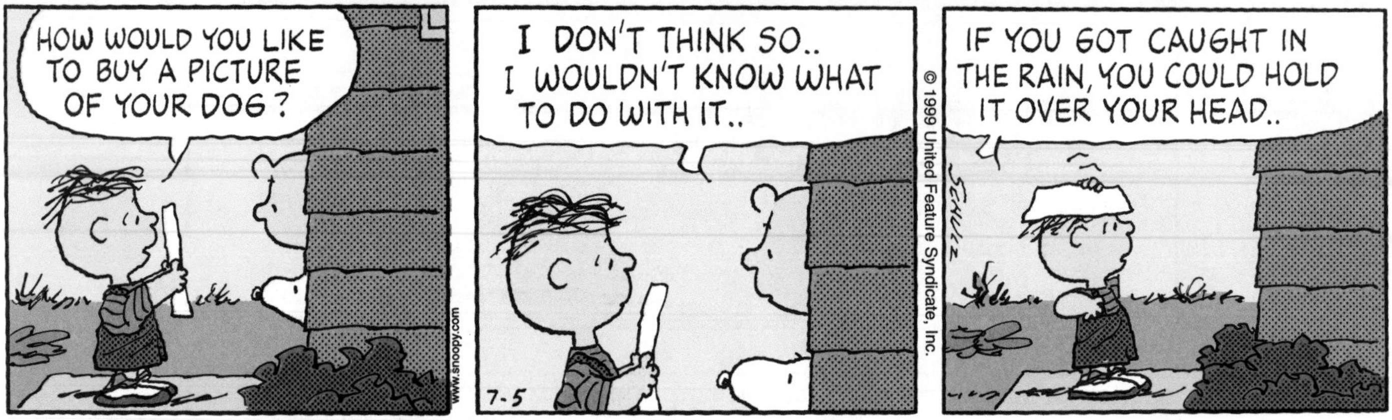
HOW WOULD YOU LIKE TO BUY A PICTURE OF YOUR DOG?
www.snoopy.com
7-5
I DON'T THINK SO.. I WOULDN'T KNOW WHAT TO DO WITH IT..
© 1999 United Feature Syndicate, Inc.
IF YOU GOT CAUGHT IN THE RAIN, YOU COULD HOLD IT OVER YOUR HEAD..
SCHULZ

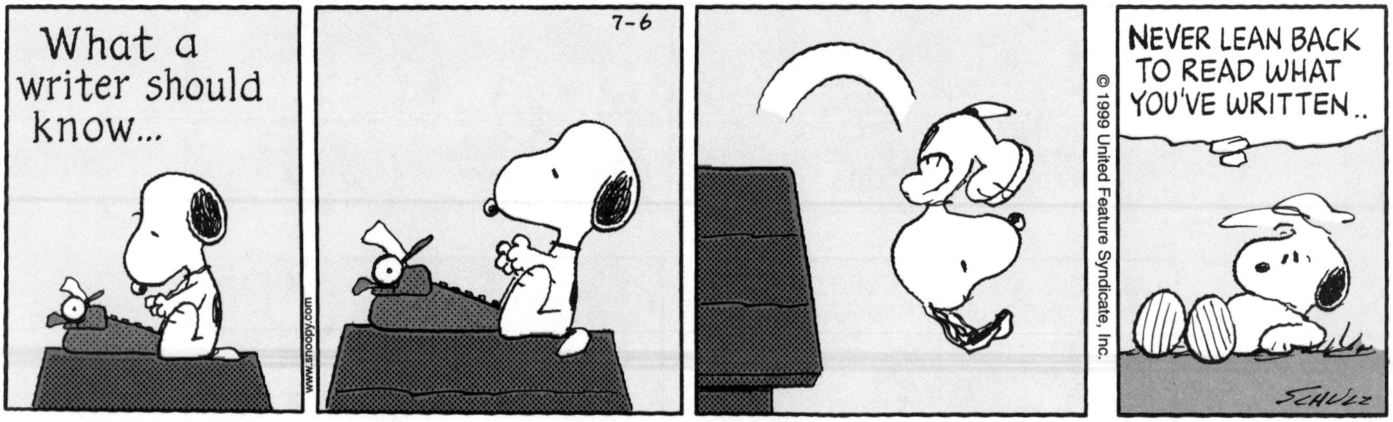
What a writer should know...
www.snoopy.com
7-6
© 1999 United Feature Syndicate, Inc.
NEVER LEAN BACK TO READ WHAT YOU'VE WRITTEN..
SCHULZ

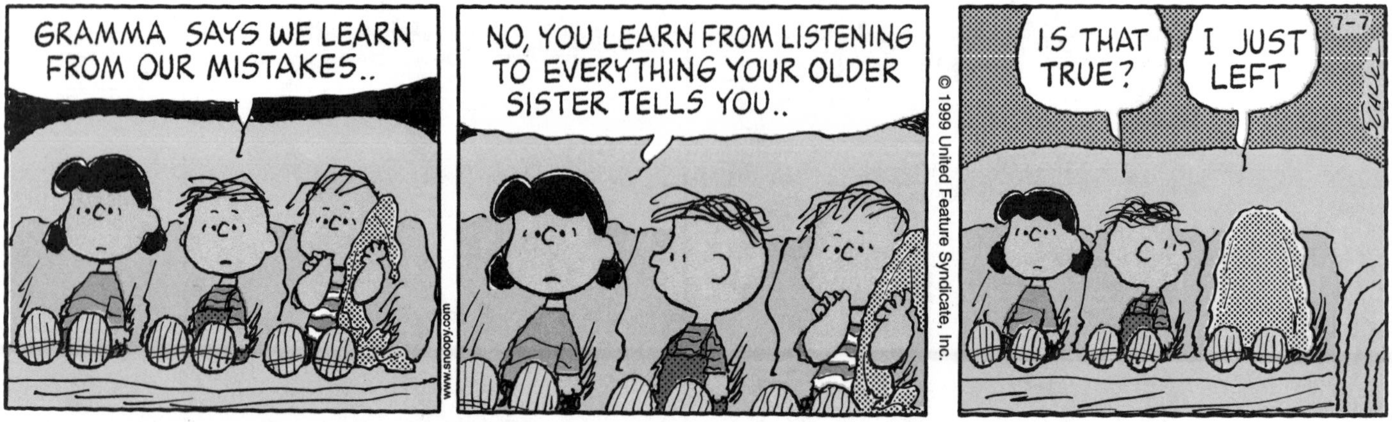
GRAMMA SAYS WE LEARN FROM OUR MISTAKES..
www.snoopy.com
NO, YOU LEARN FROM LISTENING TO EVERYTHING YOUR OLDER SISTER TELLS YOU..
© 1999 United Feature Syndicate, Inc.
7-7
IS THAT TRUE?
I JUST LEFT
SCHULZ

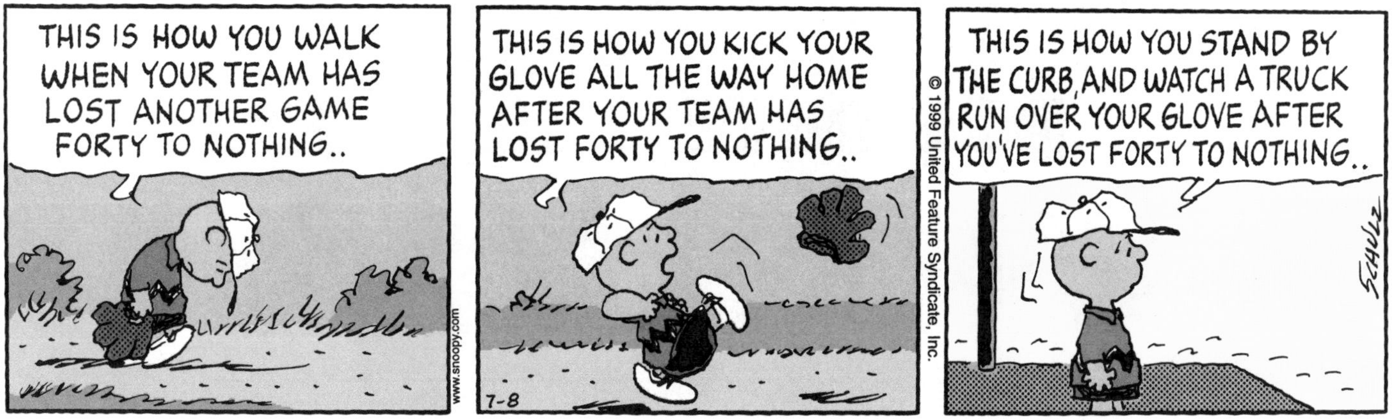
THIS IS HOW YOU WALK WHEN YOUR TEAM HAS LOST ANOTHER GAME FORTY TO NOTHING..
THIS IS HOW YOU KICK YOUR GLOVE ALL THE WAY HOME AFTER YOUR TEAM HAS LOST FORTY TO NOTHING..
THIS IS HOW YOU STAND BY THE CURB, AND WATCH A TRUCK RUN OVER YOUR GLOVE AFTER YOU'VE LOST FORTY TO NOTHING..
7-8
SCHULZ
www.snoopy.com

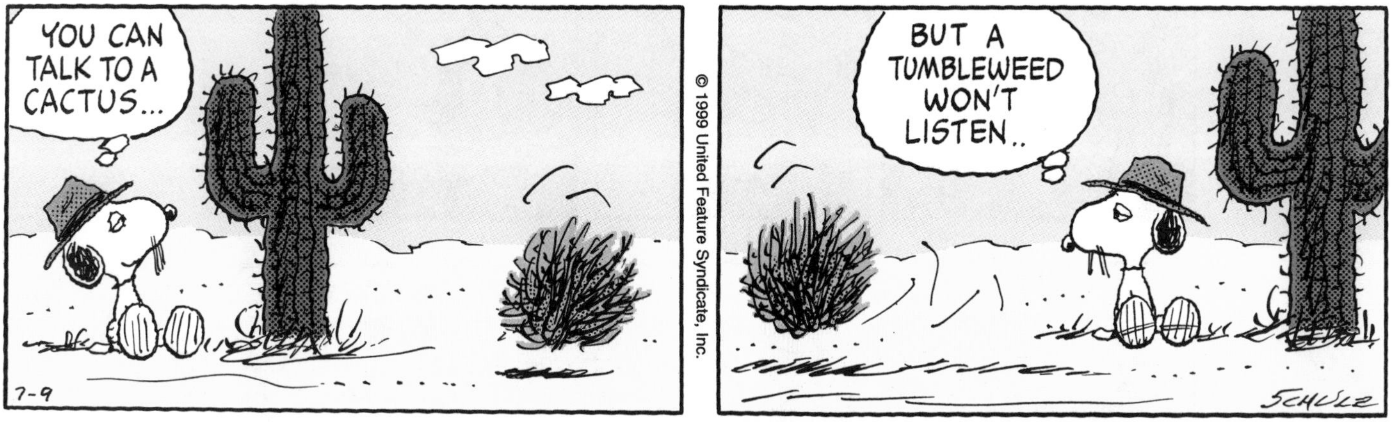
YOU CAN TALK TO A CACTUS...
BUT A TUMBLEWEED WON'T LISTEN..
7-9
SCHULZ

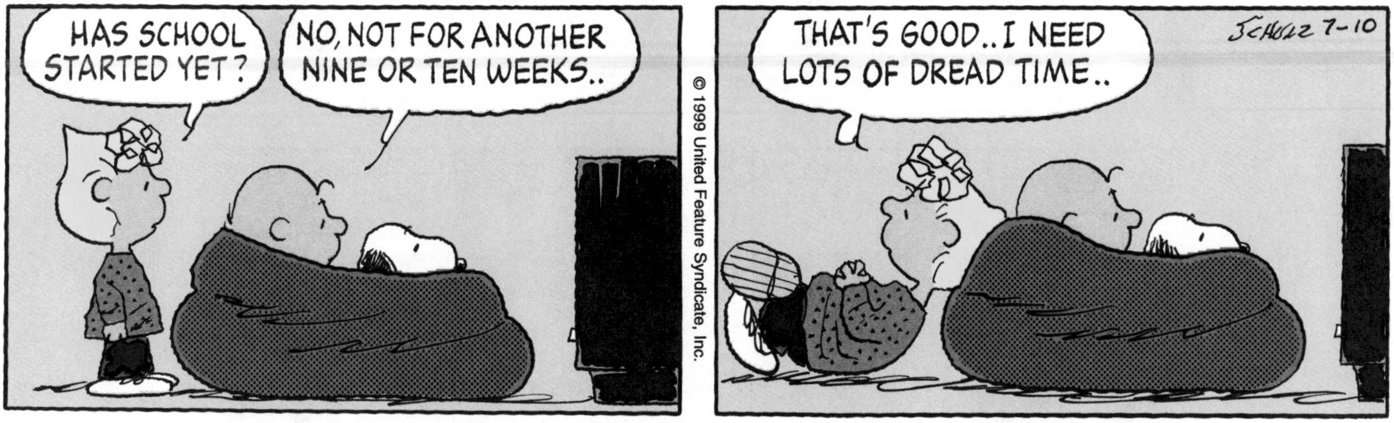
HAS SCHOOL STARTED YET?
NO, NOT FOR ANOTHER NINE OR TEN WEEKS..
THAT'S GOOD..I NEED LOTS OF DREAD TIME..
SCHULZ 7-10

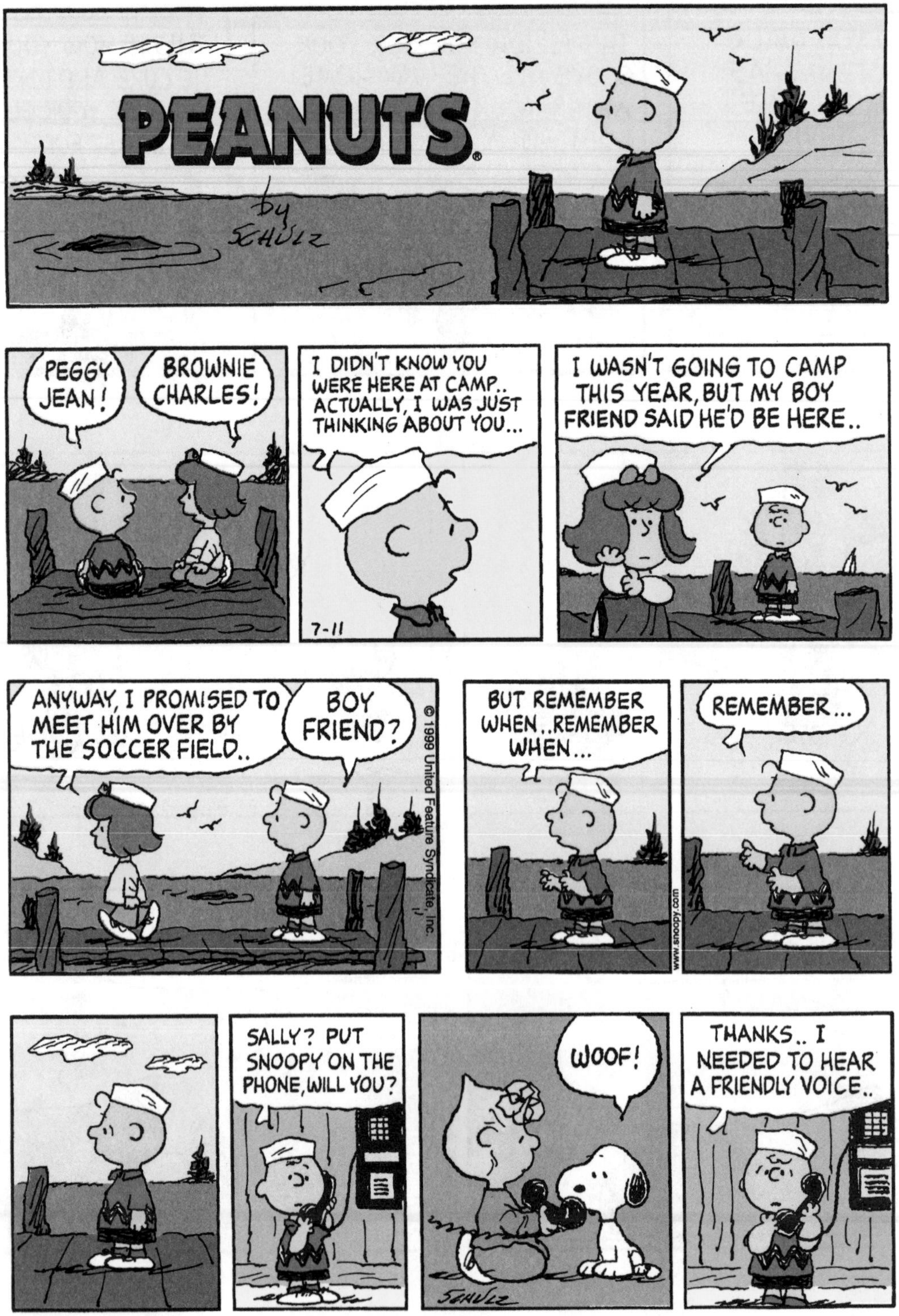
PEANUTS
by SCHULZ
PEGGY JEAN!
BROWNIE CHARLES!
I DIDN'T KNOW YOU WERE HERE AT CAMP.. ACTUALLY, I WAS JUST THINKING ABOUT YOU...
7-11
I WASN'T GOING TO CAMP THIS YEAR, BUT MY BOY FRIEND SAID HE'D BE HERE..
ANYWAY, I PROMISED TO MEET HIM OVER BY THE SOCCER FIELD..
BOY FRIEND?
© 1999 United Feature Syndicate, Inc.
BUT REMEMBER WHEN..REMEMBER WHEN...
www.snoopy.com
REMEMBER...
SALLY? PUT SNOOPY ON THE PHONE, WILL YOU?
WOOF!
SCHULZ
THANKS.. I NEEDED TO HEAR A FRIENDLY VOICE..

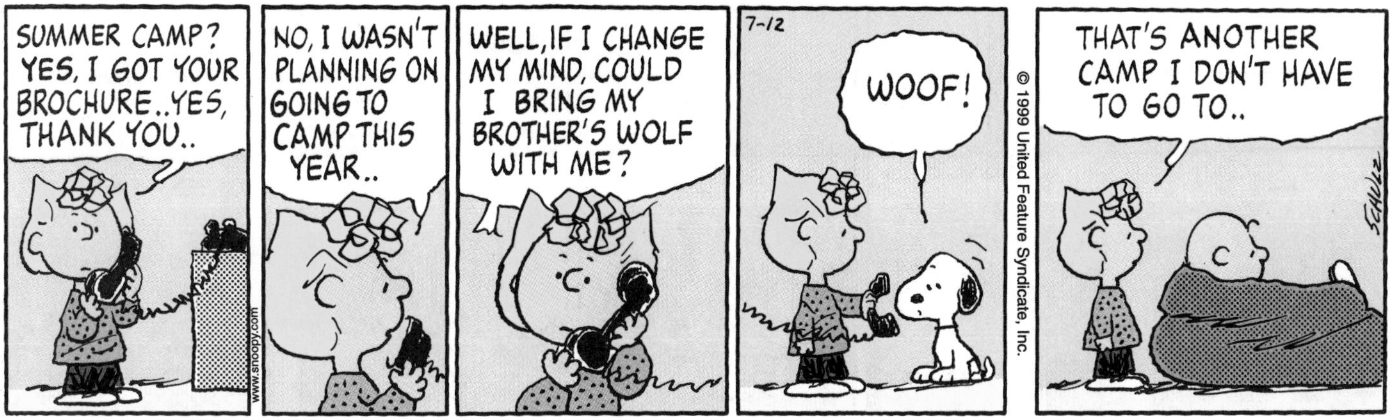
7-12
SUMMER CAMP? YES, I GOT YOUR BROCHURE..YES, THANK YOU..
NO, I WASN'T PLANNING ON GOING TO CAMP THIS YEAR..
WELL, IF I CHANGE MY MIND, COULD I BRING MY BROTHER'S WOLF WITH ME?
WOOF!
THAT'S ANOTHER CAMP I DON'T HAVE TO GO TO..
www.snoopy.com
© 1999 United Feature Syndicate, Inc.

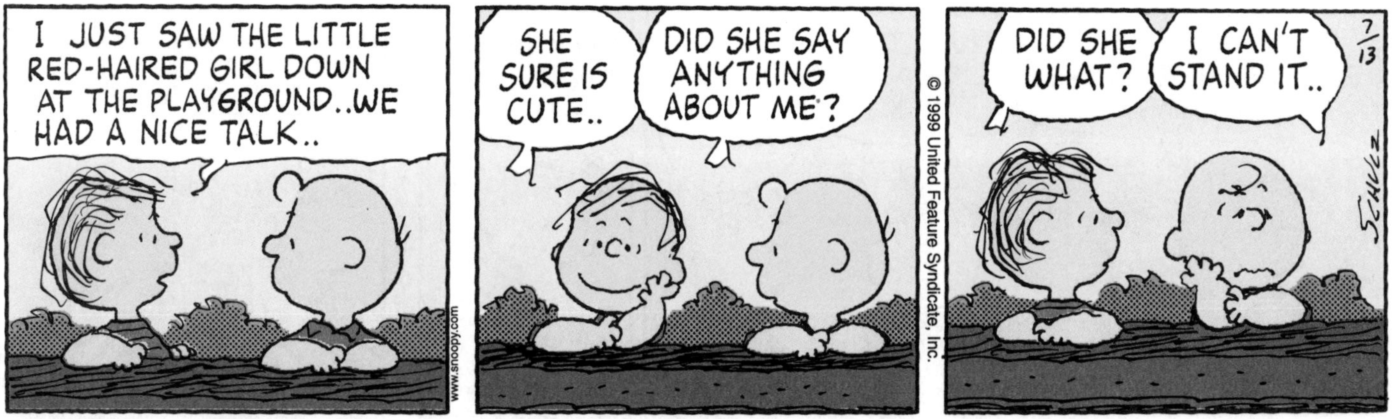
7/13
I JUST SAW THE LITTLE RED-HAIRED GIRL DOWN AT THE PLAYGROUND..WE HAD A NICE TALK..
SHE SURE IS CUTE..
DID SHE SAY ANYTHING ABOUT ME?
DID SHE WHAT?
I CAN'T STAND IT..
www.snoopy.com
© 1999 United Feature Syndicate, Inc.

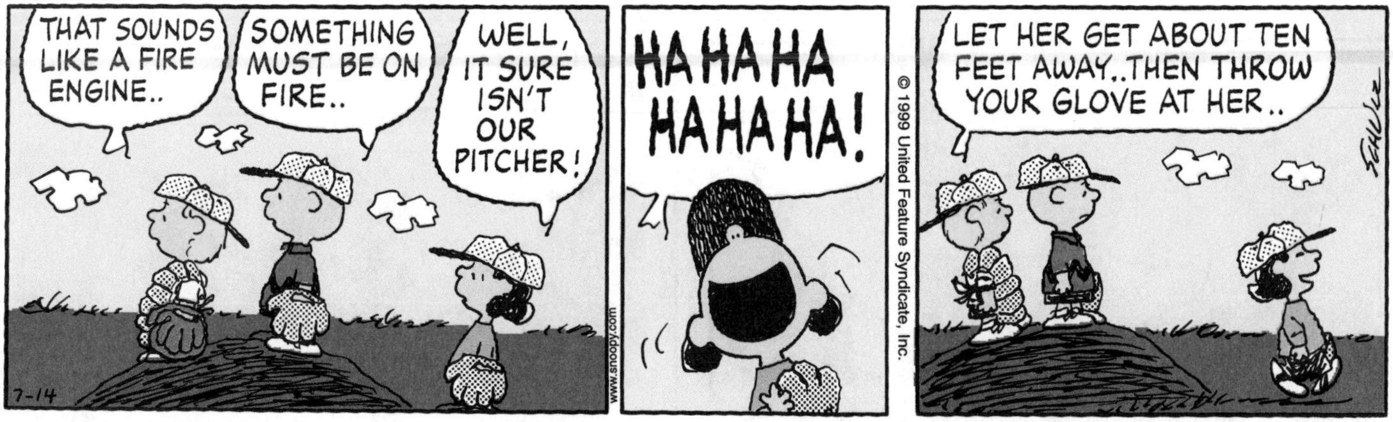
7-14
THAT SOUNDS LIKE A FIRE ENGINE..
SOMETHING MUST BE ON FIRE..
WELL, IT SURE ISN'T OUR PITCHER!
HA HA HA HA HA HA!
LET HER GET ABOUT TEN FEET AWAY..THEN THROW YOUR GLOVE AT HER..
www.snoopy.com
© 1999 United Feature Syndicate, Inc.

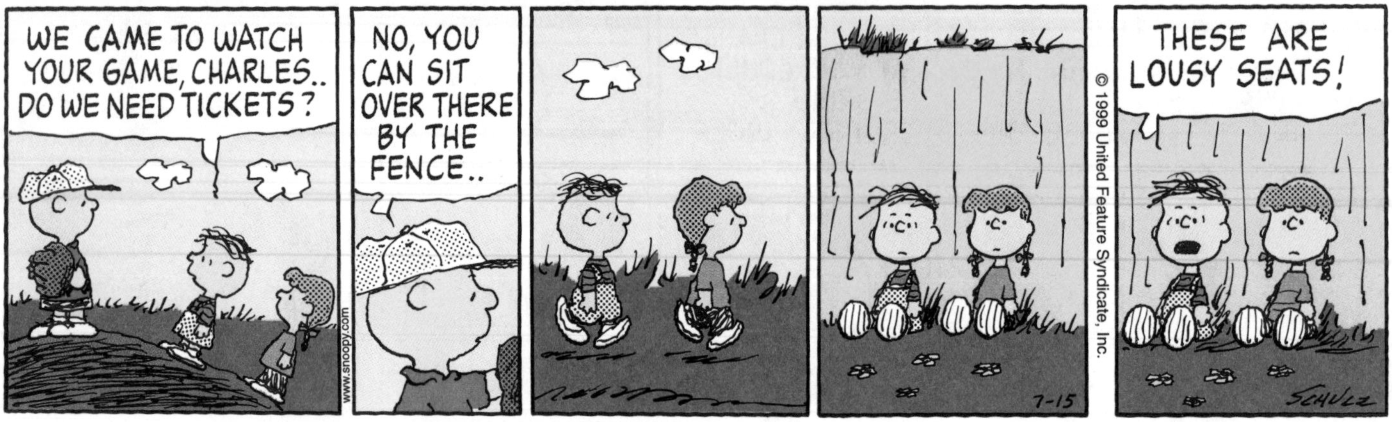
WE CAME TO WATCH YOUR GAME, CHARLES.. DO WE NEED TICKETS?
NO, YOU CAN SIT OVER THERE BY THE FENCE..
THESE ARE LOUSY SEATS!
www.snoopy.com
© 1999 United Feature Syndicate, Inc.
7-15
SCHULZ

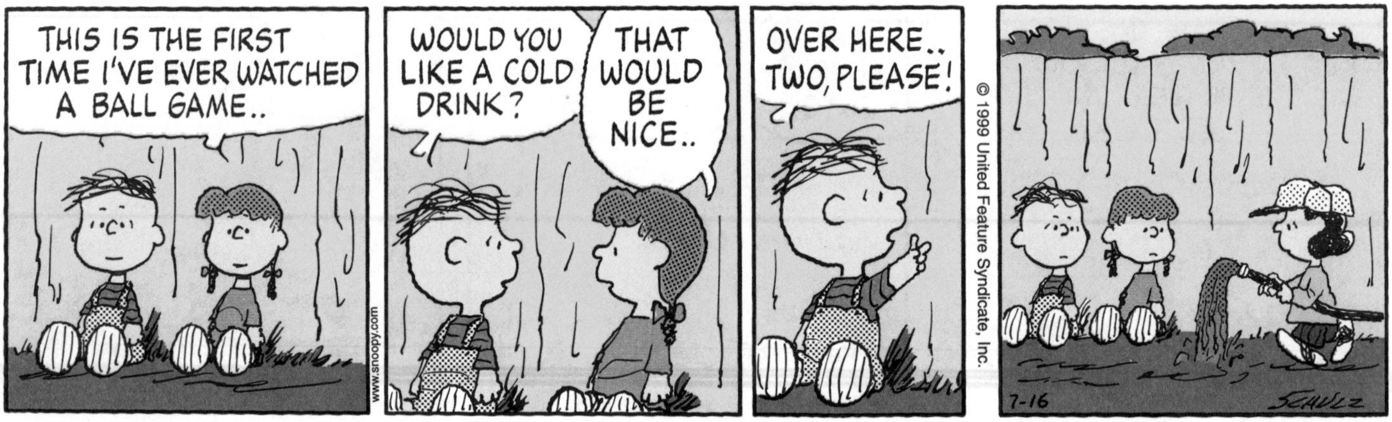
THIS IS THE FIRST TIME I'VE EVER WATCHED A BALL GAME..
WOULD YOU LIKE A COLD DRINK?
THAT WOULD BE NICE..
OVER HERE.. TWO, PLEASE!
www.snoopy.com
© 1999 United Feature Syndicate, Inc.
7-16
SCHULZ

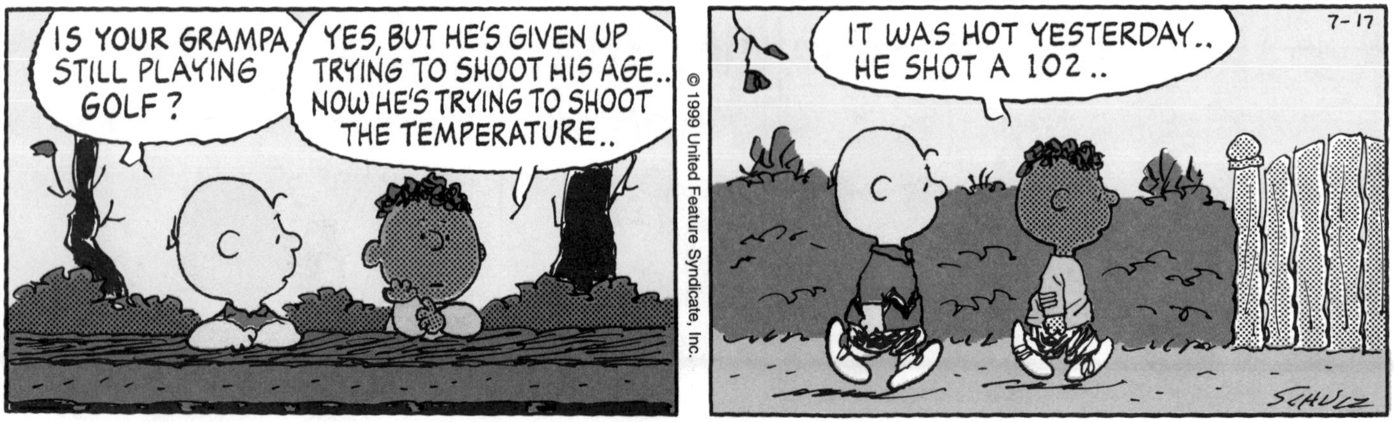
IS YOUR GRAMPA STILL PLAYING GOLF?
YES, BUT HE'S GIVEN UP TRYING TO SHOOT HIS AGE.. NOW HE'S TRYING TO SHOOT THE TEMPERATURE..
IT WAS HOT YESTERDAY.. HE SHOT A 102..
© 1999 United Feature Syndicate, Inc.
7-17
SCHULZ

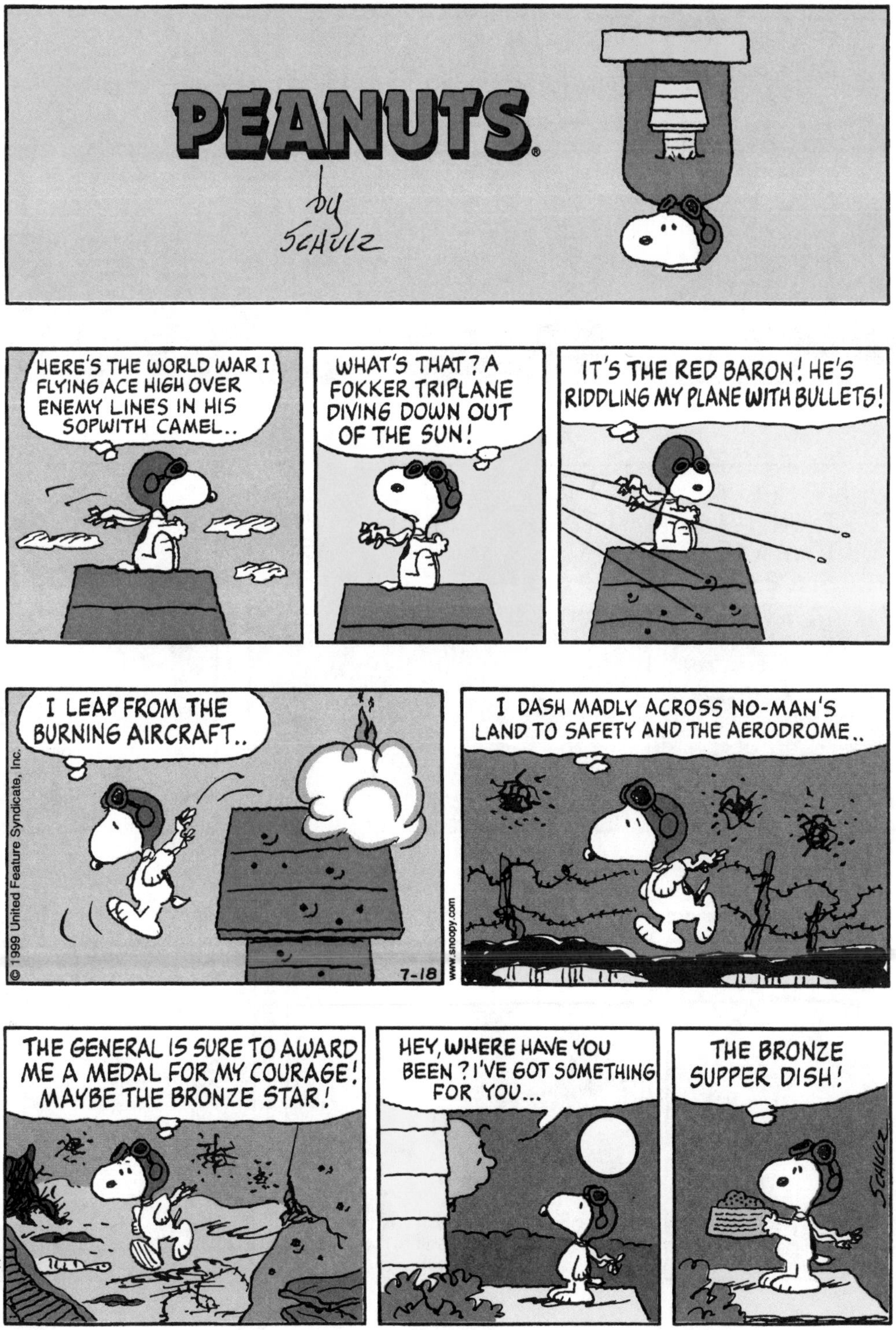
PEANUTS
by SCHULZ
HERE'S THE WORLD WAR I FLYING ACE HIGH OVER ENEMY LINES IN HIS SOPWITH CAMEL..
WHAT'S THAT? A FOKKER TRIPLANE DIVING DOWN OUT OF THE SUN!
IT'S THE RED BARON! HE'S RIDDLING MY PLANE WITH BULLETS!
I LEAP FROM THE BURNING AIRCRAFT..
© 1999 United Feature Syndicate, Inc.
7-18
www.snoopy.com
I DASH MADLY ACROSS NO-MAN'S LAND TO SAFETY AND THE AERODROME..
THE GENERAL IS SURE TO AWARD ME A MEDAL FOR MY COURAGE! MAYBE THE BRONZE STAR!
HEY, WHERE HAVE YOU BEEN? I'VE GOT SOMETHING FOR YOU...
THE BRONZE SUPPER DISH!
SCHULZ

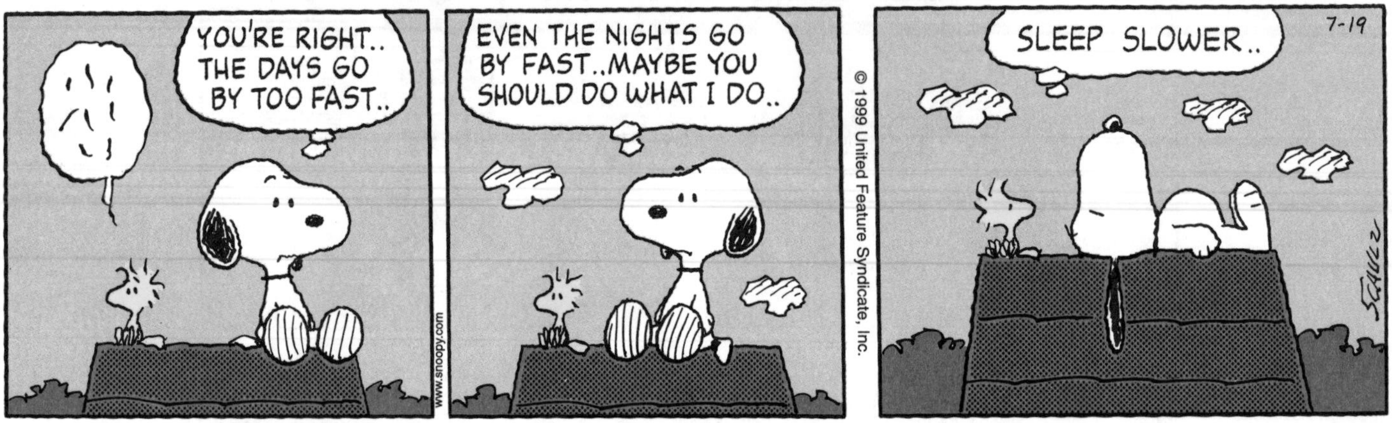
YOU'RE RIGHT.. THE DAYS GO BY TOO FAST..
EVEN THE NIGHTS GO BY FAST..MAYBE YOU SHOULD DO WHAT I DO..
SLEEP SLOWER..
7-19
www.snoopy.com
© 1999 United Feature Syndicate, Inc.
SCHULZ

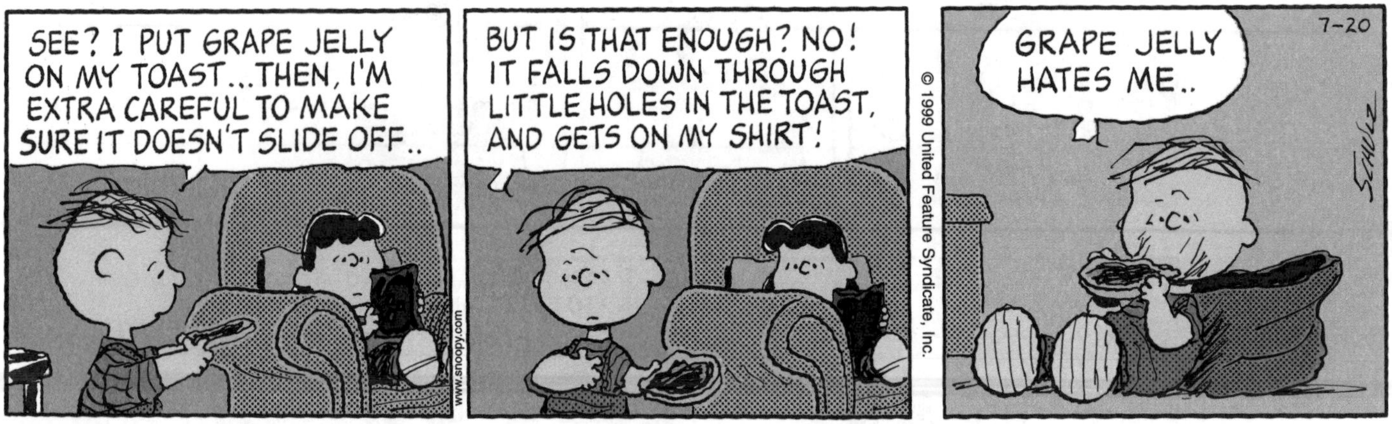
SEE? I PUT GRAPE JELLY ON MY TOAST...THEN, I'M EXTRA CAREFUL TO MAKE SURE IT DOESN'T SLIDE OFF..
BUT IS THAT ENOUGH? NO! IT FALLS DOWN THROUGH LITTLE HOLES IN THE TOAST, AND GETS ON MY SHIRT!
GRAPE JELLY HATES ME..
7-20
www.snoopy.com
© 1999 United Feature Syndicate, Inc.
SCHULZ

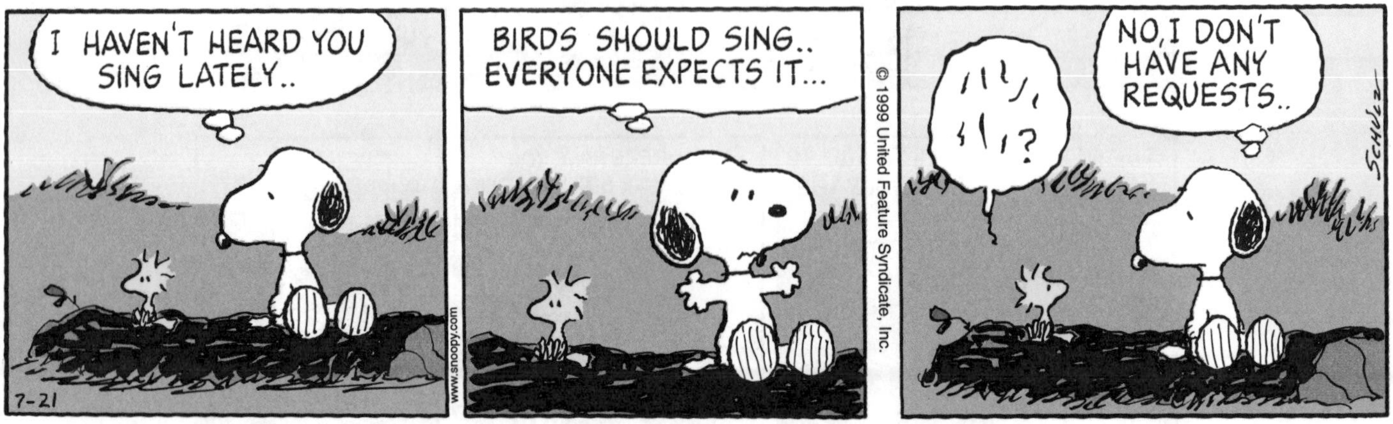
I HAVEN'T HEARD YOU SING LATELY..
BIRDS SHOULD SING.. EVERYONE EXPECTS IT...
NO, I DON'T HAVE ANY REQUESTS..
7-21
www.snoopy.com
© 1999 United Feature Syndicate, Inc.
SCHULZ

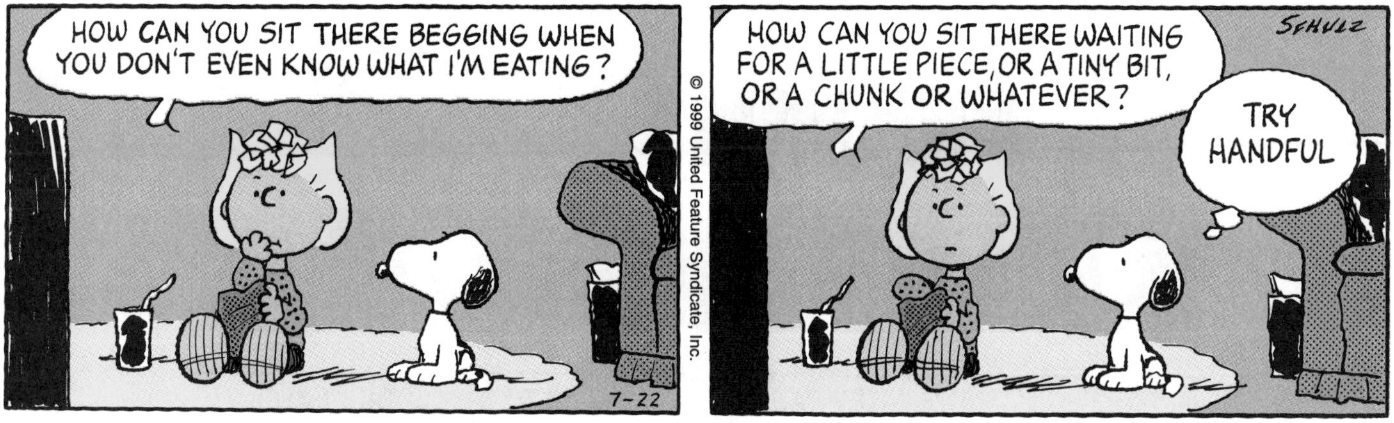
HOW CAN YOU SIT THERE BEGGING WHEN YOU DON'T EVEN KNOW WHAT I'M EATING?
HOW CAN YOU SIT THERE WAITING FOR A LITTLE PIECE, OR A TINY BIT, OR A CHUNK OR WHATEVER?
TRY HANDFUL
SCHULZ
7-22
© 1999 United Feature Syndicate, Inc.

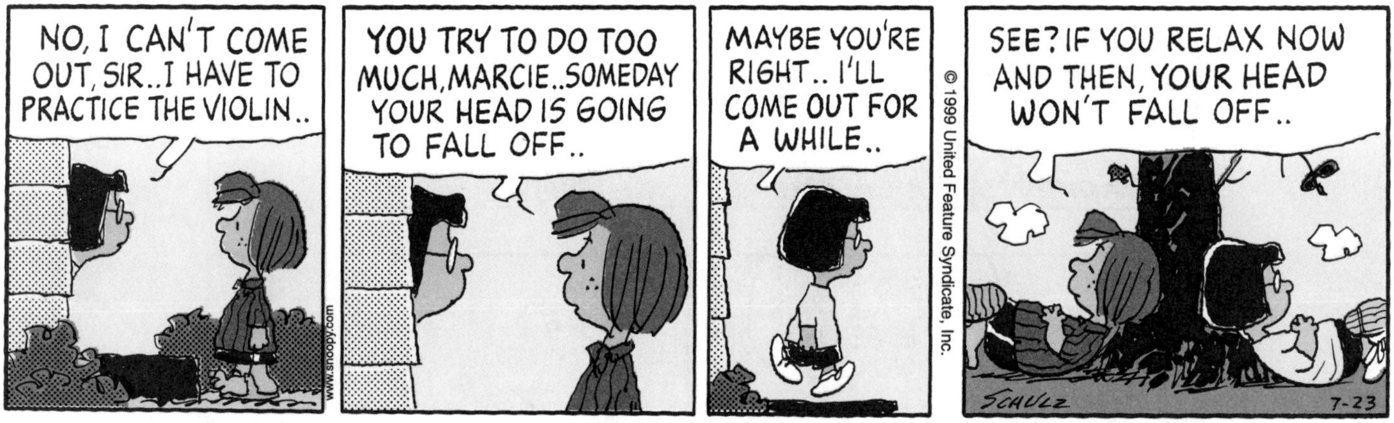
NO, I CAN'T COME OUT, SIR..I HAVE TO PRACTICE THE VIOLIN..
YOU TRY TO DO TOO MUCH, MARCIE..SOMEDAY YOUR HEAD IS GOING TO FALL OFF..
MAYBE YOU'RE RIGHT.. I'LL COME OUT FOR A WHILE..
SEE? IF YOU RELAX NOW AND THEN, YOUR HEAD WON'T FALL OFF..
SCHULZ
7-23
www.snoopy.com
© 1999 United Feature Syndicate, Inc.

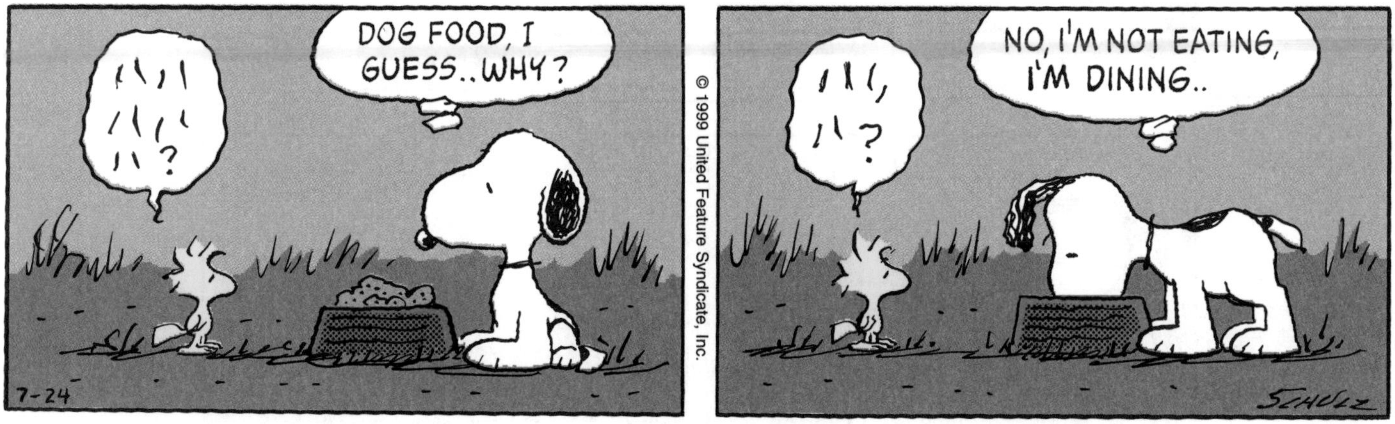
DOG FOOD, I GUESS..WHY?
NO, I'M NOT EATING, I'M DINING..
SCHULZ
7-24
© 1999 United Feature Syndicate, Inc.

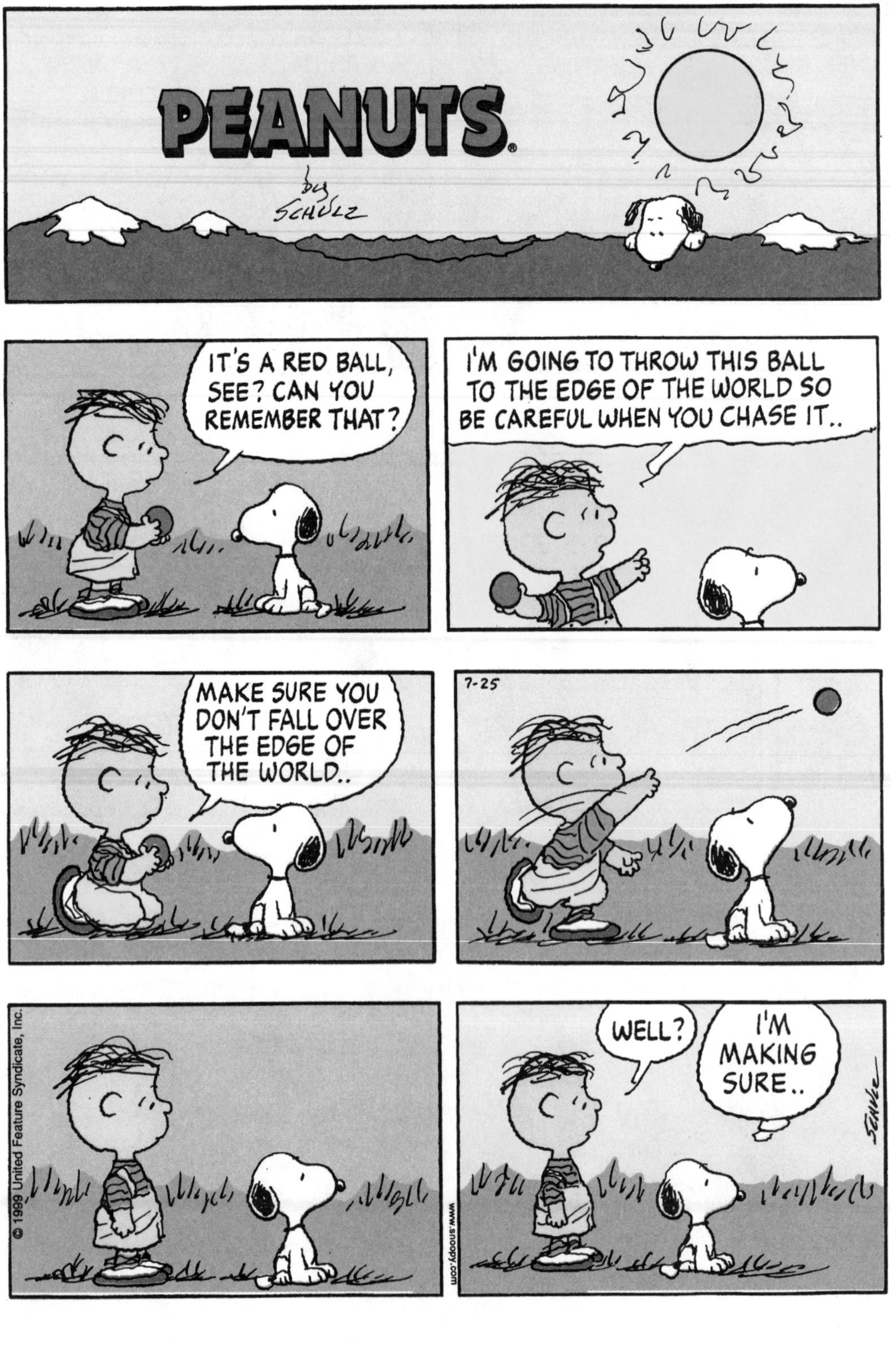
PEANUTS®
by SCHULZ
IT'S A RED BALL, SEE? CAN YOU REMEMBER THAT?
I'M GOING TO THROW THIS BALL TO THE EDGE OF THE WORLD SO BE CAREFUL WHEN YOU CHASE IT..
MAKE SURE YOU DON'T FALL OVER THE EDGE OF THE WORLD..
7-25
© 1999 United Feature Syndicate, Inc.
www.snoopy.com
WELL?
I'M MAKING SURE..
SCHULZ

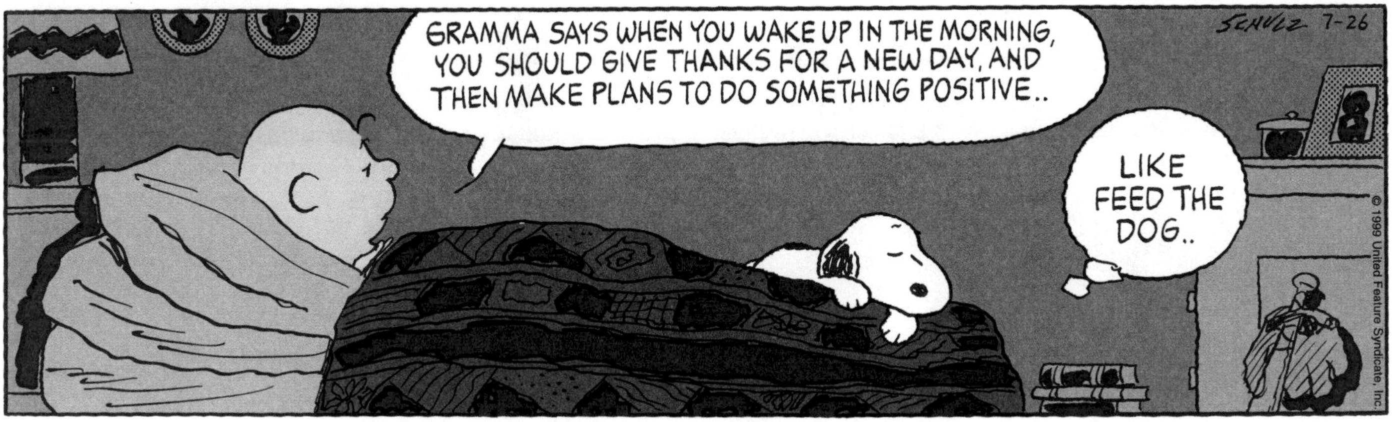
SCHULZ 7-26
GRAMMA SAYS WHEN YOU WAKE UP IN THE MORNING, YOU SHOULD GIVE THANKS FOR A NEW DAY, AND THEN MAKE PLANS TO DO SOMETHING POSITIVE..
LIKE FEED THE DOG..
© 1999 United Feature Syndicate, Inc.

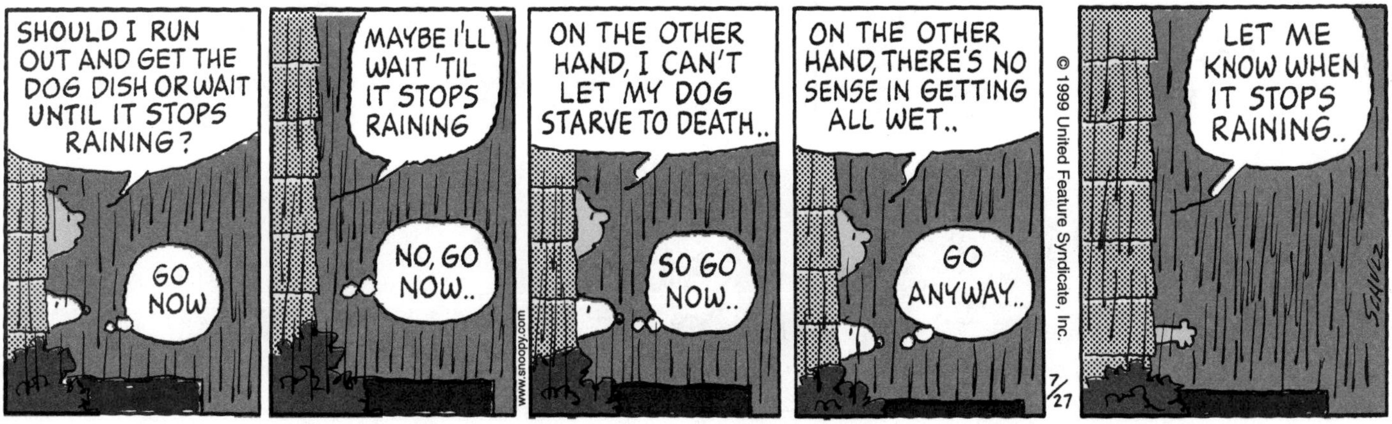
SHOULD I RUN OUT AND GET THE DOG DISH OR WAIT UNTIL IT STOPS RAINING?
GO NOW
MAYBE I'LL WAIT 'TIL IT STOPS RAINING
NO, GO NOW..
www.snoopy.com
ON THE OTHER HAND, I CAN'T LET MY DOG STARVE TO DEATH..
SO GO NOW..
ON THE OTHER HAND, THERE'S NO SENSE IN GETTING ALL WET..
GO ANYWAY..
7/27
© 1999 United Feature Syndicate, Inc.
LET ME KNOW WHEN IT STOPS RAINING..
SCHULZ

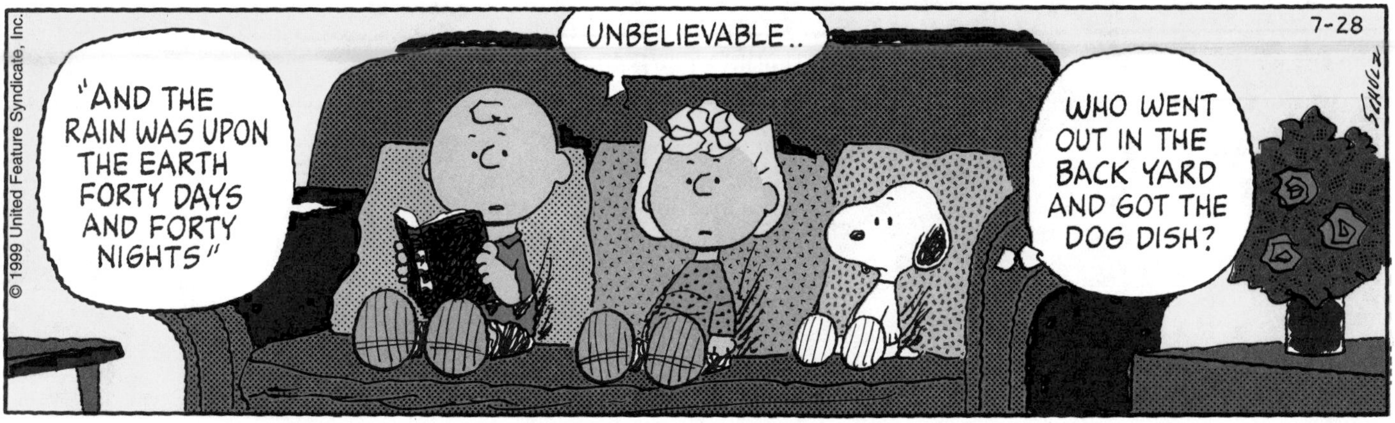
7-28
SCHULZ
"AND THE RAIN WAS UPON THE EARTH FORTY DAYS AND FORTY NIGHTS"
UNBELIEVABLE..
WHO WENT OUT IN THE BACK YARD AND GOT THE DOG DISH?
© 1999 United Feature Syndicate, Inc.

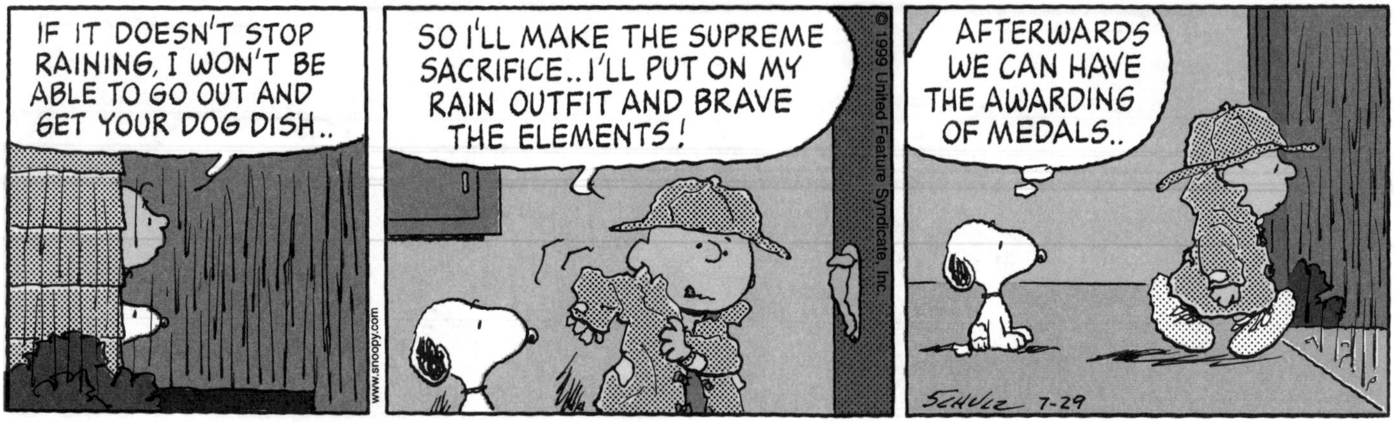
IF IT DOESN'T STOP RAINING, I WON'T BE ABLE TO GO OUT AND GET YOUR DOG DISH..
www.snoopy.com
SO I'LL MAKE THE SUPREME SACRIFICE..I'LL PUT ON MY RAIN OUTFIT AND BRAVE THE ELEMENTS!
© 1999 United Feature Syndicate, Inc.
AFTERWARDS WE CAN HAVE THE AWARDING OF MEDALS..
SCHULZ 7-29

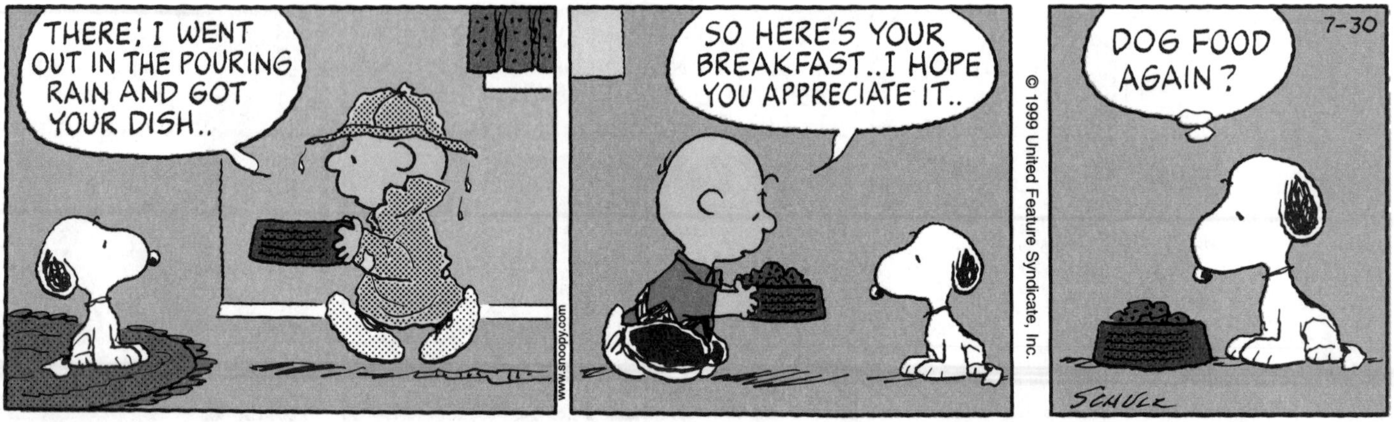
THERE! I WENT OUT IN THE POURING RAIN AND GOT YOUR DISH..
www.snoopy.com
SO HERE'S YOUR BREAKFAST..I HOPE YOU APPRECIATE IT..
© 1999 United Feature Syndicate, Inc.
7-30
DOG FOOD AGAIN?
SCHULZ

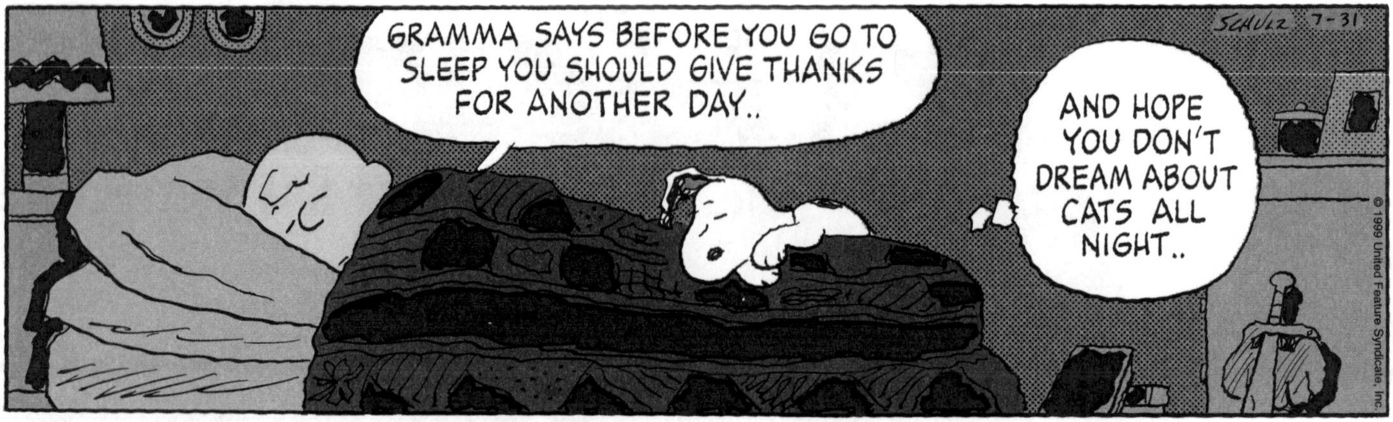
SCHULZ 7-31
GRAMMA SAYS BEFORE YOU GO TO SLEEP YOU SHOULD GIVE THANKS FOR ANOTHER DAY..
AND HOPE YOU DON'T DREAM ABOUT CATS ALL NIGHT..
© 1999 United Feature Syndicate, Inc.

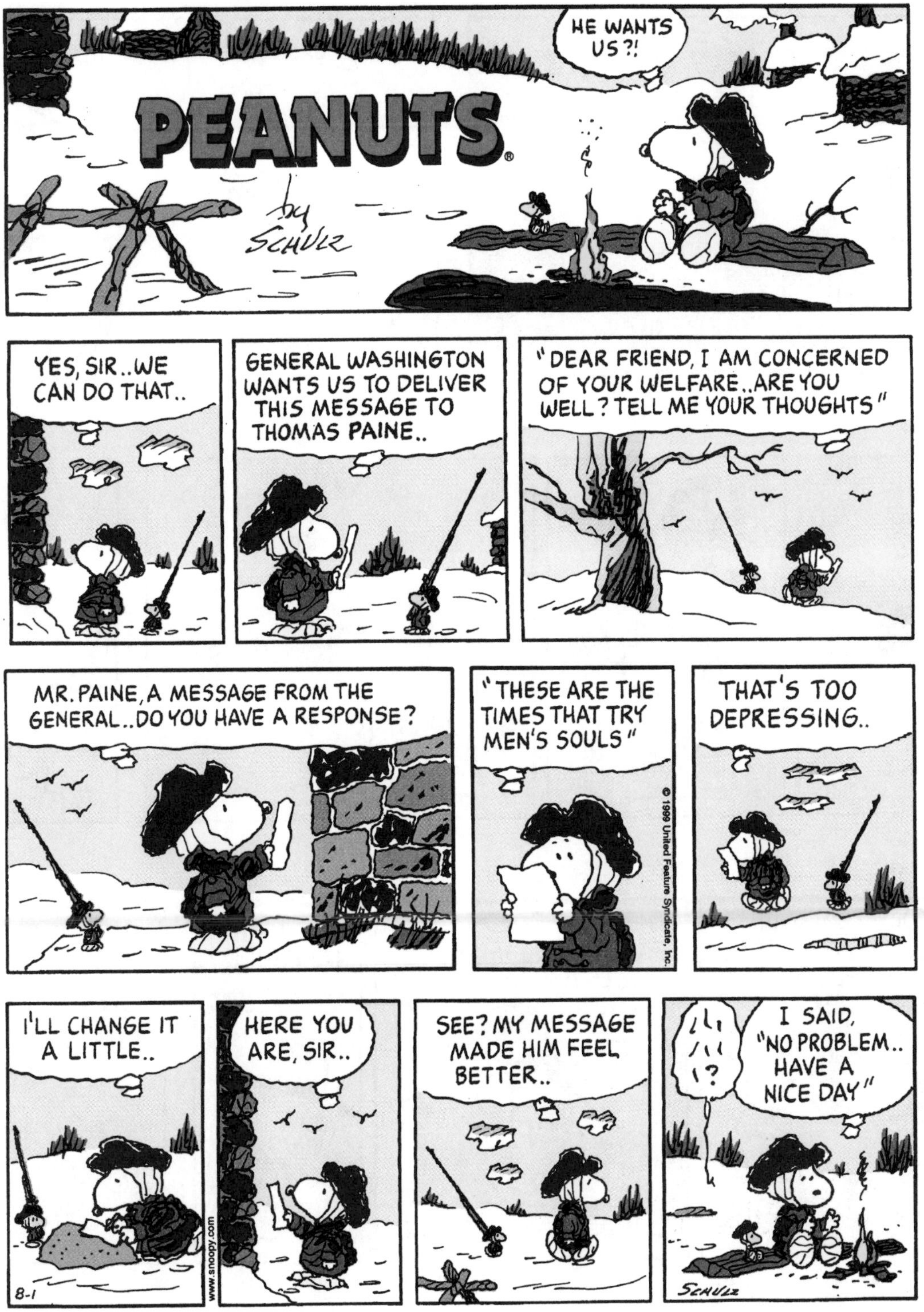
PEANUTS
by SCHULZ
HE WANTS US?!
YES, SIR..WE CAN DO THAT..
GENERAL WASHINGTON WANTS US TO DELIVER THIS MESSAGE TO THOMAS PAINE..
"DEAR FRIEND, I AM CONCERNED OF YOUR WELFARE..ARE YOU WELL? TELL ME YOUR THOUGHTS"
MR. PAINE, A MESSAGE FROM THE GENERAL..DO YOU HAVE A RESPONSE?
"THESE ARE THE TIMES THAT TRY MEN'S SOULS"
© 1999 United Feature Syndicate, Inc.
THAT'S TOO DEPRESSING..
I'LL CHANGE IT A LITTLE..
8-1
www.snoopy.com
HERE YOU ARE, SIR..
SEE? MY MESSAGE MADE HIM FEEL BETTER..
I SAID, "NO PROBLEM.. HAVE A NICE DAY"
SCHULZ

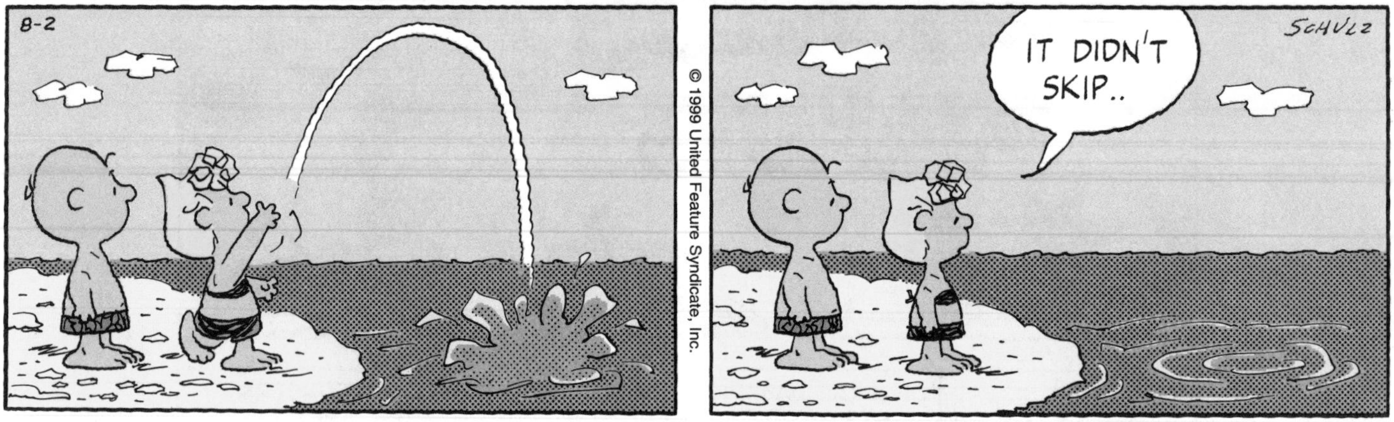
8-2
© 1999 United Feature Syndicate, Inc.
SCHULZ
IT DIDN'T SKIP..

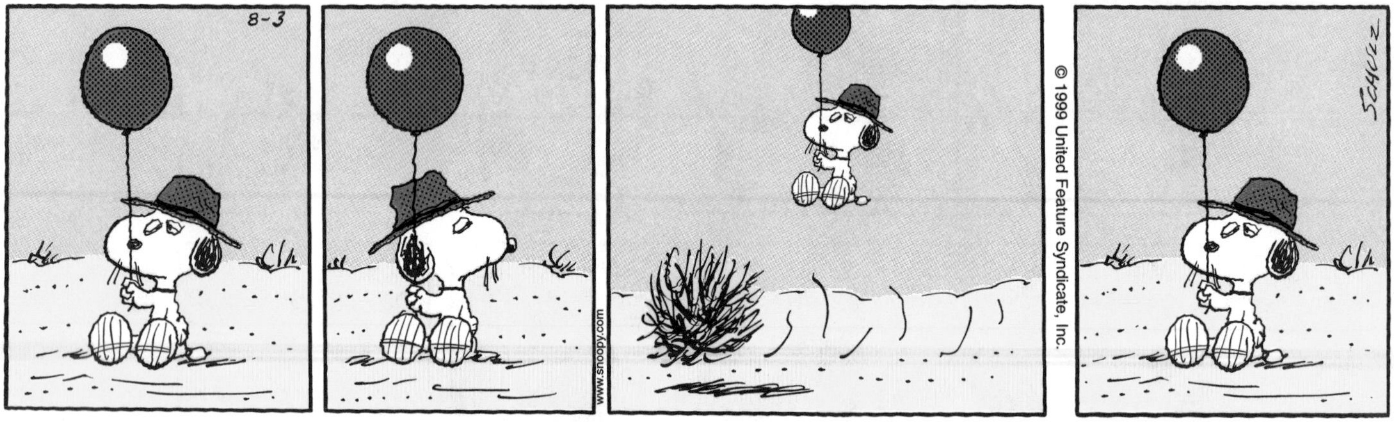
8-3
www.snoopy.com
© 1999 United Feature Syndicate, Inc.
SCHULZ

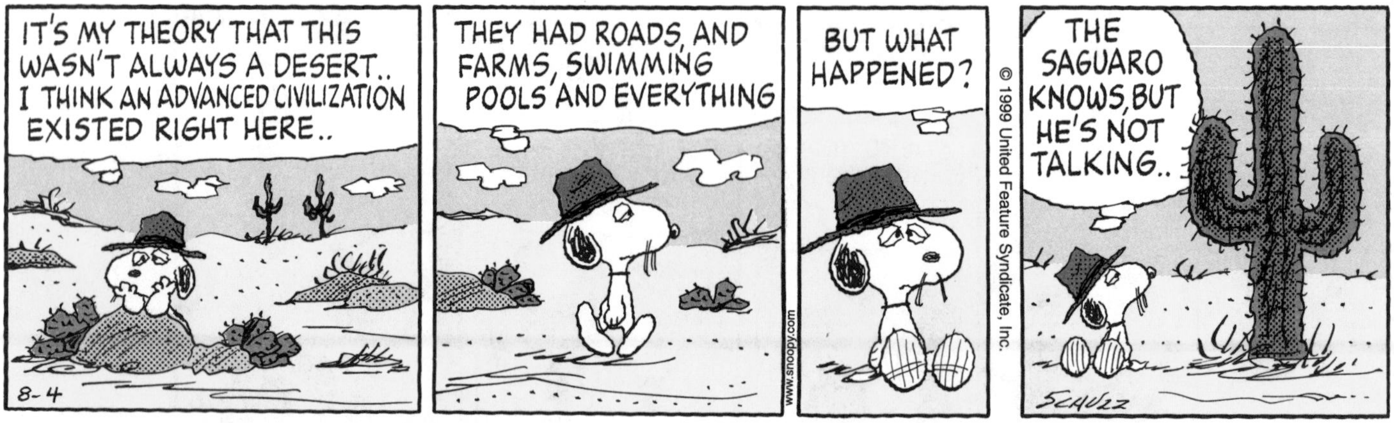
IT'S MY THEORY THAT THIS WASN'T ALWAYS A DESERT.. I THINK AN ADVANCED CIVILIZATION EXISTED RIGHT HERE..
8-4
THEY HAD ROADS, AND FARMS, SWIMMING POOLS AND EVERYTHING
www.snoopy.com
BUT WHAT HAPPENED?
© 1999 United Feature Syndicate, Inc.
THE SAGUARO KNOWS, BUT HE'S NOT TALKING..
SCHULZ

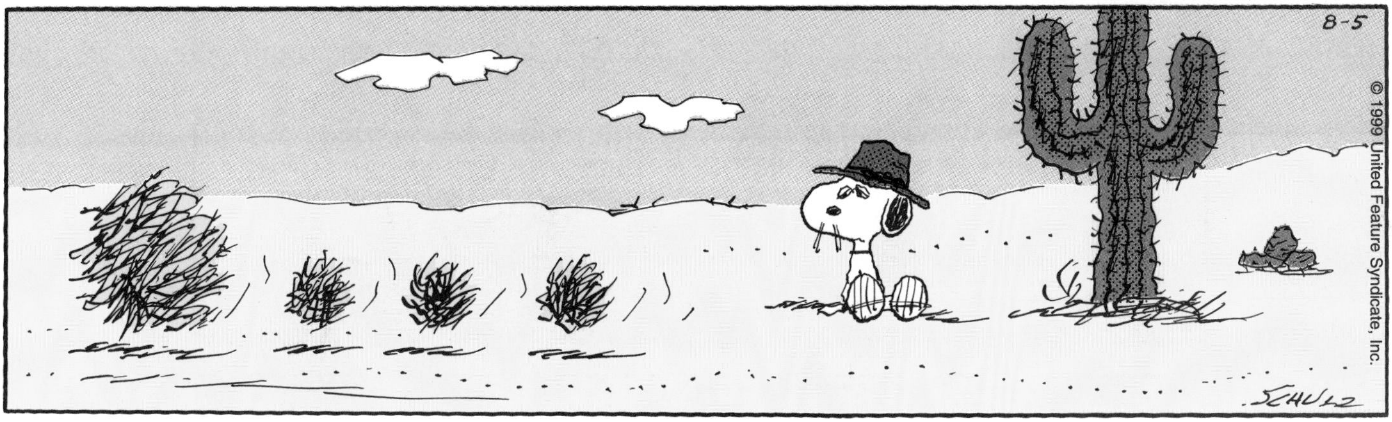
8-5
© 1999 United Feature Syndicate, Inc.
SCHULZ

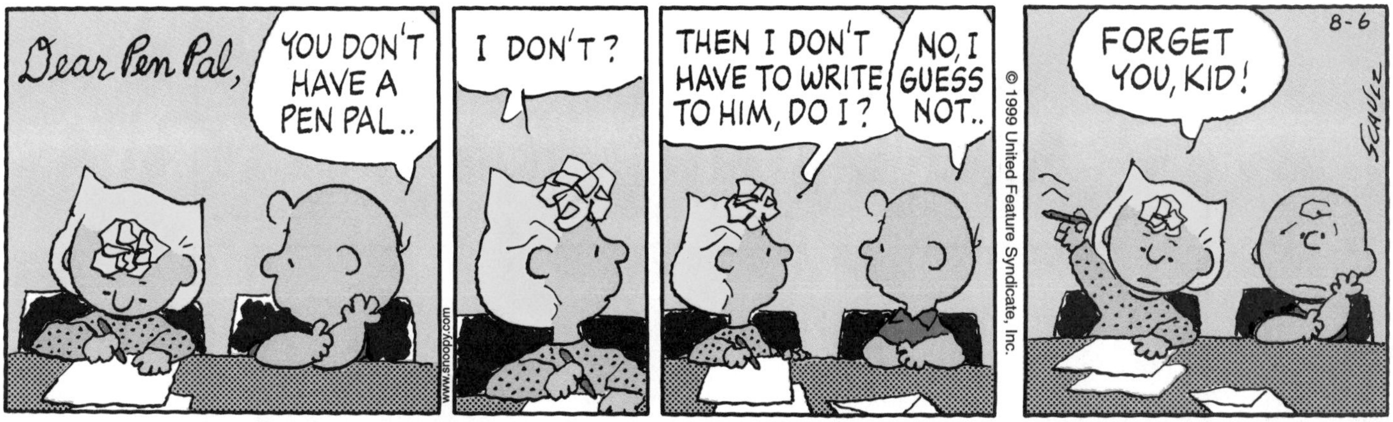
Dear Pen Pal,
YOU DON'T HAVE A PEN PAL..
I DON'T?
THEN I DON'T HAVE TO WRITE TO HIM, DO I?
NO, I GUESS NOT..
FORGET YOU, KID!
8-6
SCHULZ
www.snoopy.com
© 1999 United Feature Syndicate, Inc.

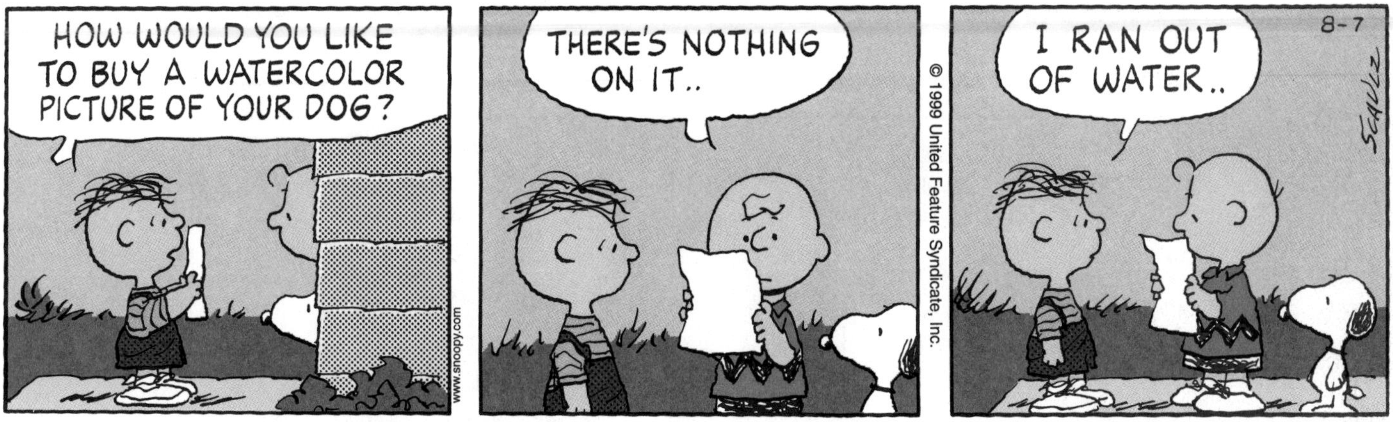
HOW WOULD YOU LIKE TO BUY A WATERCOLOR PICTURE OF YOUR DOG?
THERE'S NOTHING ON IT..
I RAN OUT OF WATER..
8-7
SCHULZ
www.snoopy.com
© 1999 United Feature Syndicate, Inc.

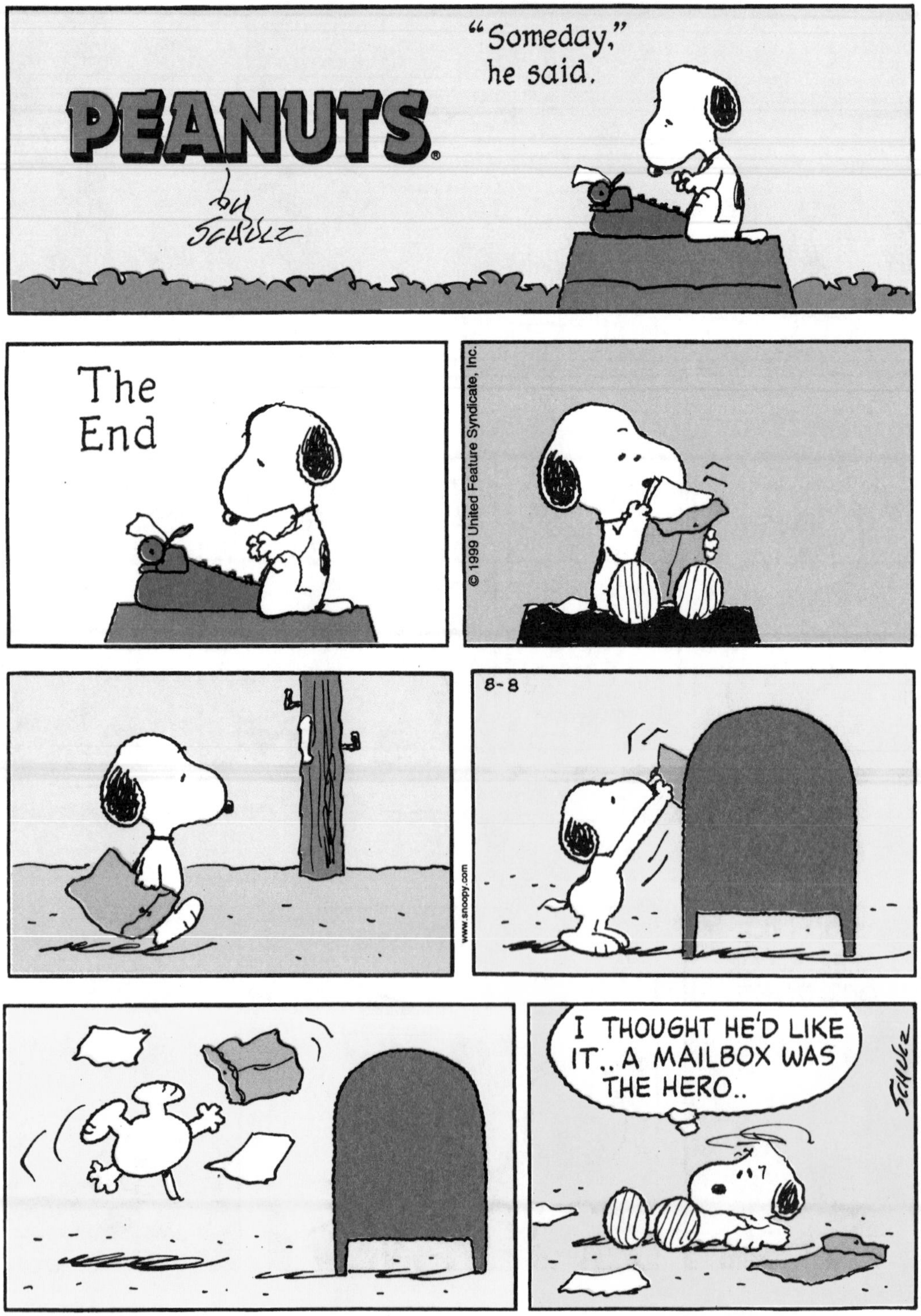
"Someday," he said.
PEANUTS
by SCHULZ
The End
© 1999 United Feature Syndicate, Inc.
8-8
www.snoopy.com
I THOUGHT HE'D LIKE IT.. A MAILBOX WAS THE HERO..
SCHULZ

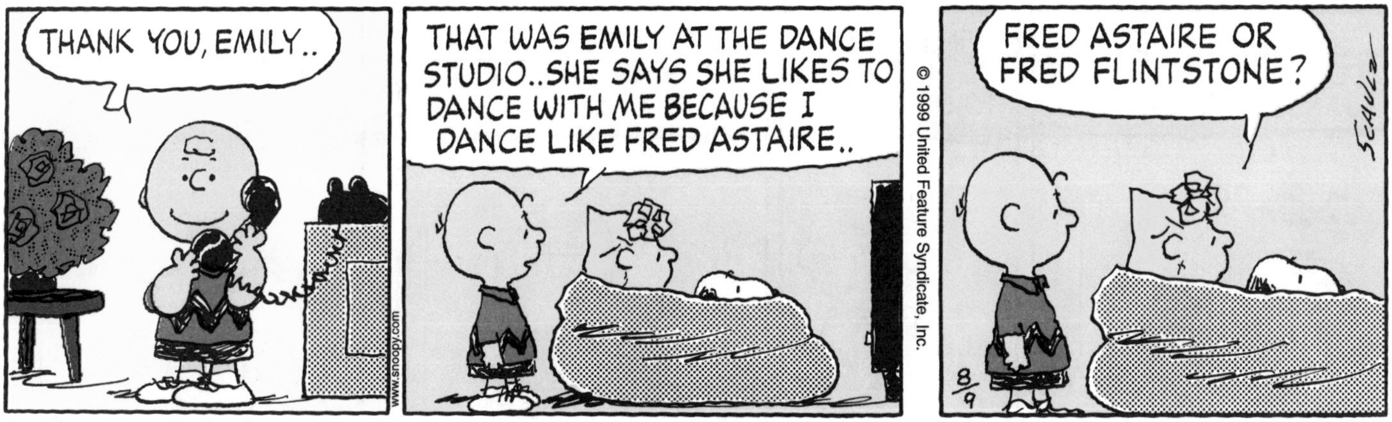
THANK YOU, EMILY..
www.snoopy.com
THAT WAS EMILY AT THE DANCE STUDIO..SHE SAYS SHE LIKES TO DANCE WITH ME BECAUSE I DANCE LIKE FRED ASTAIRE..
© 1999 United Feature Syndicate, Inc.
FRED ASTAIRE OR FRED FLINTSTONE?
SCHULZ
8/9

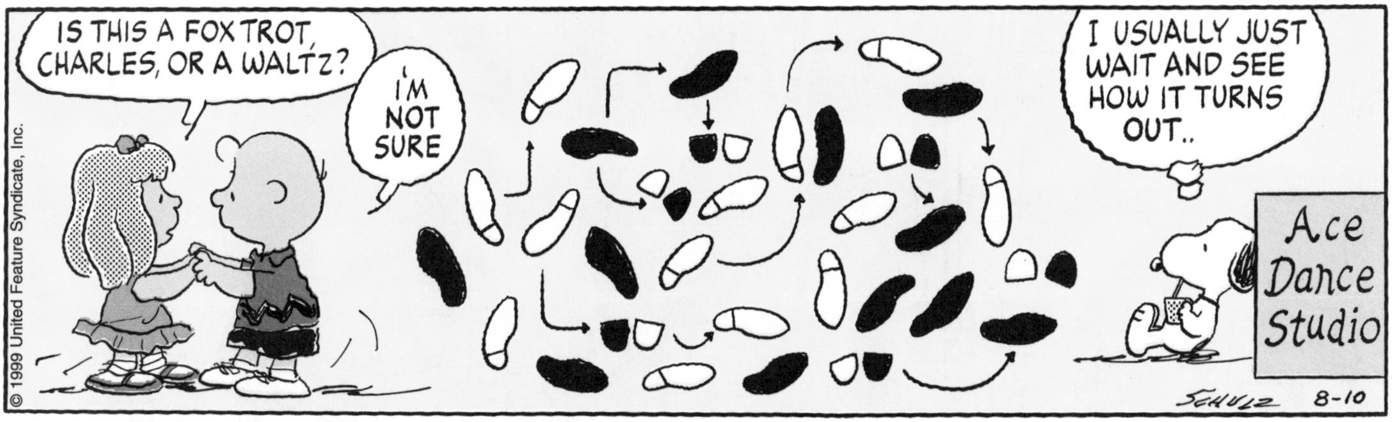
IS THIS A FOXTROT, CHARLES, OR A WALTZ?
I'M NOT SURE
I USUALLY JUST WAIT AND SEE HOW IT TURNS OUT..
Ace Dance Studio
© 1999 United Feature Syndicate, Inc.
SCHULZ 8-10

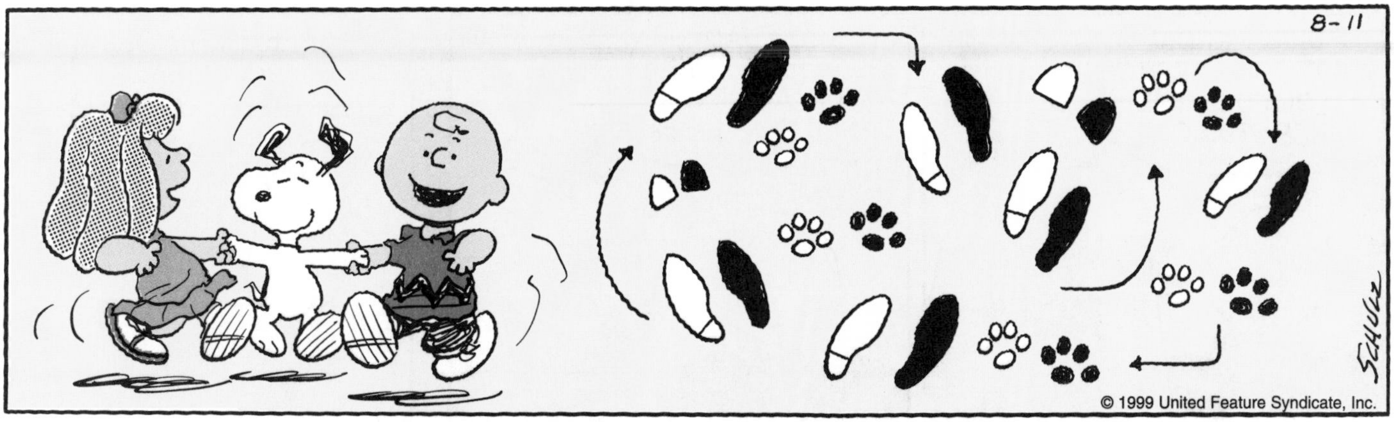
8-11
SCHULZ
© 1999 United Feature Syndicate, Inc.

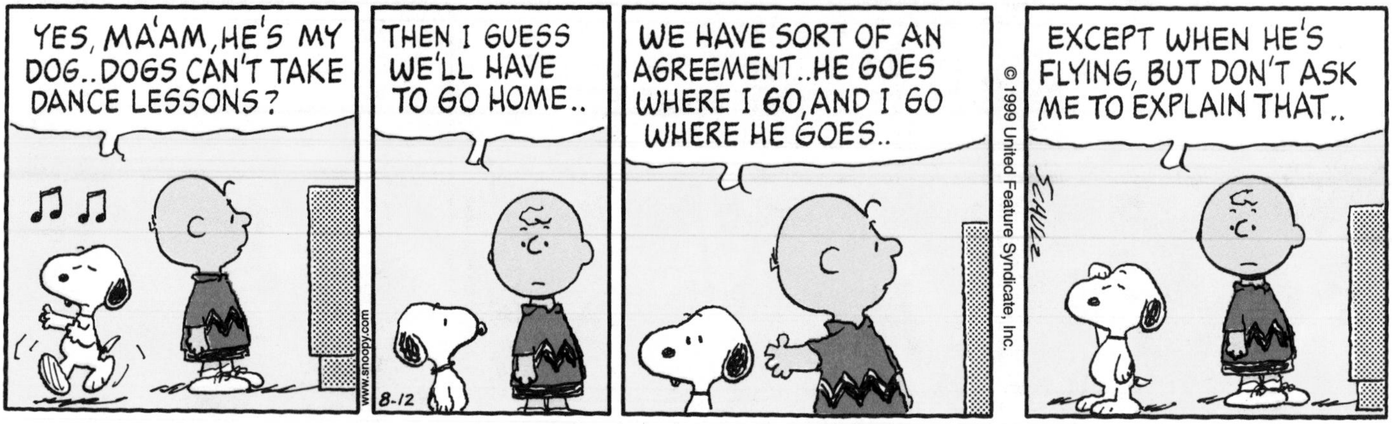
YES, MA'AM, HE'S MY DOG.. DOGS CAN'T TAKE DANCE LESSONS?
www.snoopy.com
8-12
THEN I GUESS WE'LL HAVE TO GO HOME..
WE HAVE SORT OF AN AGREEMENT..HE GOES WHERE I GO, AND I GO WHERE HE GOES..
© 1999 United Feature Syndicate, Inc.
SCHULZ
EXCEPT WHEN HE'S FLYING, BUT DON'T ASK ME TO EXPLAIN THAT..

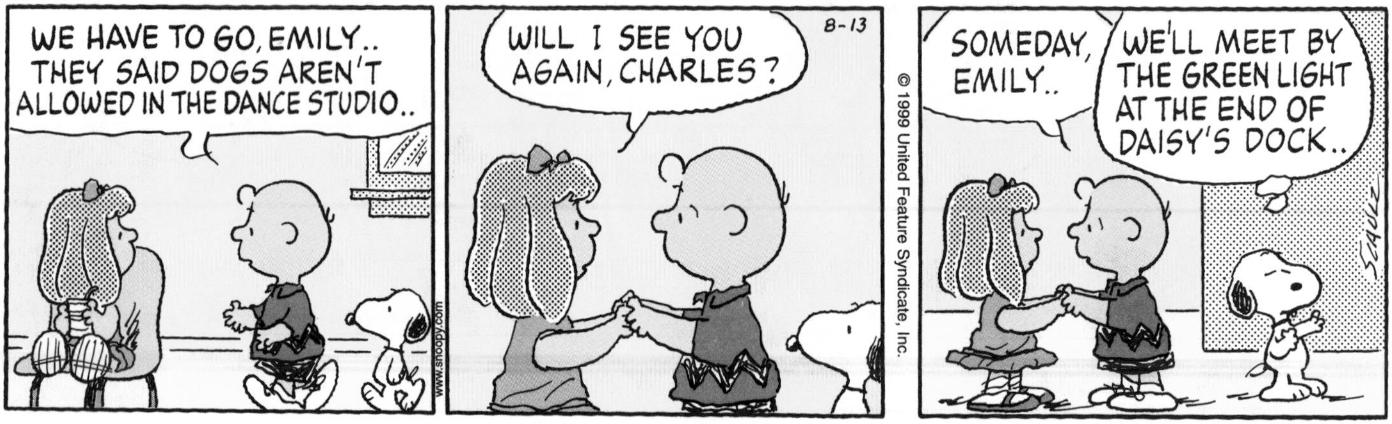
WE HAVE TO GO, EMILY.. THEY SAID DOGS AREN'T ALLOWED IN THE DANCE STUDIO..
www.snoopy.com
8-13
WILL I SEE YOU AGAIN, CHARLES?
© 1999 United Feature Syndicate, Inc.
SOMEDAY, EMILY..
WE'LL MEET BY THE GREEN LIGHT AT THE END OF DAISY'S DOCK..
SCHULZ

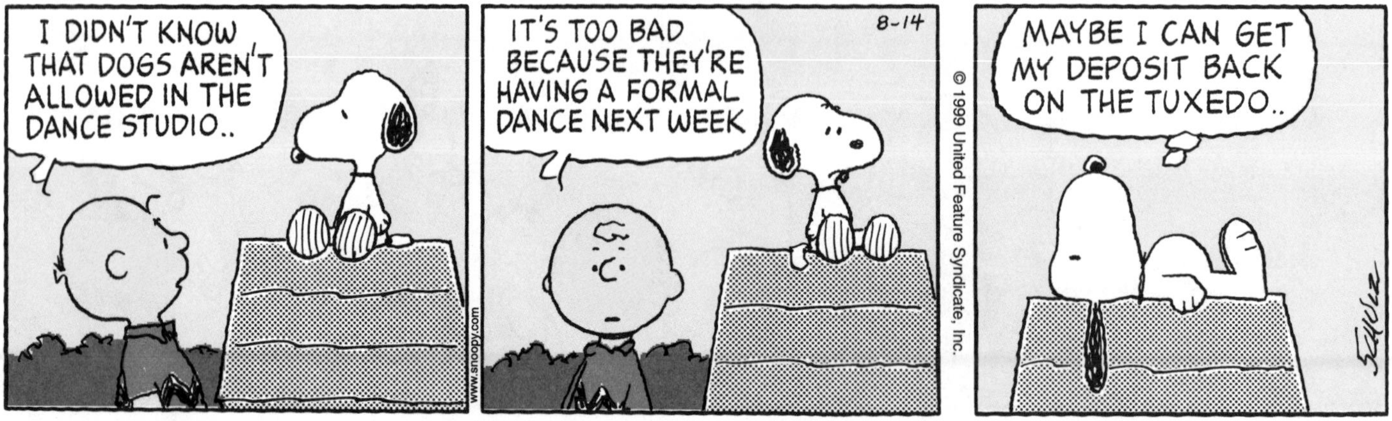
I DIDN'T KNOW THAT DOGS AREN'T ALLOWED IN THE DANCE STUDIO..
www.snoopy.com
8-14
IT'S TOO BAD BECAUSE THEY'RE HAVING A FORMAL DANCE NEXT WEEK
© 1999 United Feature Syndicate, Inc.
MAYBE I CAN GET MY DEPOSIT BACK ON THE TUXEDO..
SCHULZ

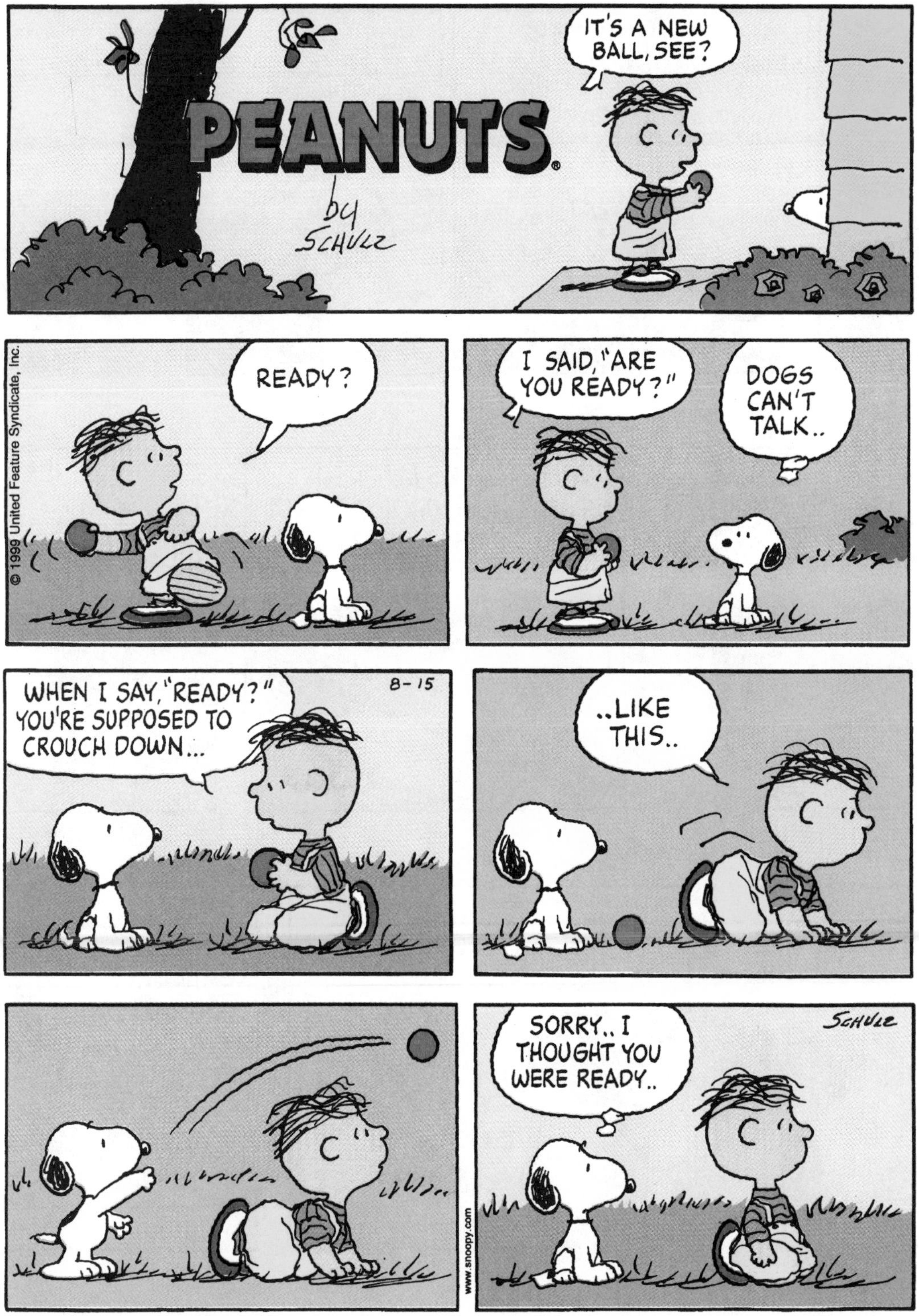
IT'S A NEW BALL, SEE?
PEANUTS
by SCHULZ
© 1999 United Feature Syndicate, Inc.
READY?
I SAID, "ARE YOU READY?"
DOGS CAN'T TALK..
8-15
WHEN I SAY, "READY?" YOU'RE SUPPOSED TO CROUCH DOWN...
..LIKE THIS..
www.snoopy.com
SCHULZ
SORRY.. I THOUGHT YOU WERE READY..

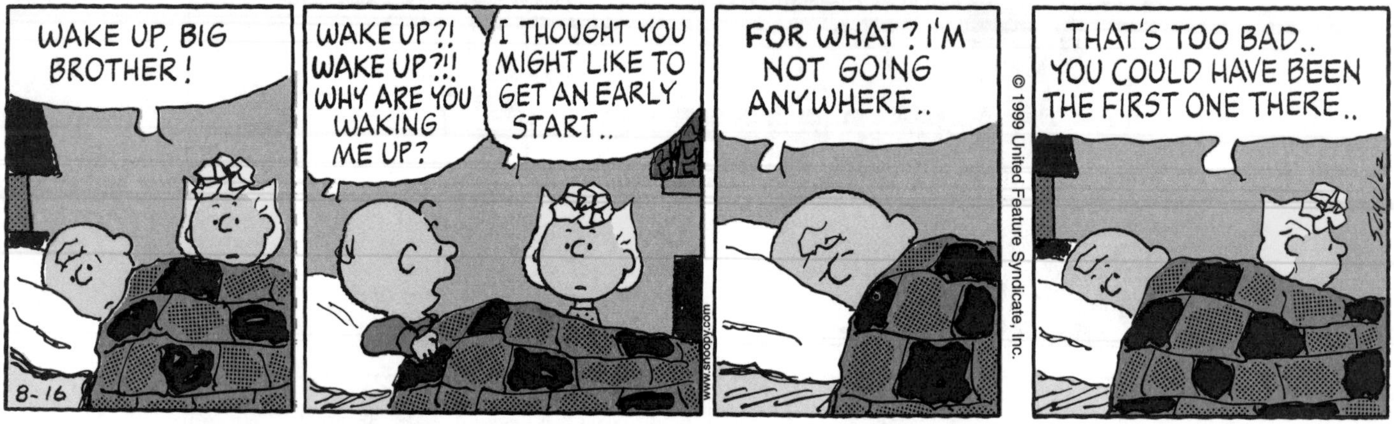
WAKE UP, BIG BROTHER!
WAKE UP?! WAKE UP?!! WHY ARE YOU WAKING ME UP?
I THOUGHT YOU MIGHT LIKE TO GET AN EARLY START..
FOR WHAT? I'M NOT GOING ANYWHERE..
THAT'S TOO BAD.. YOU COULD HAVE BEEN THE FIRST ONE THERE..
8-16
www.snoopy.com
© 1999 United Feature Syndicate, Inc.
SCHULZ

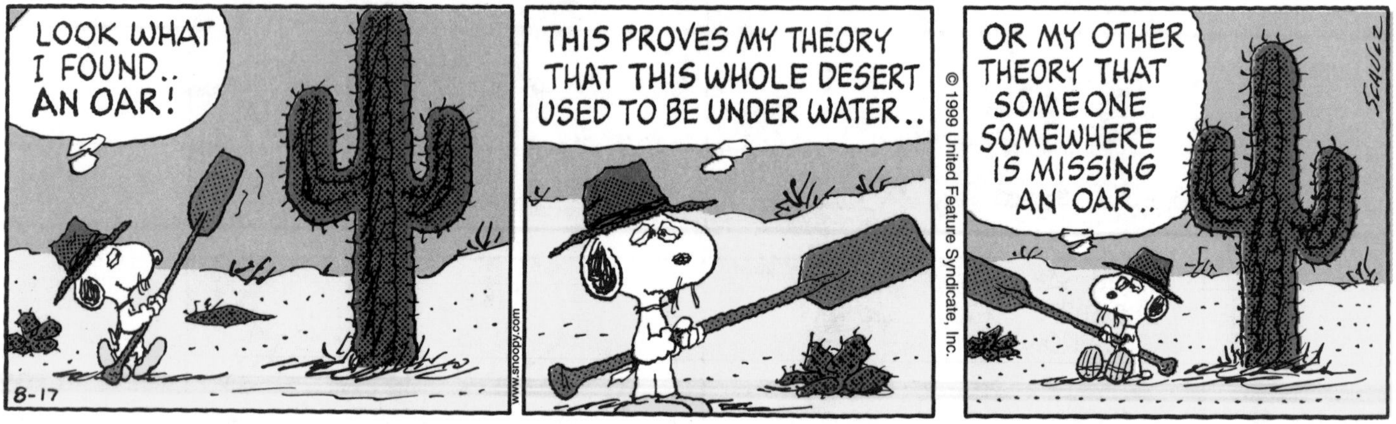
LOOK WHAT I FOUND.. AN OAR!
THIS PROVES MY THEORY THAT THIS WHOLE DESERT USED TO BE UNDER WATER..
OR MY OTHER THEORY THAT SOMEONE SOMEWHERE IS MISSING AN OAR..
8-17
www.snoopy.com
© 1999 United Feature Syndicate, Inc.
SCHULZ

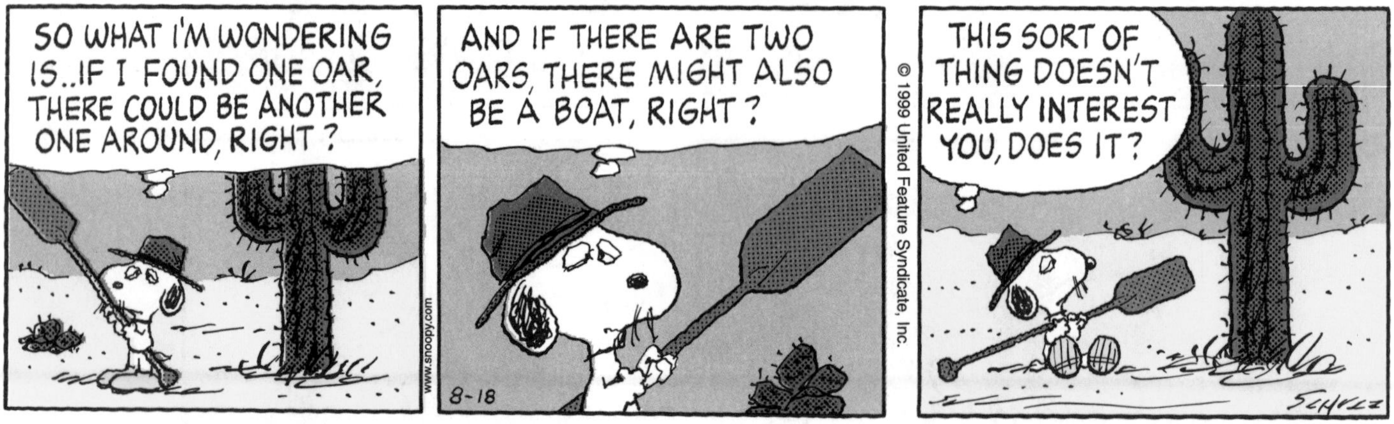
SO WHAT I'M WONDERING IS..IF I FOUND ONE OAR, THERE COULD BE ANOTHER ONE AROUND, RIGHT?
AND IF THERE ARE TWO OARS, THERE MIGHT ALSO BE A BOAT, RIGHT?
THIS SORT OF THING DOESN'T REALLY INTEREST YOU, DOES IT?
8-18
www.snoopy.com
© 1999 United Feature Syndicate, Inc.
SCHULZ

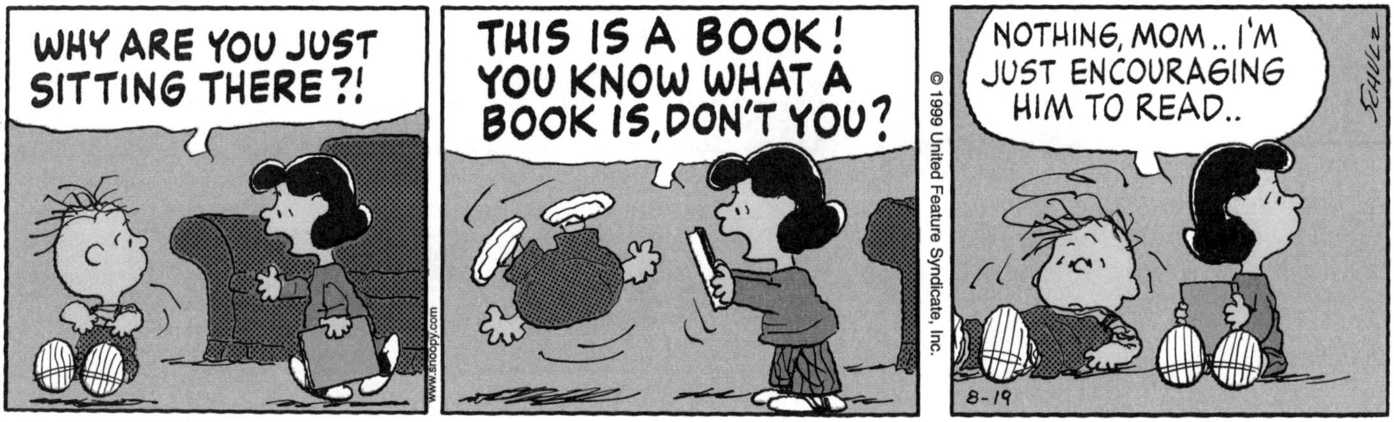
WHY ARE YOU JUST SITTING THERE ?!
THIS IS A BOOK! YOU KNOW WHAT A BOOK IS, DON'T YOU?
NOTHING, MOM.. I'M JUST ENCOURAGING HIM TO READ..
www.snoopy.com
© 1999 United Feature Syndicate, Inc.
8-19

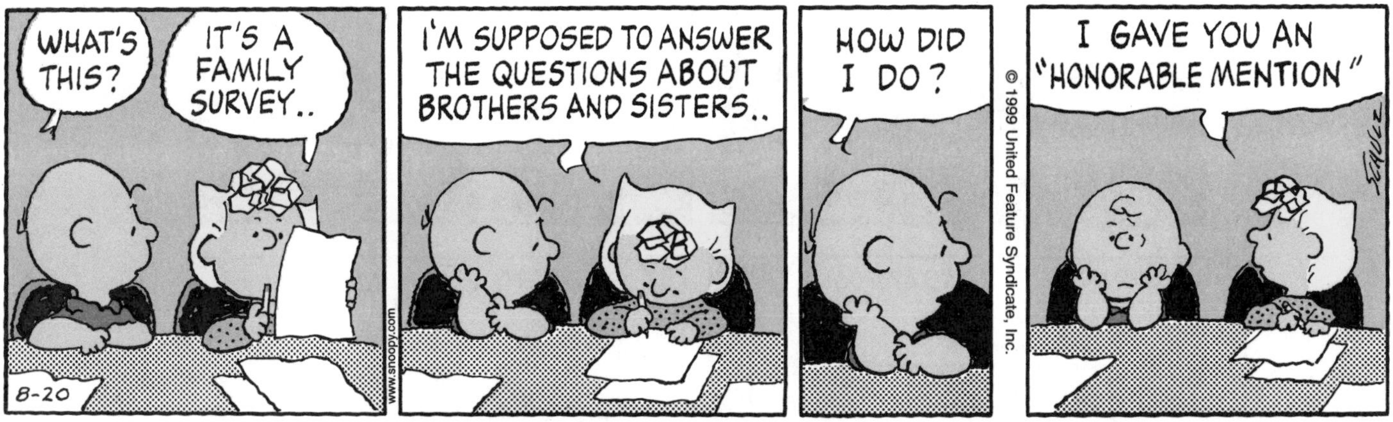
WHAT'S THIS?
IT'S A FAMILY SURVEY..
I'M SUPPOSED TO ANSWER THE QUESTIONS ABOUT BROTHERS AND SISTERS..
HOW DID I DO?
I GAVE YOU AN "HONORABLE MENTION"
8-20
www.snoopy.com
© 1999 United Feature Syndicate, Inc.

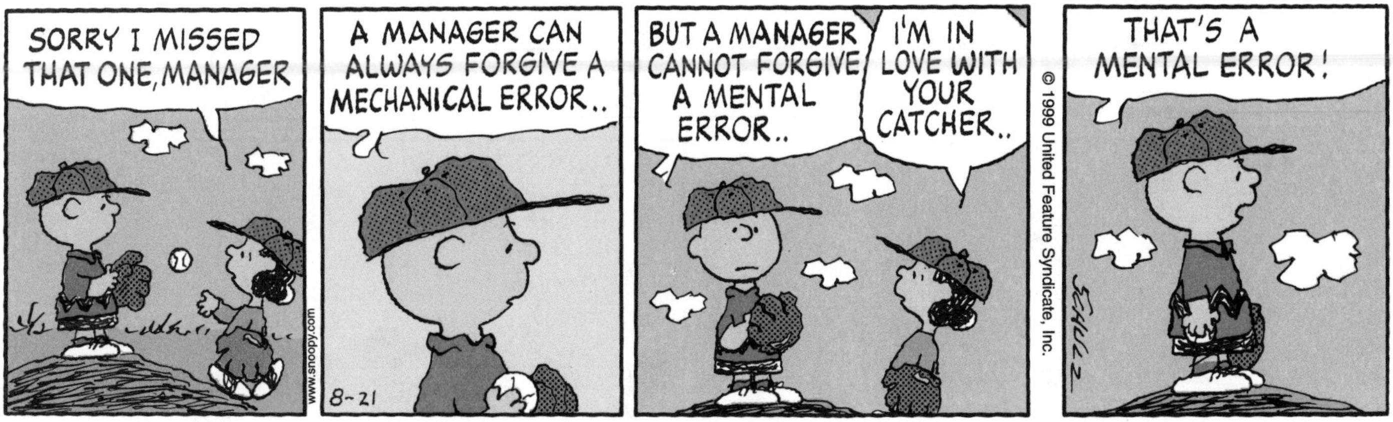
SORRY I MISSED THAT ONE, MANAGER
A MANAGER CAN ALWAYS FORGIVE A MECHANICAL ERROR..
BUT A MANAGER CANNOT FORGIVE A MENTAL ERROR..
I'M IN LOVE WITH YOUR CATCHER..
THAT'S A MENTAL ERROR!
www.snoopy.com
8-21
© 1999 United Feature Syndicate, Inc.

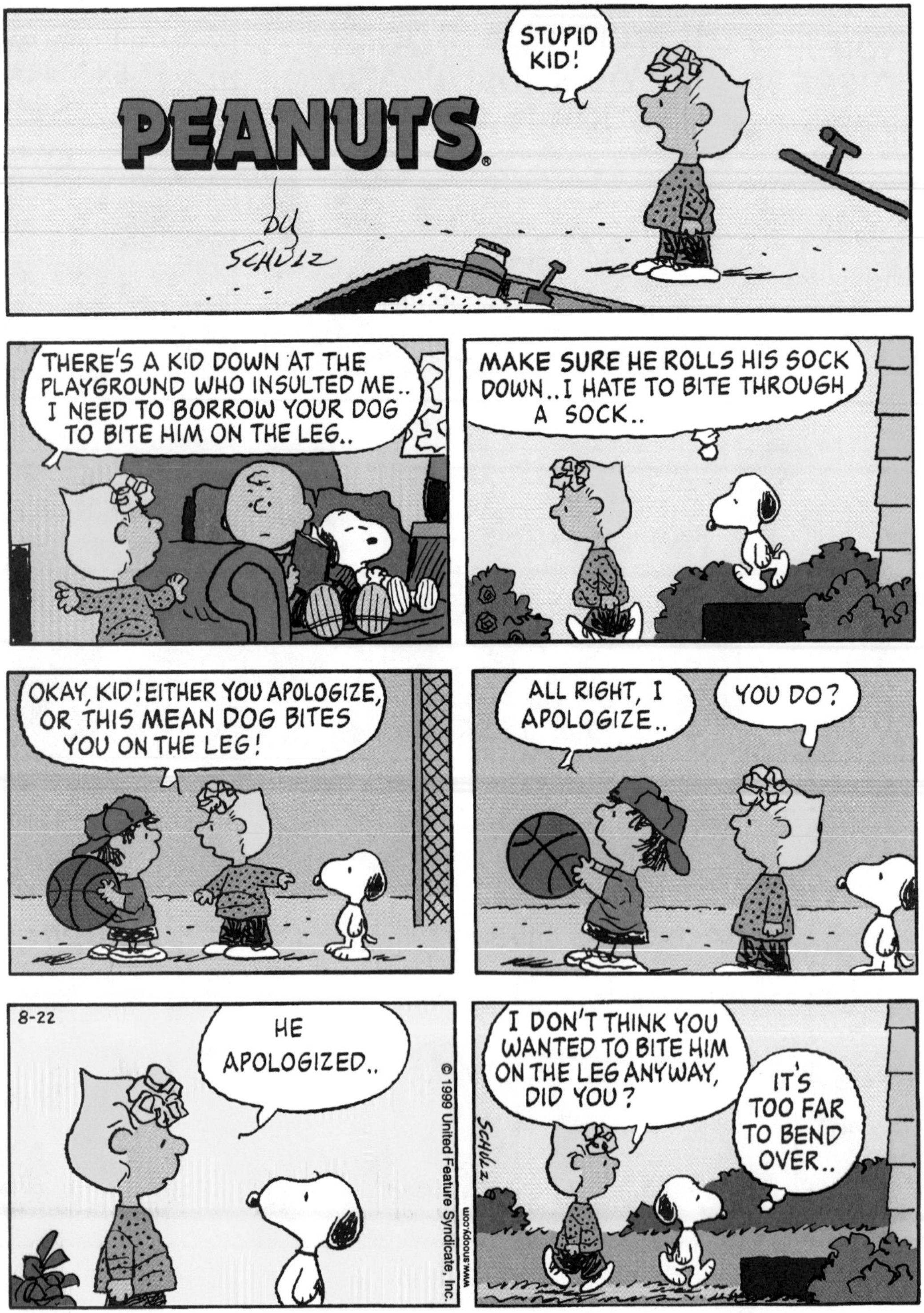
PEANUTS
by SCHULZ
STUPID KID!
THERE'S A KID DOWN AT THE PLAYGROUND WHO INSULTED ME.. I NEED TO BORROW YOUR DOG TO BITE HIM ON THE LEG..
MAKE SURE HE ROLLS HIS SOCK DOWN..I HATE TO BITE THROUGH A SOCK..
OKAY, KID! EITHER YOU APOLOGIZE, OR THIS MEAN DOG BITES YOU ON THE LEG!
ALL RIGHT, I APOLOGIZE..
YOU DO?
8-22
HE APOLOGIZED..
© 1999 United Feature Syndicate, Inc.
www.snoopy.com
I DON'T THINK YOU WANTED TO BITE HIM ON THE LEG ANYWAY, DID YOU?
IT'S TOO FAR TO BEND OVER..
SCHULZ

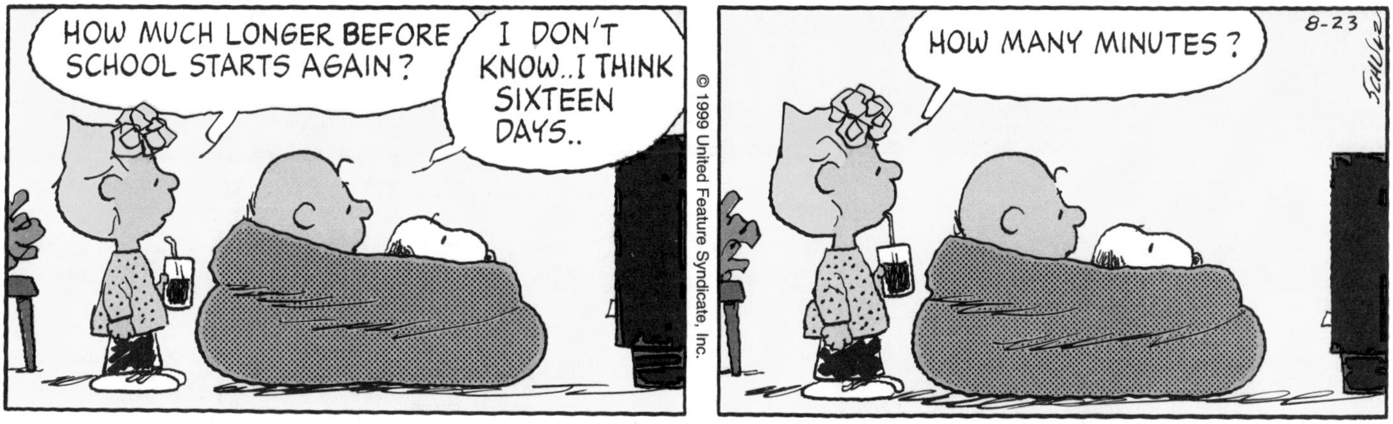
HOW MUCH LONGER BEFORE SCHOOL STARTS AGAIN?
I DON'T KNOW..I THINK SIXTEEN DAYS..
© 1999 United Feature Syndicate, Inc.
8-23
HOW MANY MINUTES?
SCHULZ

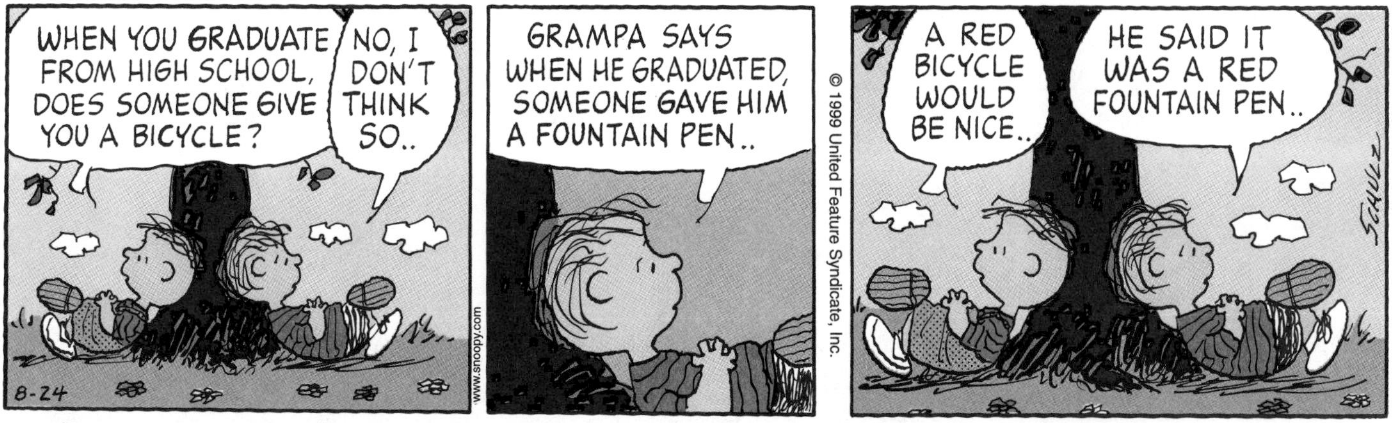
WHEN YOU GRADUATE FROM HIGH SCHOOL, DOES SOMEONE GIVE YOU A BICYCLE?
NO, I DON'T THINK SO..
8-24
www.snoopy.com
GRAMPA SAYS WHEN HE GRADUATED, SOMEONE GAVE HIM A FOUNTAIN PEN..
© 1999 United Feature Syndicate, Inc.
A RED BICYCLE WOULD BE NICE..
HE SAID IT WAS A RED FOUNTAIN PEN..
SCHULZ

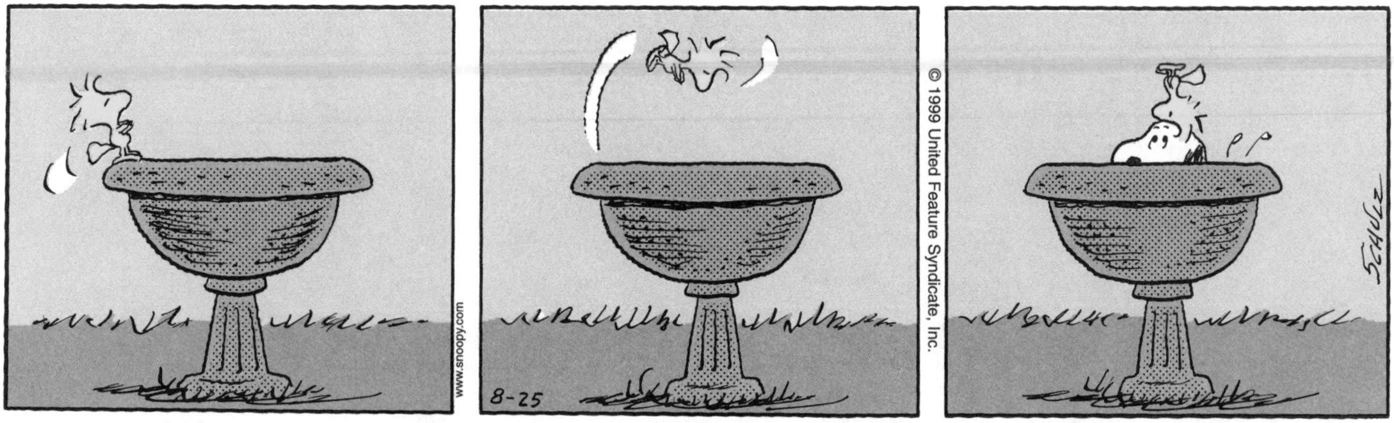
www.snoopy.com
8-25
© 1999 United Feature Syndicate, Inc.
SCHULZ

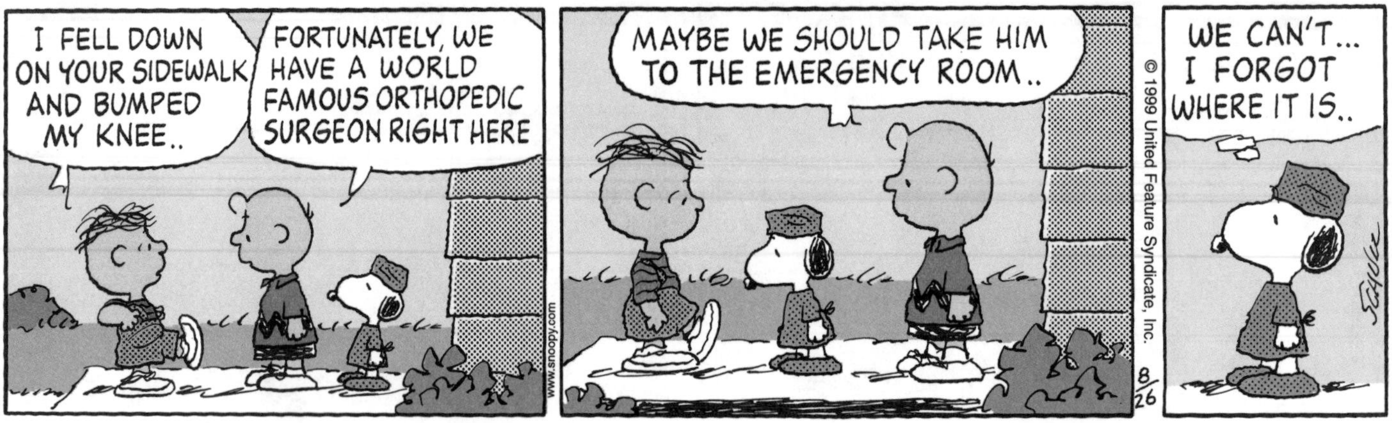
I FELL DOWN ON YOUR SIDEWALK AND BUMPED MY KNEE..
FORTUNATELY, WE HAVE A WORLD FAMOUS ORTHOPEDIC SURGEON RIGHT HERE
www.snoopy.com
MAYBE WE SHOULD TAKE HIM TO THE EMERGENCY ROOM..
© 1999 United Feature Syndicate, Inc.
8/26
WE CAN'T... I FORGOT WHERE IT IS..

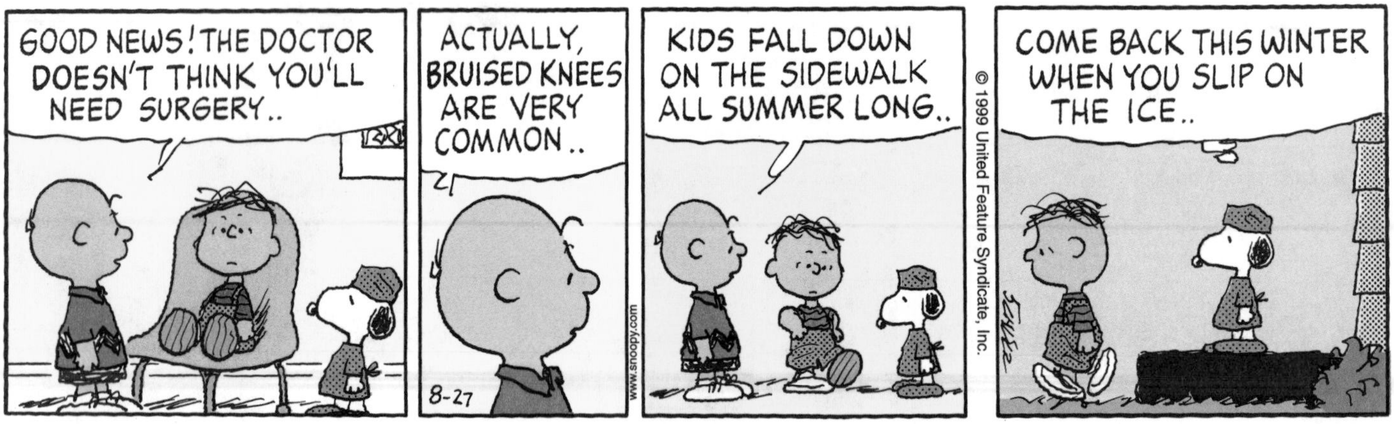
GOOD NEWS! THE DOCTOR DOESN'T THINK YOU'LL NEED SURGERY..
ACTUALLY, BRUISED KNEES ARE VERY COMMON..
8-27
www.snoopy.com
KIDS FALL DOWN ON THE SIDEWALK ALL SUMMER LONG..
© 1999 United Feature Syndicate, Inc.
COME BACK THIS WINTER WHEN YOU SLIP ON THE ICE..

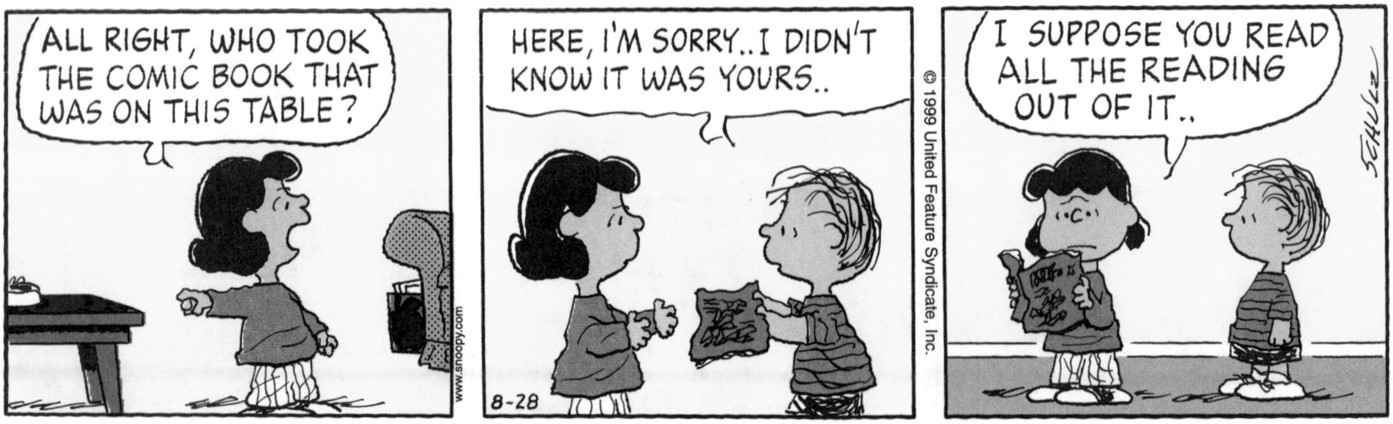
ALL RIGHT, WHO TOOK THE COMIC BOOK THAT WAS ON THIS TABLE?
www.snoopy.com
HERE, I'M SORRY..I DIDN'T KNOW IT WAS YOURS..
8-28
© 1999 United Feature Syndicate, Inc.
I SUPPOSE YOU READ ALL THE READING OUT OF IT..

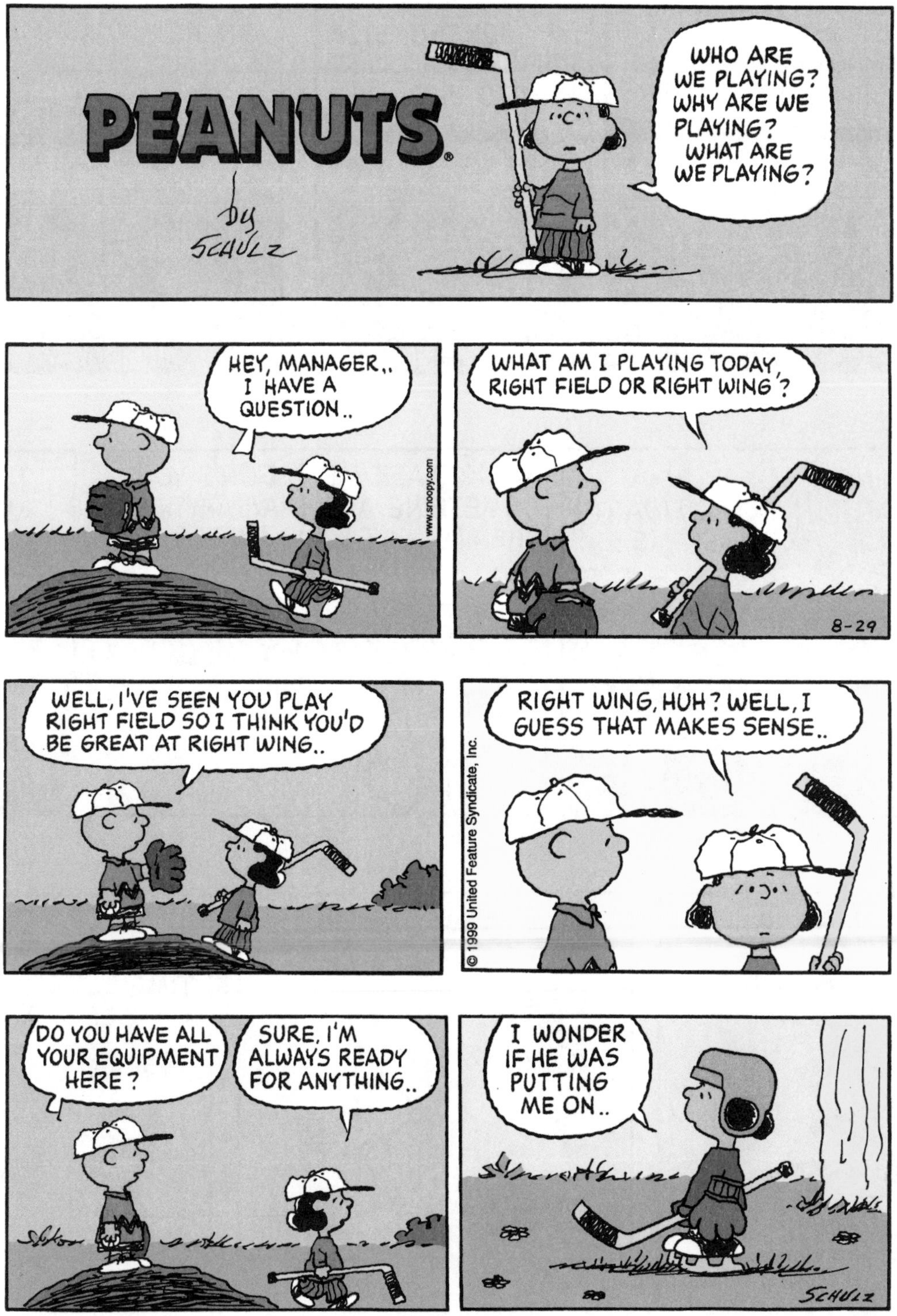
PEANUTS
by SCHULZ
WHO ARE WE PLAYING? WHY ARE WE PLAYING? WHAT ARE WE PLAYING?
HEY, MANAGER.. I HAVE A QUESTION..
www.snoopy.com
WHAT AM I PLAYING TODAY, RIGHT FIELD OR RIGHT WING?
8-29
WELL, I'VE SEEN YOU PLAY RIGHT FIELD SO I THINK YOU'D BE GREAT AT RIGHT WING..
© 1999 United Feature Syndicate, Inc.
RIGHT WING, HUH? WELL, I GUESS THAT MAKES SENSE..
DO YOU HAVE ALL YOUR EQUIPMENT HERE?
SURE, I'M ALWAYS READY FOR ANYTHING..
I WONDER IF HE WAS PUTTING ME ON..
SCHULZ

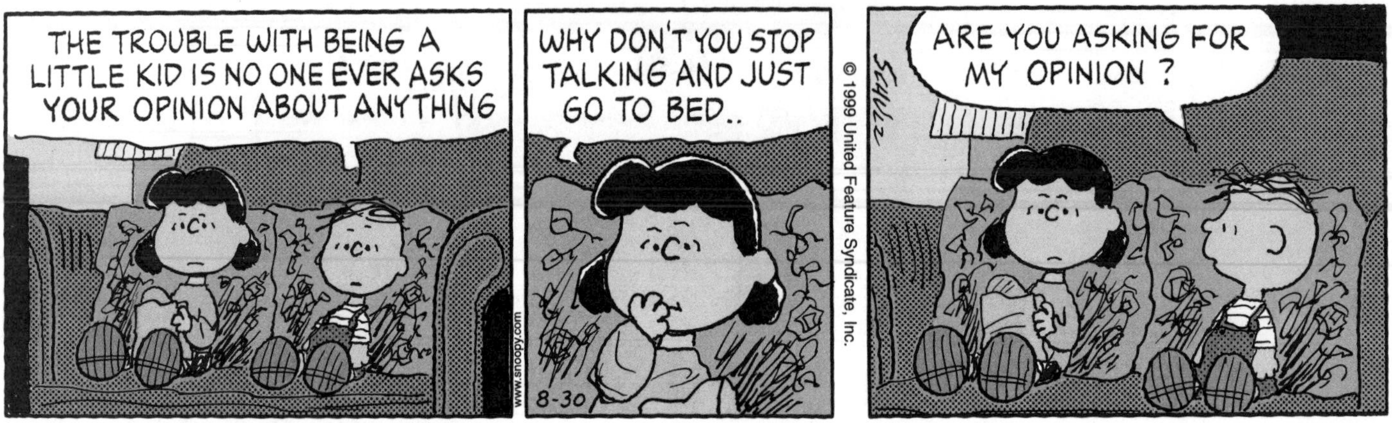
THE TROUBLE WITH BEING A LITTLE KID IS NO ONE EVER ASKS YOUR OPINION ABOUT ANYTHING
WHY DON'T YOU STOP TALKING AND JUST GO TO BED..
ARE YOU ASKING FOR MY OPINION ?
8-30
www.snoopy.com
© 1999 United Feature Syndicate, Inc.

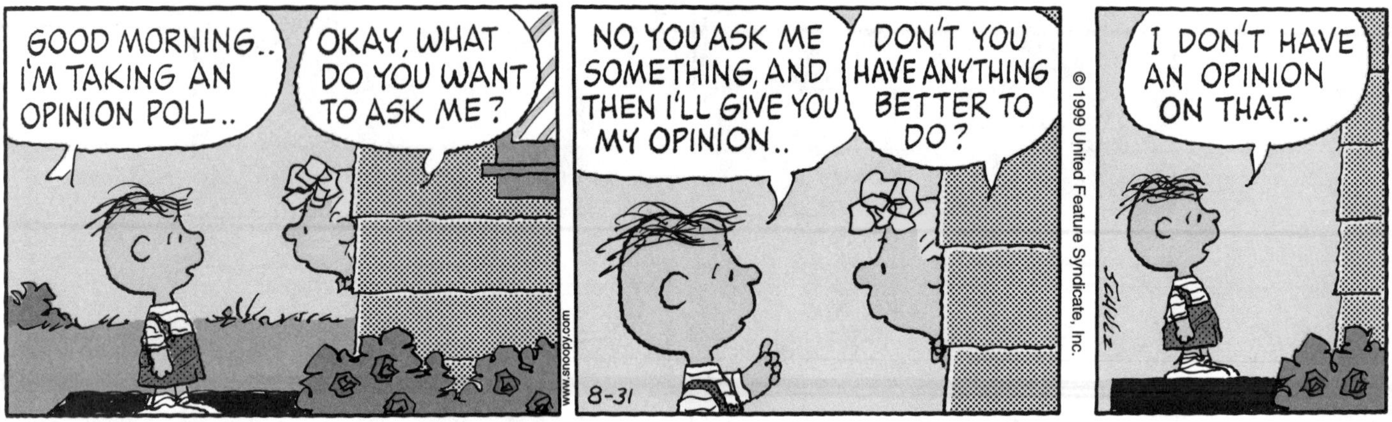
GOOD MORNING.. I'M TAKING AN OPINION POLL..
OKAY, WHAT DO YOU WANT TO ASK ME ?
NO, YOU ASK ME SOMETHING, AND THEN I'LL GIVE YOU MY OPINION..
DON'T YOU HAVE ANYTHING BETTER TO DO ?
I DON'T HAVE AN OPINION ON THAT..
8-31
www.snoopy.com
© 1999 United Feature Syndicate, Inc.

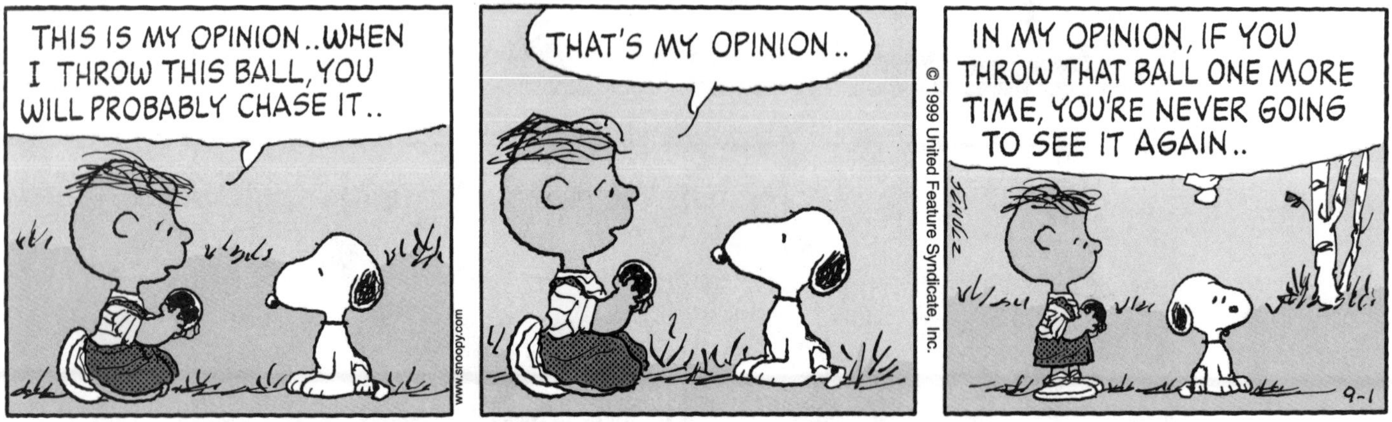
THIS IS MY OPINION..WHEN I THROW THIS BALL, YOU WILL PROBABLY CHASE IT..
THAT'S MY OPINION..
IN MY OPINION, IF YOU THROW THAT BALL ONE MORE TIME, YOU'RE NEVER GOING TO SEE IT AGAIN..
9-1
www.snoopy.com
© 1999 United Feature Syndicate, Inc.

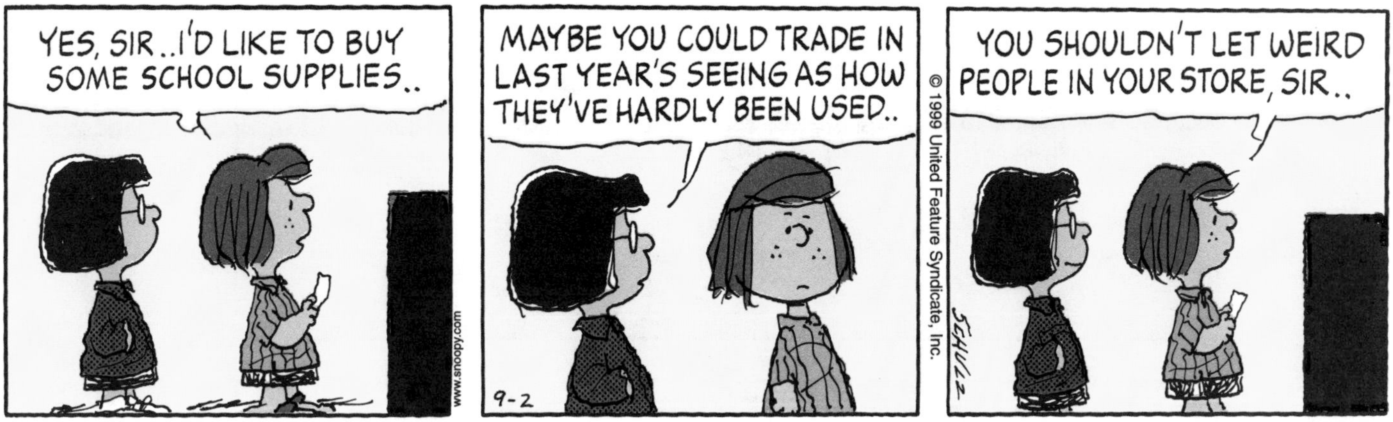
YES, SIR..I'D LIKE TO BUY SOME SCHOOL SUPPLIES..
www.snoopy.com
9-2
MAYBE YOU COULD TRADE IN LAST YEAR'S SEEING AS HOW THEY'VE HARDLY BEEN USED..
© 1999 United Feature Syndicate, Inc.
YOU SHOULDN'T LET WEIRD PEOPLE IN YOUR STORE, SIR..
SCHULZ

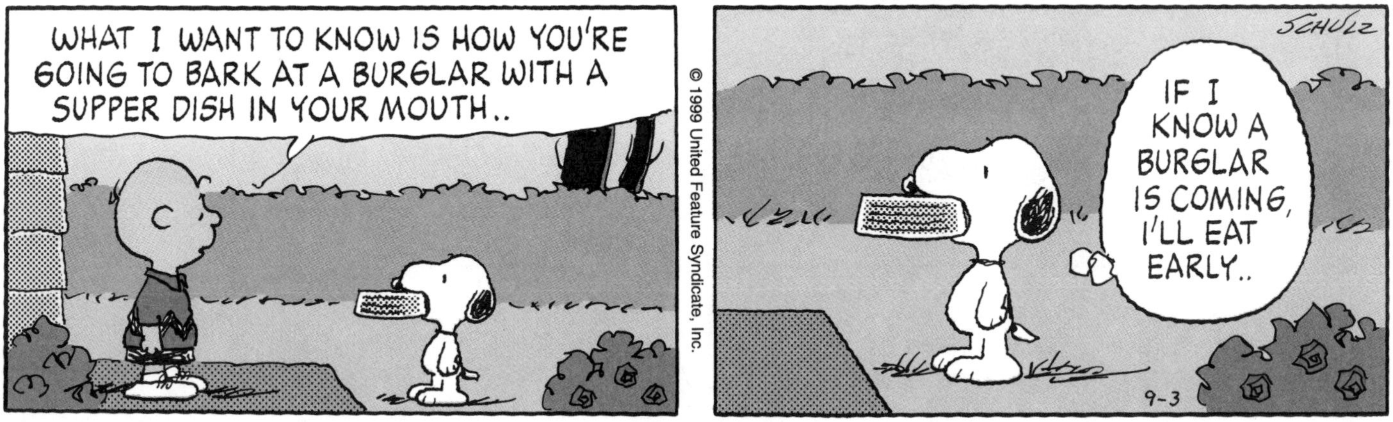
WHAT I WANT TO KNOW IS HOW YOU'RE GOING TO BARK AT A BURGLAR WITH A SUPPER DISH IN YOUR MOUTH..
© 1999 United Feature Syndicate, Inc.
SCHULZ
IF I KNOW A BURGLAR IS COMING, I'LL EAT EARLY..
9-3

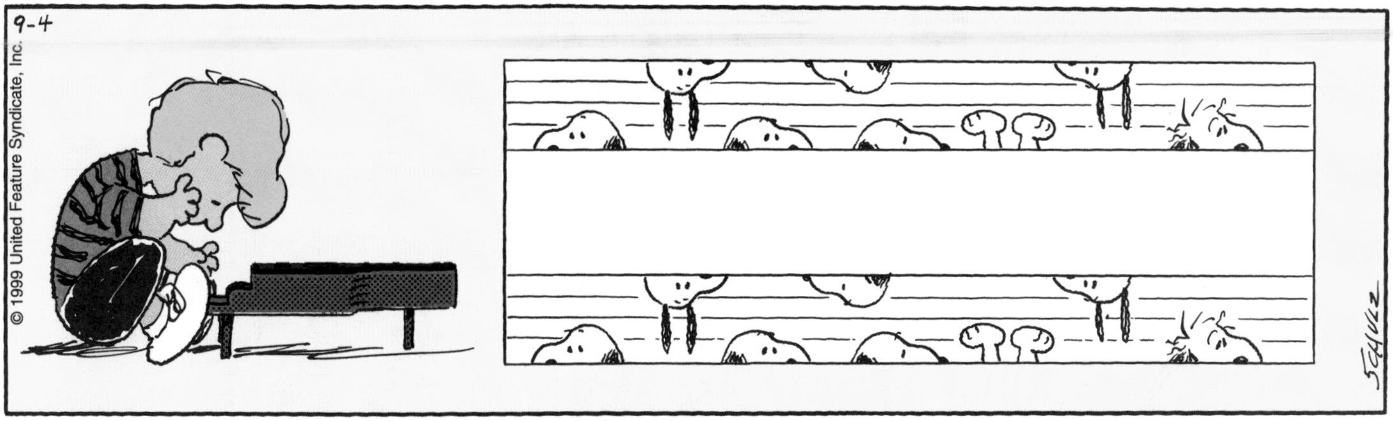
9-4
© 1999 United Feature Syndicate, Inc.
SCHULZ

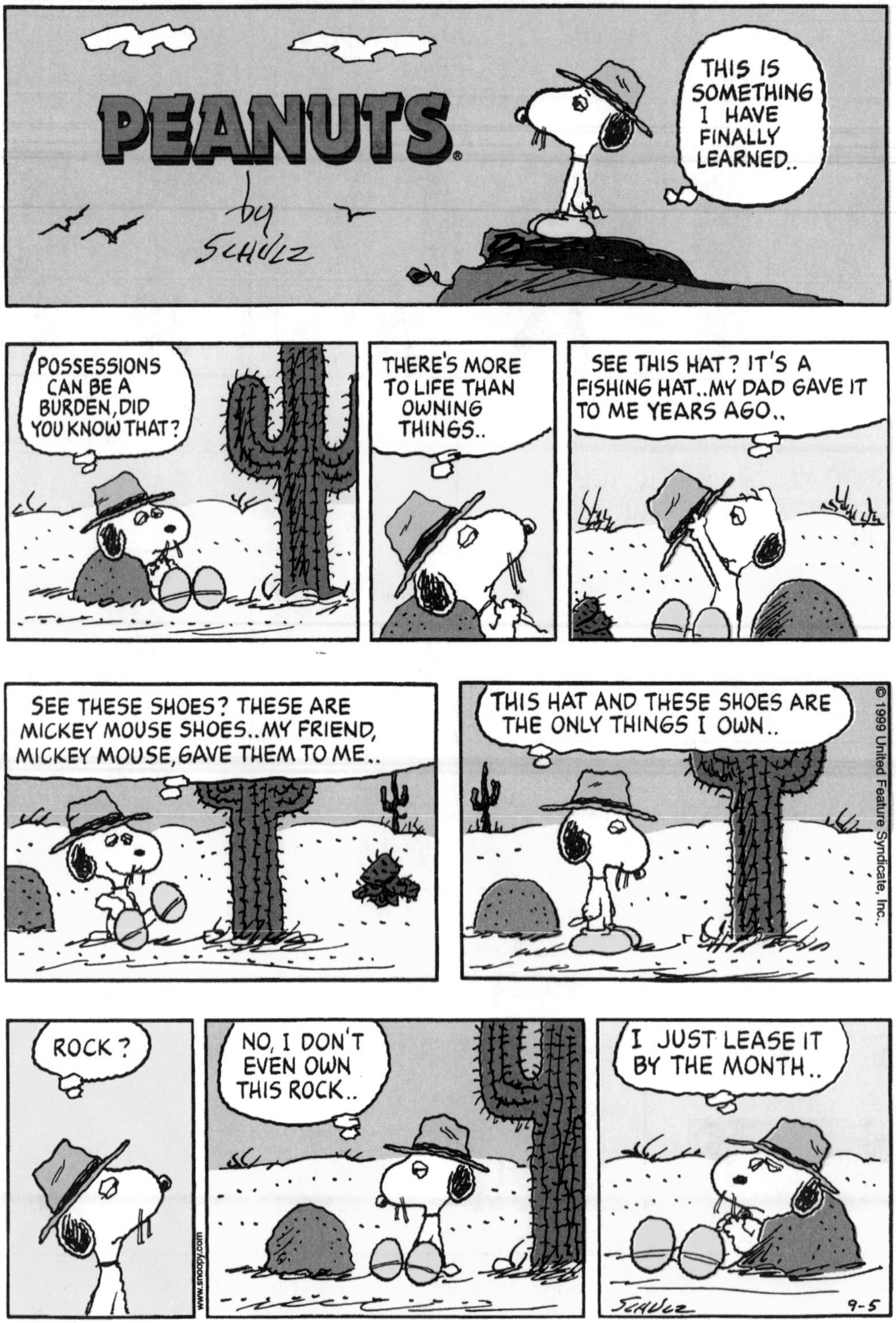
PEANUTS
by SCHULZ
THIS IS SOMETHING I HAVE FINALLY LEARNED..
POSSESSIONS CAN BE A BURDEN, DID YOU KNOW THAT?
THERE'S MORE TO LIFE THAN OWNING THINGS..
SEE THIS HAT? IT'S A FISHING HAT..MY DAD GAVE IT TO ME YEARS AGO..
SEE THESE SHOES? THESE ARE MICKEY MOUSE SHOES..MY FRIEND, MICKEY MOUSE, GAVE THEM TO ME..
THIS HAT AND THESE SHOES ARE THE ONLY THINGS I OWN..
© 1999 United Feature Syndicate, Inc.
ROCK?
www.snoopy.com
NO, I DON'T EVEN OWN THIS ROCK..
I JUST LEASE IT BY THE MONTH..
SCHULZ
9-5

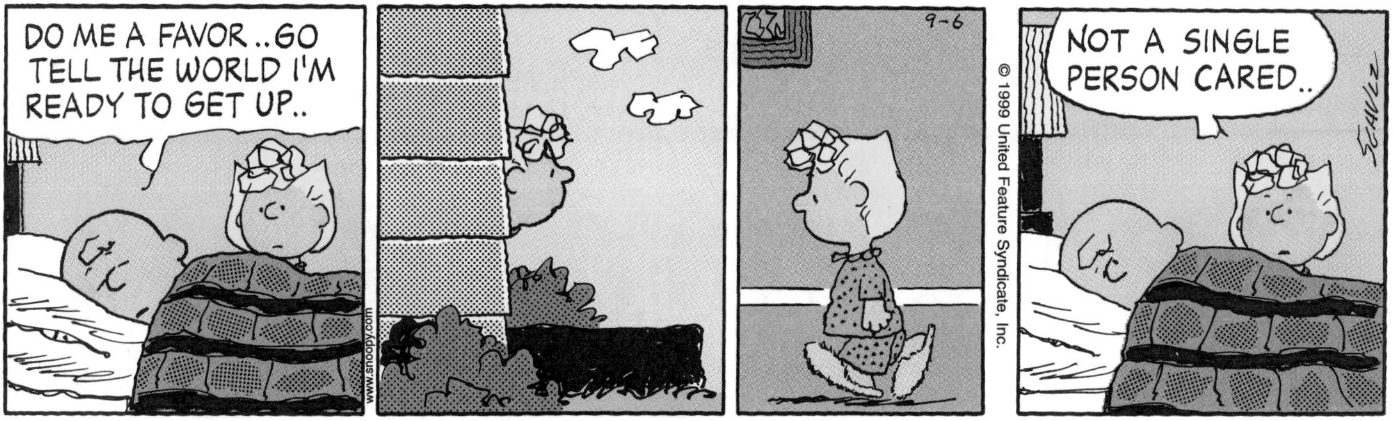
DO ME A FAVOR..GO TELL THE WORLD I'M READY TO GET UP..
www.snoopy.com
9-6
© 1999 United Feature Syndicate, Inc.
NOT A SINGLE PERSON CARED..
SCHULZ

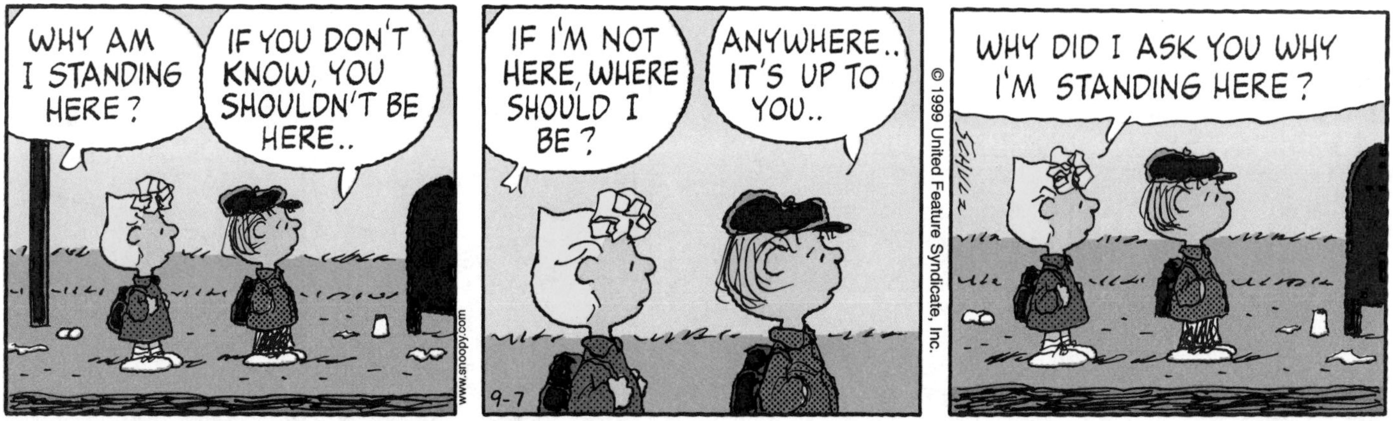
WHY AM I STANDING HERE?
IF YOU DON'T KNOW, YOU SHOULDN'T BE HERE..
www.snoopy.com
IF I'M NOT HERE, WHERE SHOULD I BE?
ANYWHERE.. IT'S UP TO YOU..
9-7
© 1999 United Feature Syndicate, Inc.
WHY DID I ASK YOU WHY I'M STANDING HERE?
SCHULZ

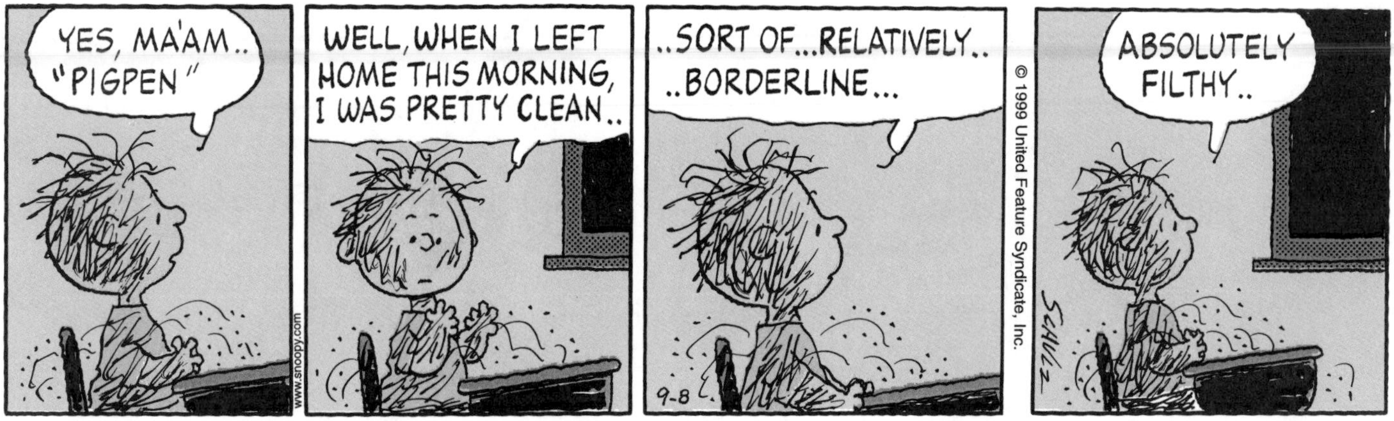
YES, MA'AM.. "PIGPEN"
www.snoopy.com
WELL, WHEN I LEFT HOME THIS MORNING, I WAS PRETTY CLEAN..
..SORT OF...RELATIVELY.. ..BORDERLINE...
9-8
© 1999 United Feature Syndicate, Inc.
ABSOLUTELY FILTHY..
SCHULZ

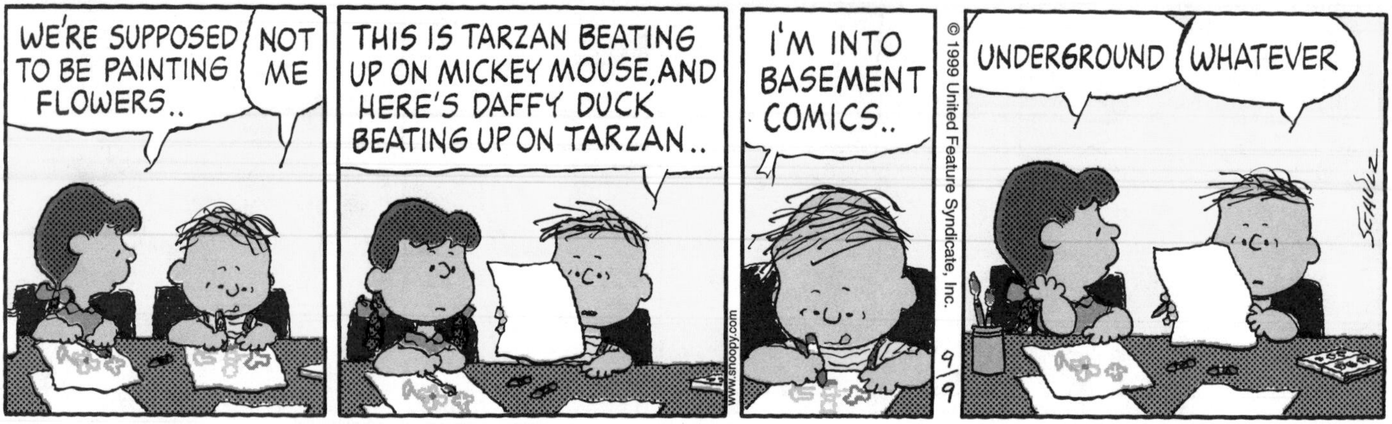
WE'RE SUPPOSED TO BE PAINTING FLOWERS..
NOT ME
THIS IS TARZAN BEATING UP ON MICKEY MOUSE, AND HERE'S DAFFY DUCK BEATING UP ON TARZAN..
I'M INTO BASEMENT COMICS..
UNDERGROUND
WHATEVER
© 1999 United Feature Syndicate, Inc.
www.snoopy.com
9/9
SCHULZ

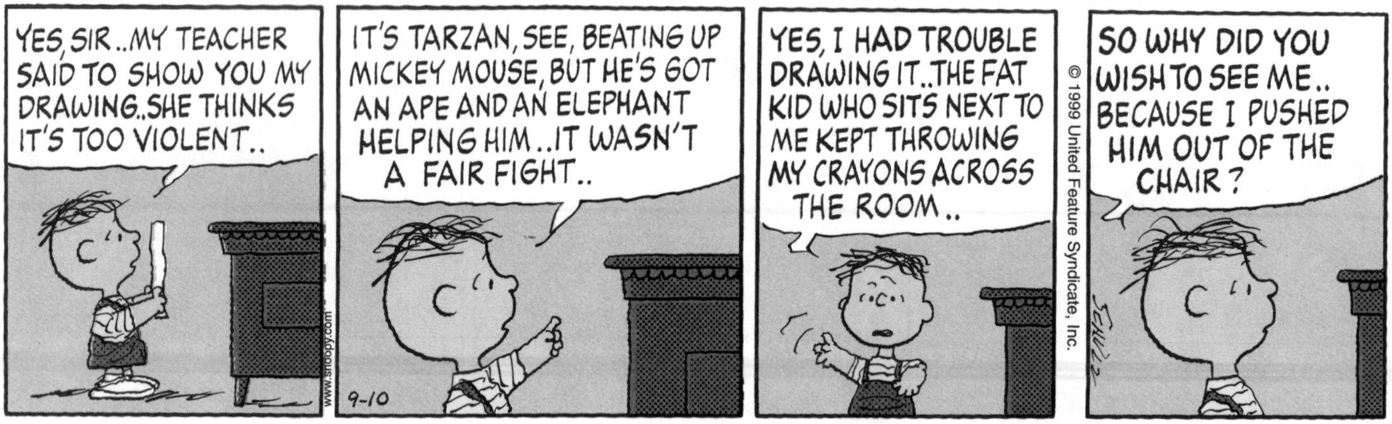
YES, SIR..MY TEACHER SAID TO SHOW YOU MY DRAWING..SHE THINKS IT'S TOO VIOLENT..
IT'S TARZAN, SEE, BEATING UP MICKEY MOUSE, BUT HE'S GOT AN APE AND AN ELEPHANT HELPING HIM..IT WASN'T A FAIR FIGHT..
YES, I HAD TROUBLE DRAWING IT..THE FAT KID WHO SITS NEXT TO ME KEPT THROWING MY CRAYONS ACROSS THE ROOM..
SO WHY DID YOU WISH TO SEE ME.. BECAUSE I PUSHED HIM OUT OF THE CHAIR?
www.snoopy.com
9-10
© 1999 United Feature Syndicate, Inc.
SCHULZ

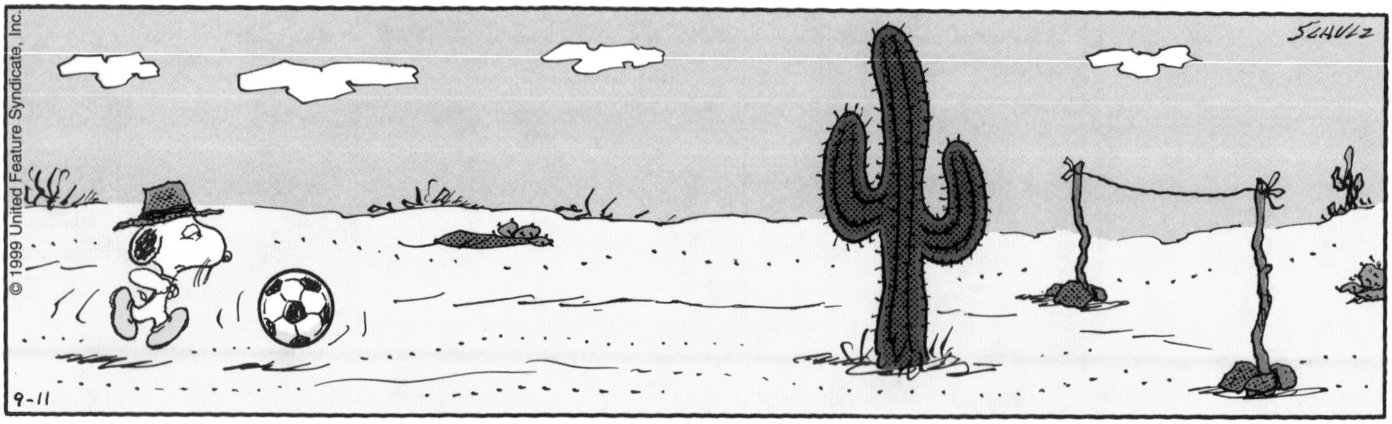
© 1999 United Feature Syndicate, Inc.
SCHULZ
9-11

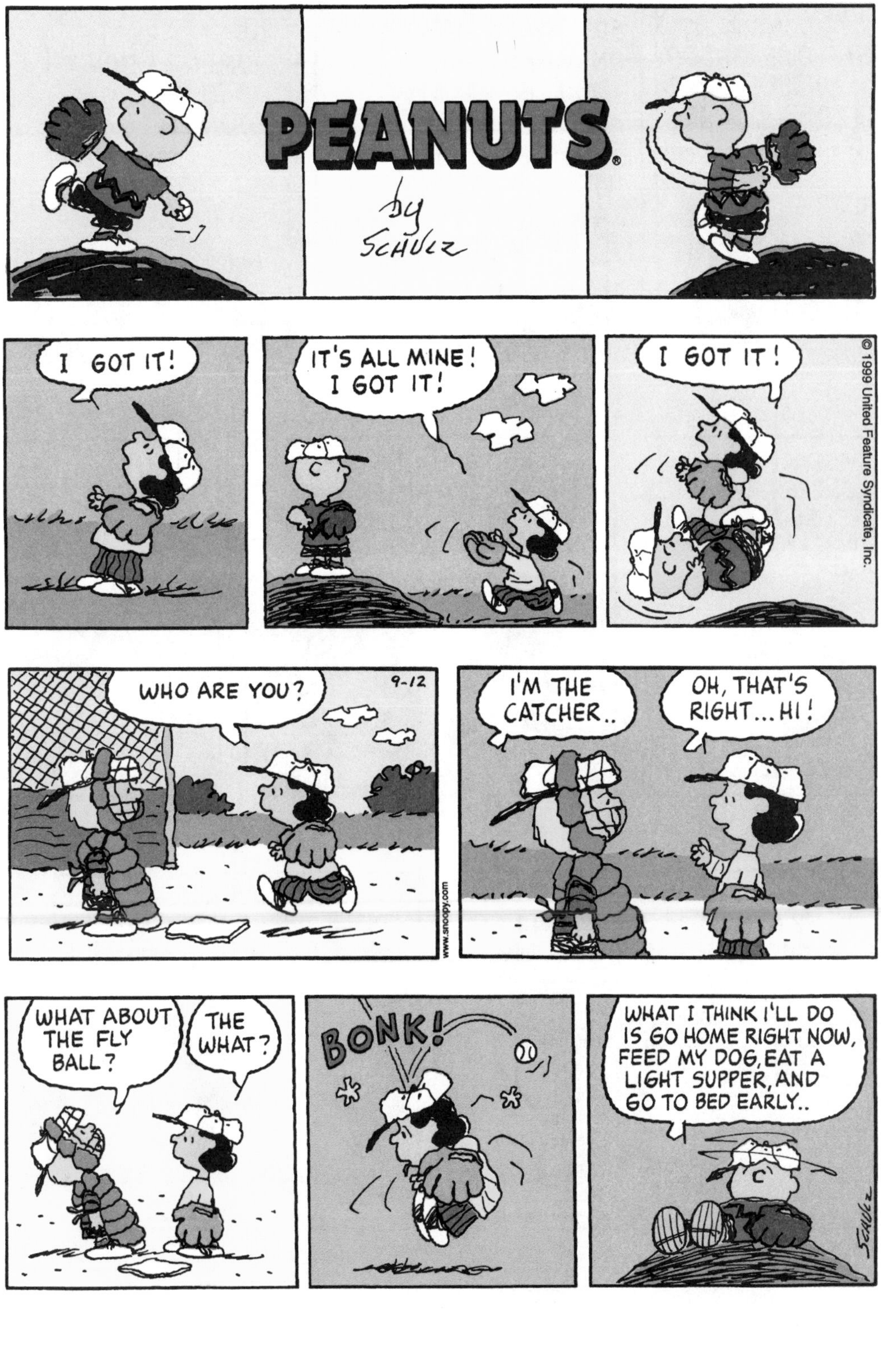
PEANUTS®
by SCHULZ
I GOT IT!
IT'S ALL MINE! I GOT IT!
I GOT IT!
© 1999 United Feature Syndicate, Inc.
WHO ARE YOU?
9-12
www.snoopy.com
I'M THE CATCHER..
OH, THAT'S RIGHT... HI!
WHAT ABOUT THE FLY BALL?
THE WHAT?
BONK!
WHAT I THINK I'LL DO IS GO HOME RIGHT NOW, FEED MY DOG, EAT A LIGHT SUPPER, AND GO TO BED EARLY..
SCHULZ

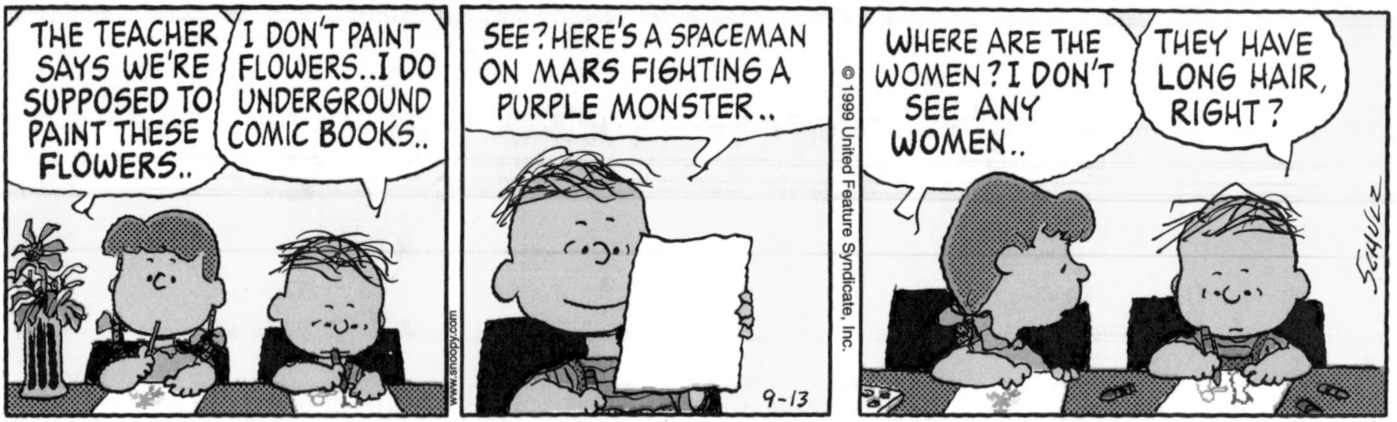
THE TEACHER SAYS WE'RE SUPPOSED TO PAINT THESE FLOWERS..
I DON'T PAINT FLOWERS..I DO UNDERGROUND COMIC BOOKS..
SEE? HERE'S A SPACEMAN ON MARS FIGHTING A PURPLE MONSTER..
WHERE ARE THE WOMEN? I DON'T SEE ANY WOMEN..
THEY HAVE LONG HAIR, RIGHT?
www.snoopy.com
© 1999 United Feature Syndicate, Inc.
9-13
SCHULZ

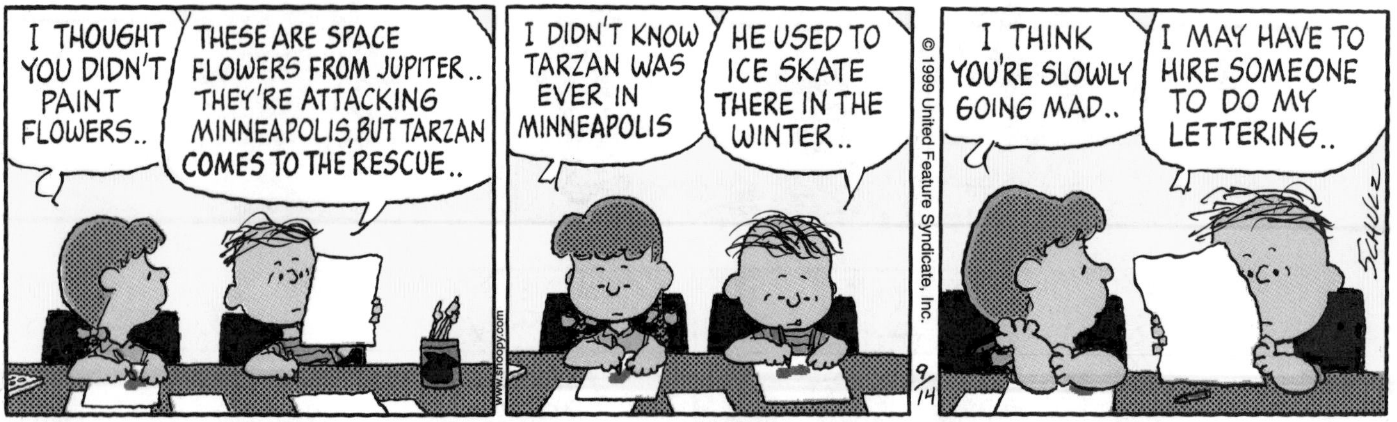
I THOUGHT YOU DIDN'T PAINT FLOWERS..
THESE ARE SPACE FLOWERS FROM JUPITER.. THEY'RE ATTACKING MINNEAPOLIS, BUT TARZAN COMES TO THE RESCUE..
I DIDN'T KNOW TARZAN WAS EVER IN MINNEAPOLIS
HE USED TO ICE SKATE THERE IN THE WINTER..
I THINK YOU'RE SLOWLY GOING MAD..
I MAY HAVE TO HIRE SOMEONE TO DO MY LETTERING..
www.snoopy.com
© 1999 United Feature Syndicate, Inc.
9/14
SCHULZ

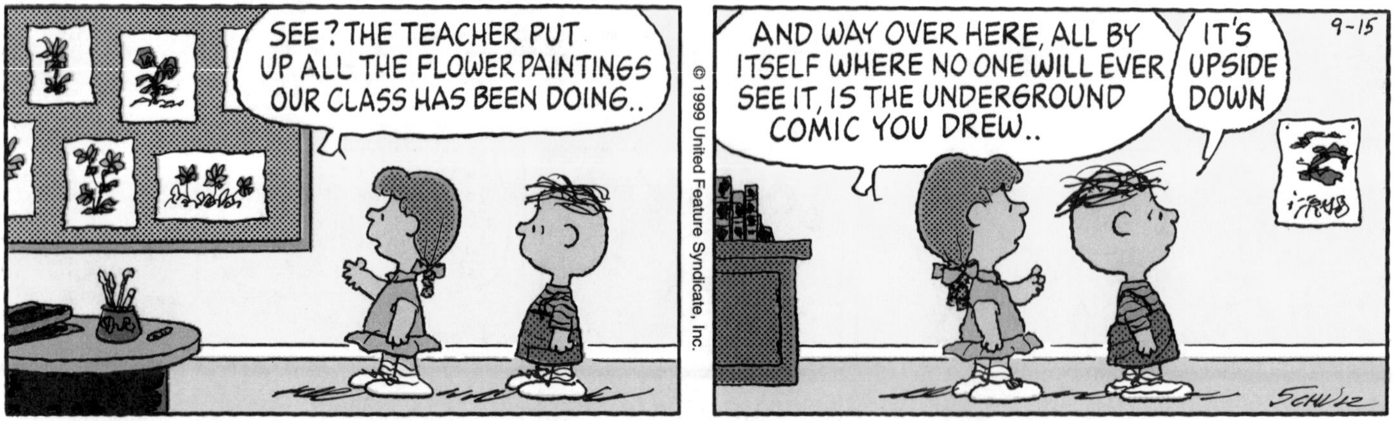
SEE? THE TEACHER PUT UP ALL THE FLOWER PAINTINGS OUR CLASS HAS BEEN DOING..
AND WAY OVER HERE, ALL BY ITSELF WHERE NO ONE WILL EVER SEE IT, IS THE UNDERGROUND COMIC YOU DREW..
IT'S UPSIDE DOWN
© 1999 United Feature Syndicate, Inc.
9-15
SCHULZ

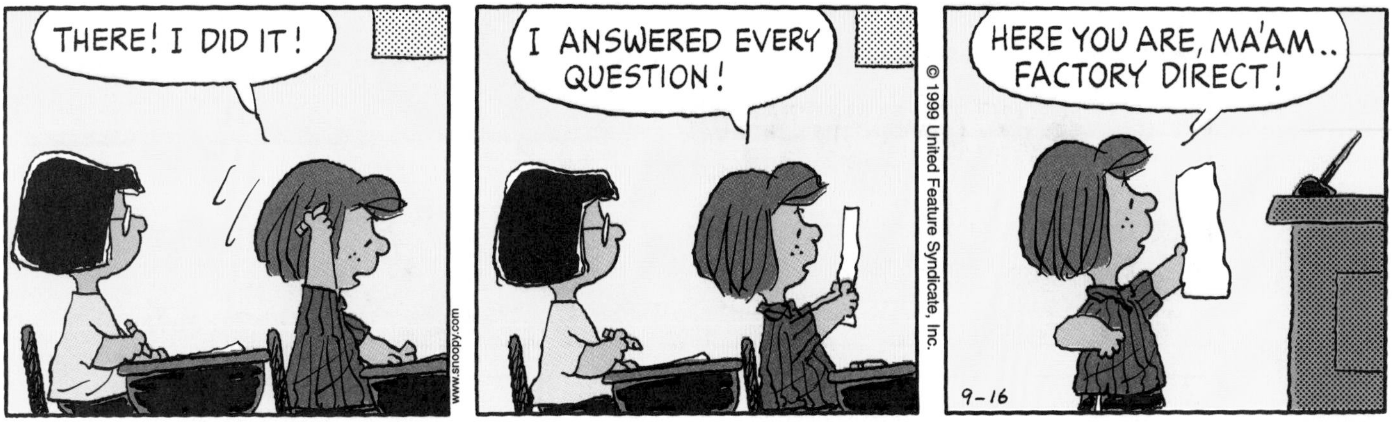
THERE! I DID IT!
www.snoopy.com
I ANSWERED EVERY QUESTION!
© 1999 United Feature Syndicate, Inc.
HERE YOU ARE, MA'AM.. FACTORY DIRECT!
9-16

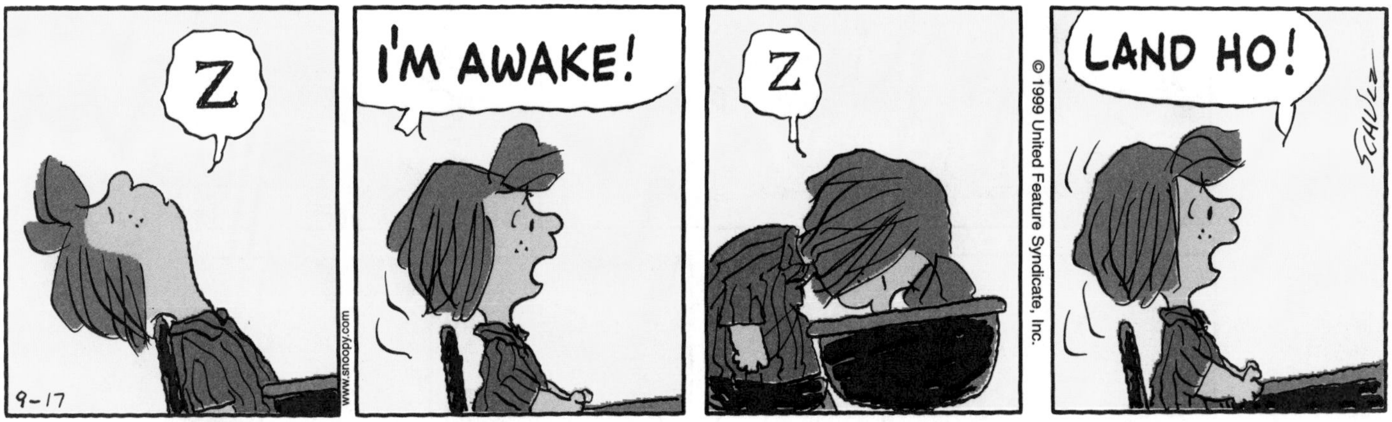
Z
9-17
www.snoopy.com
I'M AWAKE!
Z
© 1999 United Feature Syndicate, Inc.
LAND HO!
SCHULZ

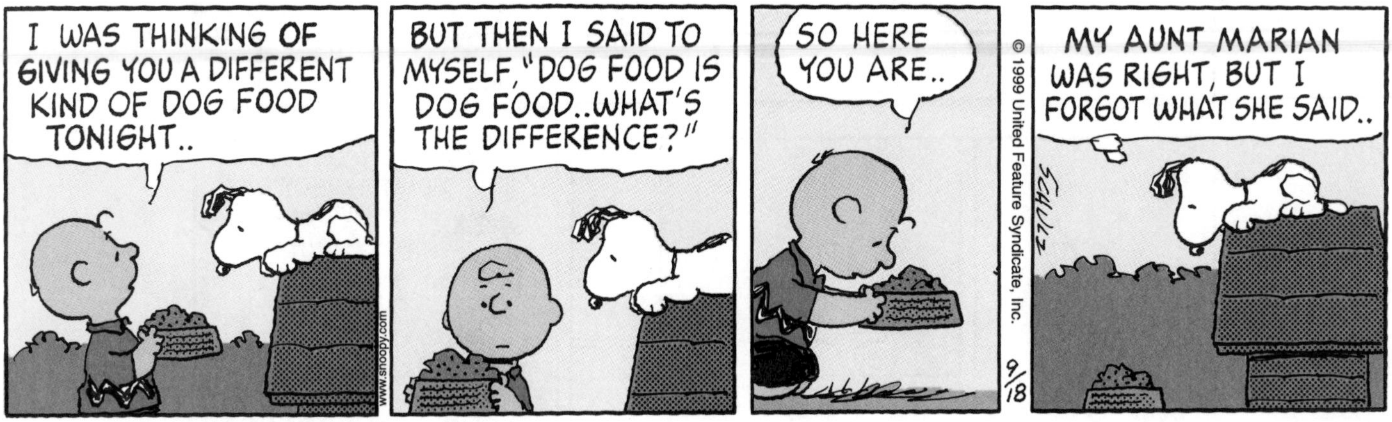
I WAS THINKING OF GIVING YOU A DIFFERENT KIND OF DOG FOOD TONIGHT..
www.snoopy.com
BUT THEN I SAID TO MYSELF, "DOG FOOD IS DOG FOOD..WHAT'S THE DIFFERENCE?"
SO HERE YOU ARE..
9/18
© 1999 United Feature Syndicate, Inc.
SCHULZ
MY AUNT MARIAN WAS RIGHT, BUT I FORGOT WHAT SHE SAID..

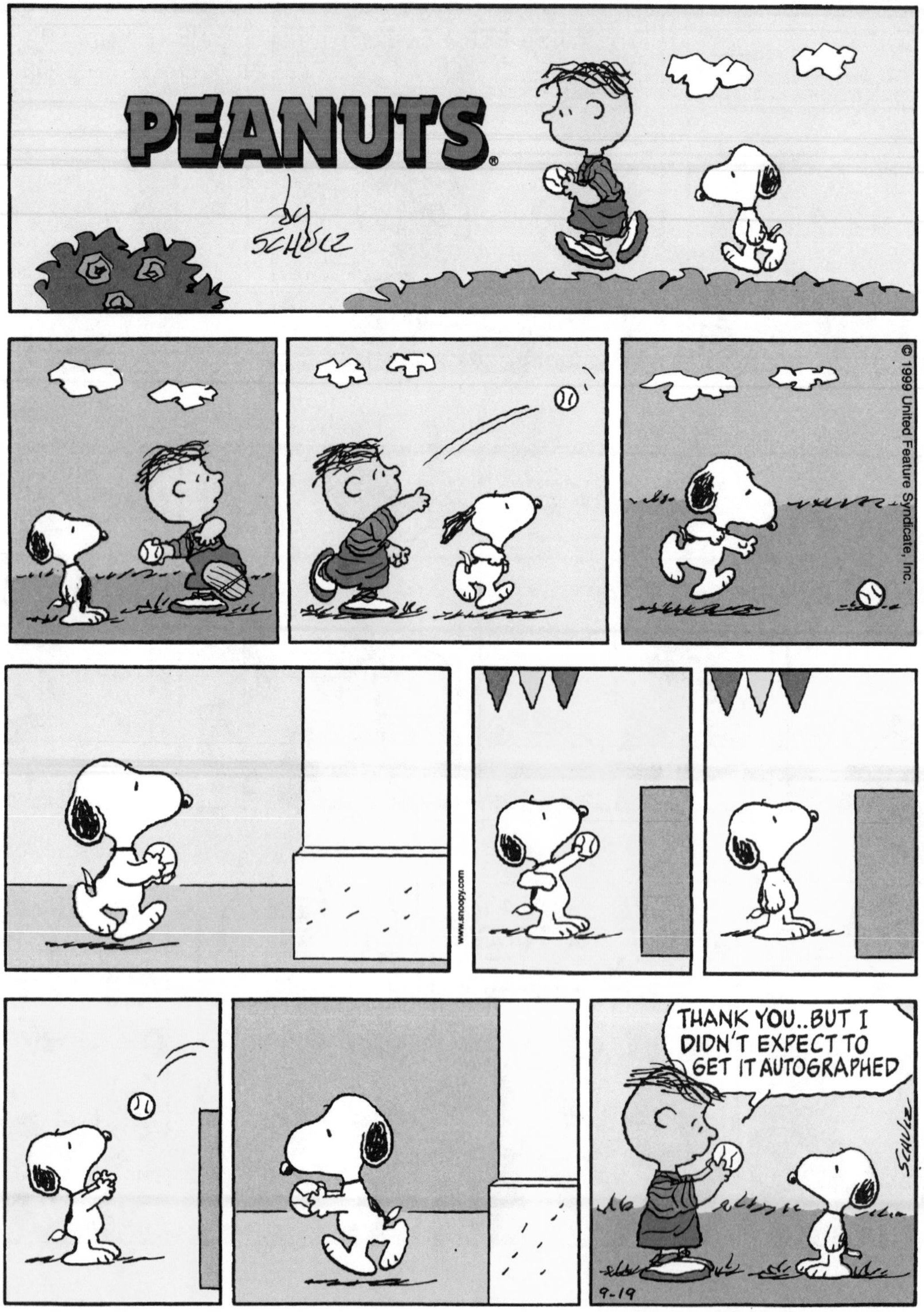
PEANUTS
by SCHULZ
© 1999 United Feature Syndicate, Inc.
www.snoopy.com
THANK YOU..BUT I DIDN'T EXPECT TO GET IT AUTOGRAPHED
SCHULZ
9-19

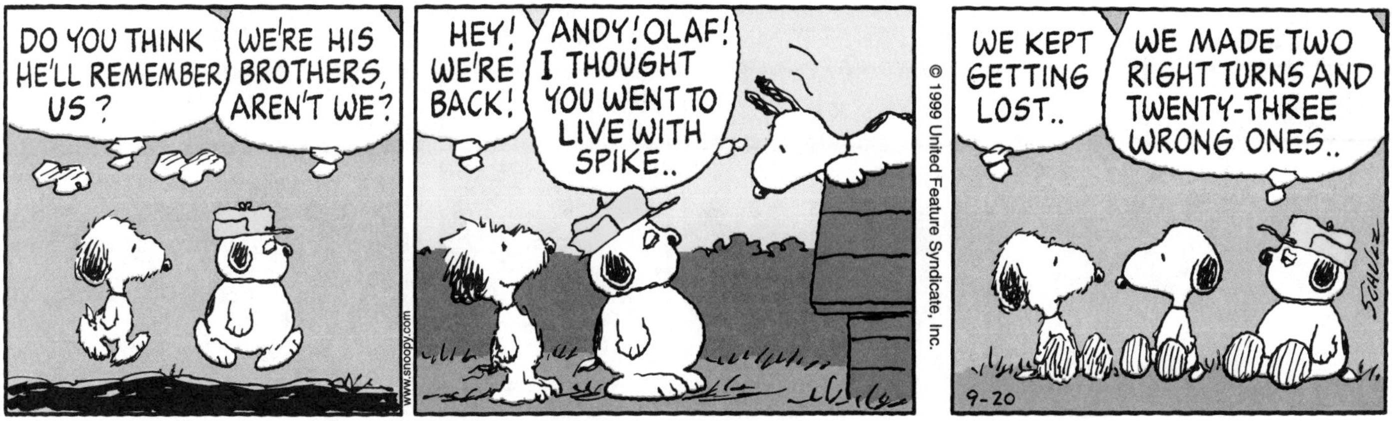
DO YOU THINK HE'LL REMEMBER US?
WE'RE HIS BROTHERS, AREN'T WE?
www.snoopy.com
HEY! WE'RE BACK!
ANDY! OLAF! I THOUGHT YOU WENT TO LIVE WITH SPIKE..
© 1999 United Feature Syndicate, Inc.
WE KEPT GETTING LOST..
WE MADE TWO RIGHT TURNS AND TWENTY-THREE WRONG ONES..
SCHULZ
9-20

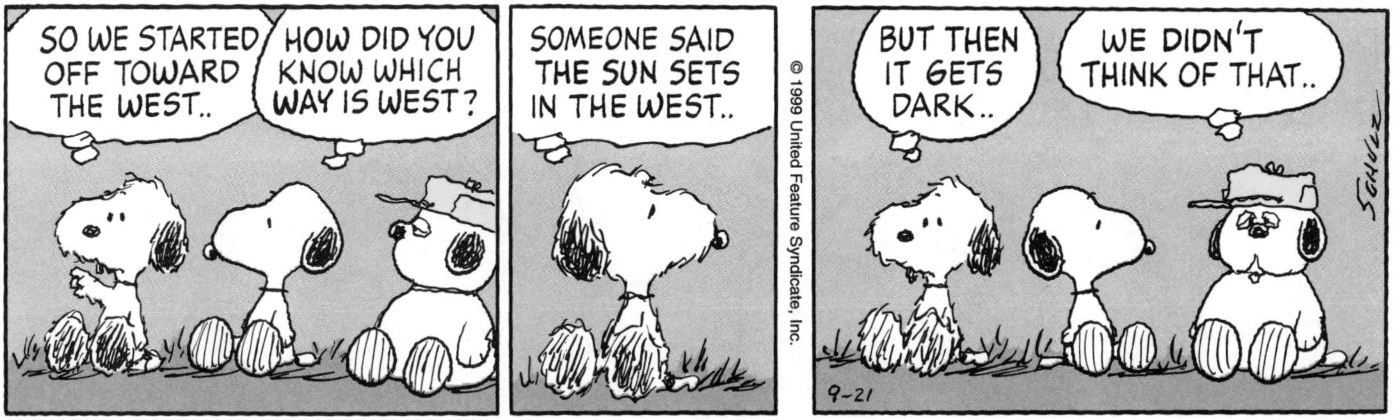
SO WE STARTED OFF TOWARD THE WEST..
HOW DID YOU KNOW WHICH WAY IS WEST?
SOMEONE SAID THE SUN SETS IN THE WEST..
© 1999 United Feature Syndicate, Inc.
BUT THEN IT GETS DARK..
WE DIDN'T THINK OF THAT..
SCHULZ
9-21

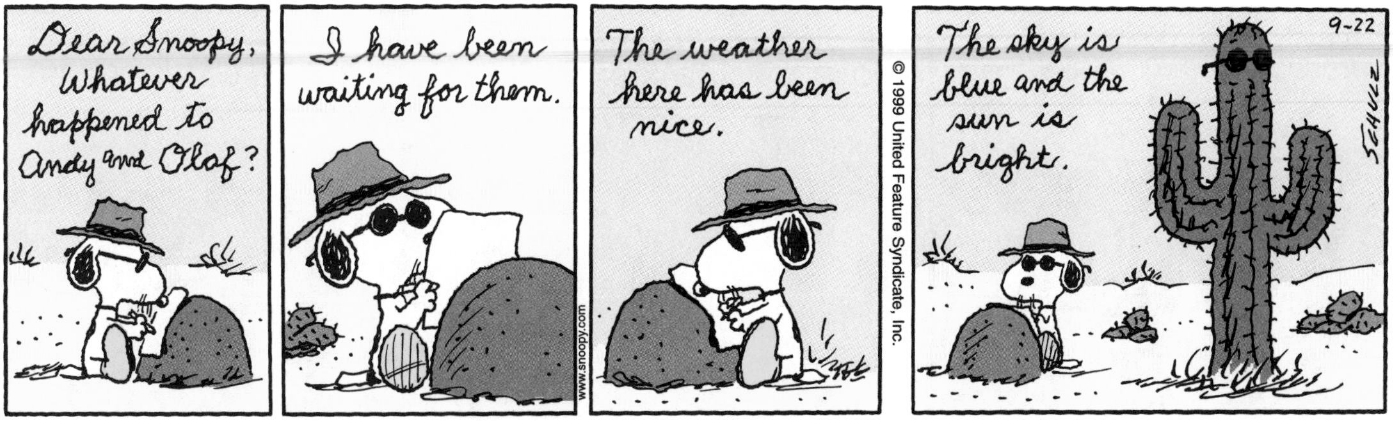
Dear Snoopy, Whatever happened to Andy and Olaf?
I have been waiting for them.
www.snoopy.com
The weather here has been nice.
© 1999 United Feature Syndicate, Inc.
The sky is blue and the sun is bright.
9-22
SCHULZ

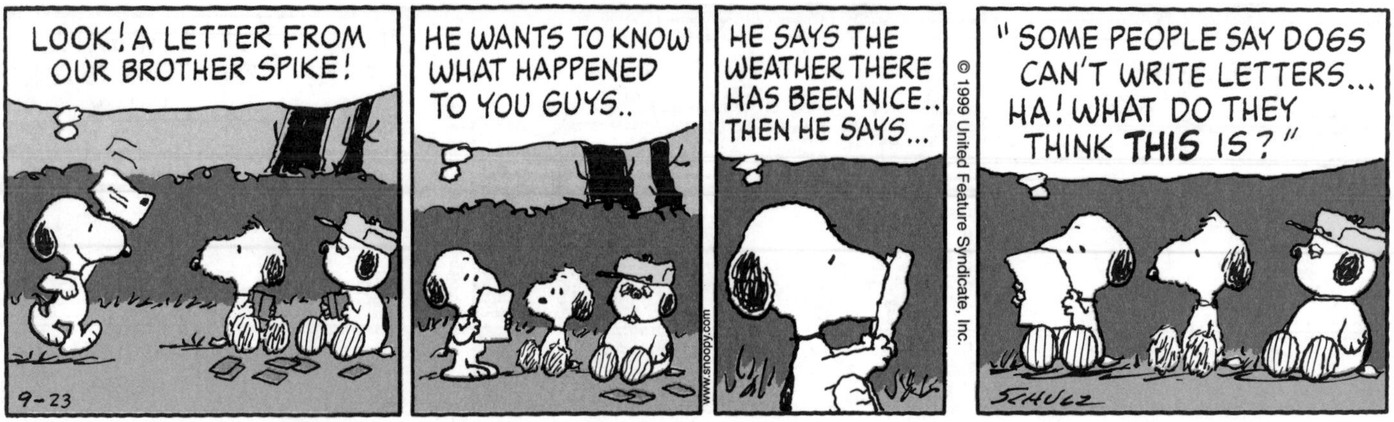
LOOK! A LETTER FROM OUR BROTHER SPIKE!
HE WANTS TO KNOW WHAT HAPPENED TO YOU GUYS..
HE SAYS THE WEATHER THERE HAS BEEN NICE.. THEN HE SAYS...
"SOME PEOPLE SAY DOGS CAN'T WRITE LETTERS... HA! WHAT DO THEY THINK **THIS** IS?"
9-23
www.snoopy.com
© 1999 United Feature Syndicate, Inc.
SCHULZ

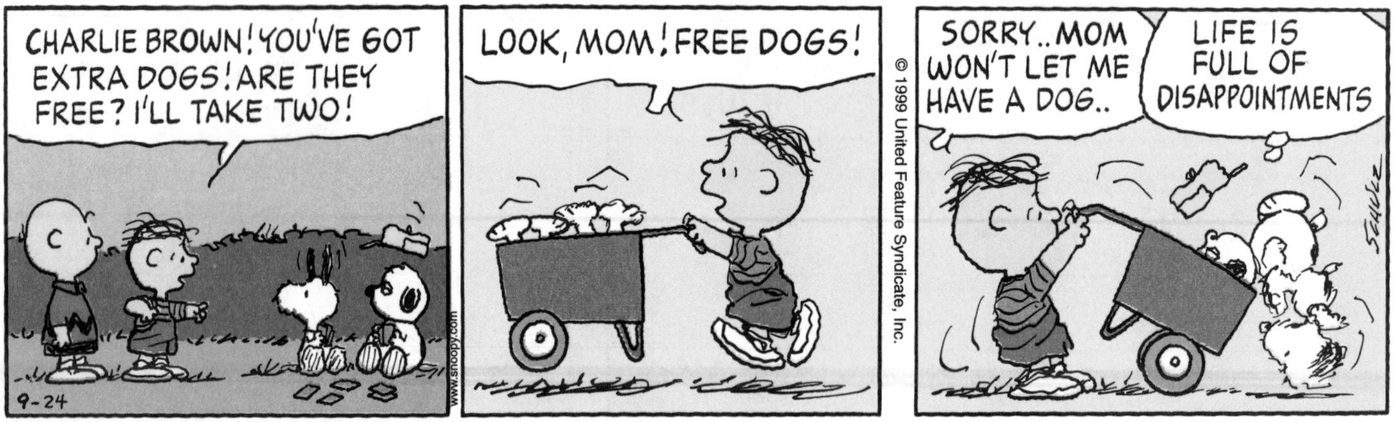
CHARLIE BROWN! YOU'VE GOT EXTRA DOGS! ARE THEY FREE? I'LL TAKE TWO!
LOOK, MOM! FREE DOGS!
SORRY.. MOM WON'T LET ME HAVE A DOG..
LIFE IS FULL OF DISAPPOINTMENTS
9-24
www.snoopy.com
© 1999 United Feature Syndicate, Inc.
SCHULZ

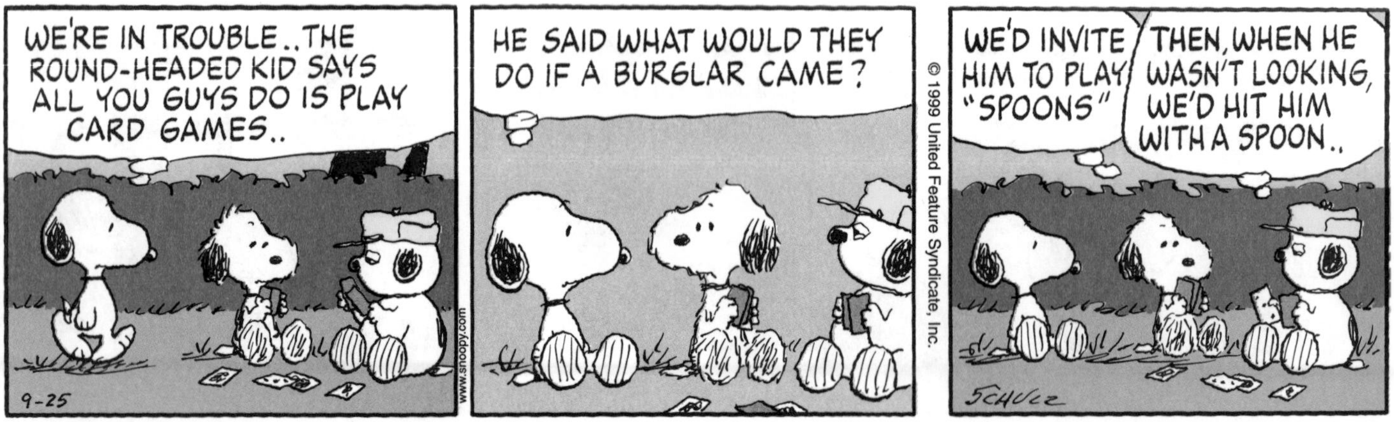
WE'RE IN TROUBLE..THE ROUND-HEADED KID SAYS ALL YOU GUYS DO IS PLAY CARD GAMES..
HE SAID WHAT WOULD THEY DO IF A BURGLAR CAME?
WE'D INVITE HIM TO PLAY "SPOONS"
THEN, WHEN HE WASN'T LOOKING, WE'D HIT HIM WITH A SPOON..
9-25
www.snoopy.com
© 1999 United Feature Syndicate, Inc.
SCHULZ

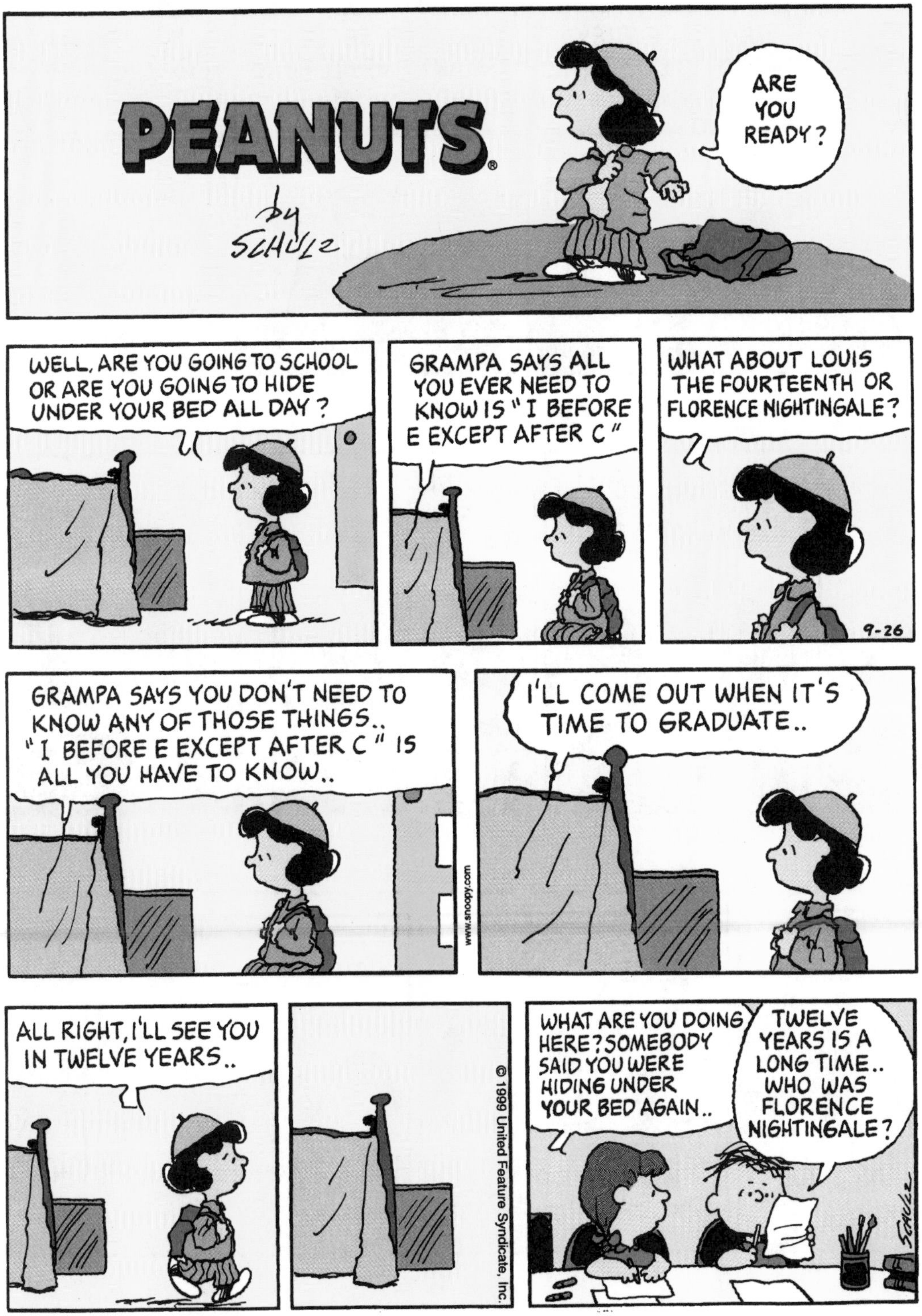
PEANUTS
by SCHULZ
ARE YOU READY?
WELL, ARE YOU GOING TO SCHOOL OR ARE YOU GOING TO HIDE UNDER YOUR BED ALL DAY?
GRAMPA SAYS ALL YOU EVER NEED TO KNOW IS "I BEFORE E EXCEPT AFTER C"
WHAT ABOUT LOUIS THE FOURTEENTH OR FLORENCE NIGHTINGALE?
9-26
GRAMPA SAYS YOU DON'T NEED TO KNOW ANY OF THOSE THINGS.. "I BEFORE E EXCEPT AFTER C" IS ALL YOU HAVE TO KNOW..
www.snoopy.com
I'LL COME OUT WHEN IT'S TIME TO GRADUATE..
ALL RIGHT, I'LL SEE YOU IN TWELVE YEARS..
© 1999 United Feature Syndicate, Inc.
WHAT ARE YOU DOING HERE? SOMEBODY SAID YOU WERE HIDING UNDER YOUR BED AGAIN..
TWELVE YEARS IS A LONG TIME.. WHO WAS FLORENCE NIGHTINGALE?
SCHULZ

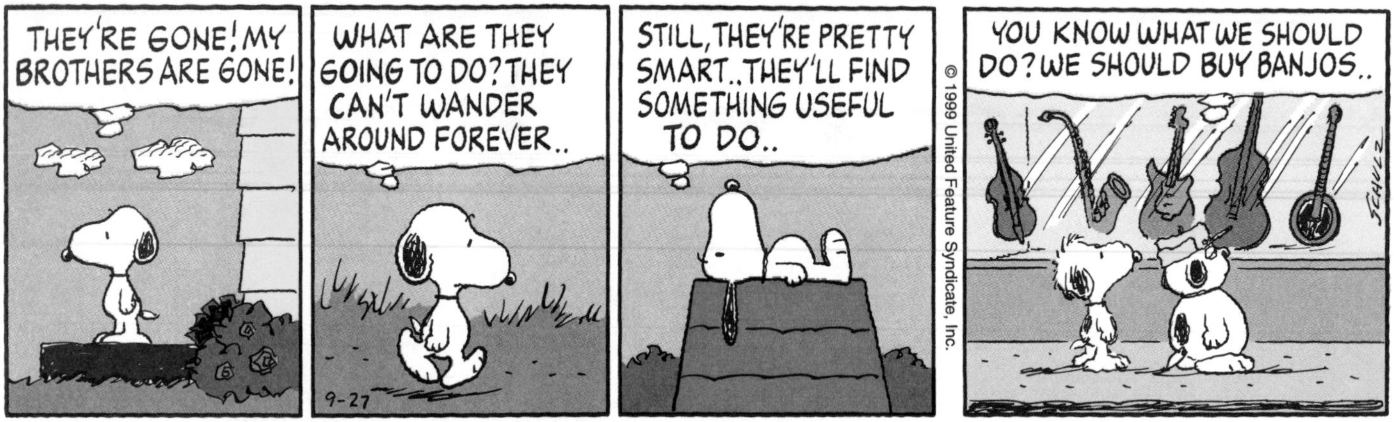
THEY'RE GONE! MY BROTHERS ARE GONE!
WHAT ARE THEY GOING TO DO? THEY CAN'T WANDER AROUND FOREVER..
9-27
STILL, THEY'RE PRETTY SMART.. THEY'LL FIND SOMETHING USEFUL TO DO..
© 1999 United Feature Syndicate, Inc.
YOU KNOW WHAT WE SHOULD DO? WE SHOULD BUY BANJOS..
SCHULZ

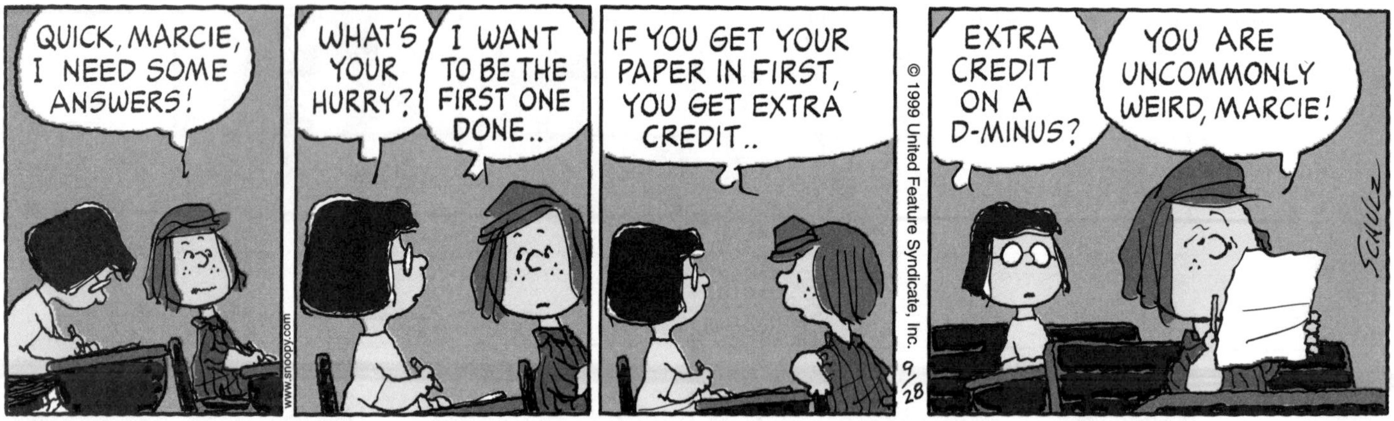
QUICK, MARCIE, I NEED SOME ANSWERS!
www.snoopy.com
WHAT'S YOUR HURRY?
I WANT TO BE THE FIRST ONE DONE..
IF YOU GET YOUR PAPER IN FIRST, YOU GET EXTRA CREDIT..
© 1999 United Feature Syndicate, Inc.
9/28
EXTRA CREDIT ON A D-MINUS?
YOU ARE UNCOMMONLY WEIRD, MARCIE!
SCHULZ

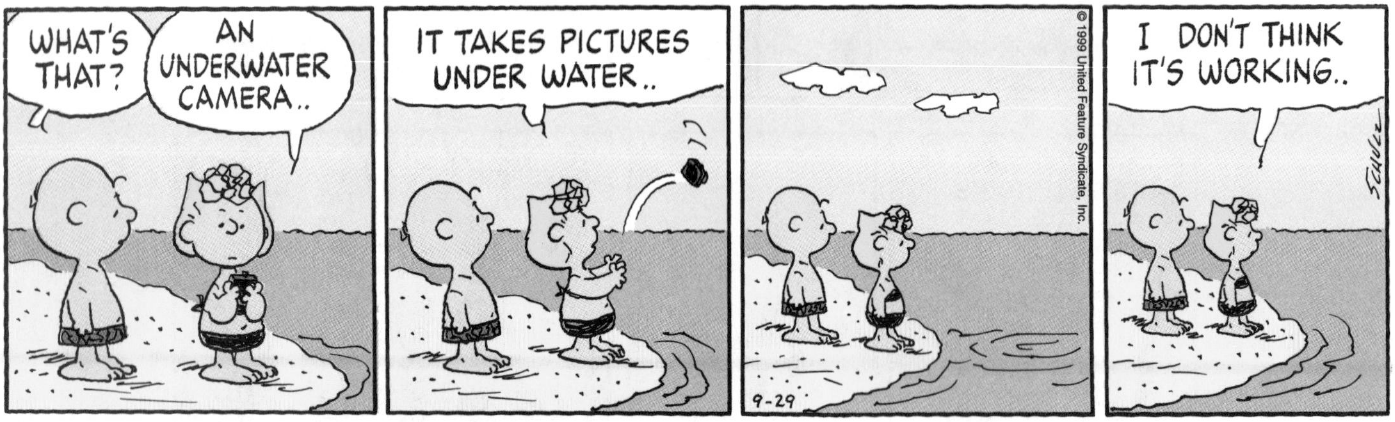
WHAT'S THAT?
AN UNDERWATER CAMERA..
IT TAKES PICTURES UNDER WATER..
9-29
© 1999 United Feature Syndicate, Inc.
I DON'T THINK IT'S WORKING..
SCHULZ

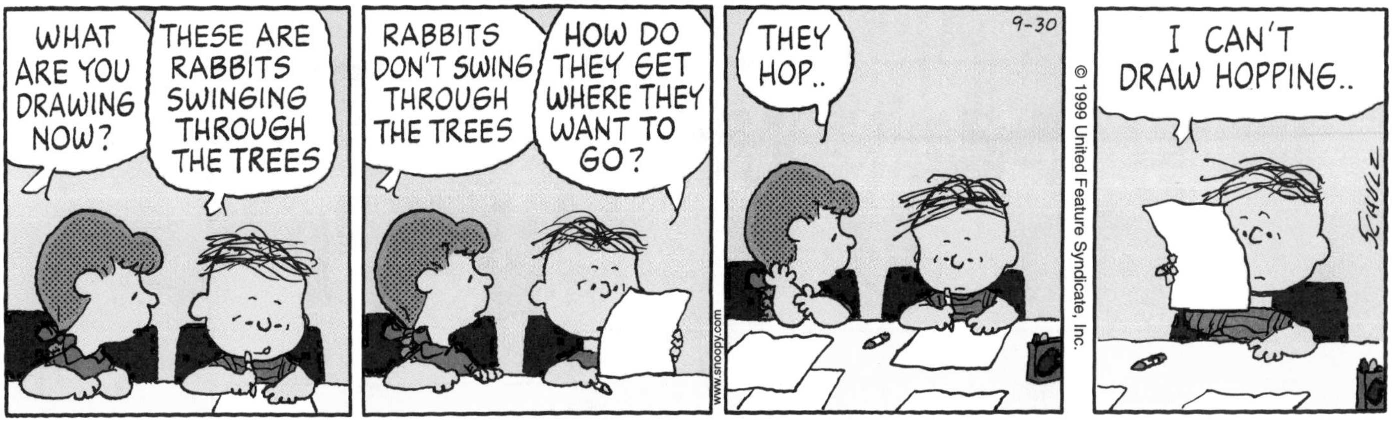
WHAT ARE YOU DRAWING NOW?
THESE ARE RABBITS SWINGING THROUGH THE TREES
RABBITS DON'T SWING THROUGH THE TREES
HOW DO THEY GET WHERE THEY WANT TO GO?
9-30
THEY HOP..
I CAN'T DRAW HOPPING..
SCHULZ

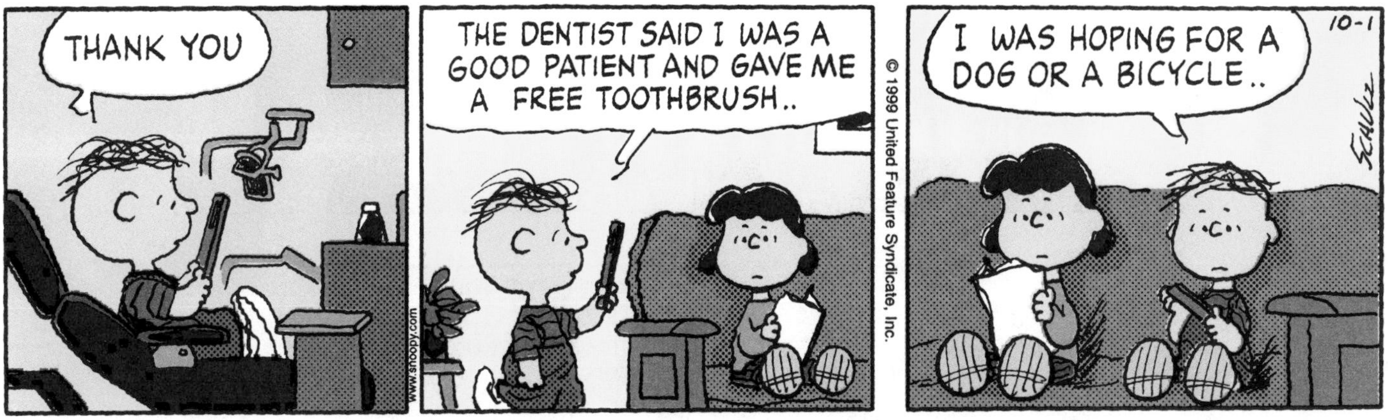
THANK YOU
THE DENTIST SAID I WAS A GOOD PATIENT AND GAVE ME A FREE TOOTHBRUSH..
10-1
I WAS HOPING FOR A DOG OR A BICYCLE..
SCHULZ

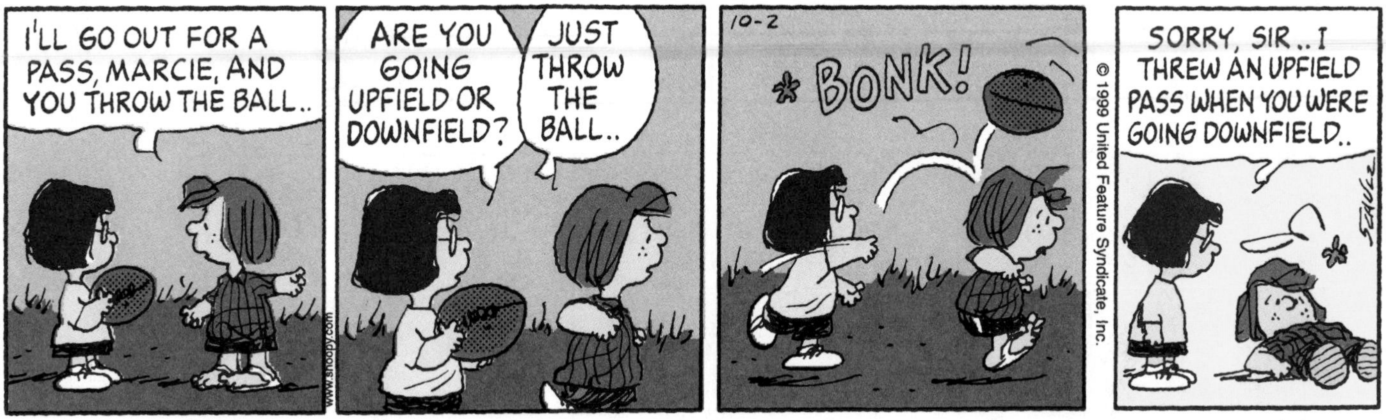
I'LL GO OUT FOR A PASS, MARCIE, AND YOU THROW THE BALL..
ARE YOU GOING UPFIELD OR DOWNFIELD?
JUST THROW THE BALL..
10-2
BONK!
SORRY, SIR.. I THREW AN UPFIELD PASS WHEN YOU WERE GOING DOWNFIELD..
SCHULZ

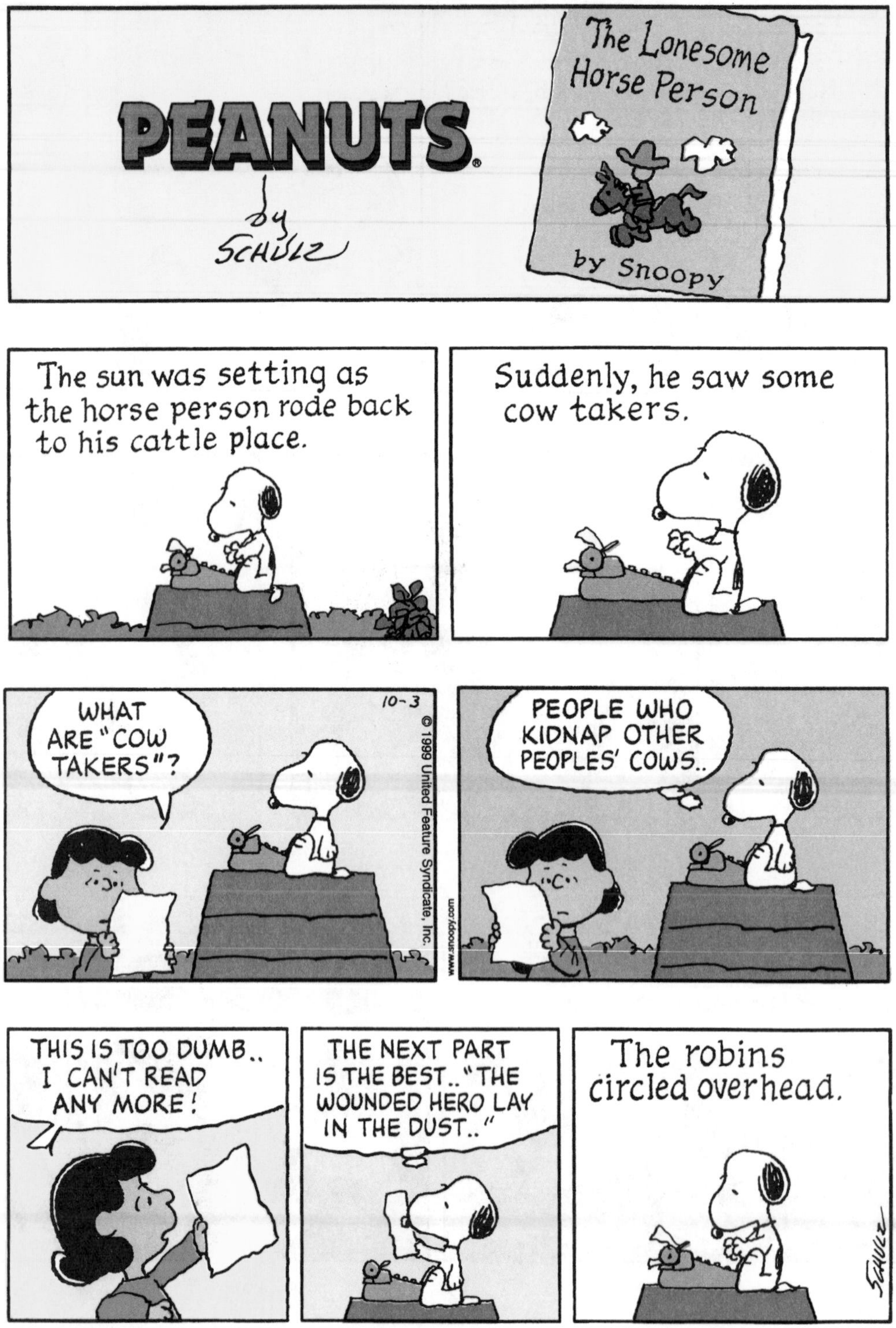
PEANUTS
by SCHULZ
The Lonesome Horse Person
by Snoopy
The sun was setting as the horse person rode back to his cattle place.
Suddenly, he saw some cow takers.
WHAT ARE "COW TAKERS"?
PEOPLE WHO KIDNAP OTHER PEOPLES' COWS..
THIS IS TOO DUMB.. I CAN'T READ ANY MORE!
THE NEXT PART IS THE BEST.."THE WOUNDED HERO LAY IN THE DUST.."
The robins circled overhead.
10-3
© 1999 United Feature Syndicate, Inc.
www.snoopy.com
SCHULZ

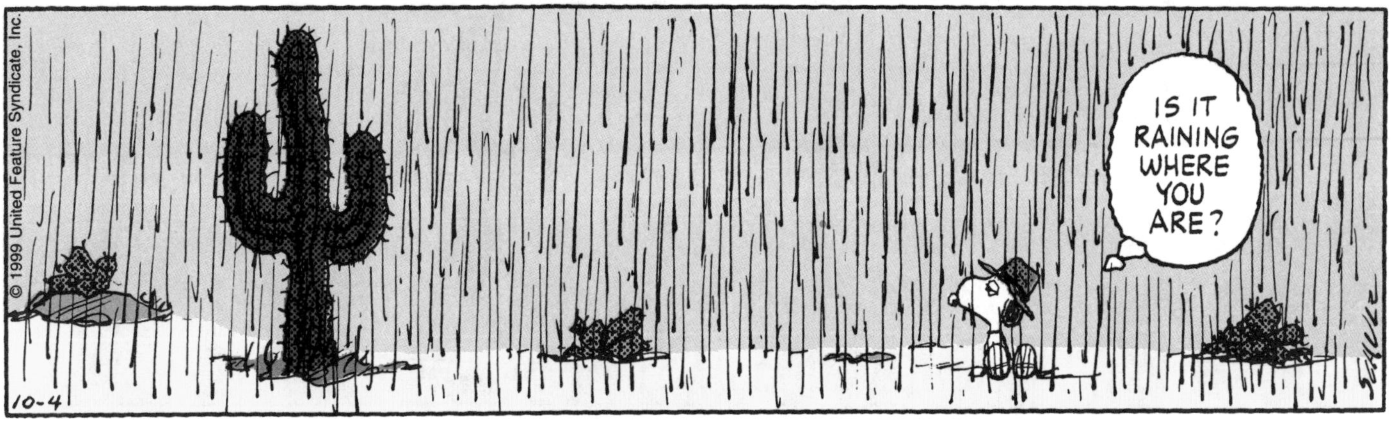
© 1999 United Feature Syndicate, Inc.
IS IT RAINING WHERE YOU ARE?
SCHULZ
10-4

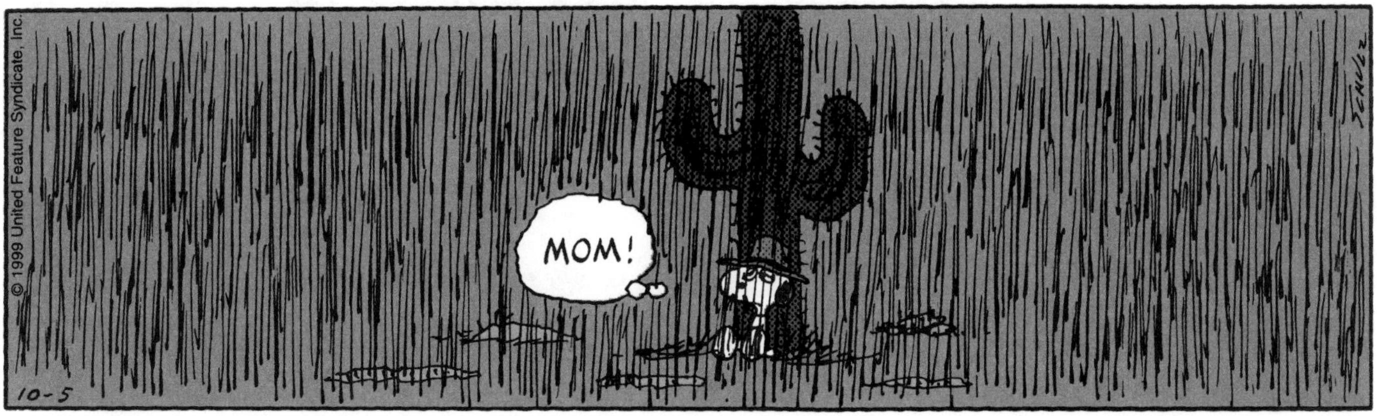
© 1999 United Feature Syndicate, Inc.
MOM!
SCHULZ
10-5

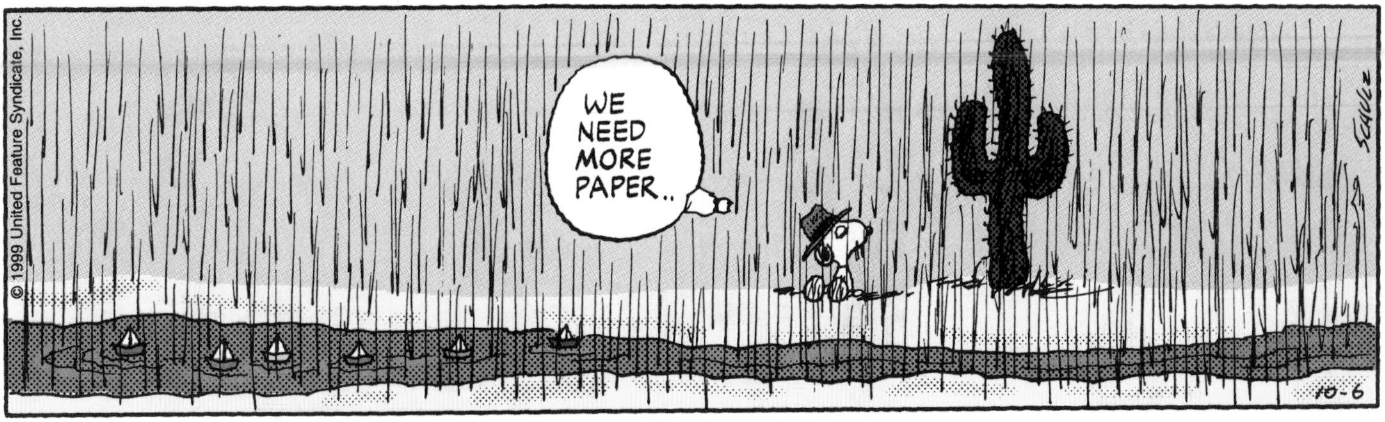
© 1999 United Feature Syndicate, Inc.
WE NEED MORE PAPER..
SCHULZ
10-6

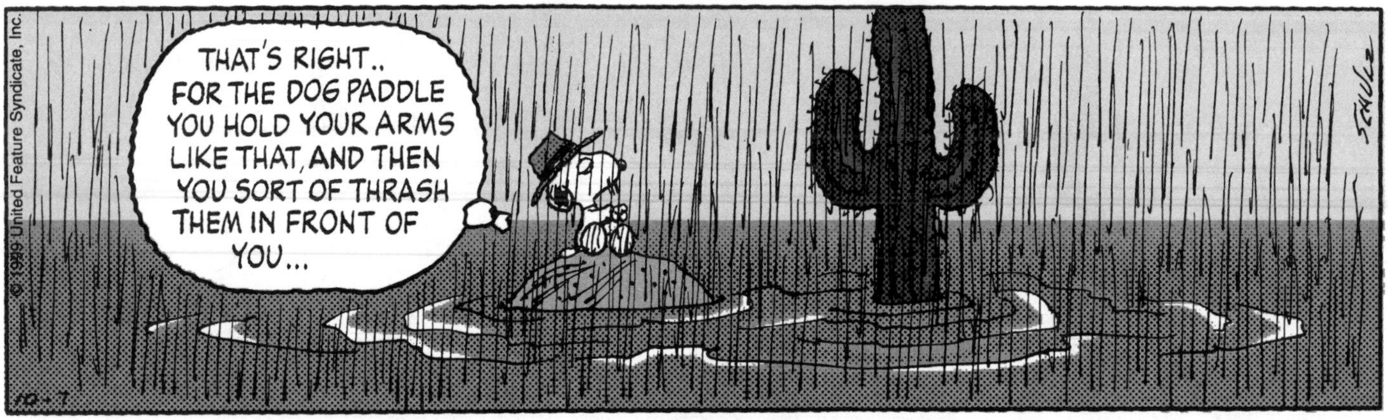
© 1999 United Feature Syndicate, Inc.
THAT'S RIGHT.. FOR THE DOG PADDLE YOU HOLD YOUR ARMS LIKE THAT, AND THEN YOU SORT OF THRASH THEM IN FRONT OF YOU...
SCHULZ
10-7

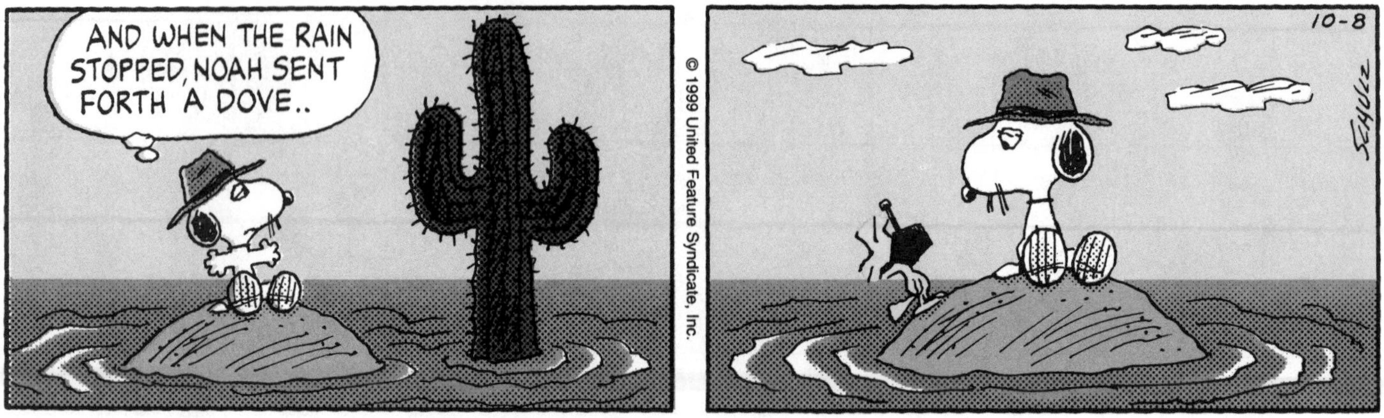
AND WHEN THE RAIN STOPPED, NOAH SENT FORTH A DOVE..
© 1999 United Feature Syndicate, Inc.
10-8
SCHULZ

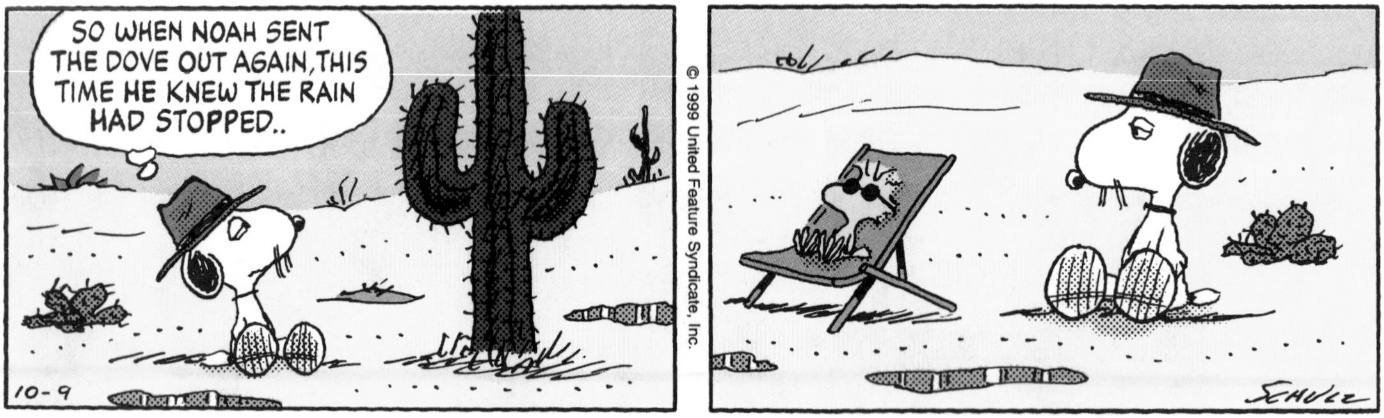
SO WHEN NOAH SENT THE DOVE OUT AGAIN, THIS TIME HE KNEW THE RAIN HAD STOPPED..
10-9
© 1999 United Feature Syndicate, Inc.
SCHULZ

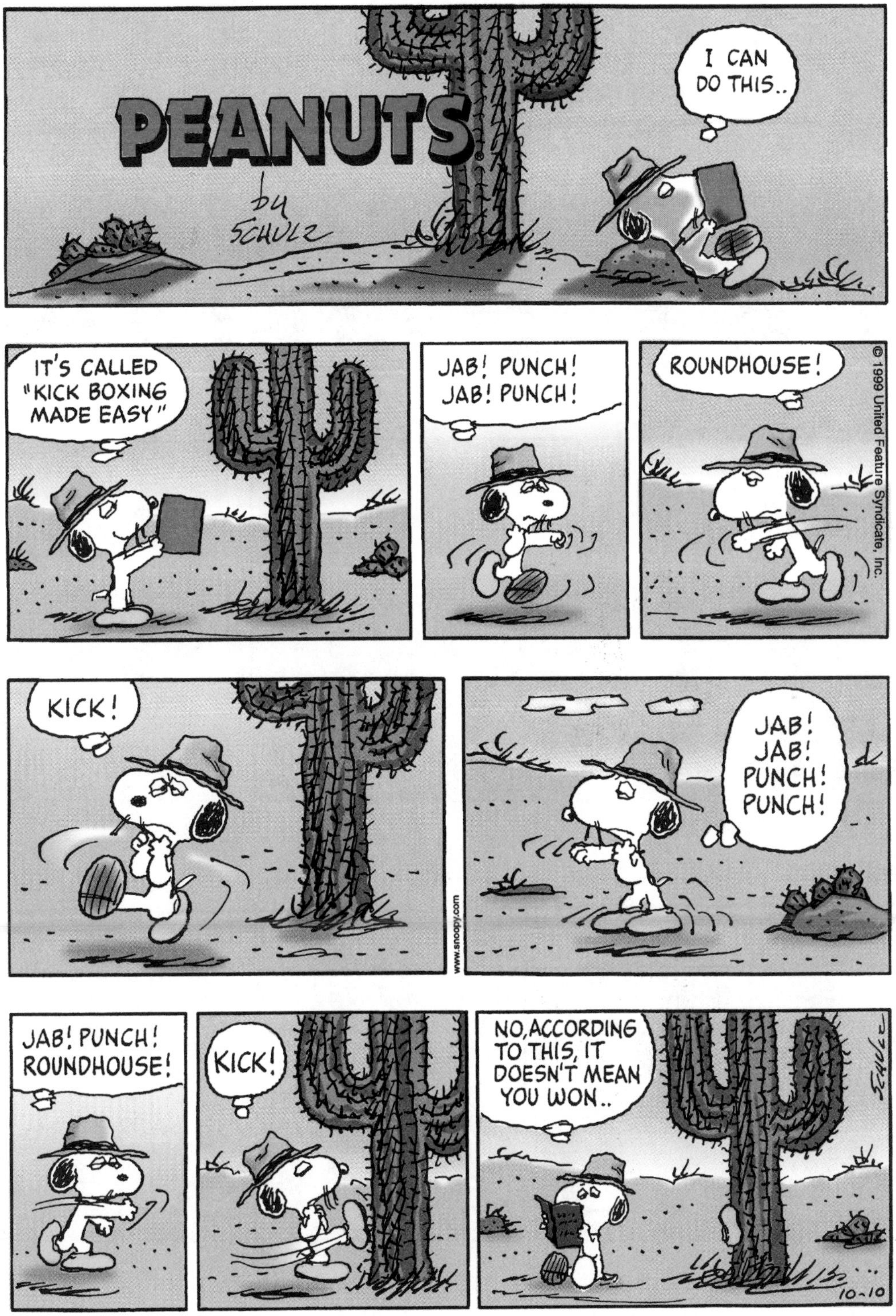
PEANUTS
by SCHULZ
I CAN DO THIS..
IT'S CALLED "KICK BOXING MADE EASY"
JAB! PUNCH! JAB! PUNCH!
ROUNDHOUSE!
© 1999 United Feature Syndicate, Inc.
KICK!
www.snoopy.com
JAB! JAB! PUNCH! PUNCH!
JAB! PUNCH! ROUNDHOUSE!
KICK!
NO, ACCORDING TO THIS, IT DOESN'T MEAN YOU WON..
SCHULZ
10-10

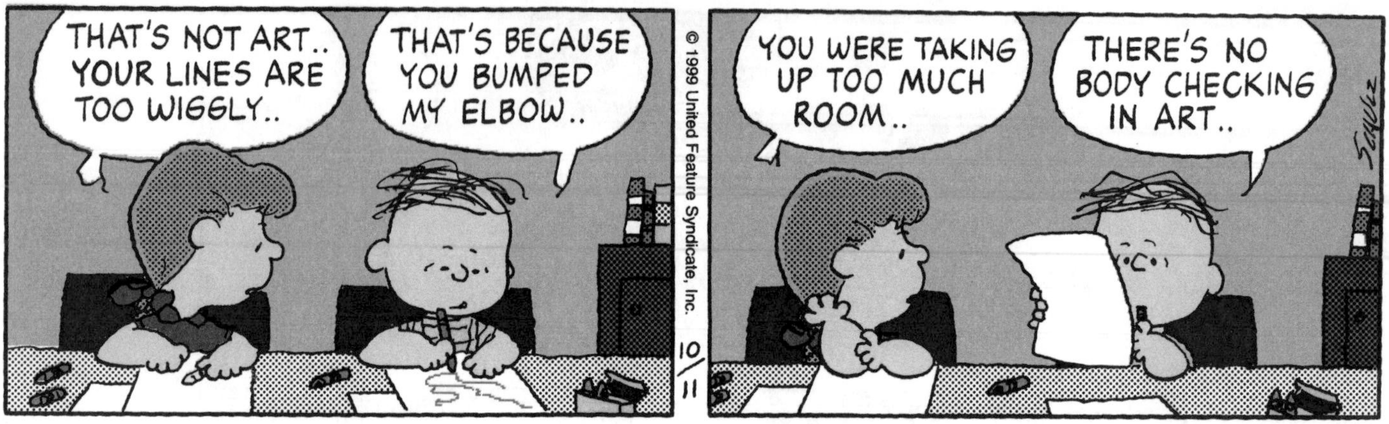
THAT'S NOT ART.. YOUR LINES ARE TOO WIGGLY..
THAT'S BECAUSE YOU BUMPED MY ELBOW..
YOU WERE TAKING UP TOO MUCH ROOM..
THERE'S NO BODY CHECKING IN ART..
© 1999 United Feature Syndicate, Inc.
10/11
SCHULZ

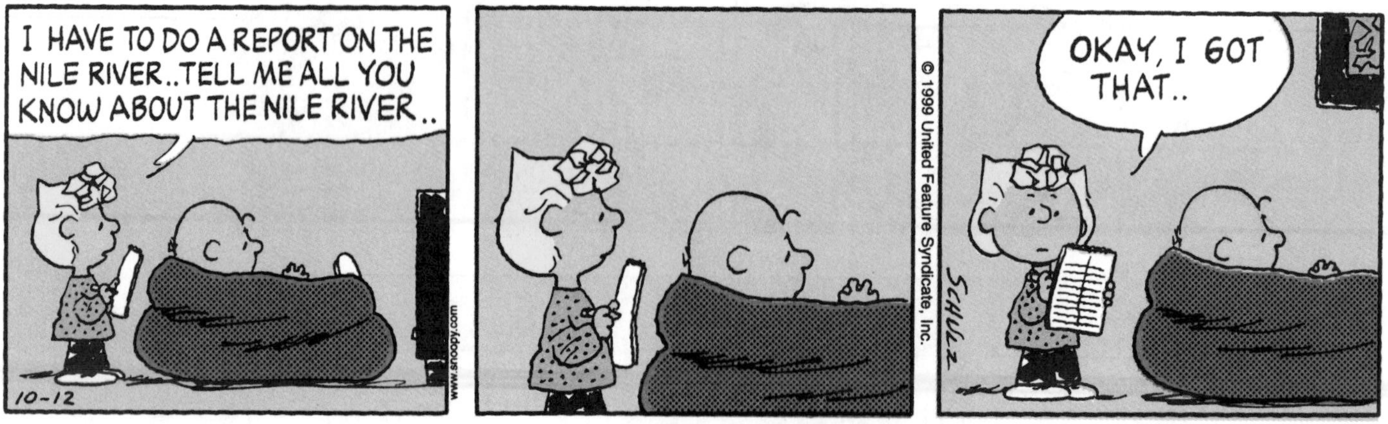
I HAVE TO DO A REPORT ON THE NILE RIVER..TELL ME ALL YOU KNOW ABOUT THE NILE RIVER..
10-12
www.snoopy.com
© 1999 United Feature Syndicate, Inc.
OKAY, I GOT THAT..
SCHULZ

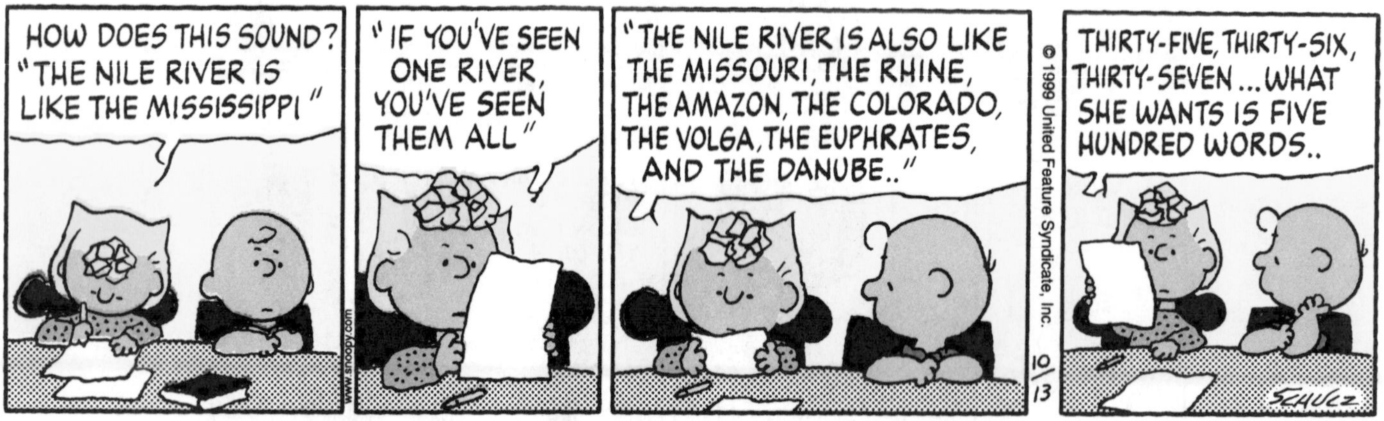
HOW DOES THIS SOUND? "THE NILE RIVER IS LIKE THE MISSISSIPPI"
www.snoopy.com
"IF YOU'VE SEEN ONE RIVER, YOU'VE SEEN THEM ALL"
"THE NILE RIVER IS ALSO LIKE THE MISSOURI, THE RHINE, THE AMAZON, THE COLORADO, THE VOLGA, THE EUPHRATES, AND THE DANUBE.."
© 1999 United Feature Syndicate, Inc.
10/13
THIRTY-FIVE, THIRTY-SIX, THIRTY-SEVEN ... WHAT SHE WANTS IS FIVE HUNDRED WORDS..
SCHULZ

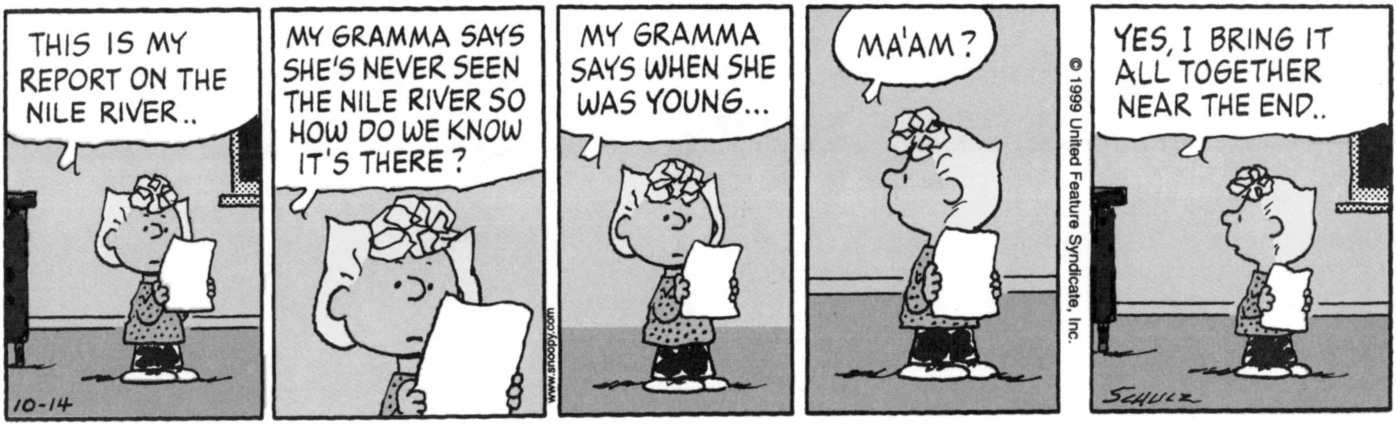
THIS IS MY REPORT ON THE NILE RIVER..
MY GRAMMA SAYS SHE'S NEVER SEEN THE NILE RIVER SO HOW DO WE KNOW IT'S THERE?
MY GRAMMA SAYS WHEN SHE WAS YOUNG...
MA'AM?
YES, I BRING IT ALL TOGETHER NEAR THE END..
10-14
www.snoopy.com
© 1999 United Feature Syndicate, Inc.
SCHULZ

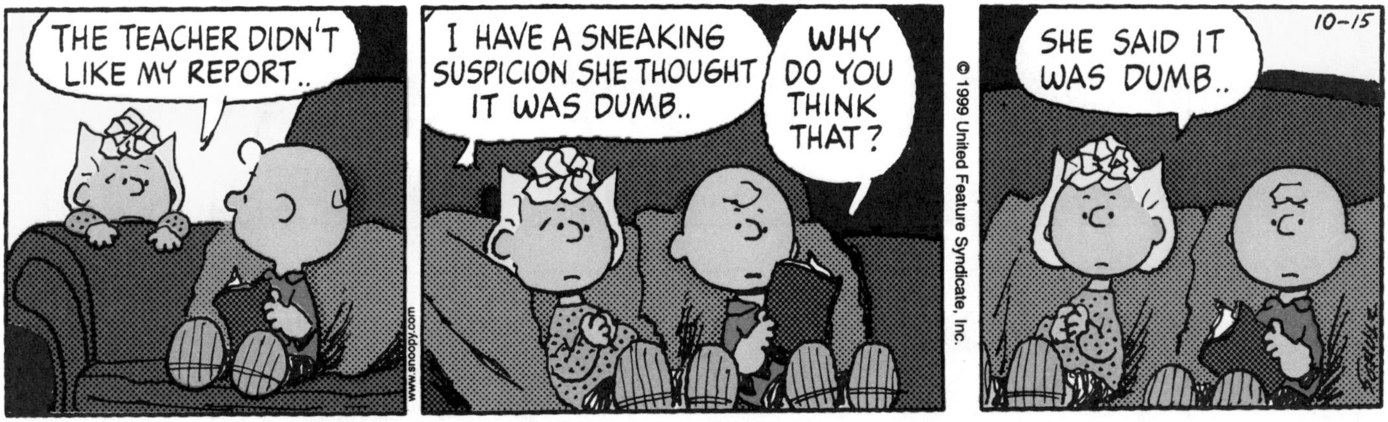
THE TEACHER DIDN'T LIKE MY REPORT..
I HAVE A SNEAKING SUSPICION SHE THOUGHT IT WAS DUMB..
WHY DO YOU THINK THAT?
SHE SAID IT WAS DUMB..
10-15
www.snoopy.com
© 1999 United Feature Syndicate, Inc.

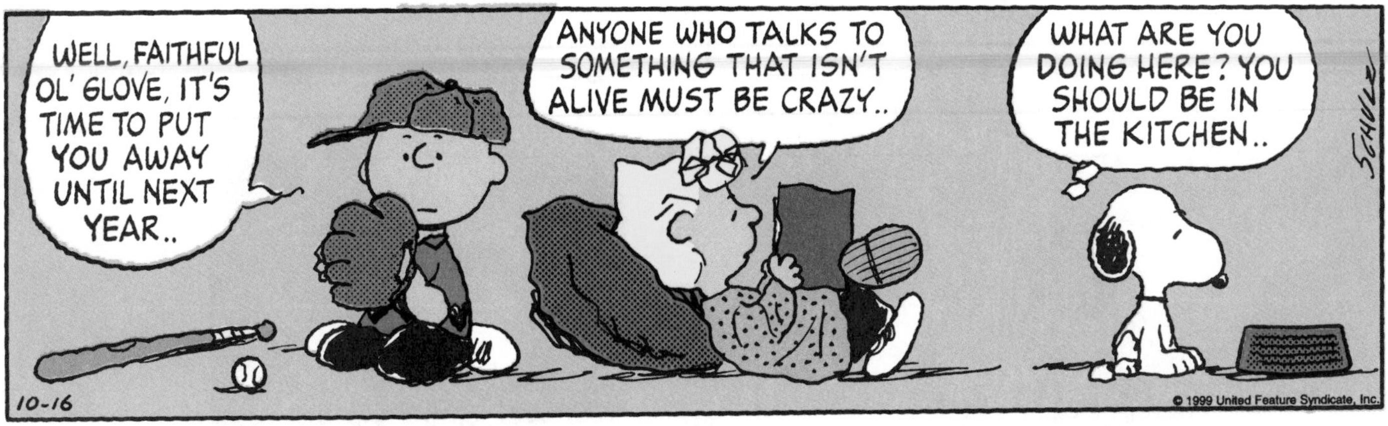
WELL, FAITHFUL OL' GLOVE, IT'S TIME TO PUT YOU AWAY UNTIL NEXT YEAR..
ANYONE WHO TALKS TO SOMETHING THAT ISN'T ALIVE MUST BE CRAZY..
WHAT ARE YOU DOING HERE? YOU SHOULD BE IN THE KITCHEN..
SCHULZ
10-16
© 1999 United Feature Syndicate, Inc.

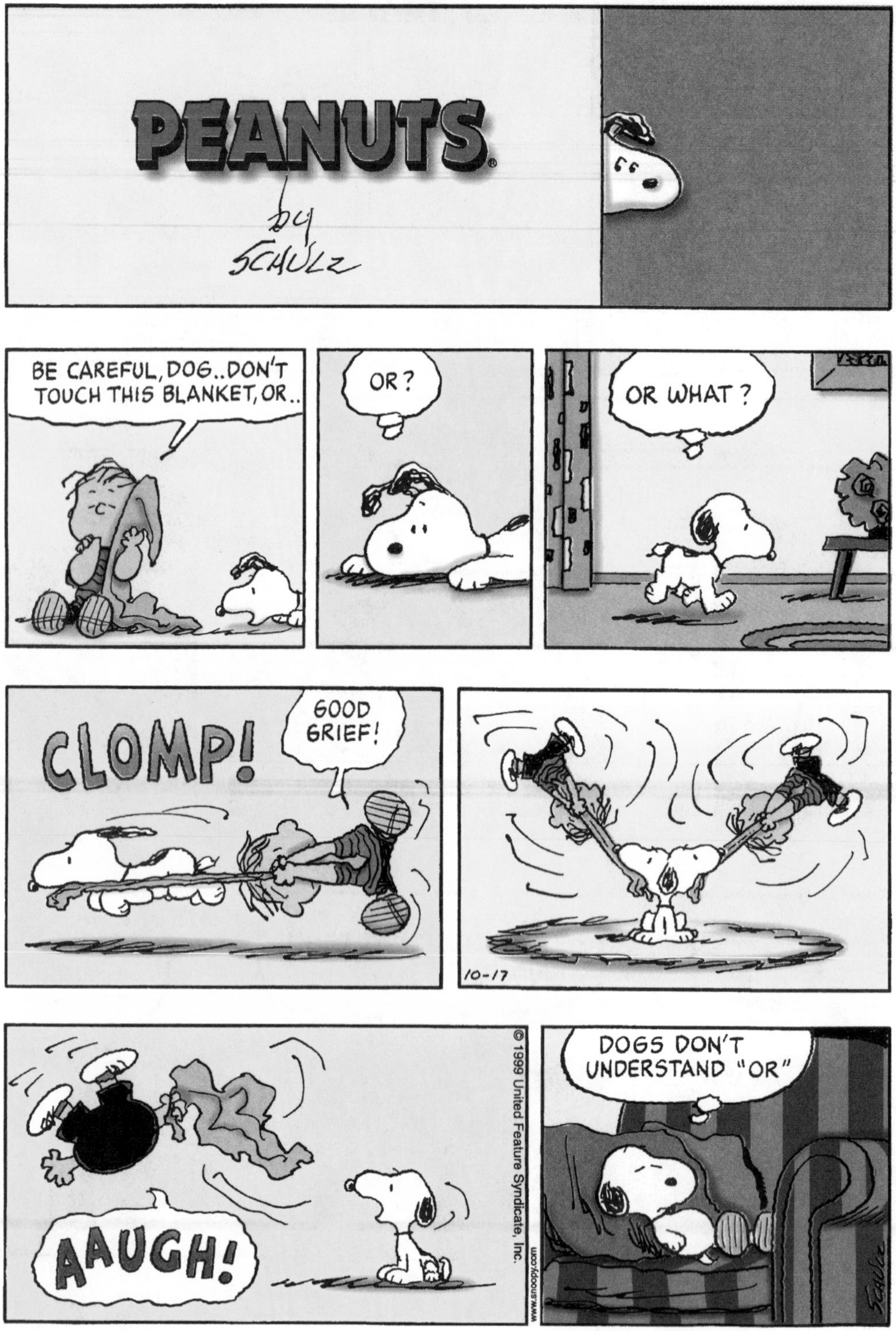
PEANUTS
by SCHULZ
BE CAREFUL, DOG..DON'T TOUCH THIS BLANKET, OR..
OR?
OR WHAT?
CLOMP!
GOOD GRIEF!
10-17
AAUGH!
© 1999 United Feature Syndicate, Inc.
www.snoopy.com
DOGS DON'T UNDERSTAND "OR"
SCHULZ

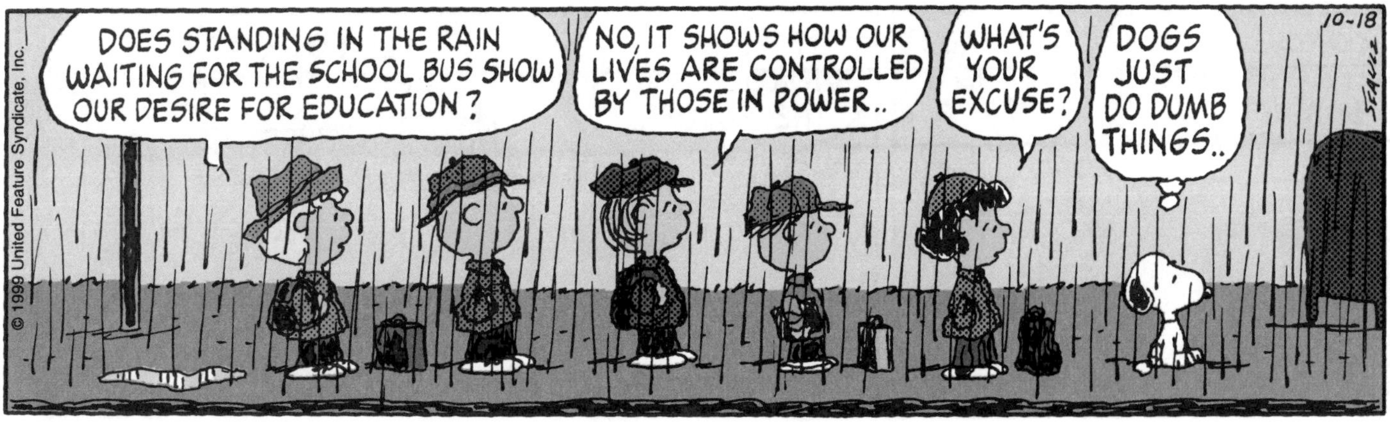
DOES STANDING IN THE RAIN WAITING FOR THE SCHOOL BUS SHOW OUR DESIRE FOR EDUCATION?
NO, IT SHOWS HOW OUR LIVES ARE CONTROLLED BY THOSE IN POWER..
WHAT'S YOUR EXCUSE?
DOGS JUST DO DUMB THINGS..
10-18
SCHULZ
© 1999 United Feature Syndicate, Inc.

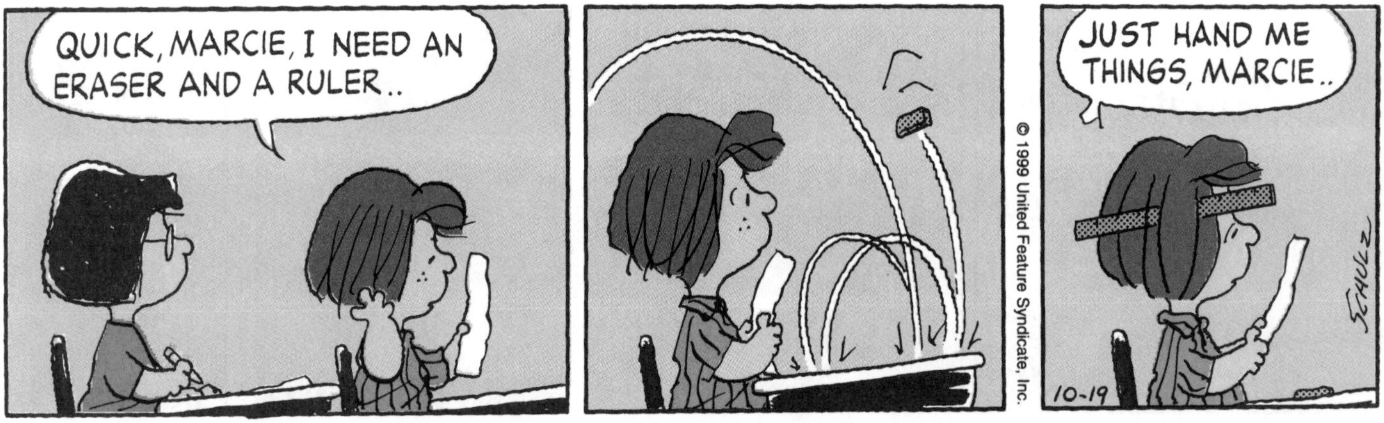
QUICK, MARCIE, I NEED AN ERASER AND A RULER..
JUST HAND ME THINGS, MARCIE..
10-19
SCHULZ
© 1999 United Feature Syndicate, Inc.

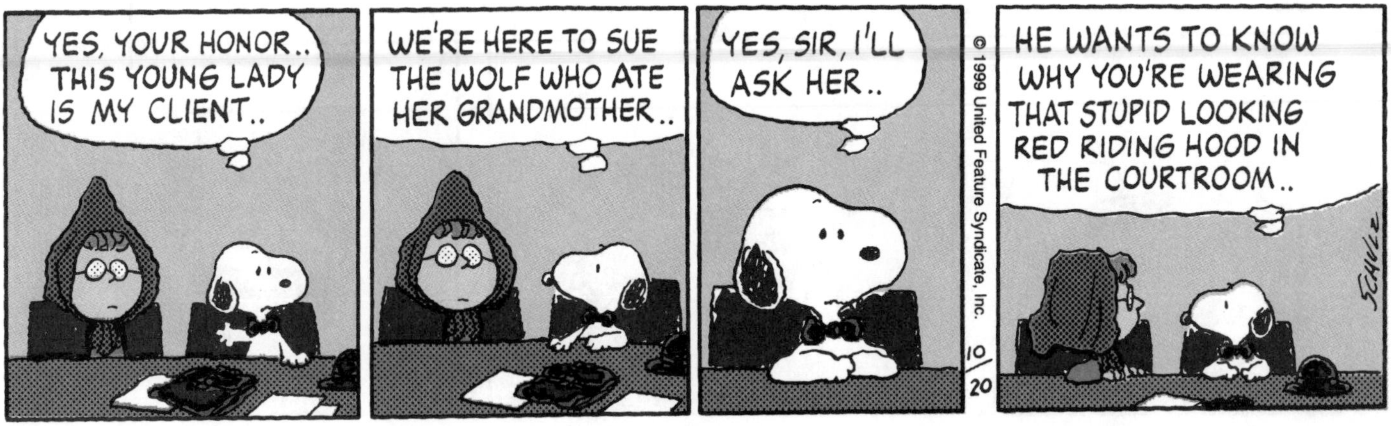
YES, YOUR HONOR.. THIS YOUNG LADY IS MY CLIENT..
WE'RE HERE TO SUE THE WOLF WHO ATE HER GRANDMOTHER..
YES, SIR, I'LL ASK HER..
HE WANTS TO KNOW WHY YOU'RE WEARING THAT STUPID LOOKING RED RIDING HOOD IN THE COURTROOM..
10/20
SCHULZ
© 1999 United Feature Syndicate, Inc.

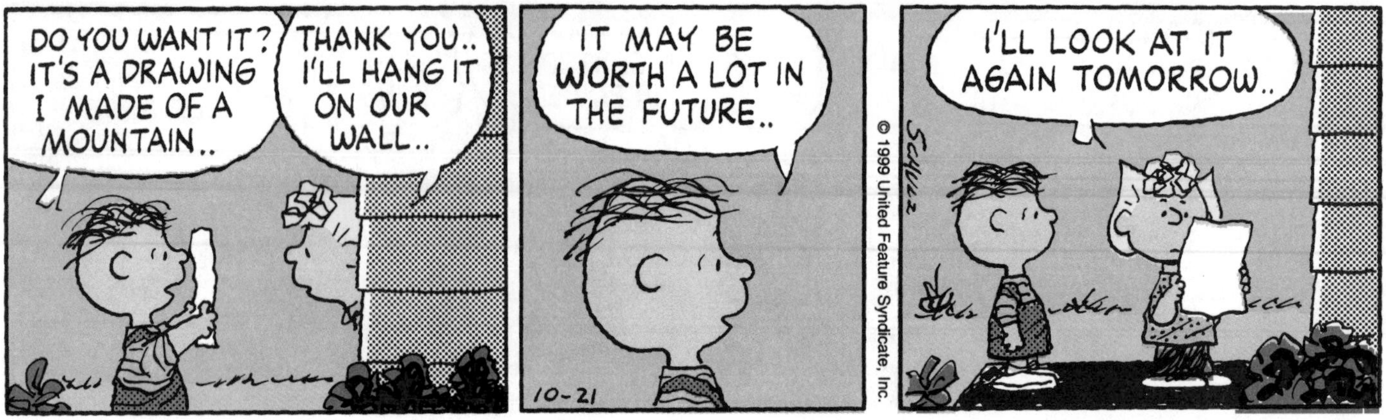
DO YOU WANT IT? IT'S A DRAWING I MADE OF A MOUNTAIN..
THANK YOU.. I'LL HANG IT ON OUR WALL..
IT MAY BE WORTH A LOT IN THE FUTURE..
10-21
I'LL LOOK AT IT AGAIN TOMORROW..
SCHULZ

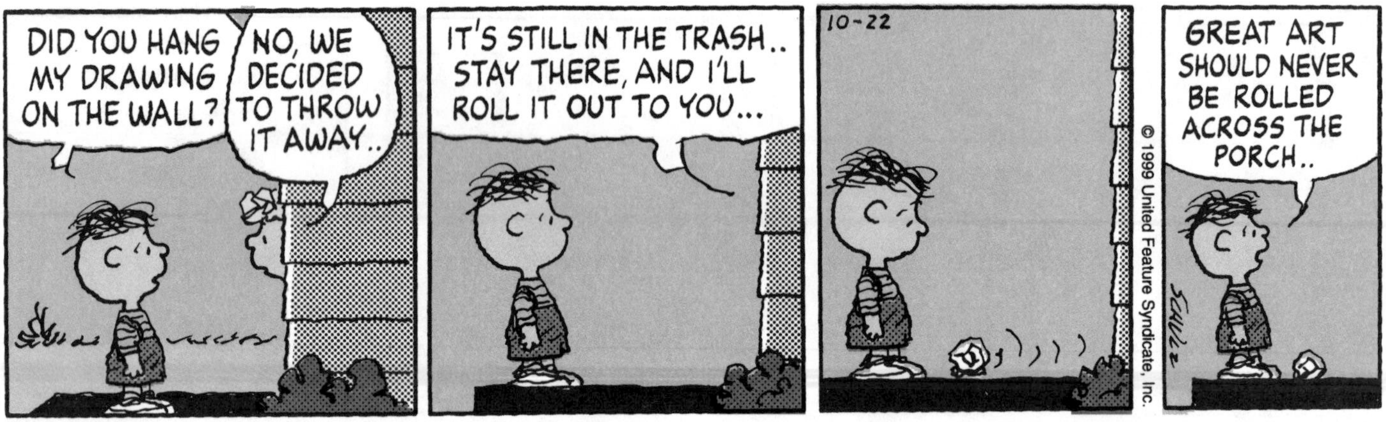
DID YOU HANG MY DRAWING ON THE WALL?
NO, WE DECIDED TO THROW IT AWAY..
IT'S STILL IN THE TRASH.. STAY THERE, AND I'LL ROLL IT OUT TO YOU...
10-22
GREAT ART SHOULD NEVER BE ROLLED ACROSS THE PORCH..
SCHULZ

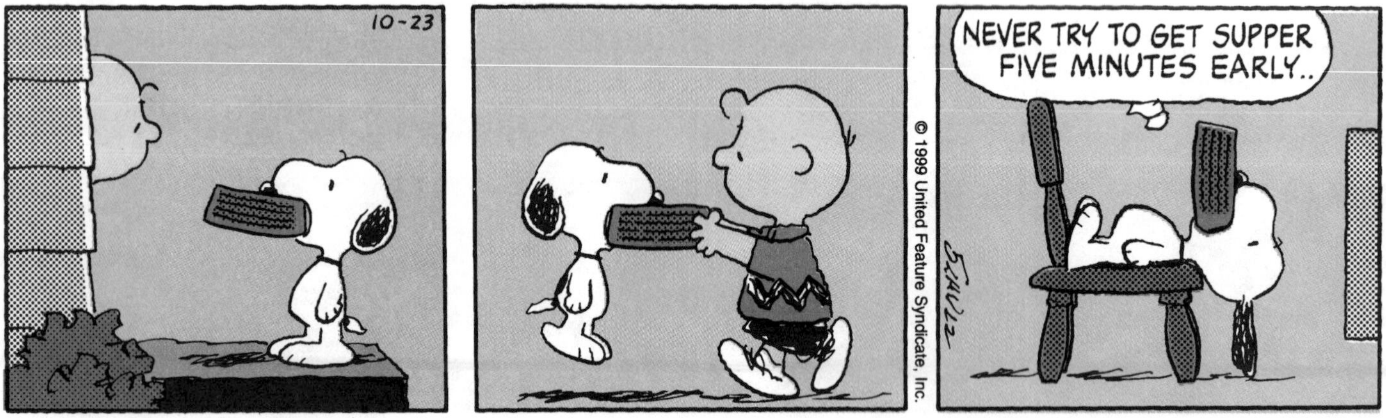
10-23
NEVER TRY TO GET SUPPER FIVE MINUTES EARLY..
SCHULZ

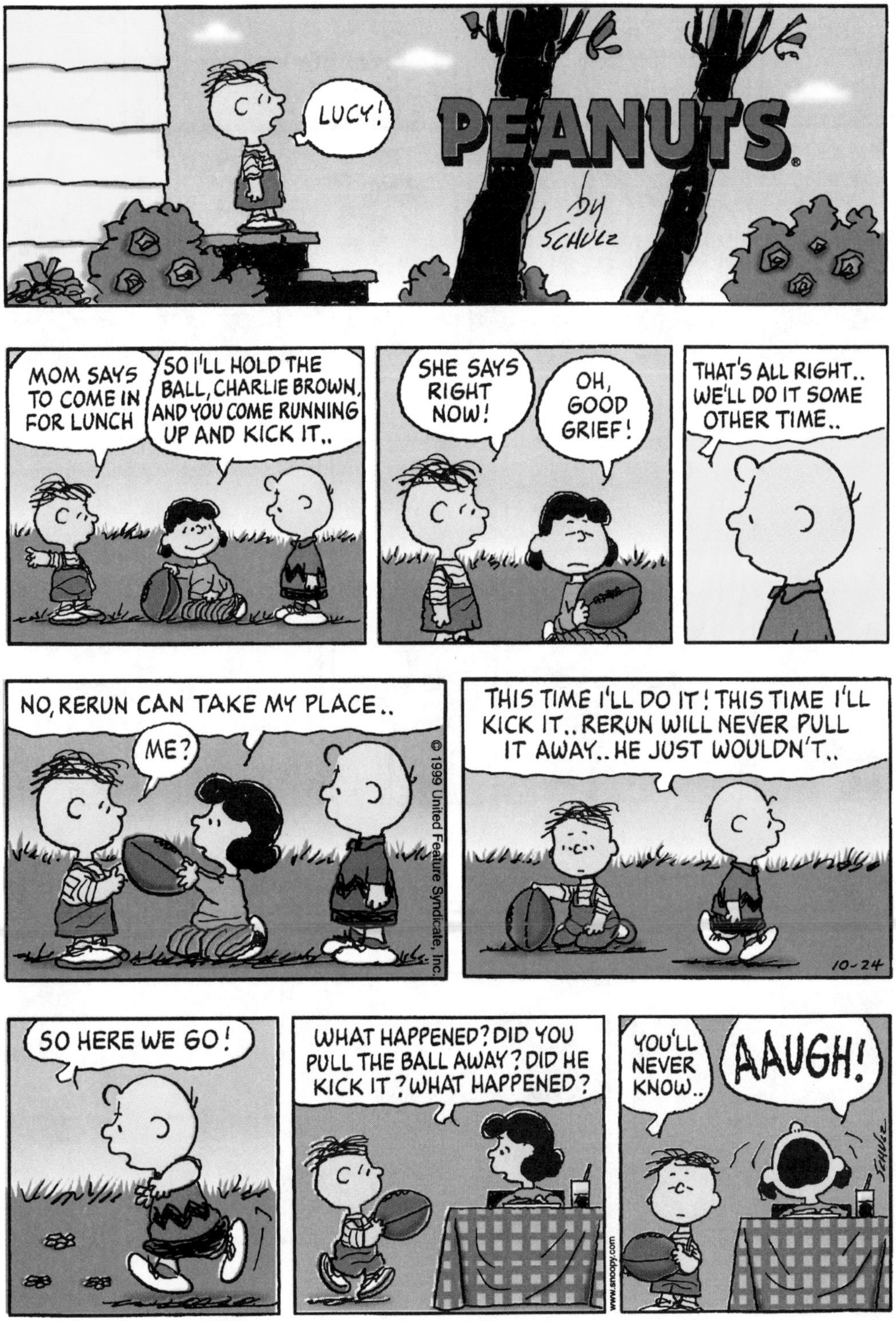
LUCY!
PEANUTS
by SCHULZ
MOM SAYS TO COME IN FOR LUNCH
SO I'LL HOLD THE BALL, CHARLIE BROWN, AND YOU COME RUNNING UP AND KICK IT..
SHE SAYS RIGHT NOW!
OH, GOOD GRIEF!
THAT'S ALL RIGHT.. WE'LL DO IT SOME OTHER TIME..
NO, RERUN CAN TAKE MY PLACE..
ME?
© 1999 United Feature Syndicate, Inc.
THIS TIME I'LL DO IT! THIS TIME I'LL KICK IT.. RERUN WILL NEVER PULL IT AWAY.. HE JUST WOULDN'T..
10-24
SO HERE WE GO!
WHAT HAPPENED? DID YOU PULL THE BALL AWAY? DID HE KICK IT? WHAT HAPPENED?
www.snoopy.com
YOU'LL NEVER KNOW..
AAUGH!
SCHULZ

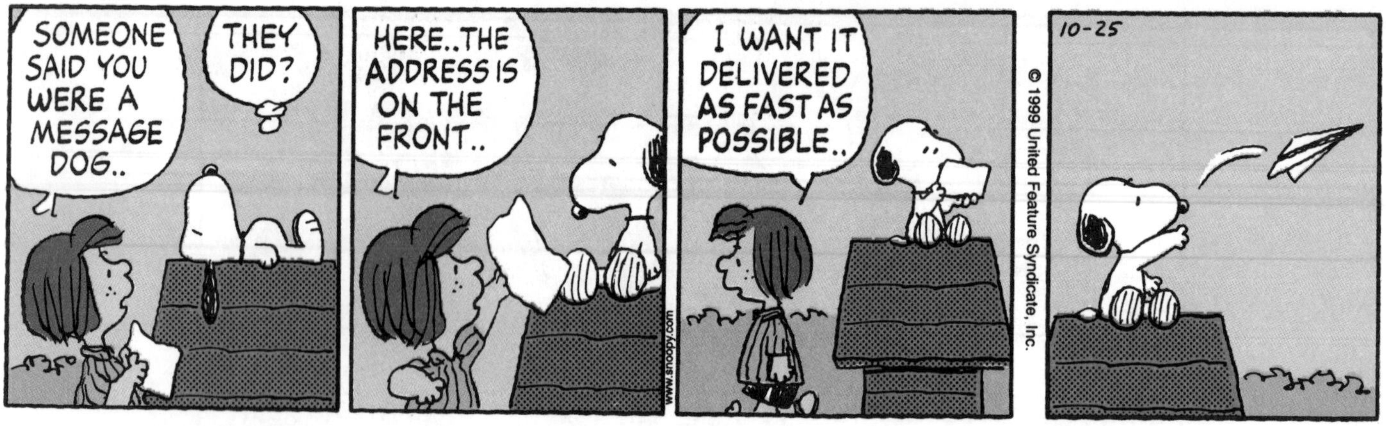
SOMEONE SAID YOU WERE A MESSAGE DOG..
THEY DID?
HERE..THE ADDRESS IS ON THE FRONT..
I WANT IT DELIVERED AS FAST AS POSSIBLE..
10-25
© 1999 United Feature Syndicate, Inc.
www.snoopy.com

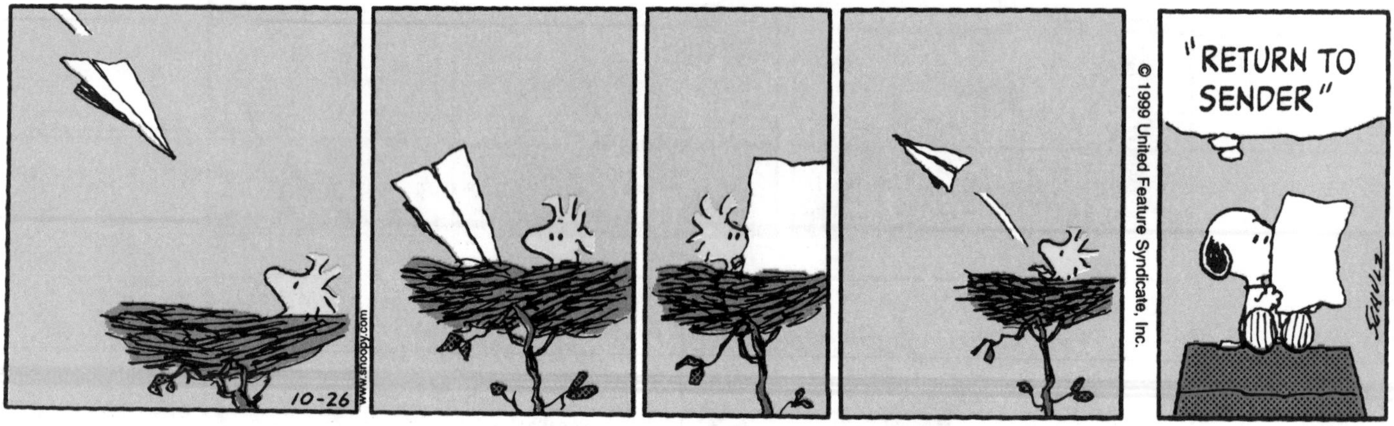
10-26
www.snoopy.com
© 1999 United Feature Syndicate, Inc.
"RETURN TO SENDER"
SCHULZ

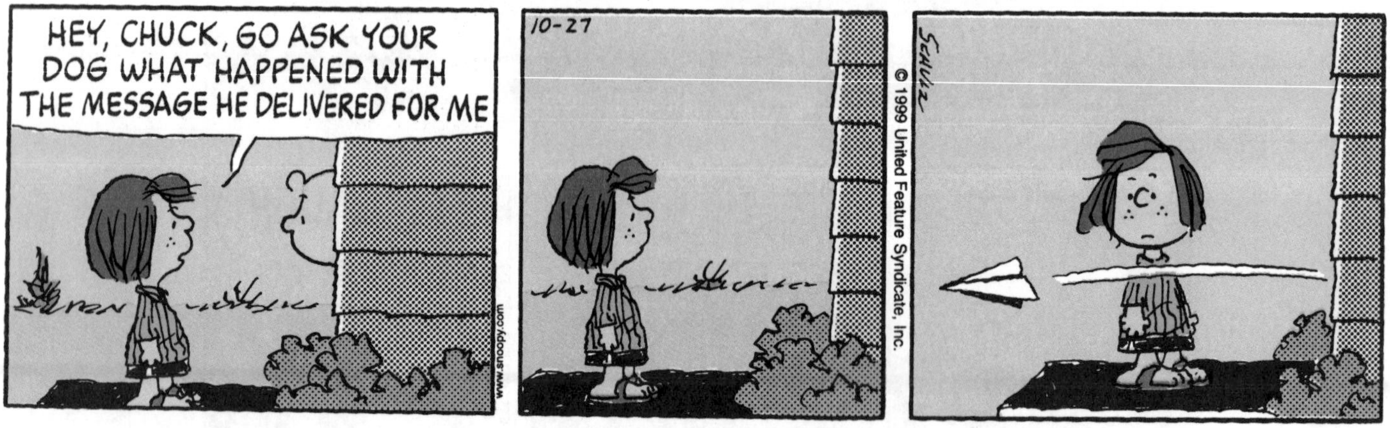
HEY, CHUCK, GO ASK YOUR DOG WHAT HAPPENED WITH THE MESSAGE HE DELIVERED FOR ME
www.snoopy.com
10-27
© 1999 United Feature Syndicate, Inc.
SCHULZ

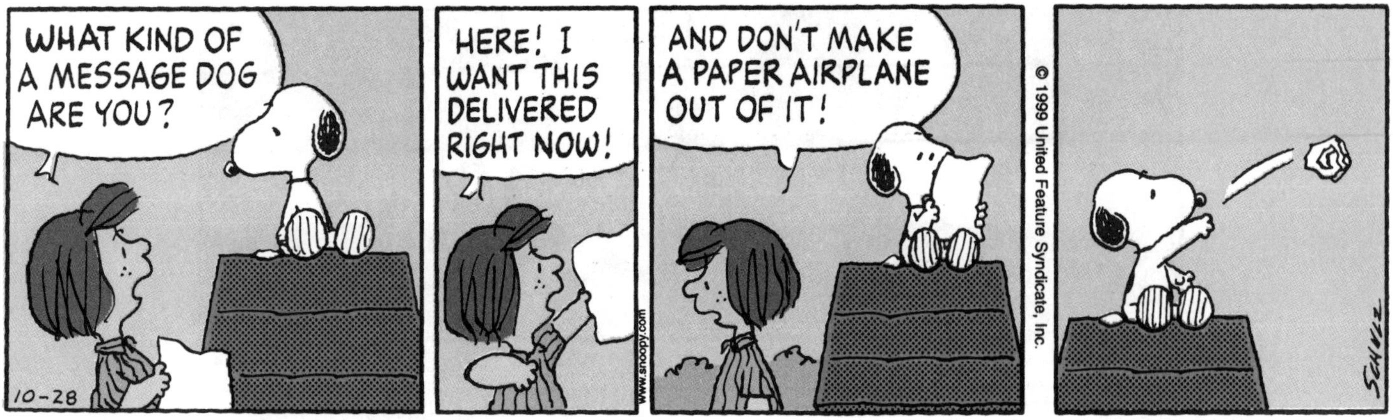
WHAT KIND OF A MESSAGE DOG ARE YOU?
HERE! I WANT THIS DELIVERED RIGHT NOW!
AND DON'T MAKE A PAPER AIRPLANE OUT OF IT!
10-28
www.snoopy.com
© 1999 United Feature Syndicate, Inc.
SCHULZ

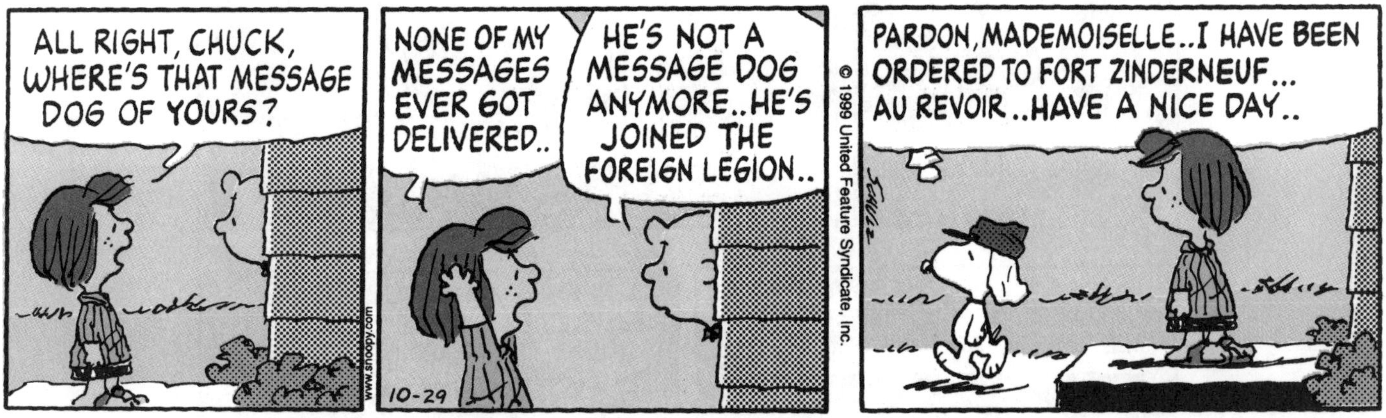
ALL RIGHT, CHUCK, WHERE'S THAT MESSAGE DOG OF YOURS?
NONE OF MY MESSAGES EVER GOT DELIVERED..
HE'S NOT A MESSAGE DOG ANYMORE..HE'S JOINED THE FOREIGN LEGION..
PARDON, MADEMOISELLE..I HAVE BEEN ORDERED TO FORT ZINDERNEUF... AU REVOIR..HAVE A NICE DAY..
10-29
www.snoopy.com
© 1999 United Feature Syndicate, Inc.
SCHULZ

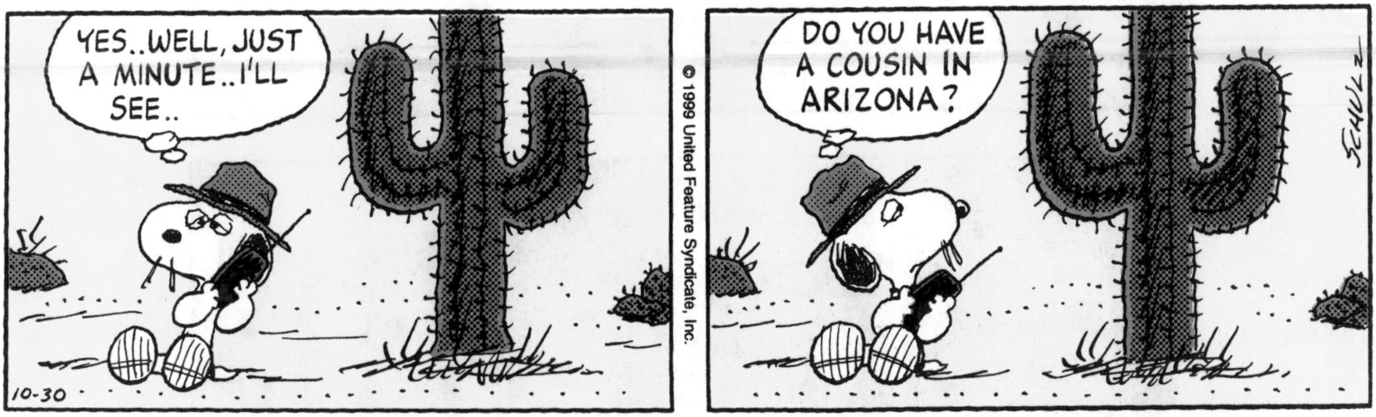
YES..WELL, JUST A MINUTE..I'LL SEE..
DO YOU HAVE A COUSIN IN ARIZONA?
10-30
© 1999 United Feature Syndicate, Inc.
SCHULZ

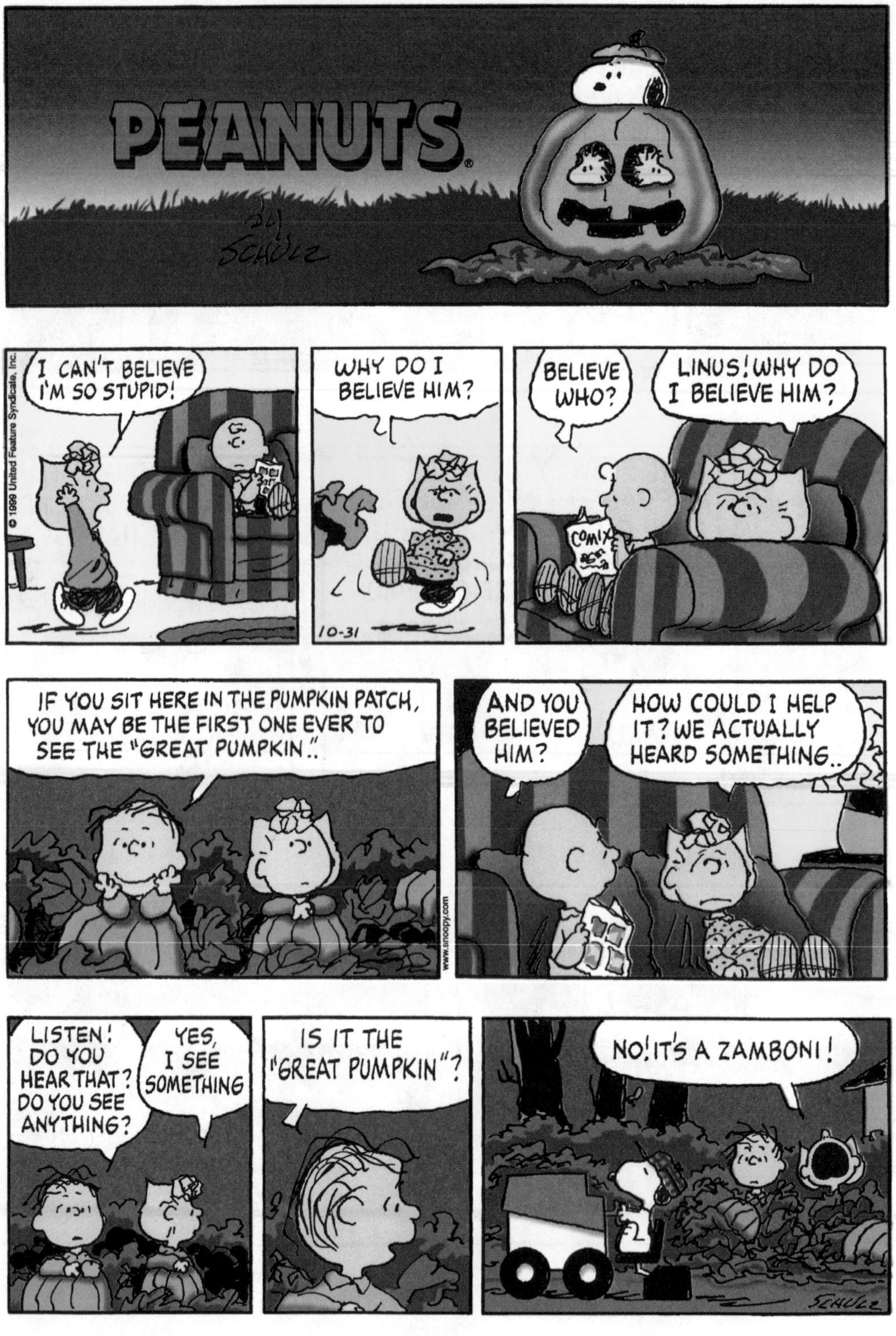
PEANUTS
SCHULZ
© 1999 United Feature Syndicate, Inc.
I CAN'T BELIEVE I'M SO STUPID!
WHY DO I BELIEVE HIM?
10-31
BELIEVE WHO?
LINUS! WHY DO I BELIEVE HIM?
COMIX
IF YOU SIT HERE IN THE PUMPKIN PATCH, YOU MAY BE THE FIRST ONE EVER TO SEE THE "GREAT PUMPKIN."
www.snoopy.com
AND YOU BELIEVED HIM?
HOW COULD I HELP IT? WE ACTUALLY HEARD SOMETHING..
LISTEN! DO YOU HEAR THAT? DO YOU SEE ANYTHING?
YES, I SEE SOMETHING
IS IT THE "GREAT PUMPKIN"?
NO! IT'S A ZAMBONI!
SCHULZ

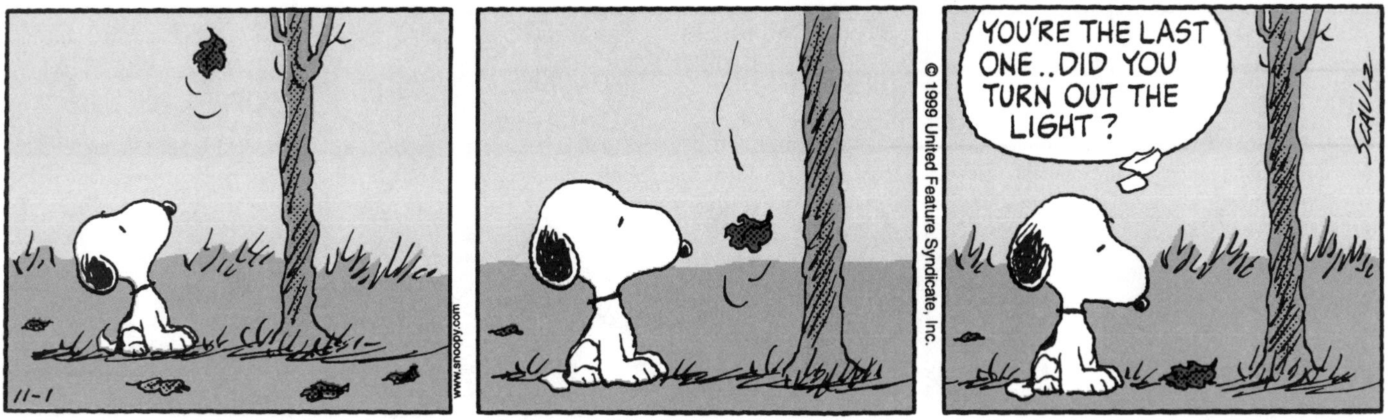
11-1
www.snoopy.com
© 1999 United Feature Syndicate, Inc.
YOU'RE THE LAST ONE..DID YOU TURN OUT THE LIGHT ?
SCHULZ

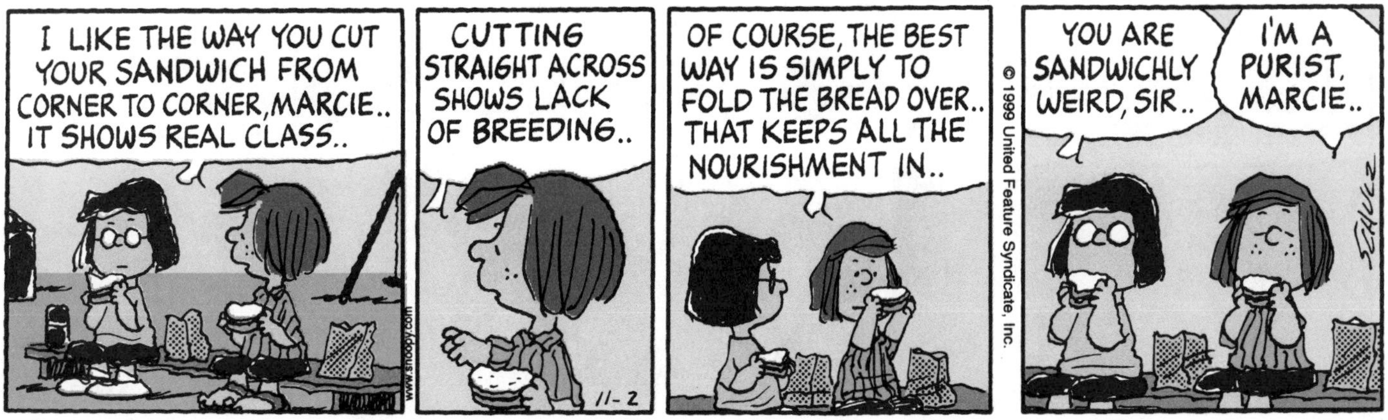
I LIKE THE WAY YOU CUT YOUR SANDWICH FROM CORNER TO CORNER, MARCIE.. IT SHOWS REAL CLASS..
www.snoopy.com
CUTTING STRAIGHT ACROSS SHOWS LACK OF BREEDING..
11-2
OF COURSE, THE BEST WAY IS SIMPLY TO FOLD THE BREAD OVER.. THAT KEEPS ALL THE NOURISHMENT IN..
© 1999 United Feature Syndicate, Inc.
YOU ARE SANDWICHLY WEIRD, SIR..
I'M A PURIST, MARCIE..
SCHULZ

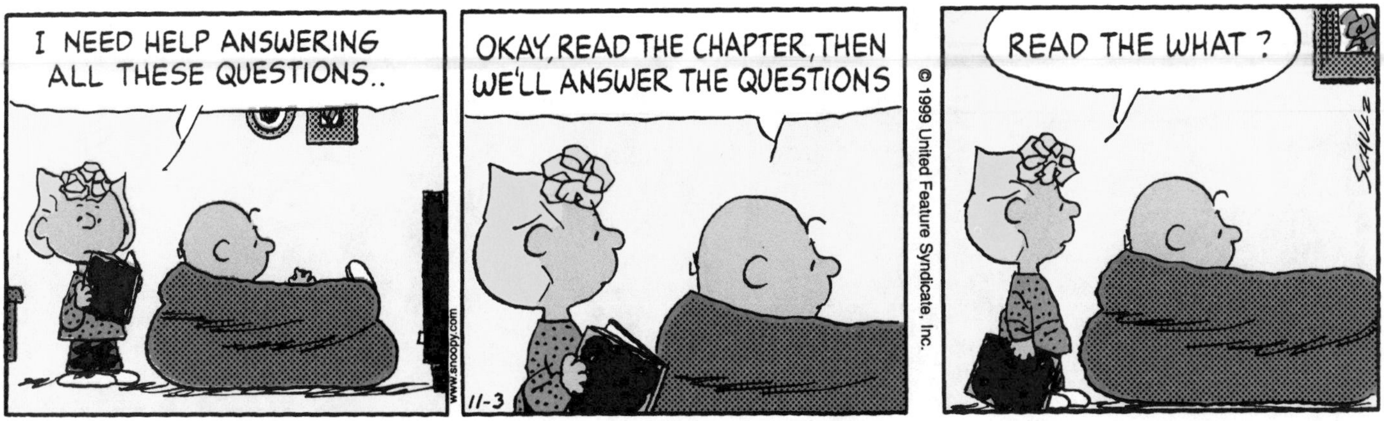
I NEED HELP ANSWERING ALL THESE QUESTIONS..
www.snoopy.com
OKAY, READ THE CHAPTER, THEN WE'LL ANSWER THE QUESTIONS
11-3
© 1999 United Feature Syndicate, Inc.
READ THE WHAT ?
SCHULZ

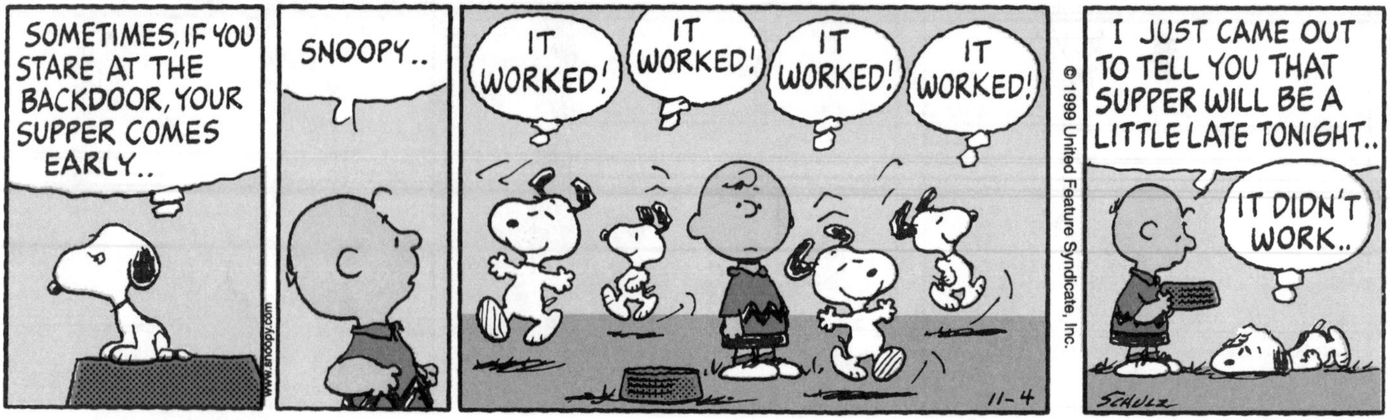
SOMETIMES, IF YOU STARE AT THE BACKDOOR, YOUR SUPPER COMES EARLY..
www.snoopy.com
SNOOPY..
IT WORKED!
IT WORKED!
IT WORKED!
IT WORKED!
11-4
© 1999 United Feature Syndicate, Inc.
I JUST CAME OUT TO TELL YOU THAT SUPPER WILL BE A LITTLE LATE TONIGHT..
IT DIDN'T WORK..
SCHULZ

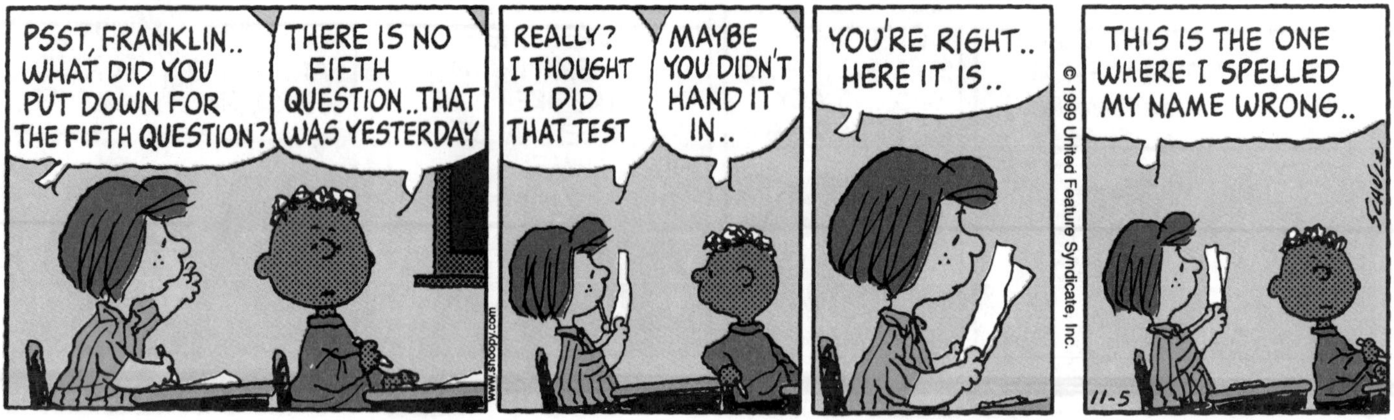
PSST, FRANKLIN.. WHAT DID YOU PUT DOWN FOR THE FIFTH QUESTION?
THERE IS NO FIFTH QUESTION..THAT WAS YESTERDAY
www.snoopy.com
REALLY? I THOUGHT I DID THAT TEST
MAYBE YOU DIDN'T HAND IT IN..
YOU'RE RIGHT.. HERE IT IS..
© 1999 United Feature Syndicate, Inc.
THIS IS THE ONE WHERE I SPELLED MY NAME WRONG..
SCHULZ
11-5

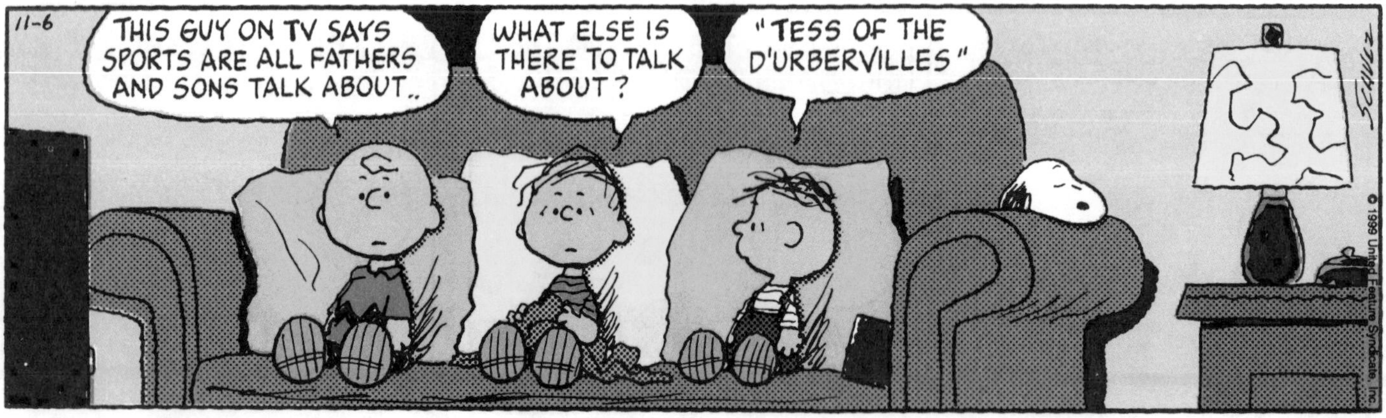
11-6
THIS GUY ON TV SAYS SPORTS ARE ALL FATHERS AND SONS TALK ABOUT..
WHAT ELSE IS THERE TO TALK ABOUT?
"TESS OF THE D'URBERVILLES"
SCHULZ
© 1999 United Feature Syndicate, Inc.

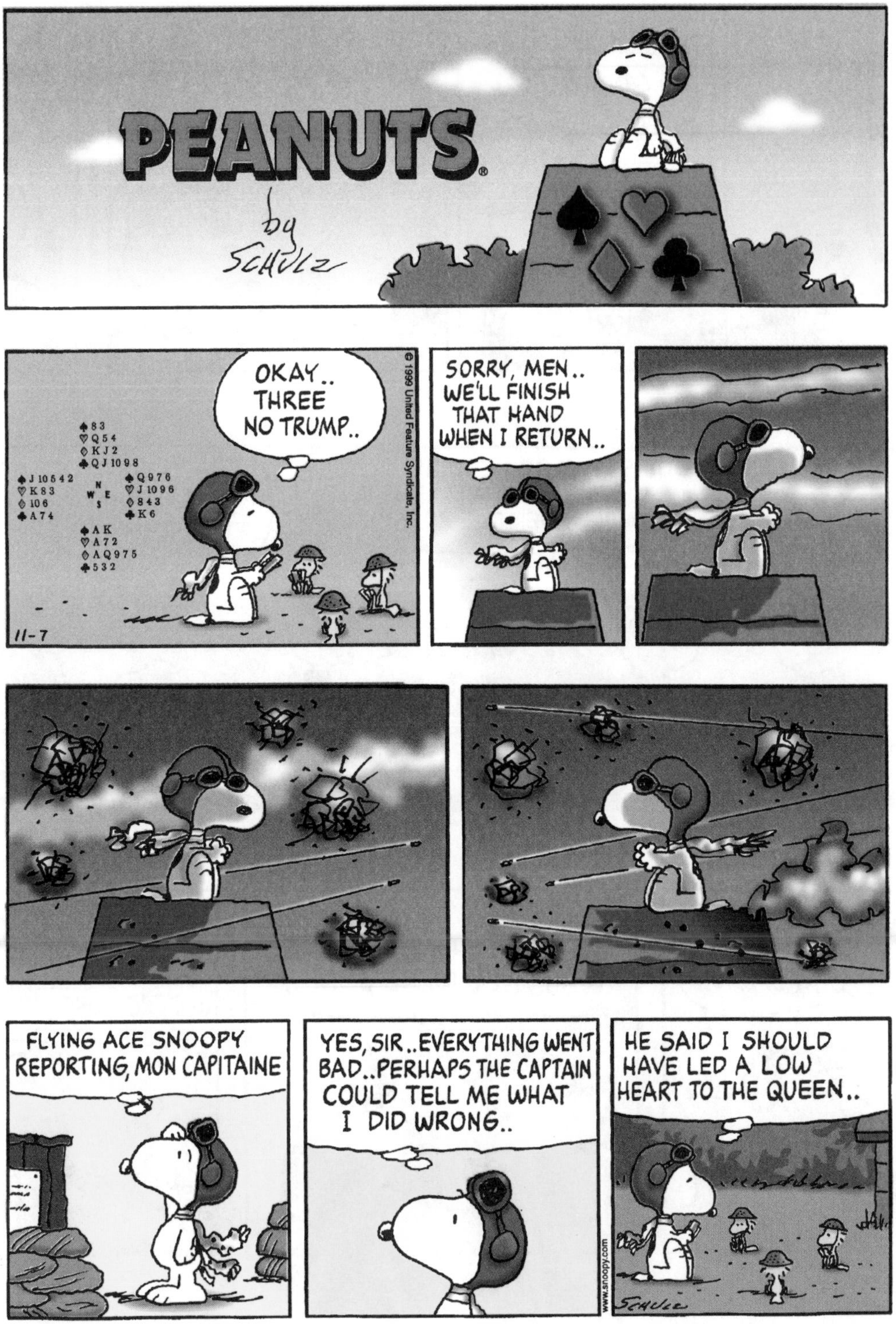
PEANUTS®
by SCHULZ
♠ 8 3
♥ Q 5 4
♦ K J 2
♣ Q J 10 9 8
♠ J 10 5 4 2
♥ K 8 3
♦ 10 6
♣ A 7 4
N W E S
♠ Q 9 7 6
♥ J 10 9 6
♦ 8 4 3
♣ K 6
♠ A K
♥ A 7 2
♦ A Q 9 7 5
♣ 5 3 2
OKAY.. THREE NO TRUMP..
© 1999 United Feature Syndicate, Inc.
11-7
SORRY, MEN.. WE'LL FINISH THAT HAND WHEN I RETURN..
FLYING ACE SNOOPY REPORTING, MON CAPITAINE
YES, SIR..EVERYTHING WENT BAD..PERHAPS THE CAPTAIN COULD TELL ME WHAT I DID WRONG..
www.snoopy.com
HE SAID I SHOULD HAVE LED A LOW HEART TO THE QUEEN..
SCHULZ

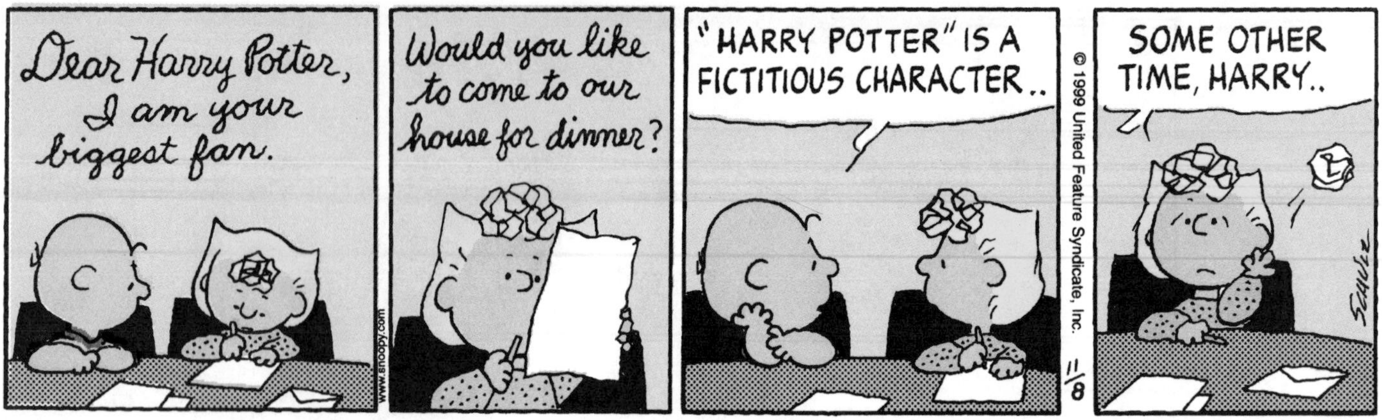
Dear Harry Potter, I am your biggest fan.
Would you like to come to our house for dinner?
"HARRY POTTER" IS A FICTITIOUS CHARACTER..
SOME OTHER TIME, HARRY..
© 1999 United Feature Syndicate, Inc.
www.snoopy.com
11/8
SCHULZ

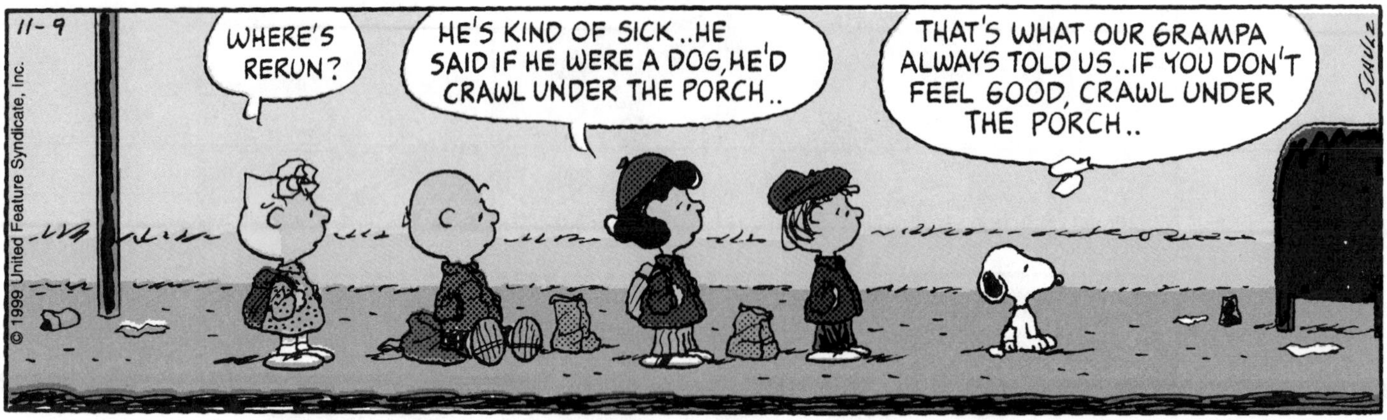
11-9
WHERE'S RERUN?
HE'S KIND OF SICK..HE SAID IF HE WERE A DOG, HE'D CRAWL UNDER THE PORCH..
THAT'S WHAT OUR GRAMPA ALWAYS TOLD US..IF YOU DON'T FEEL GOOD, CRAWL UNDER THE PORCH..
© 1999 United Feature Syndicate, Inc.
SCHULZ

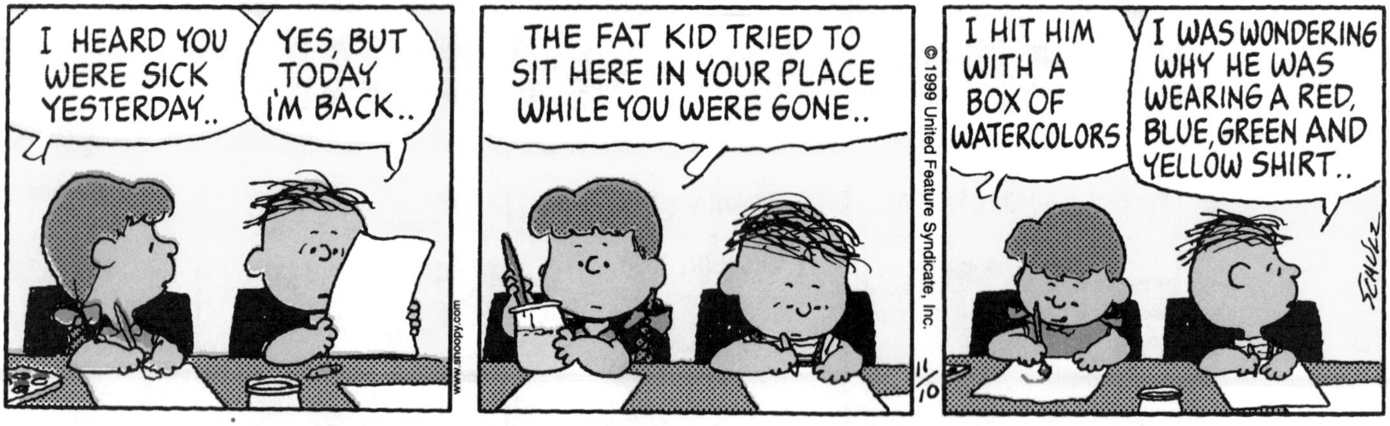
I HEARD YOU WERE SICK YESTERDAY..
YES, BUT TODAY I'M BACK..
THE FAT KID TRIED TO SIT HERE IN YOUR PLACE WHILE YOU WERE GONE..
I HIT HIM WITH A BOX OF WATERCOLORS
I WAS WONDERING WHY HE WAS WEARING A RED, BLUE, GREEN AND YELLOW SHIRT..
© 1999 United Feature Syndicate, Inc.
www.snoopy.com
11/10
SCHULZ

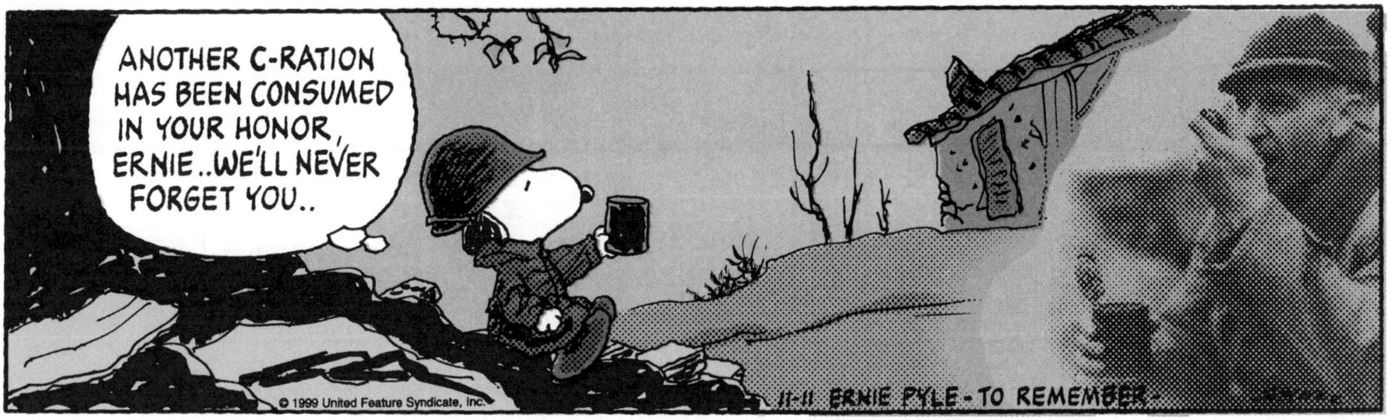
ANOTHER C-RATION HAS BEEN CONSUMED IN YOUR HONOR, ERNIE..WE'LL NEVER FORGET YOU..
© 1999 United Feature Syndicate, Inc.
11-11 ERNIE PYLE - TO REMEMBER

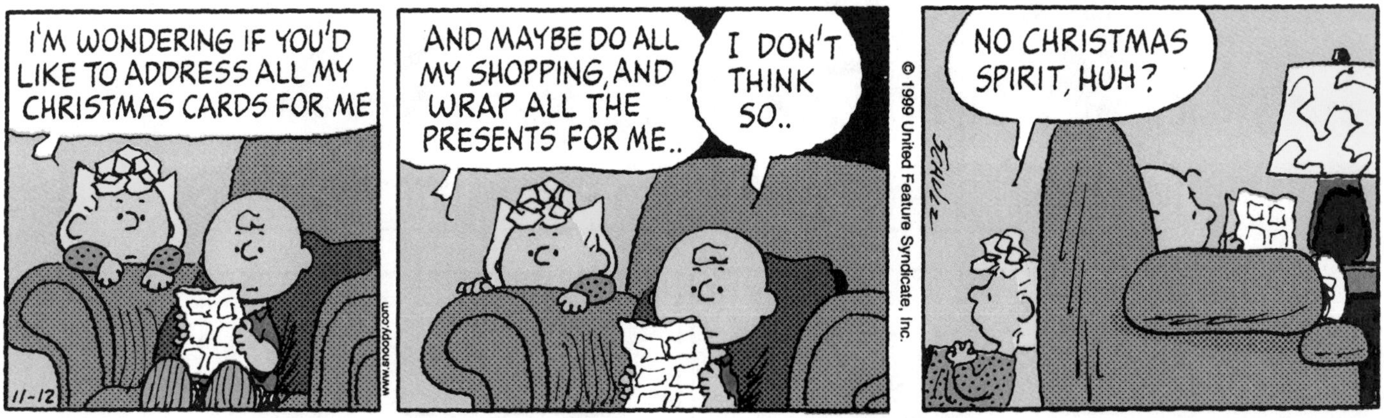
I'M WONDERING IF YOU'D LIKE TO ADDRESS ALL MY CHRISTMAS CARDS FOR ME
11-12
www.snoopy.com
AND MAYBE DO ALL MY SHOPPING, AND WRAP ALL THE PRESENTS FOR ME..
I DON'T THINK SO..
© 1999 United Feature Syndicate, Inc.
SCHULZ
NO CHRISTMAS SPIRIT, HUH?

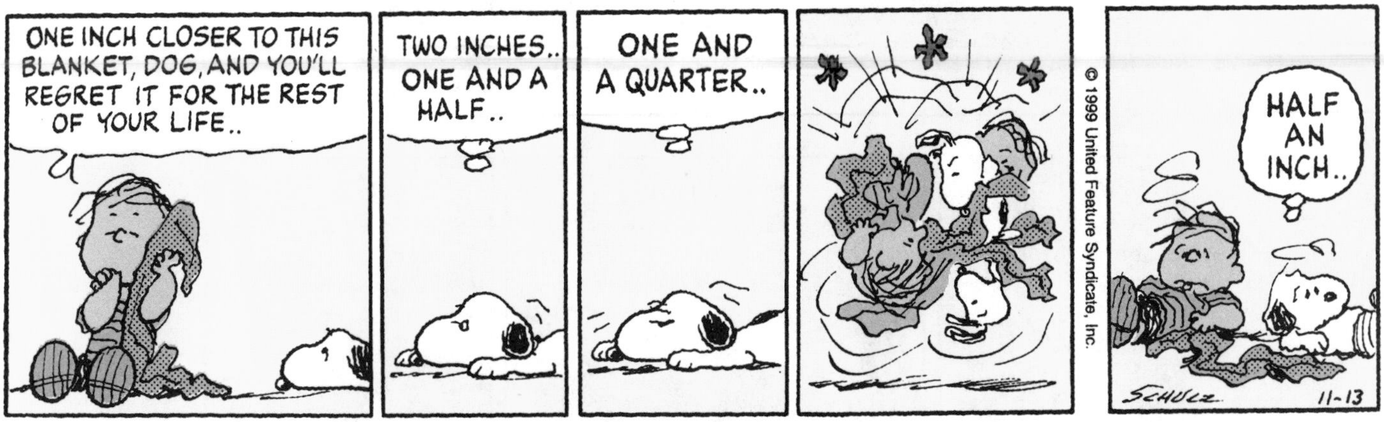
ONE INCH CLOSER TO THIS BLANKET, DOG, AND YOU'LL REGRET IT FOR THE REST OF YOUR LIFE..
TWO INCHES.. ONE AND A HALF..
ONE AND A QUARTER..
© 1999 United Feature Syndicate, Inc.
HALF AN INCH..
SCHULZ
11-13

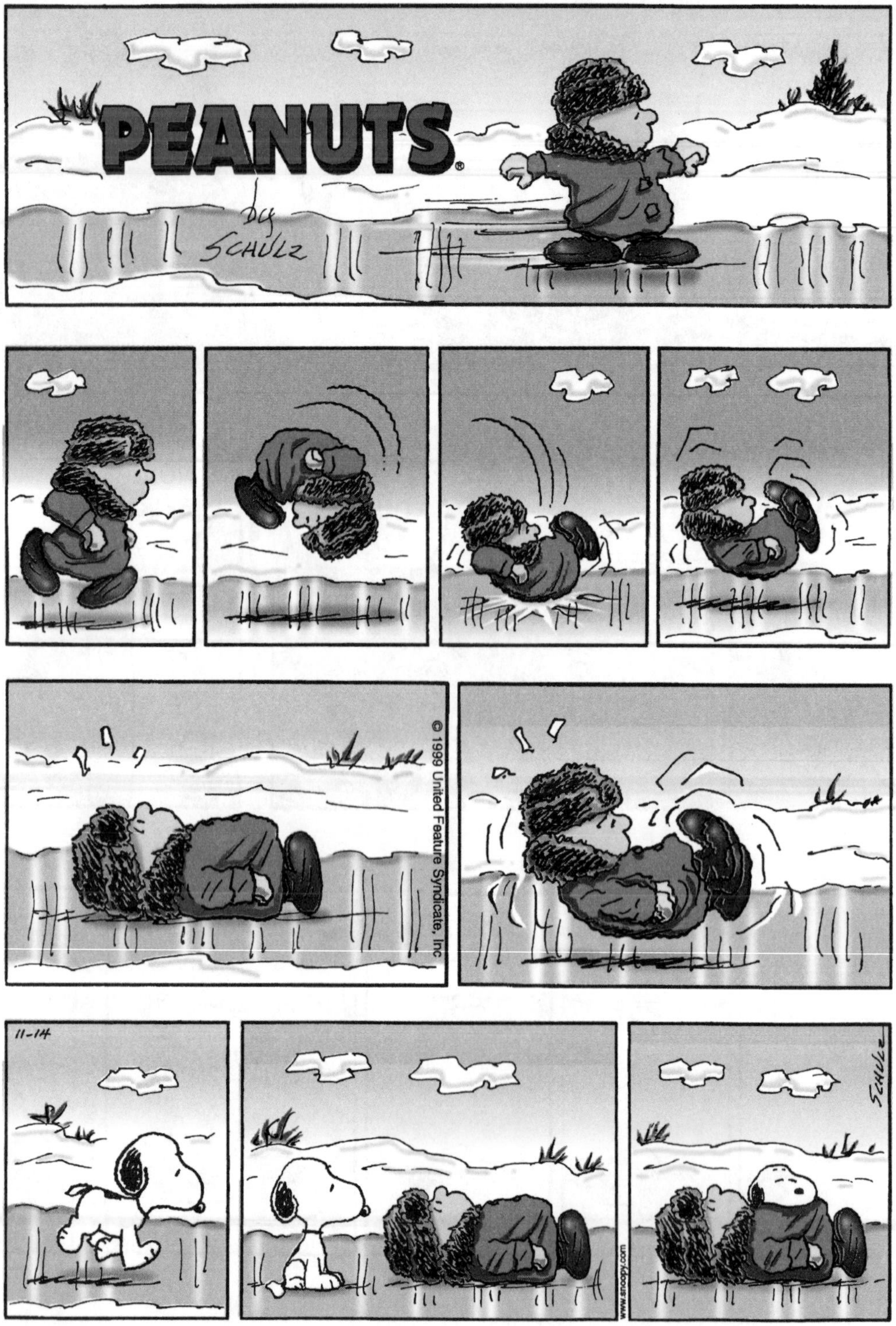

PEANUTS®
by SCHULZ
© 1999 United Feature Syndicate, Inc
11-14
www.snoopy.com
SCHULZ

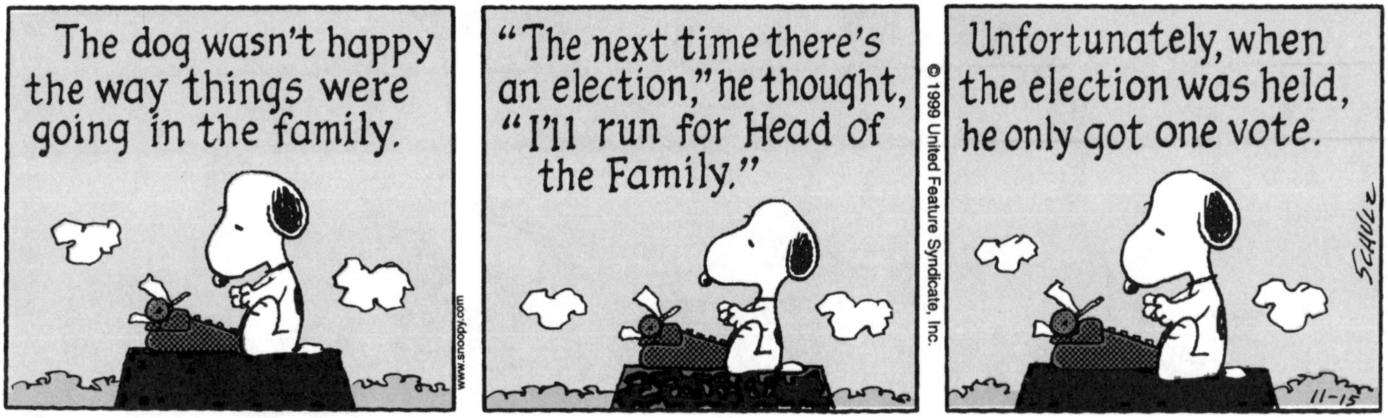
The dog wasn't happy the way things were going in the family.
www.snoopy.com
"The next time there's an election," he thought, "I'll run for Head of the Family."
© 1999 United Feature Syndicate, Inc.
Unfortunately, when the election was held, he only got one vote.
SCHULZ
11-15

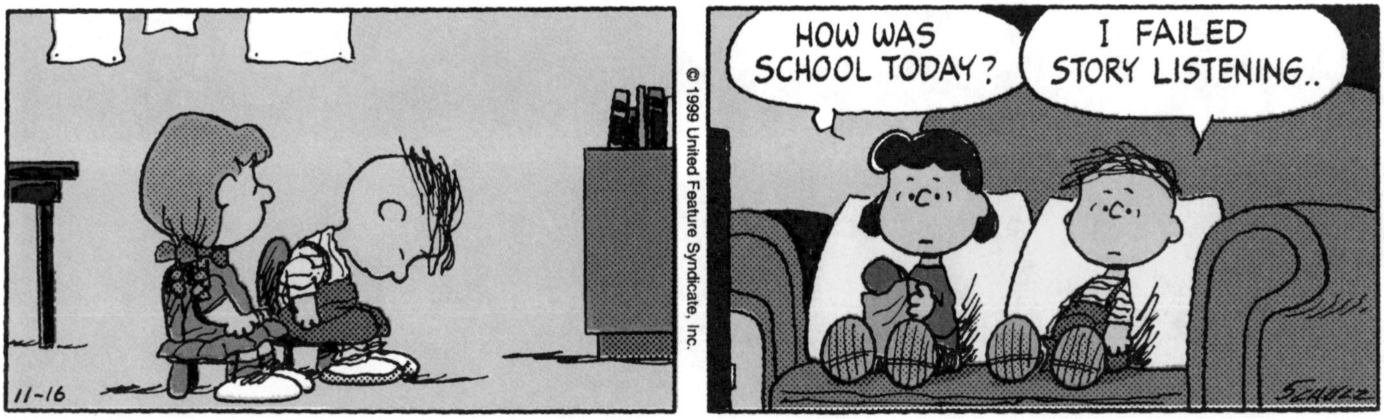
11-16
© 1999 United Feature Syndicate, Inc.
HOW WAS SCHOOL TODAY?
I FAILED STORY LISTENING..
SCHULZ

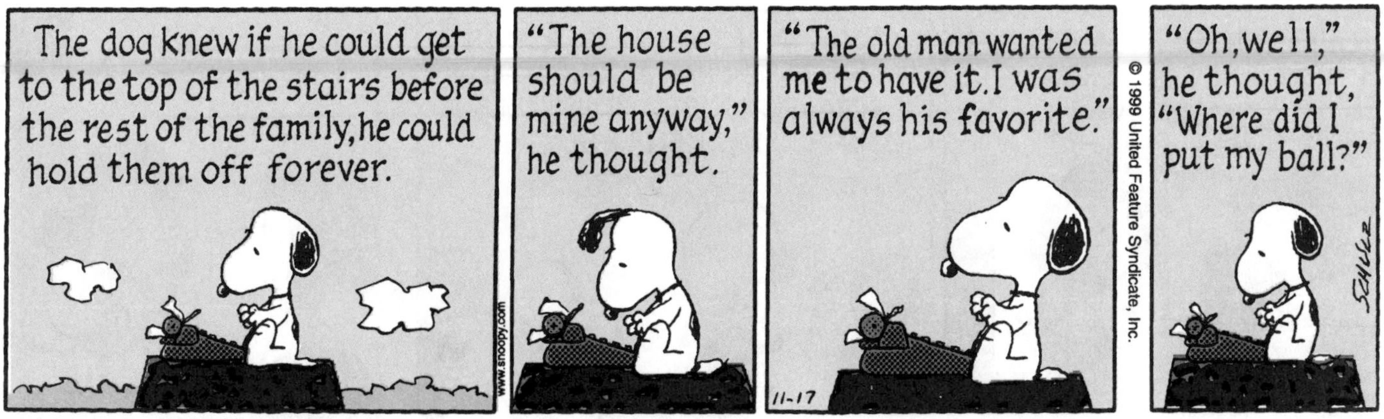
The dog knew if he could get to the top of the stairs before the rest of the family, he could hold them off forever.
www.snoopy.com
"The house should be mine anyway," he thought.
"The old man wanted me to have it. I was always his favorite."
11-17
© 1999 United Feature Syndicate, Inc.
"Oh, well," he thought, "Where did I put my ball?"
SCHULZ

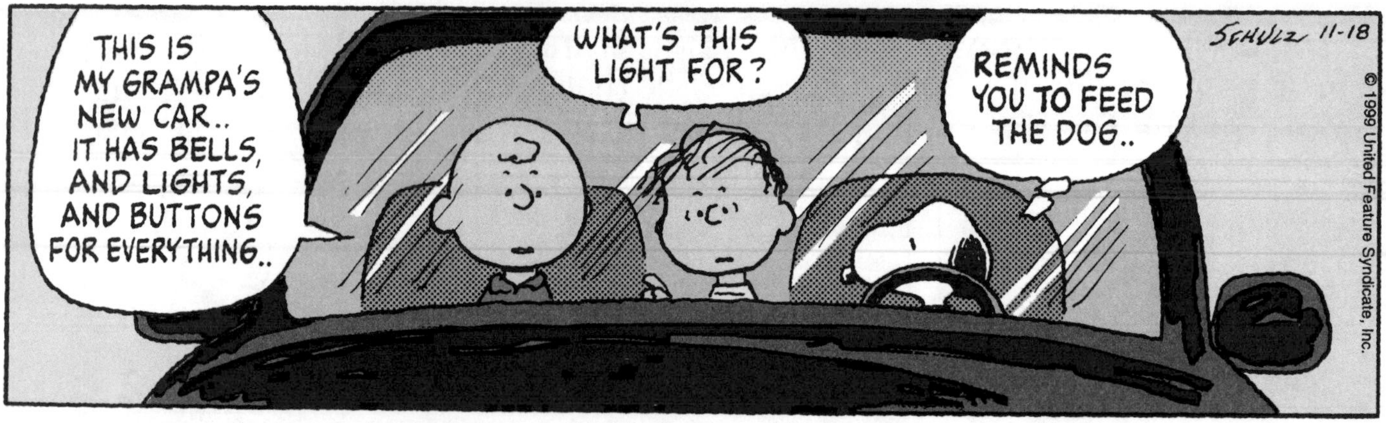
THIS IS MY GRAMPA'S NEW CAR.. IT HAS BELLS, AND LIGHTS, AND BUTTONS FOR EVERYTHING..
WHAT'S THIS LIGHT FOR?
REMINDS YOU TO FEED THE DOG..
SCHULZ 11-18
© 1999 United Feature Syndicate, Inc.

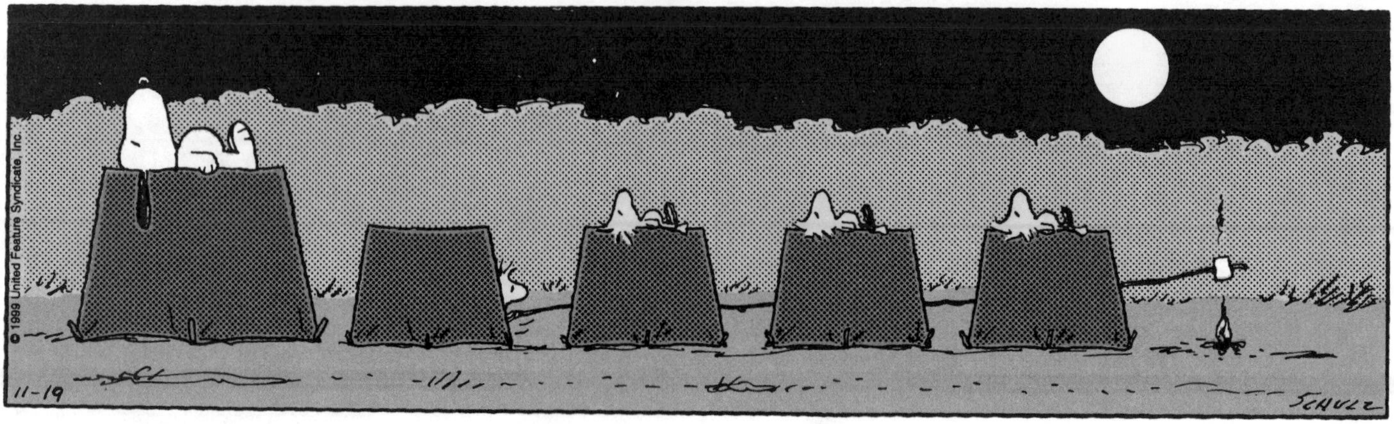
© 1999 United Feature Syndicate, Inc.
11-19
SCHULZ

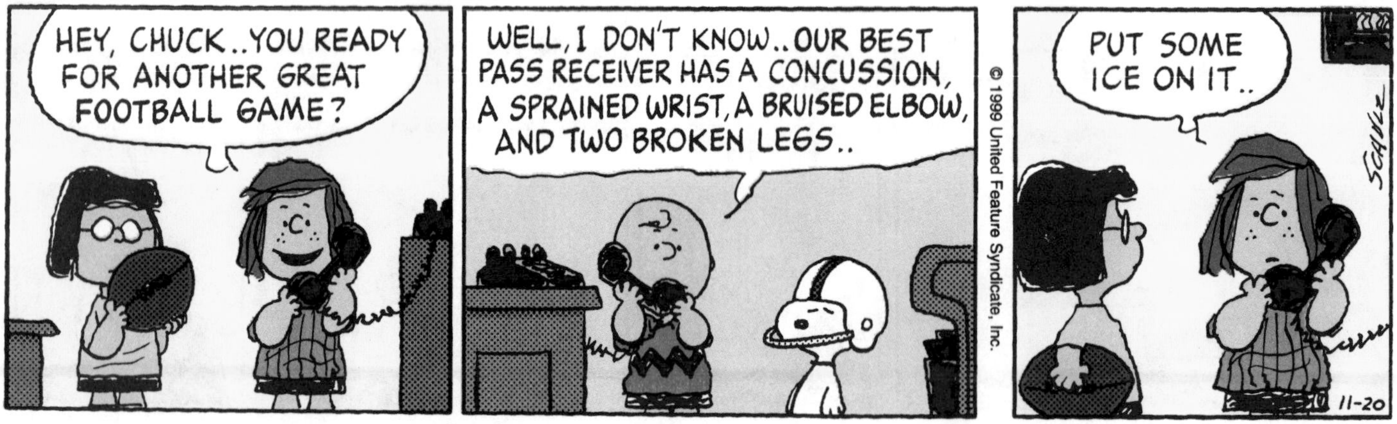
HEY, CHUCK..YOU READY FOR ANOTHER GREAT FOOTBALL GAME?
WELL, I DON'T KNOW..OUR BEST PASS RECEIVER HAS A CONCUSSION, A SPRAINED WRIST, A BRUISED ELBOW, AND TWO BROKEN LEGS..
PUT SOME ICE ON IT..
© 1999 United Feature Syndicate, Inc.
SCHULZ
11-20

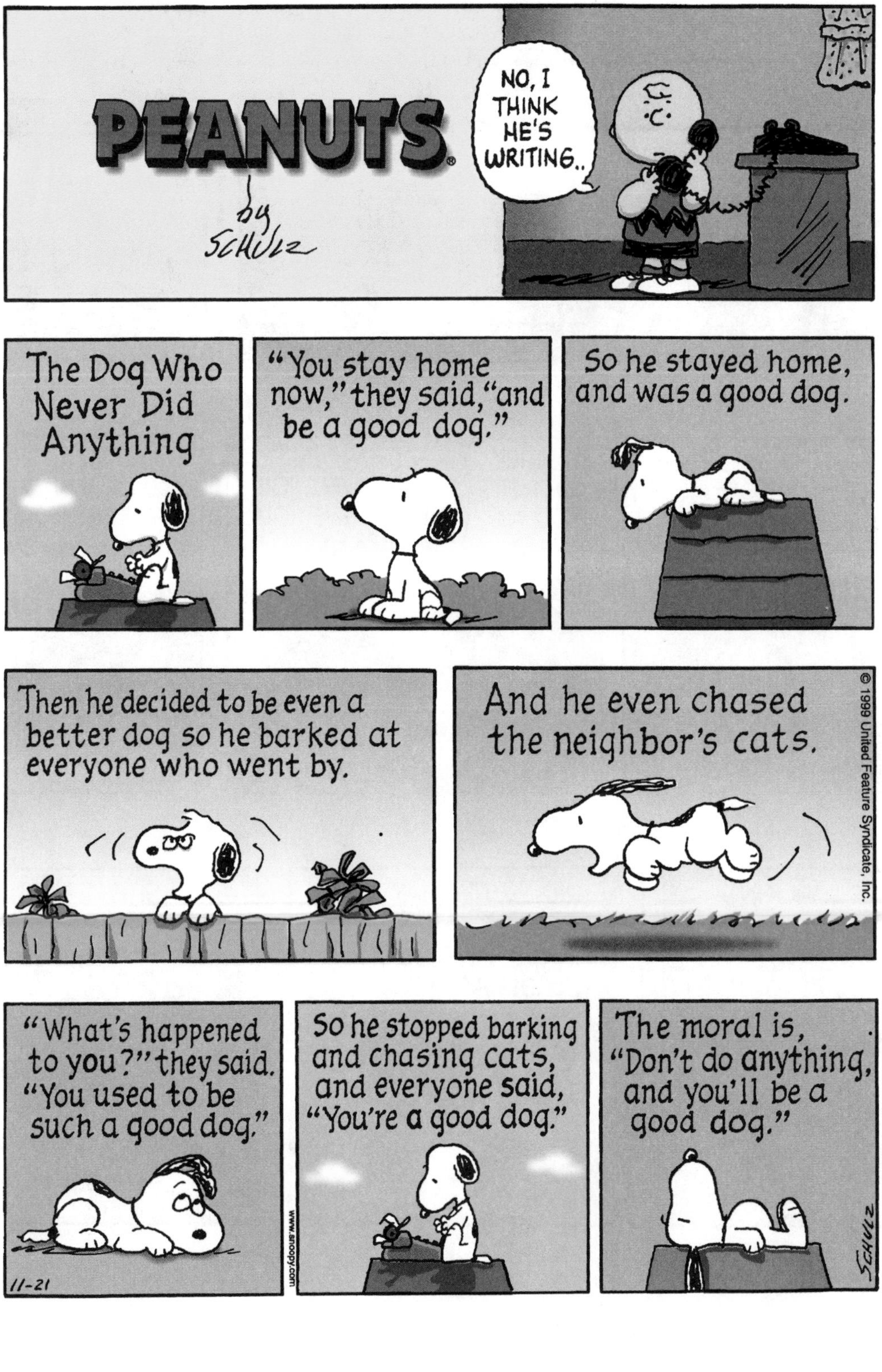
PEANUTS
by SCHULZ
NO, I THINK HE'S WRITING..
The Dog Who Never Did Anything
"You stay home now," they said, "and be a good dog."
So he stayed home, and was a good dog.
Then he decided to be even a better dog so he barked at everyone who went by.
And he even chased the neighbor's cats.
© 1999 United Feature Syndicate, Inc.
"What's happened to you?" they said. "You used to be such a good dog."
11-21
www.snoopy.com
So he stopped barking and chasing cats, and everyone said, "You're a good dog."
The moral is, "Don't do anything, and you'll be a good dog."
SCHULZ

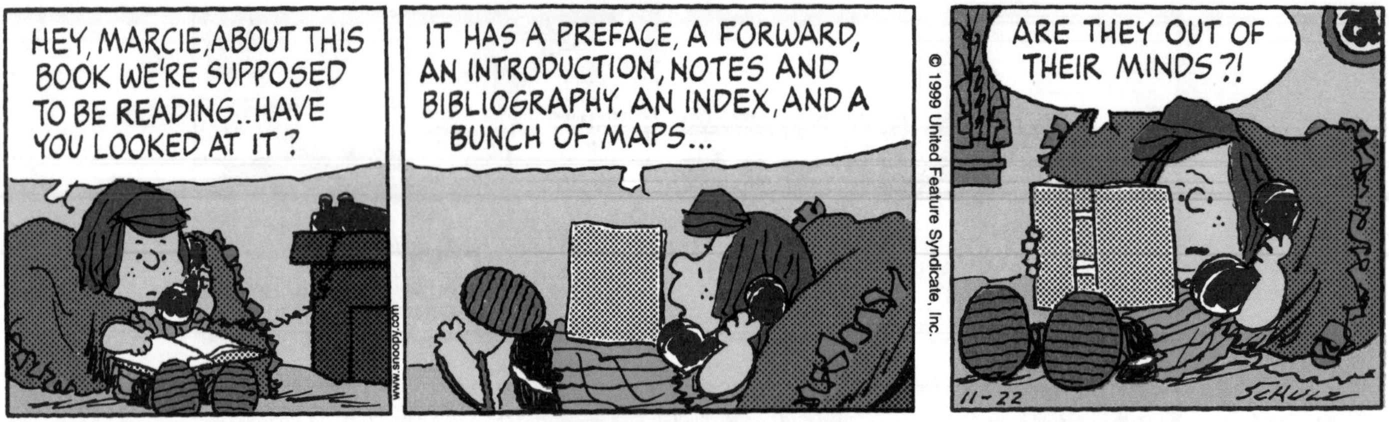
HEY, MARCIE, ABOUT THIS BOOK WE'RE SUPPOSED TO BE READING..HAVE YOU LOOKED AT IT?
IT HAS A PREFACE, A FORWARD, AN INTRODUCTION, NOTES AND BIBLIOGRAPHY, AN INDEX, AND A BUNCH OF MAPS...
ARE THEY OUT OF THEIR MINDS?!
www.snoopy.com
© 1999 United Feature Syndicate, Inc.
11-22
SCHULZ

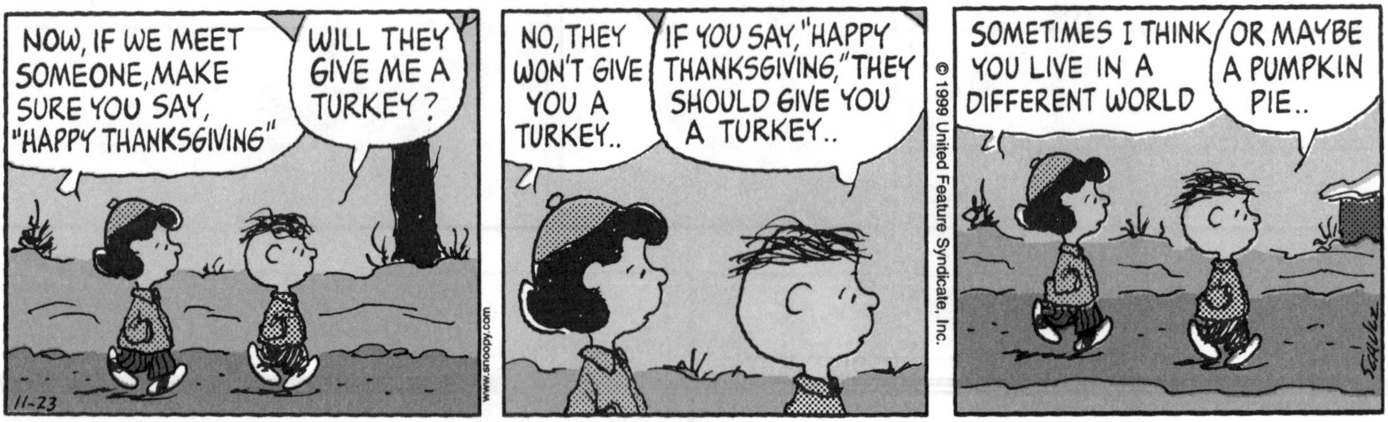
NOW, IF WE MEET SOMEONE, MAKE SURE YOU SAY, "HAPPY THANKSGIVING"
WILL THEY GIVE ME A TURKEY?
NO, THEY WON'T GIVE YOU A TURKEY..
IF YOU SAY, "HAPPY THANKSGIVING," THEY SHOULD GIVE YOU A TURKEY..
SOMETIMES I THINK YOU LIVE IN A DIFFERENT WORLD
OR MAYBE A PUMPKIN PIE..
11-23
www.snoopy.com
© 1999 United Feature Syndicate, Inc.
SCHULZ

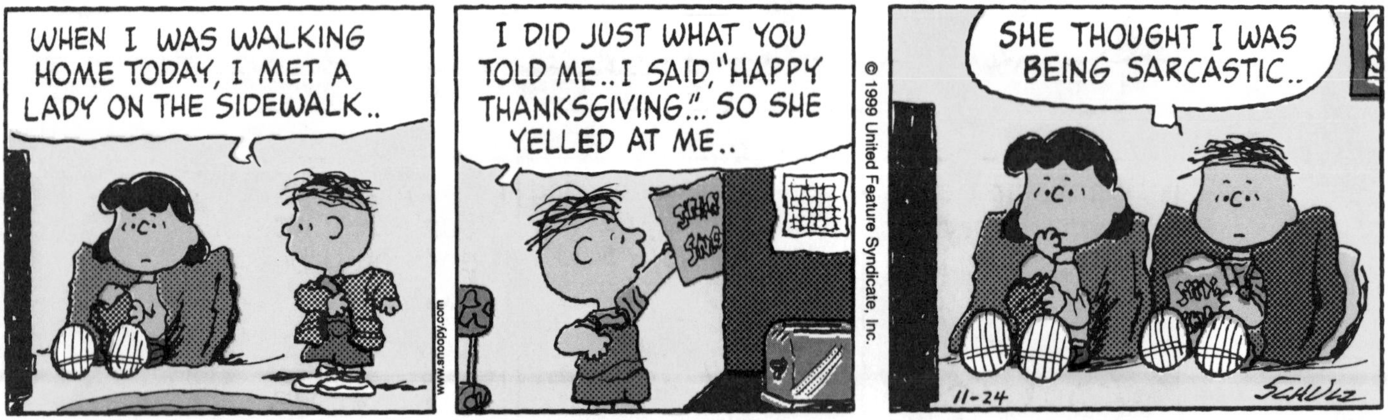
WHEN I WAS WALKING HOME TODAY, I MET A LADY ON THE SIDEWALK..
I DID JUST WHAT YOU TOLD ME..I SAID, "HAPPY THANKSGIVING".. SO SHE YELLED AT ME..
SHE THOUGHT I WAS BEING SARCASTIC..
www.snoopy.com
© 1999 United Feature Syndicate, Inc.
11-24
SCHULZ

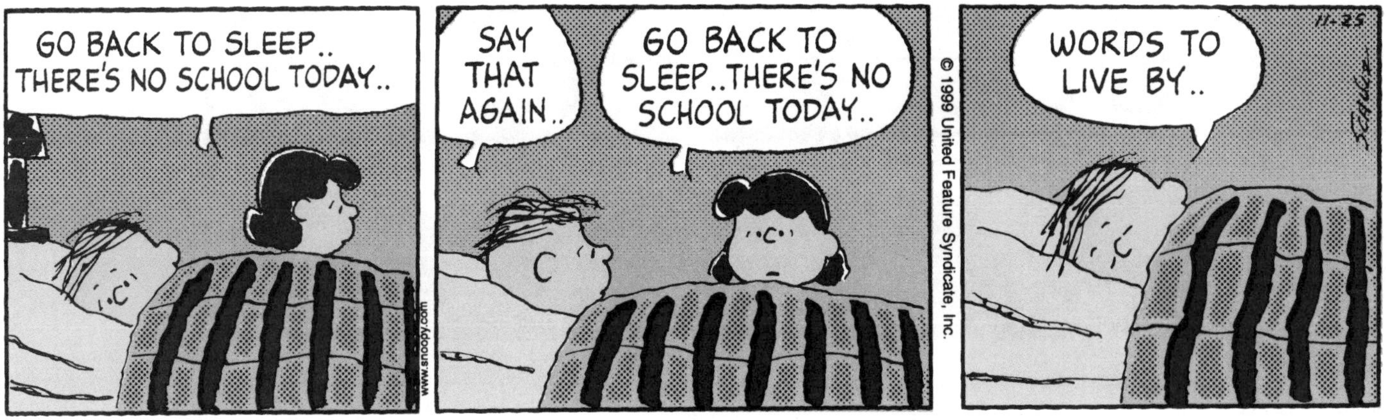
GO BACK TO SLEEP.. THERE'S NO SCHOOL TODAY..
SAY THAT AGAIN..
GO BACK TO SLEEP..THERE'S NO SCHOOL TODAY..
WORDS TO LIVE BY..

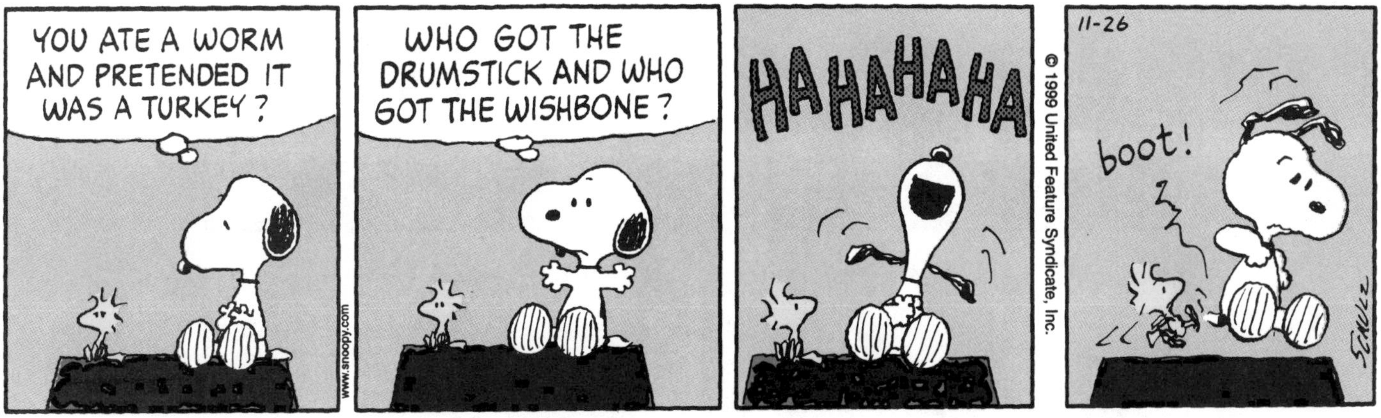
YOU ATE A WORM AND PRETENDED IT WAS A TURKEY?
WHO GOT THE DRUMSTICK AND WHO GOT THE WISHBONE?
HAHAHAHAHA
boot!

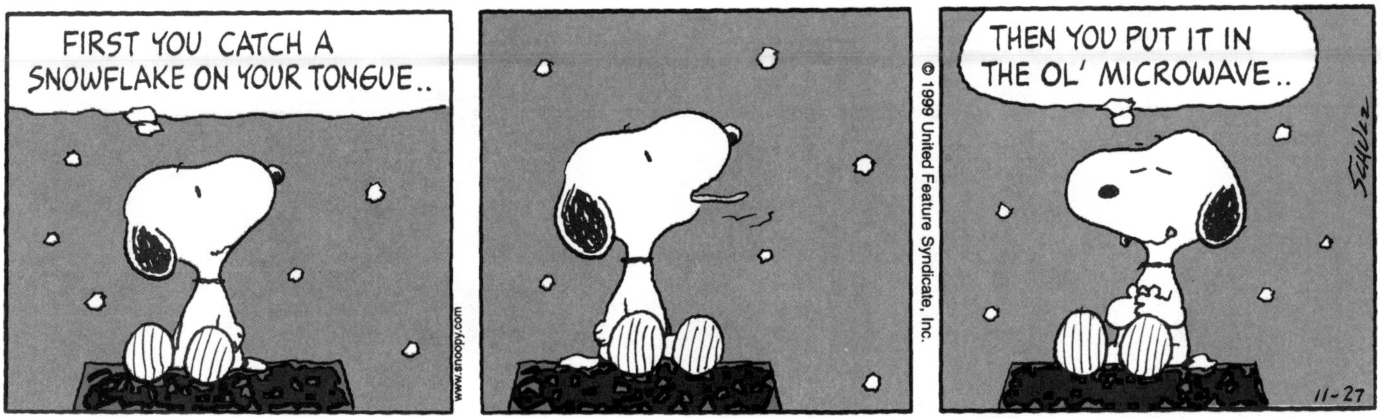
FIRST YOU CATCH A SNOWFLAKE ON YOUR TONGUE..
THEN YOU PUT IT IN THE OL' MICROWAVE..

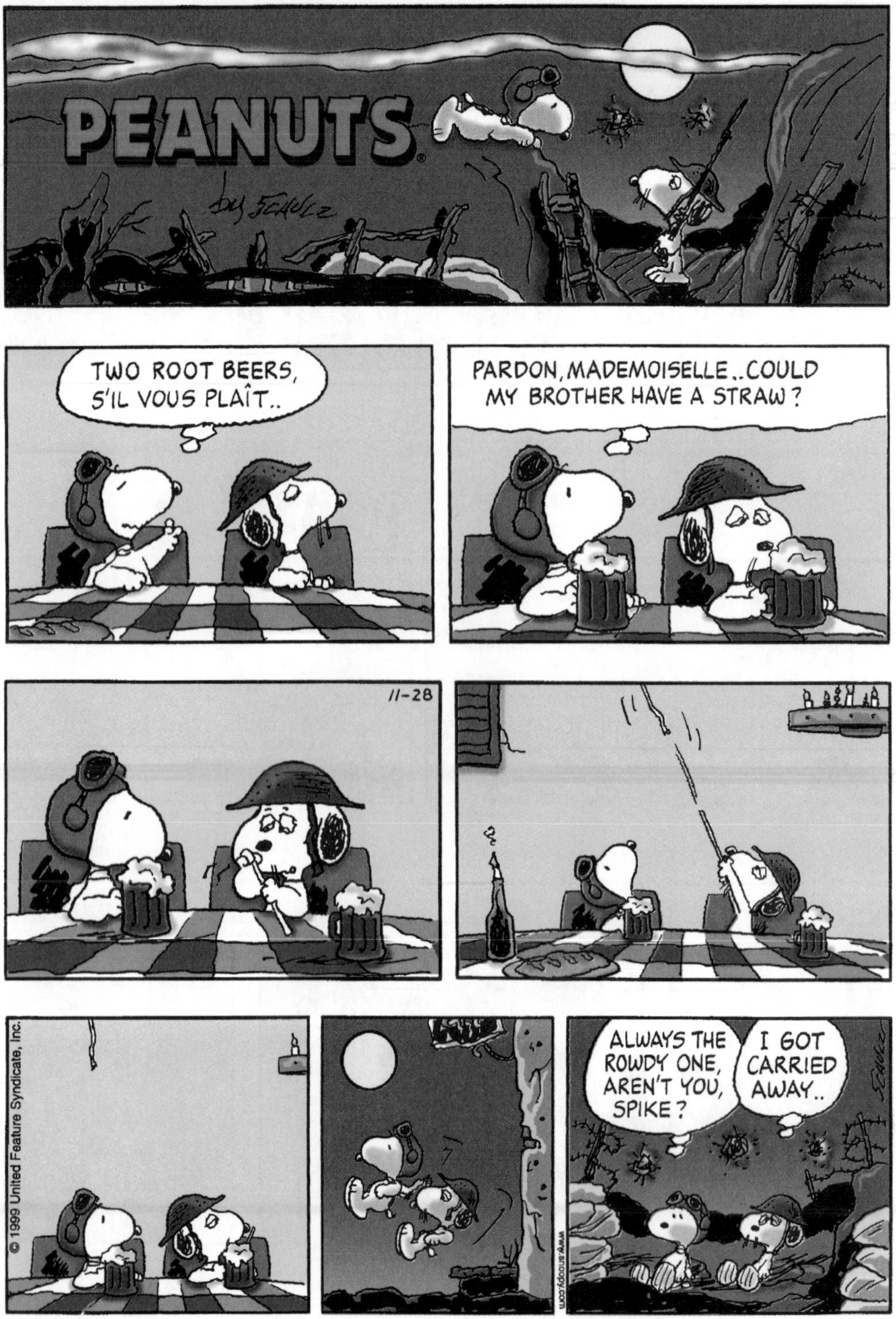
PEANUTS
by SCHULZ
TWO ROOT BEERS, S'IL VOUS PLAÎT..
PARDON, MADEMOISELLE..COULD MY BROTHER HAVE A STRAW?
11-28
© 1999 United Feature Syndicate, Inc.
www.snoopy.com
ALWAYS THE ROWDY ONE, AREN'T YOU, SPIKE?
I GOT CARRIED AWAY..
SCHULZ

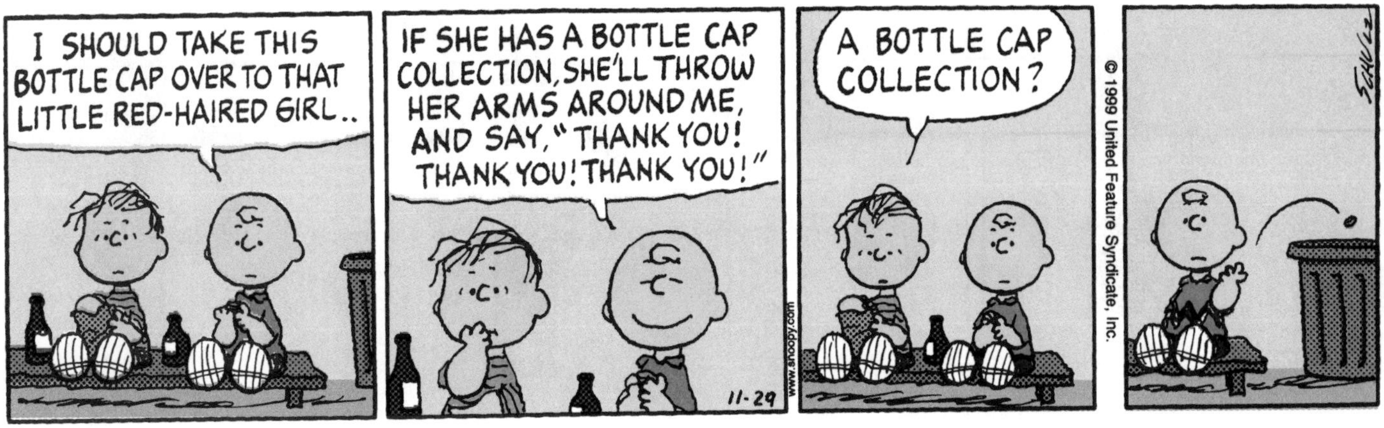
I SHOULD TAKE THIS BOTTLE CAP OVER TO THAT LITTLE RED-HAIRED GIRL..
IF SHE HAS A BOTTLE CAP COLLECTION, SHE'LL THROW HER ARMS AROUND ME, AND SAY, "THANK YOU! THANK YOU! THANK YOU!"
11-29
www.snoopy.com
A BOTTLE CAP COLLECTION?
© 1999 United Feature Syndicate, Inc.

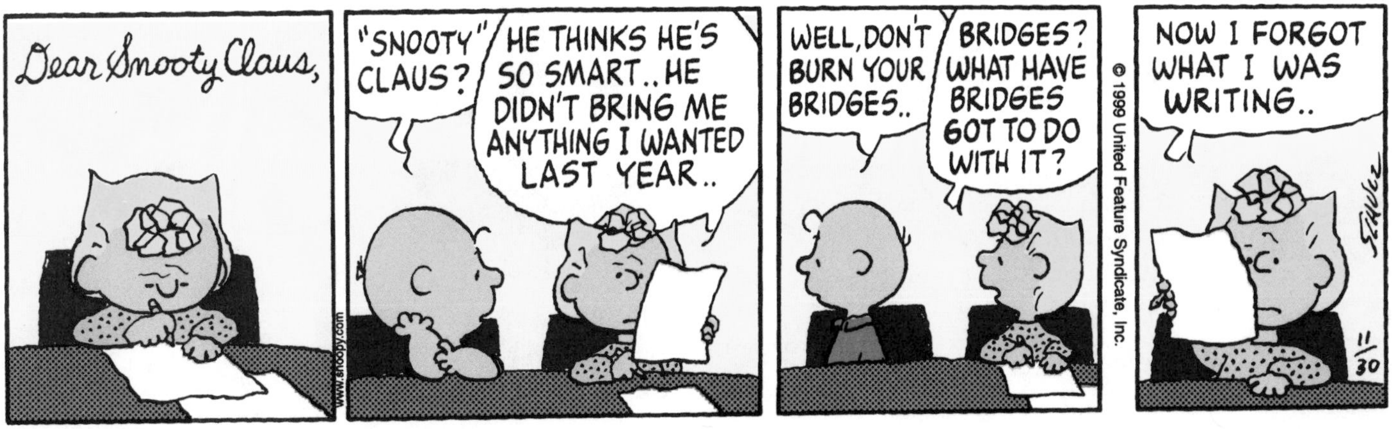
Dear Snooty Claus,
www.snoopy.com
"SNOOTY" CLAUS?
HE THINKS HE'S SO SMART.. HE DIDN'T BRING ME ANYTHING I WANTED LAST YEAR..
WELL, DON'T BURN YOUR BRIDGES..
BRIDGES? WHAT HAVE BRIDGES GOT TO DO WITH IT?
© 1999 United Feature Syndicate, Inc.
NOW I FORGOT WHAT I WAS WRITING..
11/30

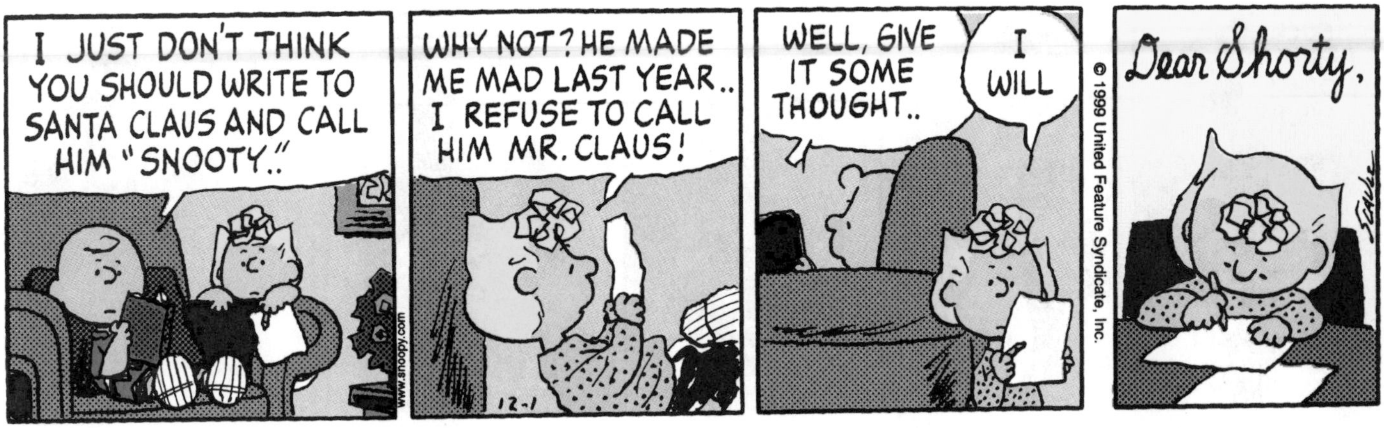
I JUST DON'T THINK YOU SHOULD WRITE TO SANTA CLAUS AND CALL HIM "SNOOTY."
www.snoopy.com
WHY NOT? HE MADE ME MAD LAST YEAR.. I REFUSE TO CALL HIM MR. CLAUS!
12-1
WELL, GIVE IT SOME THOUGHT..
I WILL
© 1999 United Feature Syndicate, Inc.
Dear Shorty,

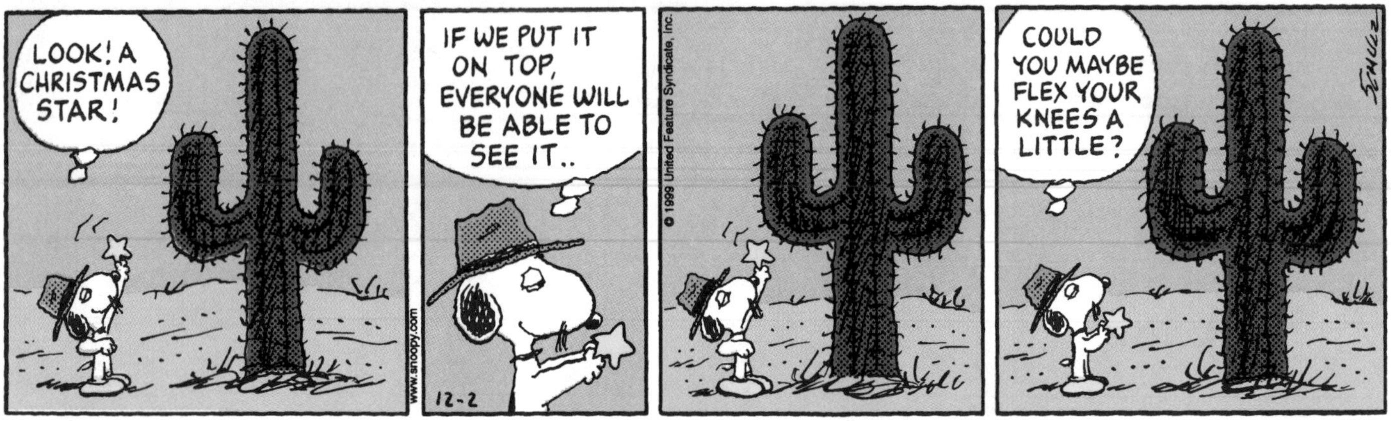
LOOK! A CHRISTMAS STAR!
www.snoopy.com
12-2
IF WE PUT IT ON TOP, EVERYONE WILL BE ABLE TO SEE IT..
© 1999 United Feature Syndicate, Inc.
COULD YOU MAYBE FLEX YOUR KNEES A LITTLE?
SCHULZ

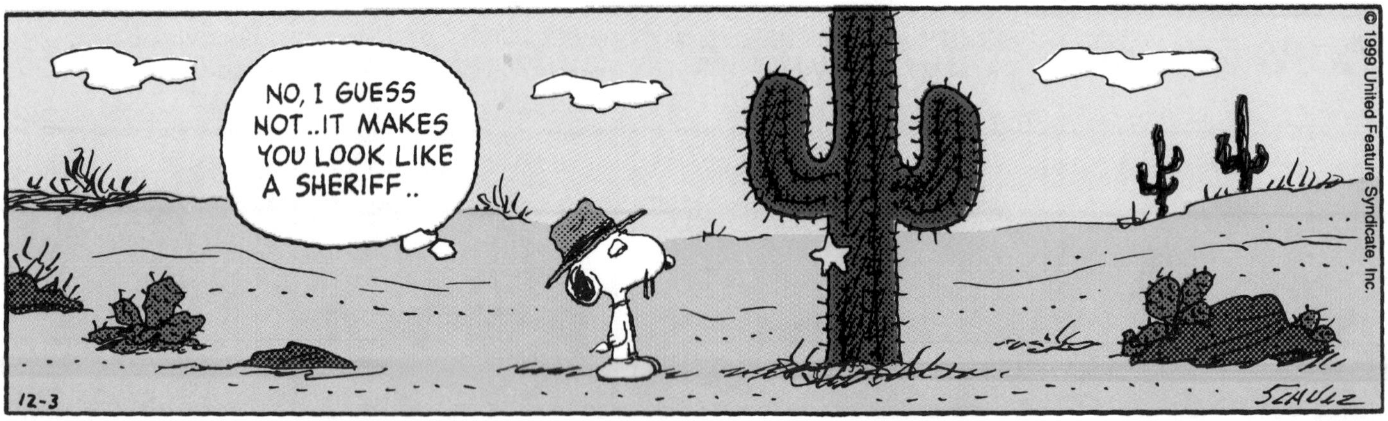
NO, I GUESS NOT..IT MAKES YOU LOOK LIKE A SHERIFF..
12-3
SCHULZ
© 1999 United Feature Syndicate, Inc.

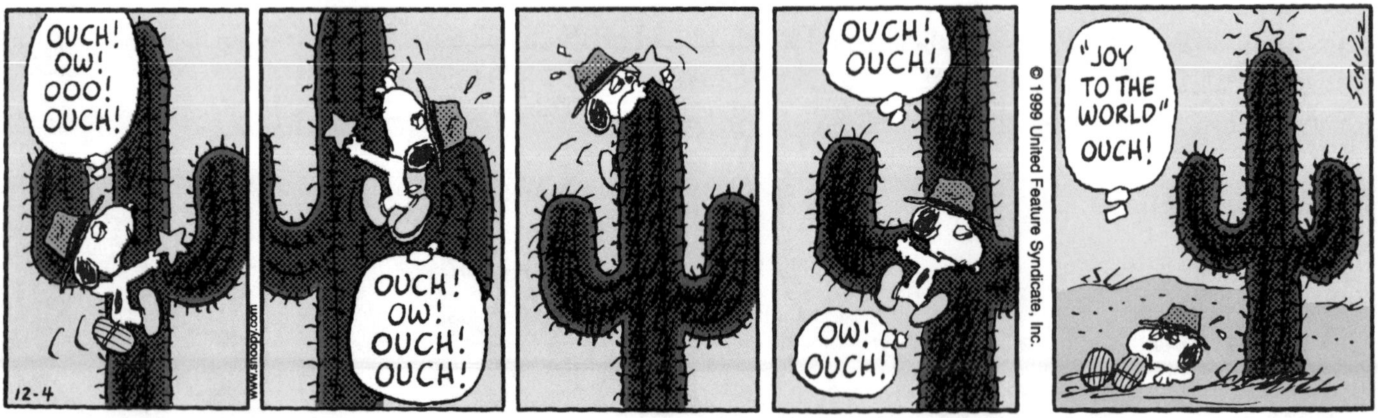
OUCH! OW! OOO! OUCH!
12-4
www.snoopy.com
OUCH! OW! OUCH! OUCH!
OUCH! OUCH!
OW! OUCH!
© 1999 United Feature Syndicate, Inc.
"JOY TO THE WORLD" OUCH!
SCHULZ

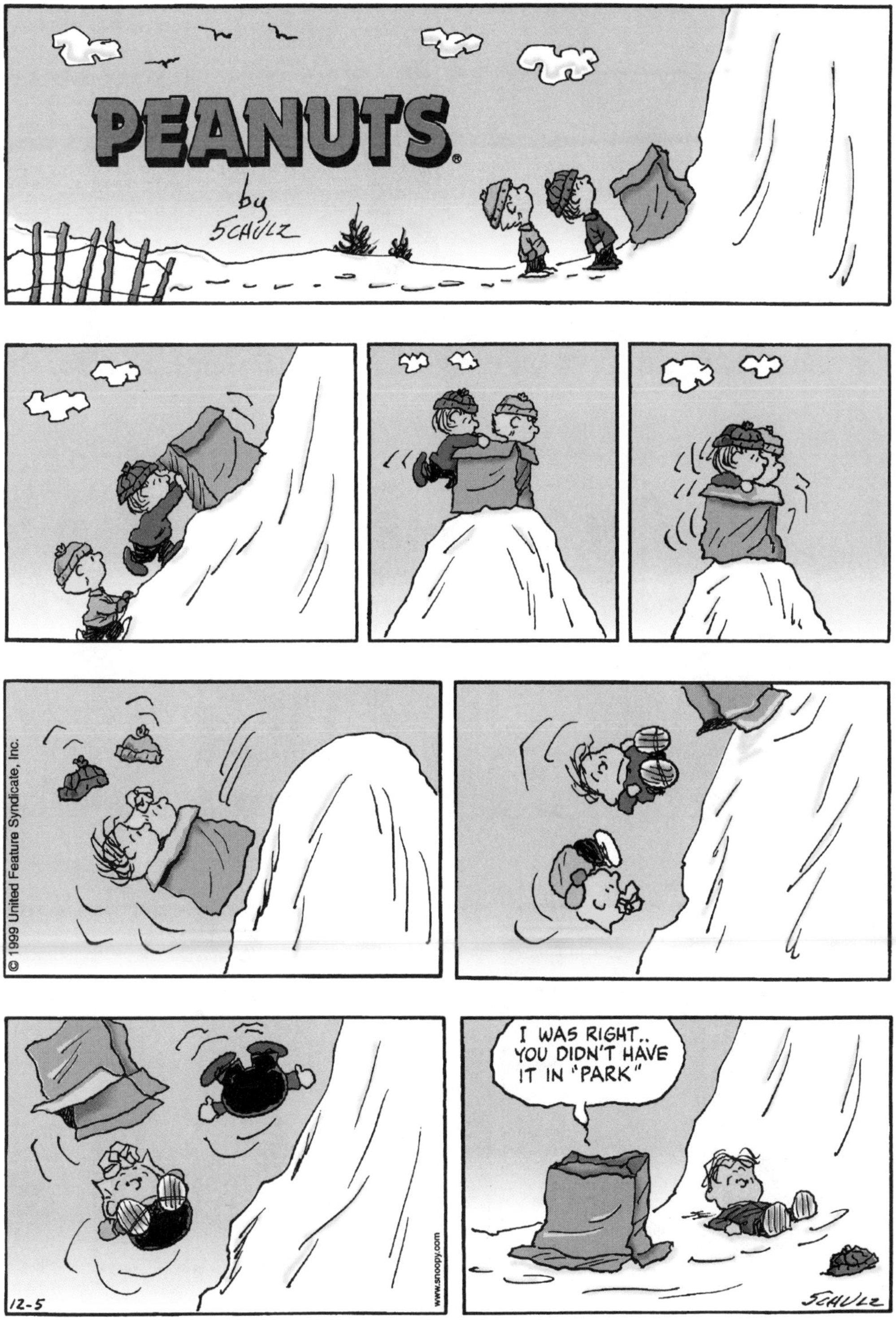
PEANUTS
by SCHULZ
© 1999 United Feature Syndicate, Inc.
12-5
www.snoopy.com
I WAS RIGHT.. YOU DIDN'T HAVE IT IN "PARK"
SCHULZ

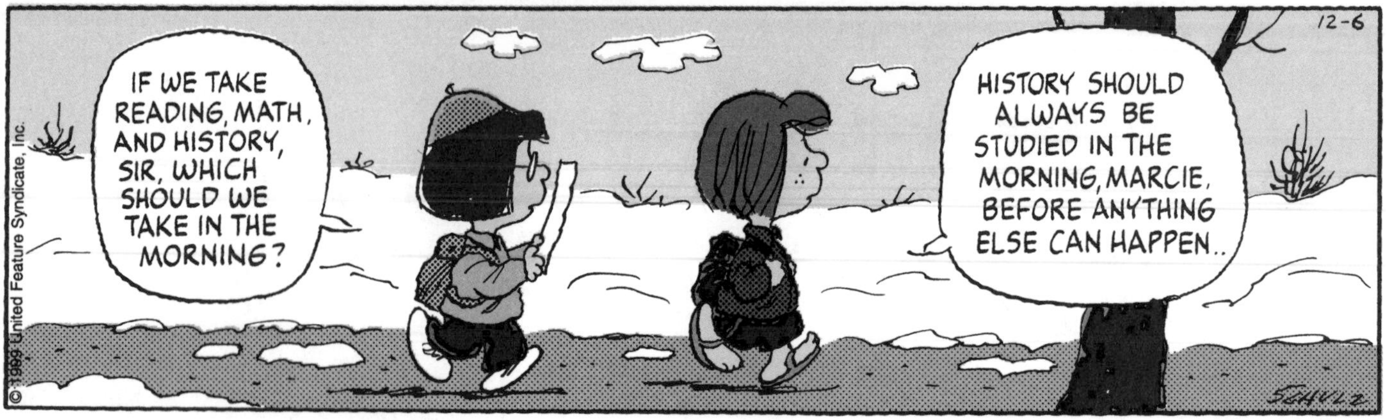
12-6
IF WE TAKE READING, MATH, AND HISTORY, SIR, WHICH SHOULD WE TAKE IN THE MORNING?
HISTORY SHOULD ALWAYS BE STUDIED IN THE MORNING, MARCIE, BEFORE ANYTHING ELSE CAN HAPPEN..
© 1999 United Feature Syndicate, Inc.
SCHULZ

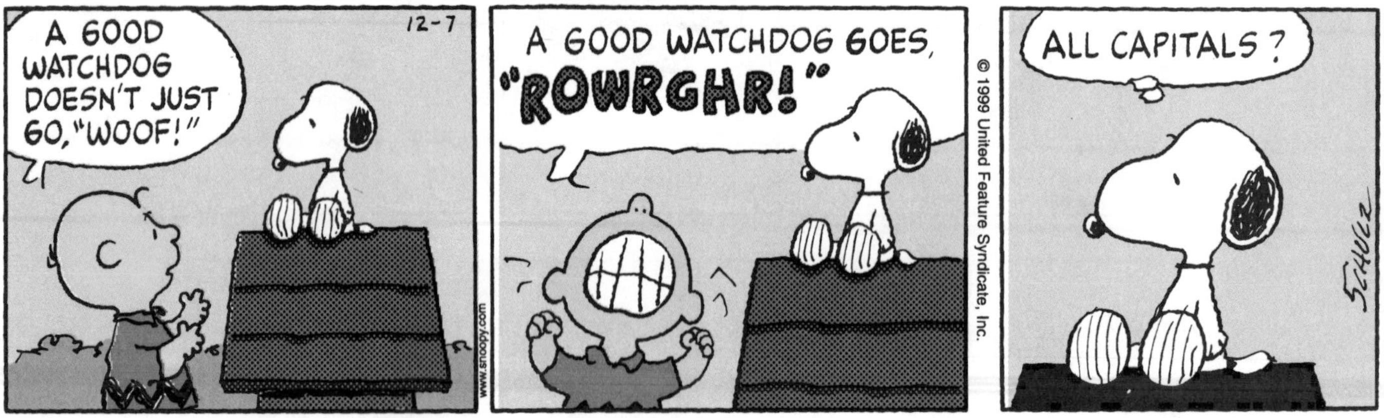
12-7
A GOOD WATCHDOG DOESN'T JUST GO, "WOOF!"
A GOOD WATCHDOG GOES,
"ROWRGHR!"
ALL CAPITALS?
© 1999 United Feature Syndicate, Inc.
www.snoopy.com
SCHULZ

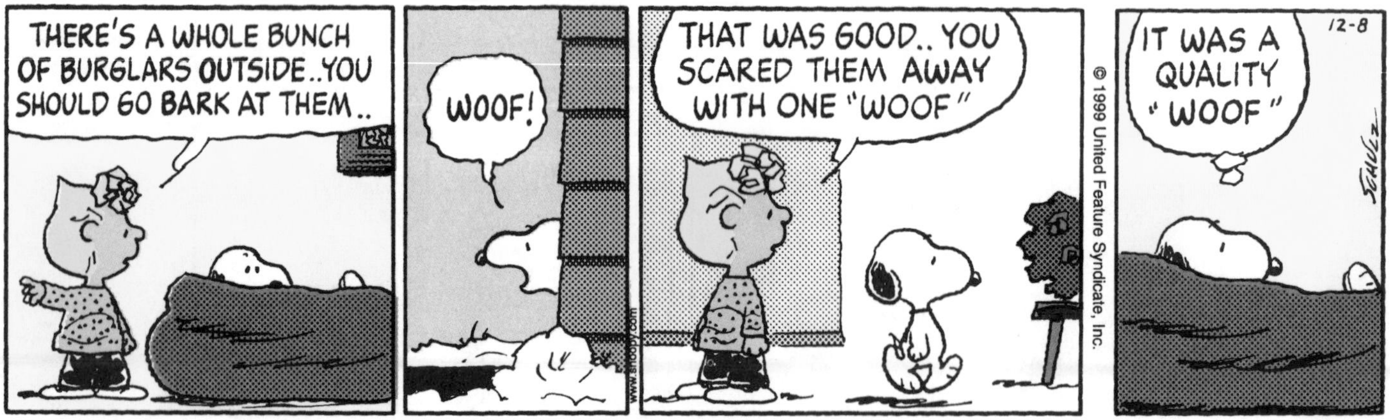
THERE'S A WHOLE BUNCH OF BURGLARS OUTSIDE..YOU SHOULD GO BARK AT THEM..
WOOF!
THAT WAS GOOD.. YOU SCARED THEM AWAY WITH ONE "WOOF"
12-8
IT WAS A QUALITY "WOOF"
© 1999 United Feature Syndicate, Inc.
www.snoopy.com
SCHULZ

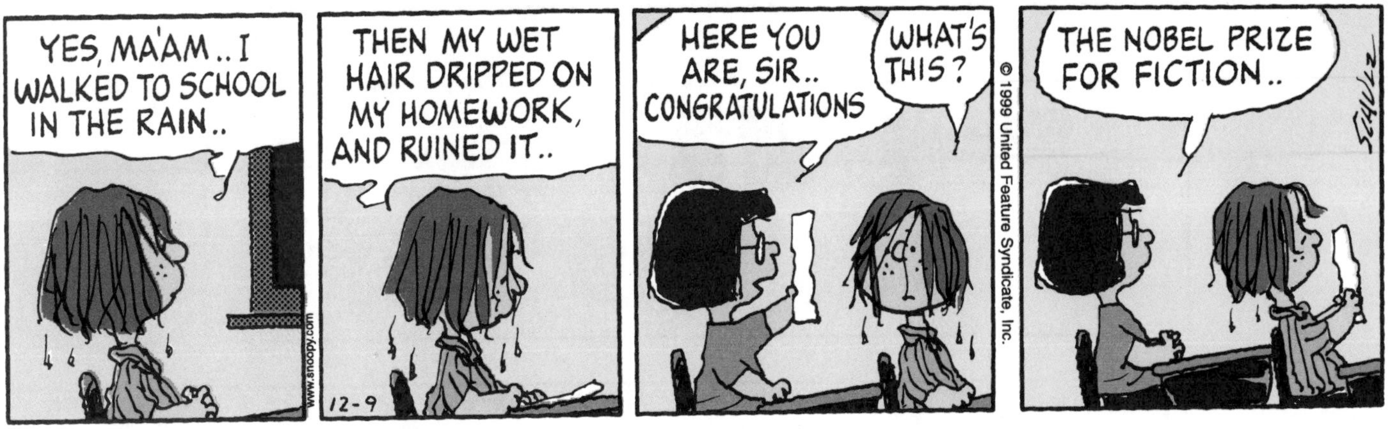
YES, MA'AM.. I WALKED TO SCHOOL IN THE RAIN..
www.snoopy.com
THEN MY WET HAIR DRIPPED ON MY HOMEWORK, AND RUINED IT..
12-9
HERE YOU ARE, SIR.. CONGRATULATIONS
WHAT'S THIS?
© 1999 United Feature Syndicate, Inc.
THE NOBEL PRIZE FOR FICTION..
SCHULZ

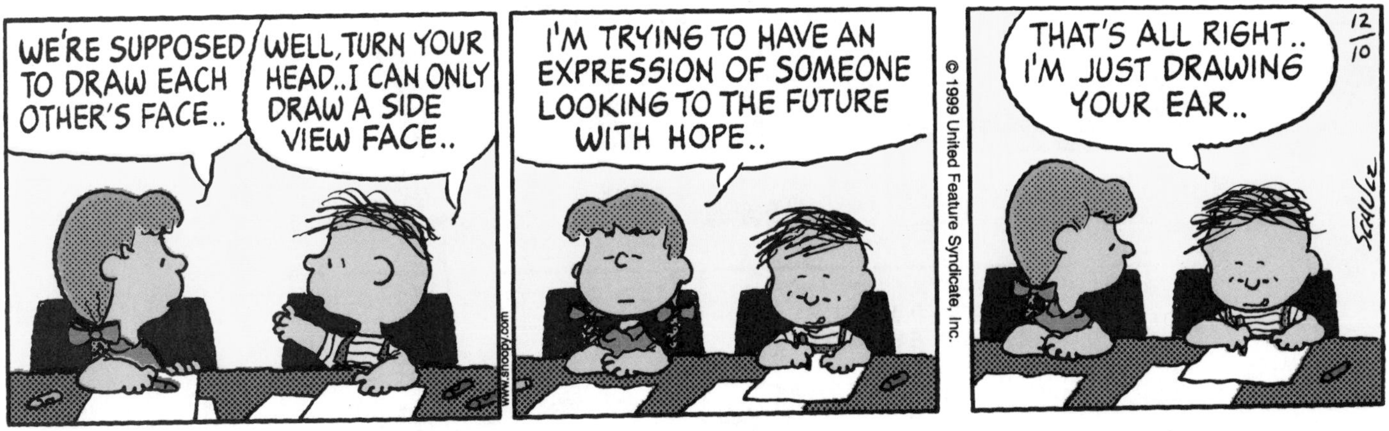
WE'RE SUPPOSED TO DRAW EACH OTHER'S FACE..
WELL, TURN YOUR HEAD..I CAN ONLY DRAW A SIDE VIEW FACE..
www.snoopy.com
I'M TRYING TO HAVE AN EXPRESSION OF SOMEONE LOOKING TO THE FUTURE WITH HOPE..
© 1999 United Feature Syndicate, Inc.
THAT'S ALL RIGHT.. I'M JUST DRAWING YOUR EAR..
12/10
SCHULZ

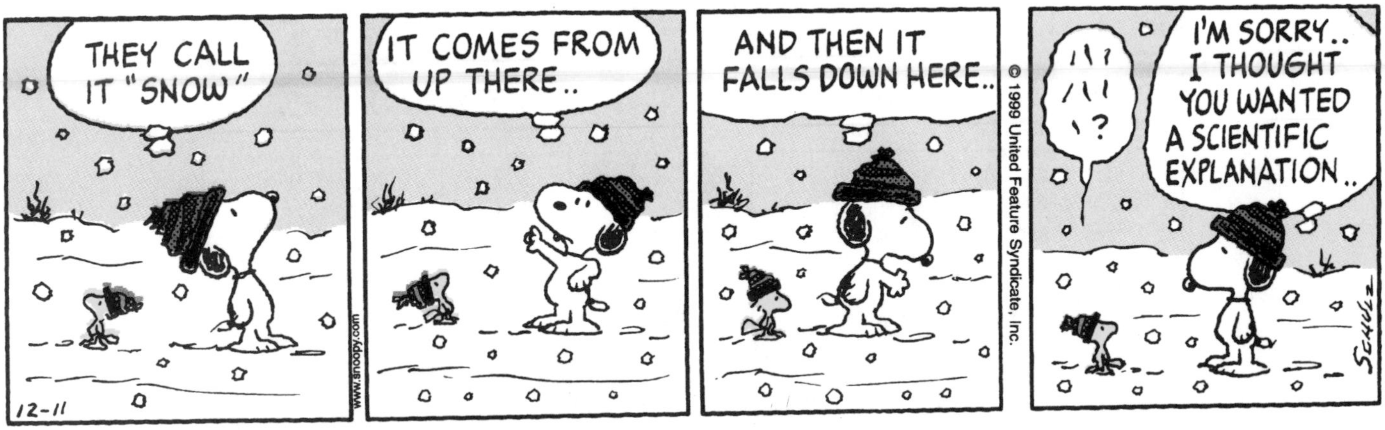
THEY CALL IT "SNOW"
12-11
www.snoopy.com
IT COMES FROM UP THERE..
AND THEN IT FALLS DOWN HERE..
© 1999 United Feature Syndicate, Inc.
?
I'M SORRY.. I THOUGHT YOU WANTED A SCIENTIFIC EXPLANATION..
SCHULZ

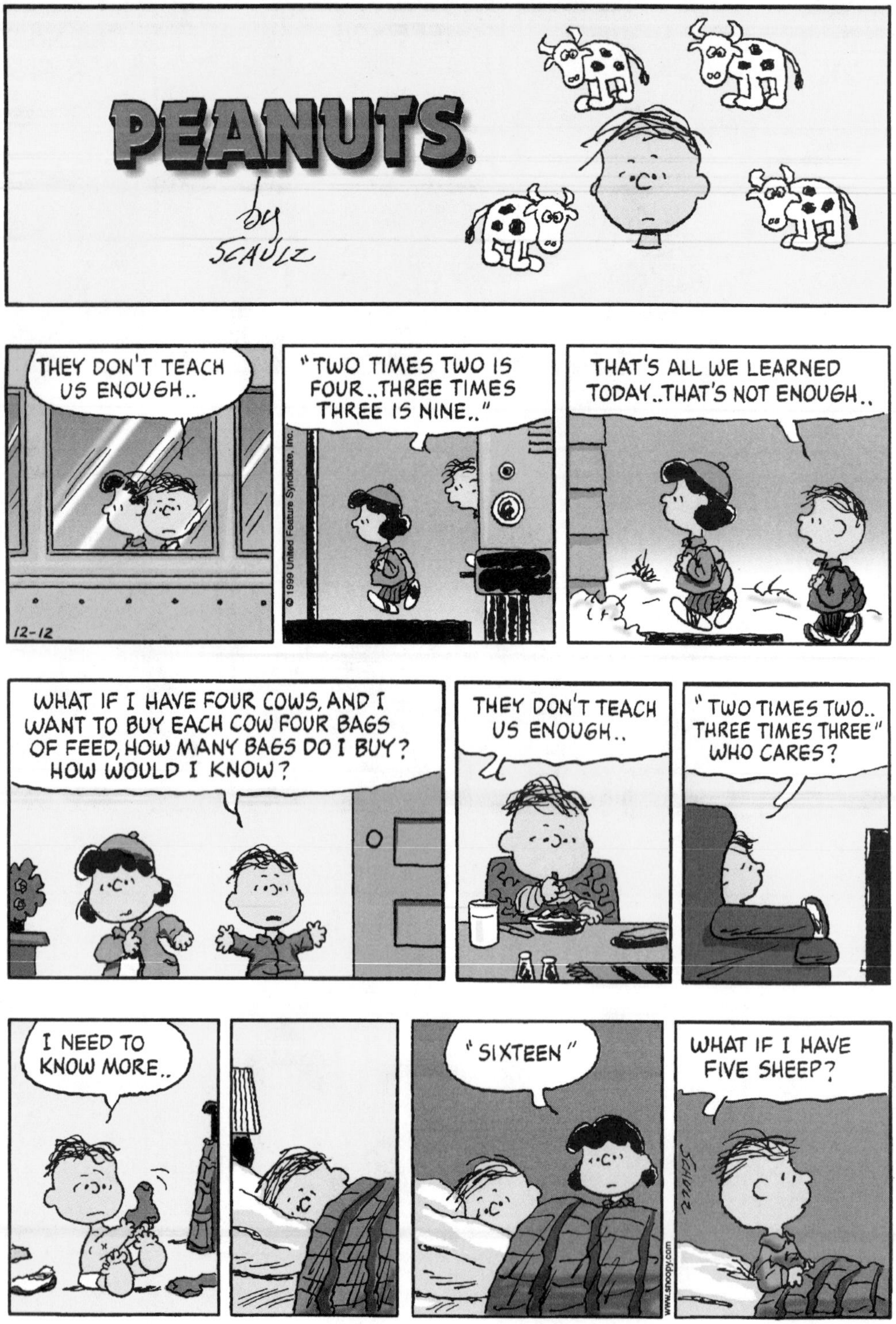
PEANUTS
by SCHULZ
THEY DON'T TEACH US ENOUGH..
12-12
"TWO TIMES TWO IS FOUR..THREE TIMES THREE IS NINE.."
© 1999 United Feature Syndicate, Inc.
THAT'S ALL WE LEARNED TODAY..THAT'S NOT ENOUGH..
WHAT IF I HAVE FOUR COWS, AND I WANT TO BUY EACH COW FOUR BAGS OF FEED, HOW MANY BAGS DO I BUY? HOW WOULD I KNOW?
THEY DON'T TEACH US ENOUGH..
"TWO TIMES TWO.. THREE TIMES THREE" WHO CARES?
I NEED TO KNOW MORE..
"SIXTEEN"
www.snoopy.com
SCHULZ
WHAT IF I HAVE FIVE SHEEP?

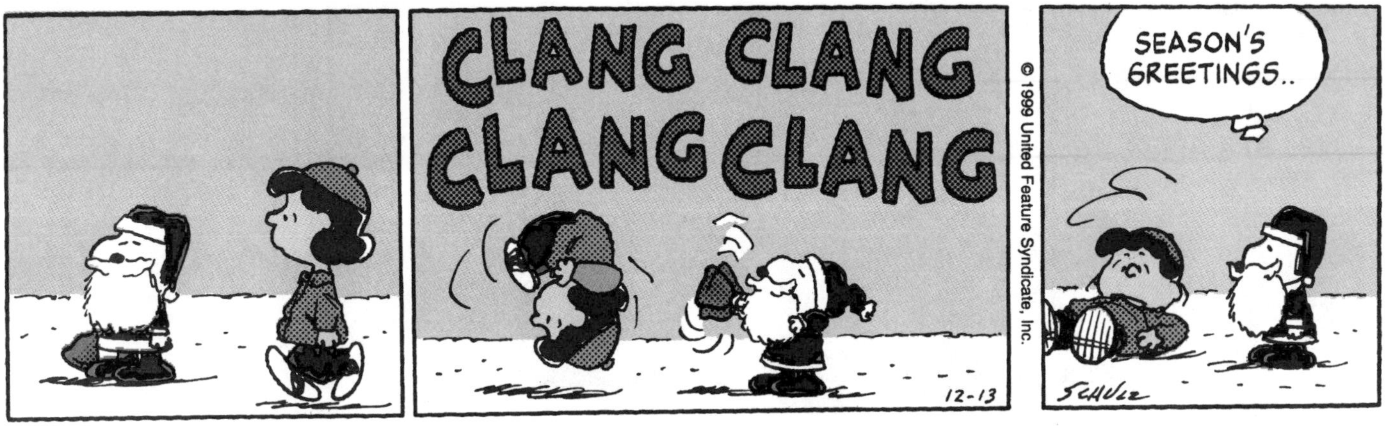
CLANG CLANG
CLANG CLANG
SEASON'S GREETINGS..
© 1999 United Feature Syndicate, Inc.
12-13
SCHULZ

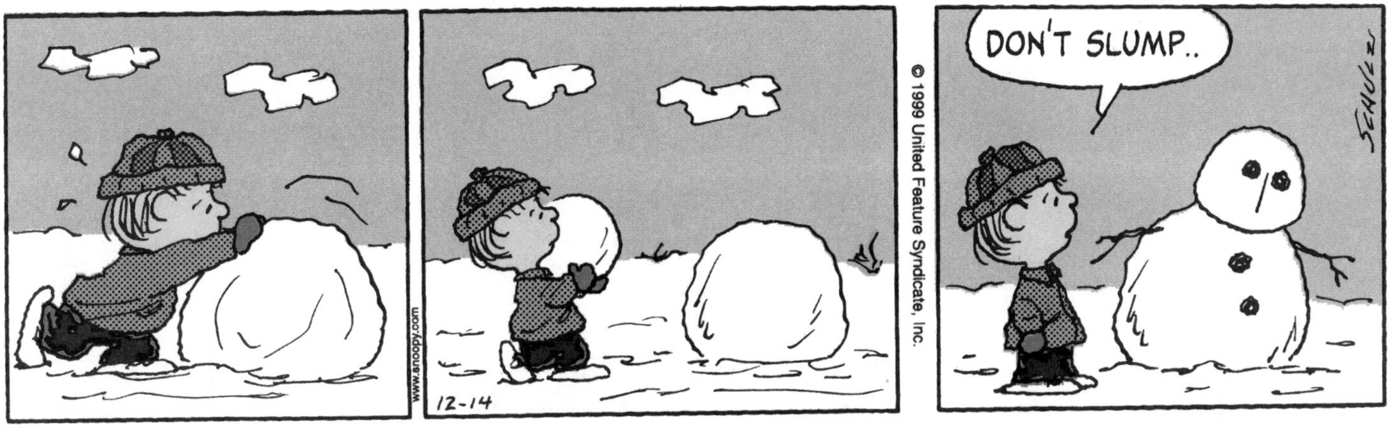
DON'T SLUMP..
© 1999 United Feature Syndicate, Inc.
www.snoopy.com
12-14
SCHULZ

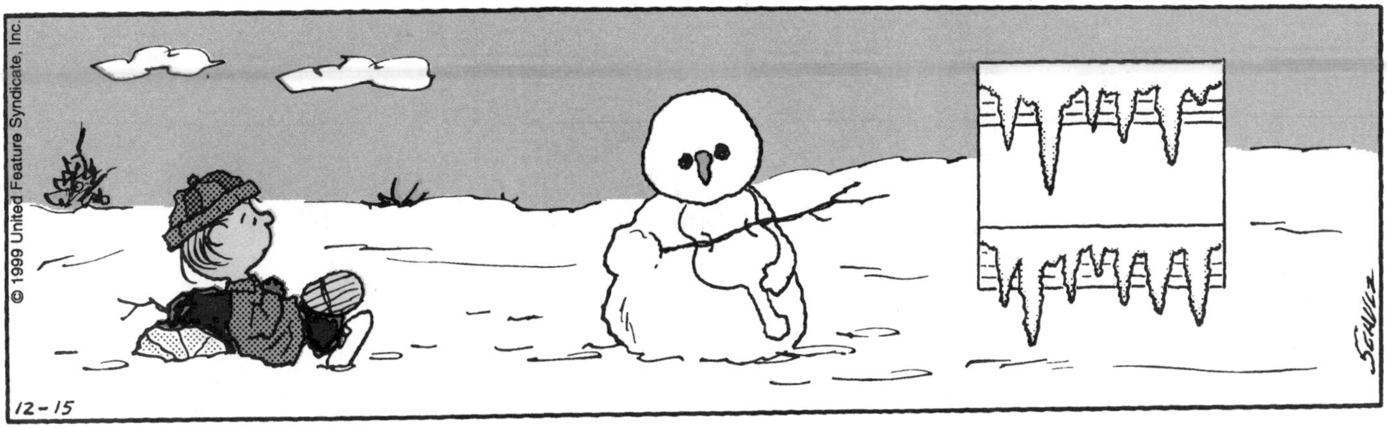
© 1999 United Feature Syndicate, Inc.
12-15
SCHULZ

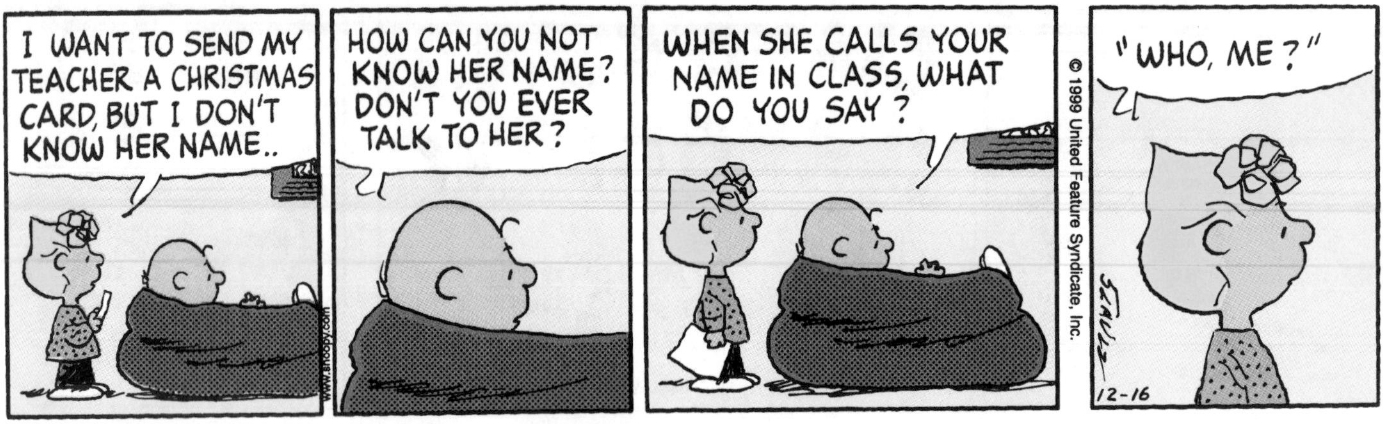
I WANT TO SEND MY TEACHER A CHRISTMAS CARD, BUT I DON'T KNOW HER NAME..
HOW CAN YOU NOT KNOW HER NAME? DON'T YOU EVER TALK TO HER?
WHEN SHE CALLS YOUR NAME IN CLASS, WHAT DO YOU SAY?
"WHO, ME?"
www.snoopy.com
© 1999 United Feature Syndicate, Inc.
12-16

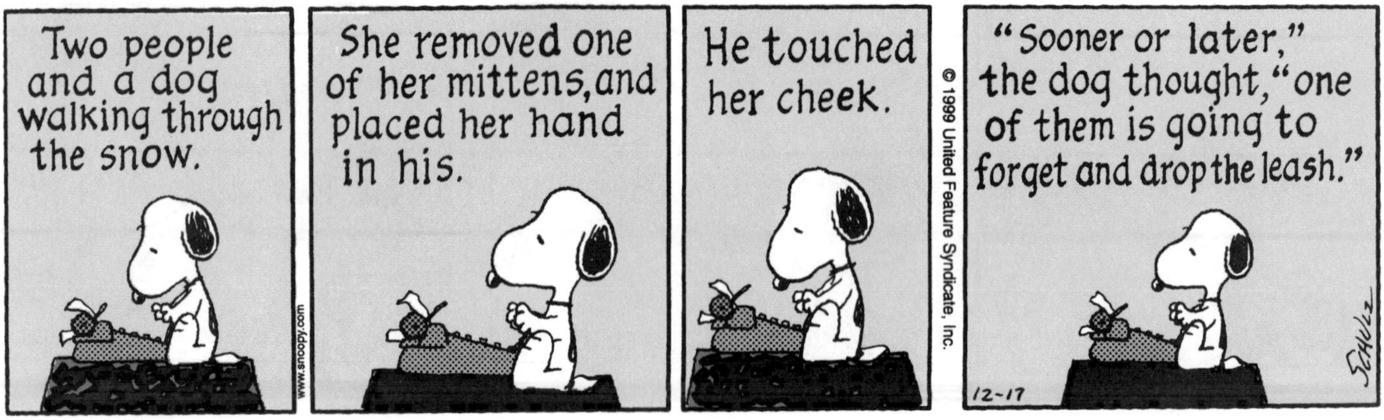
Two people and a dog walking through the snow.
She removed one of her mittens, and placed her hand in his.
He touched her cheek.
"Sooner or later," the dog thought, "one of them is going to forget and drop the leash."
www.snoopy.com
© 1999 United Feature Syndicate, Inc.
12-17

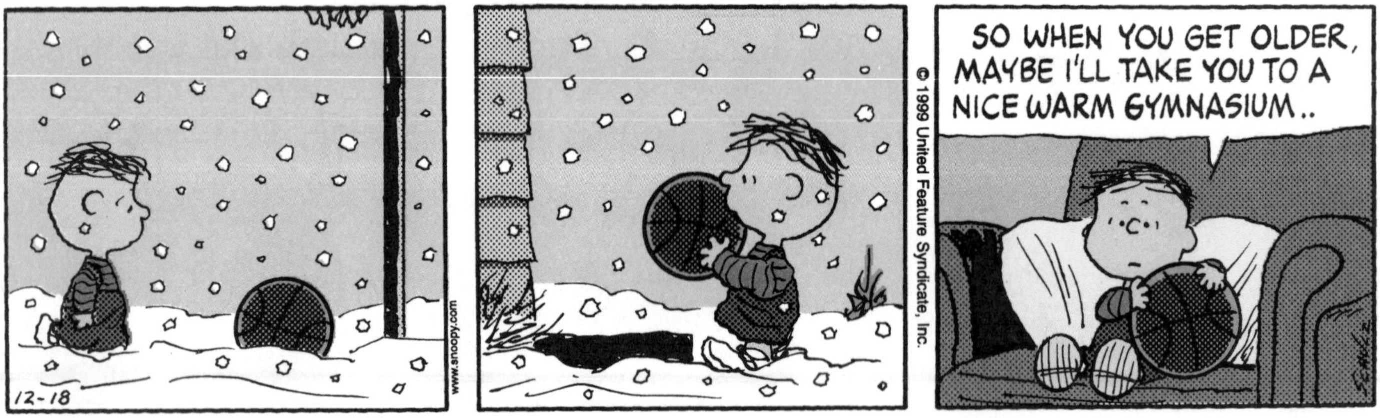
12-18
www.snoopy.com
© 1999 United Feature Syndicate, Inc.
SO WHEN YOU GET OLDER, MAYBE I'LL TAKE YOU TO A NICE WARM GYMNASIUM..

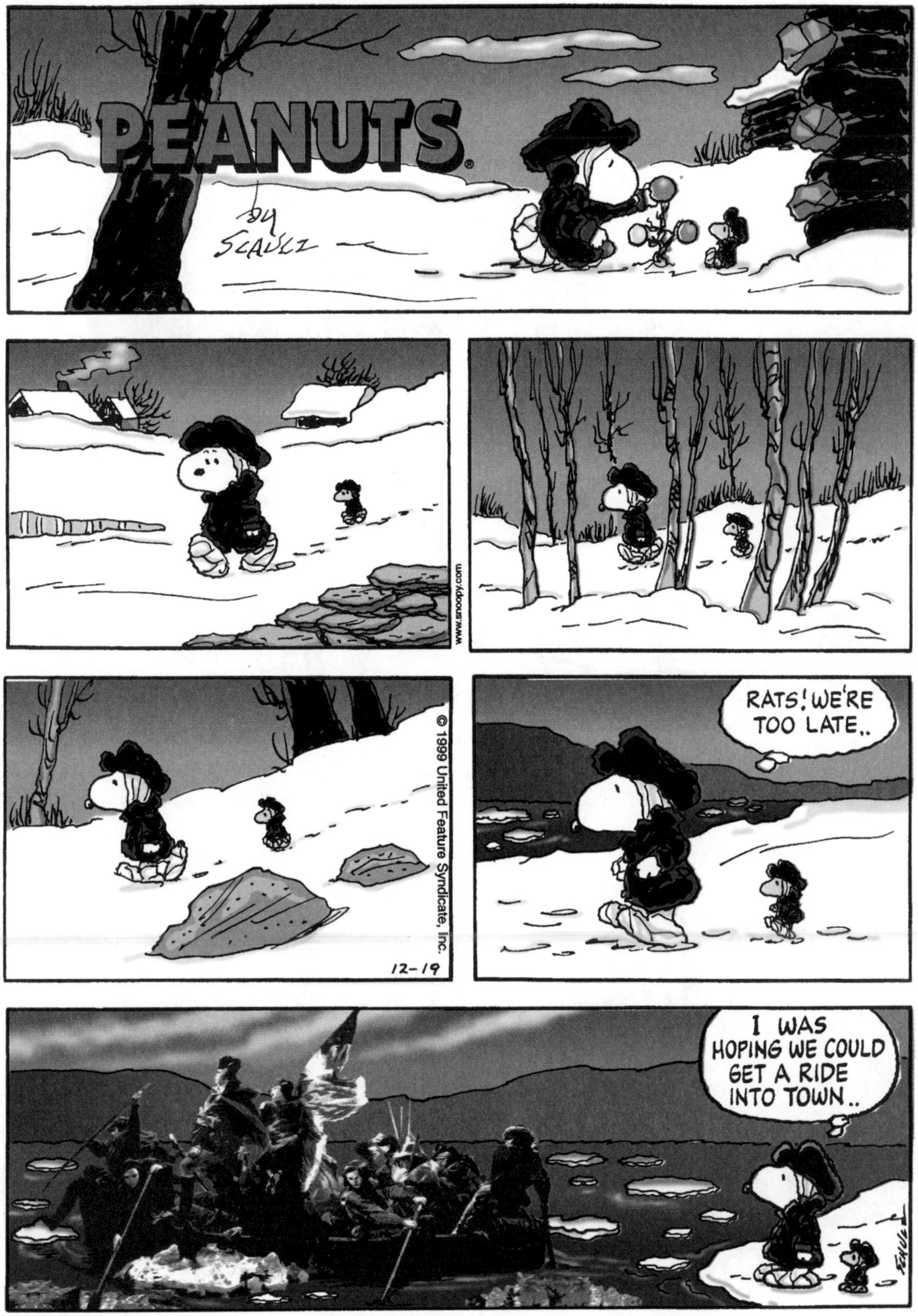
PEANUTS®
by SCHULZ
www.snoopy.com
© 1999 United Feature Syndicate, Inc.
12-19
RATS! WE'RE TOO LATE..
I WAS HOPING WE COULD GET A RIDE INTO TOWN..
SCHULZ

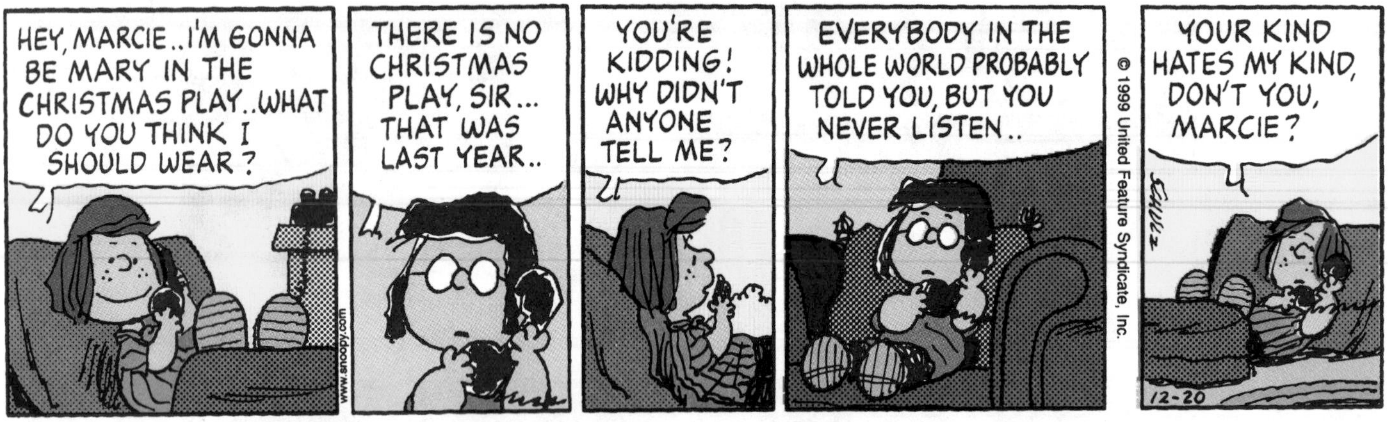
HEY, MARCIE..I'M GONNA BE MARY IN THE CHRISTMAS PLAY..WHAT DO YOU THINK I SHOULD WEAR?
THERE IS NO CHRISTMAS PLAY, SIR... THAT WAS LAST YEAR..
YOU'RE KIDDING! WHY DIDN'T ANYONE TELL ME?
EVERYBODY IN THE WHOLE WORLD PROBABLY TOLD YOU, BUT YOU NEVER LISTEN..
YOUR KIND HATES MY KIND, DON'T YOU, MARCIE?
12-20
© 1999 United Feature Syndicate, Inc.
www.snoopy.com

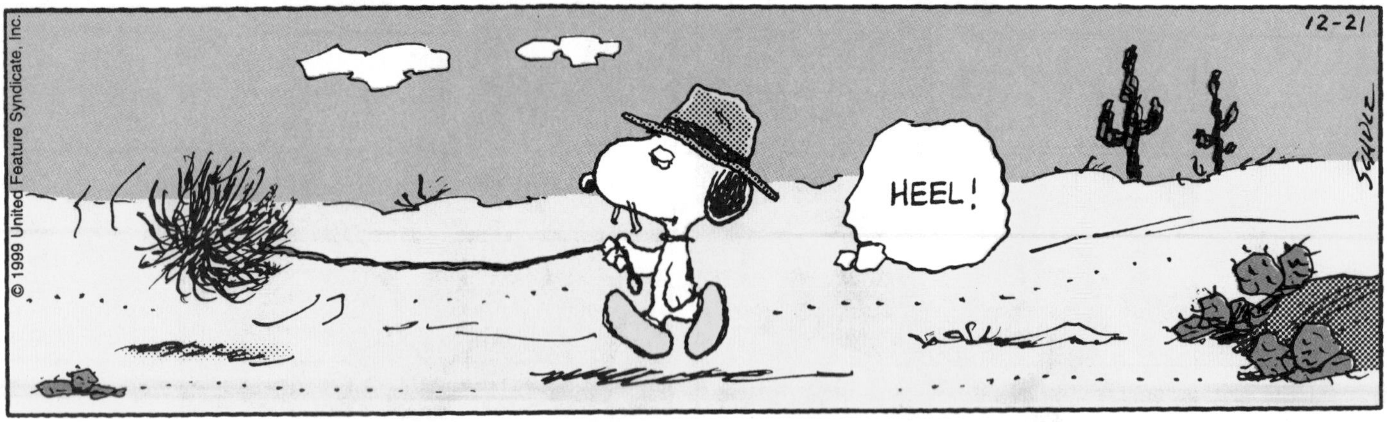
12-21
HEEL!
© 1999 United Feature Syndicate, Inc.

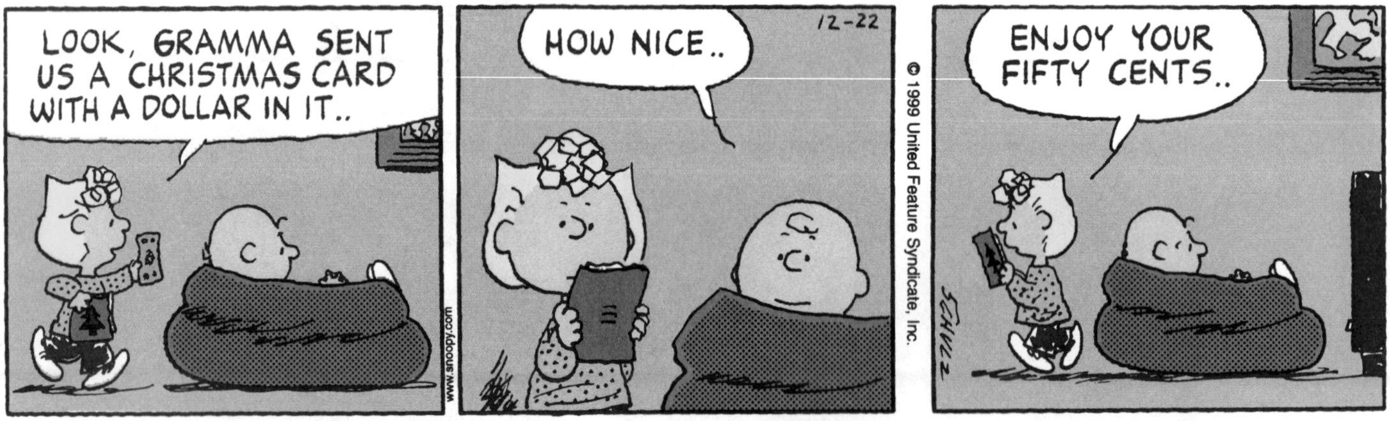
LOOK, GRAMMA SENT US A CHRISTMAS CARD WITH A DOLLAR IN IT..
HOW NICE..
12-22
ENJOY YOUR FIFTY CENTS..
© 1999 United Feature Syndicate, Inc.
www.snoopy.com

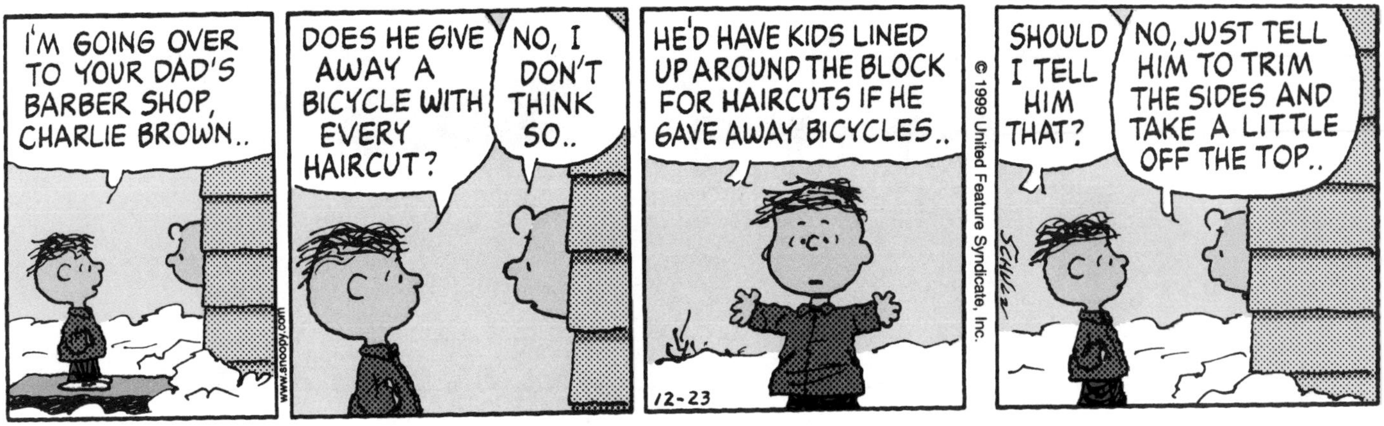
I'M GOING OVER TO YOUR DAD'S BARBER SHOP, CHARLIE BROWN..
DOES HE GIVE AWAY A BICYCLE WITH EVERY HAIRCUT?
NO, I DON'T THINK SO..
HE'D HAVE KIDS LINED UP AROUND THE BLOCK FOR HAIRCUTS IF HE GAVE AWAY BICYCLES..
SHOULD I TELL HIM THAT?
NO, JUST TELL HIM TO TRIM THE SIDES AND TAKE A LITTLE OFF THE TOP..
www.snoopy.com
12-23
© 1999 United Feature Syndicate, Inc.
SCHULZ

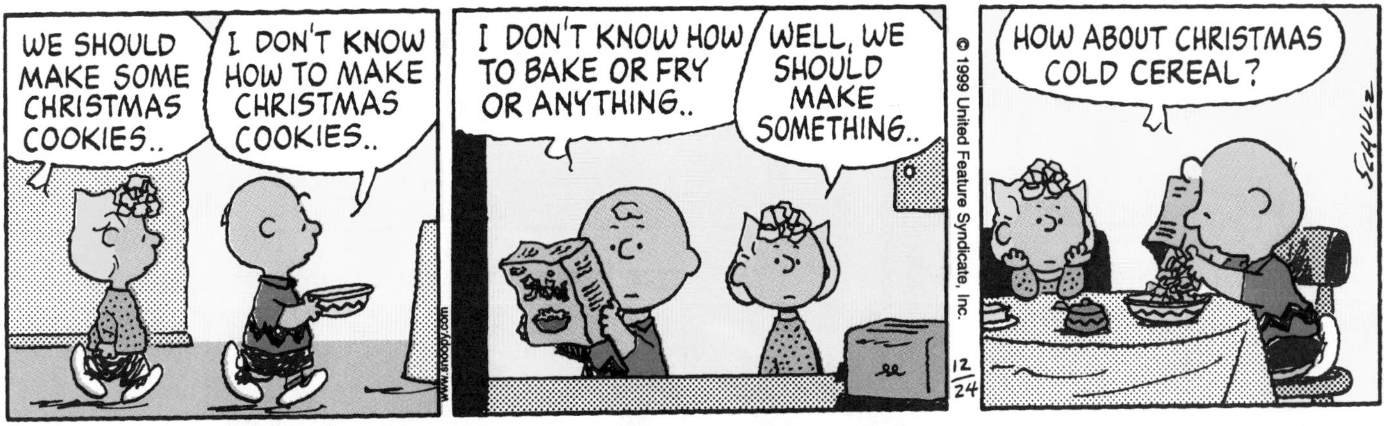
WE SHOULD MAKE SOME CHRISTMAS COOKIES..
I DON'T KNOW HOW TO MAKE CHRISTMAS COOKIES..
I DON'T KNOW HOW TO BAKE OR FRY OR ANYTHING..
WELL, WE SHOULD MAKE SOMETHING..
HOW ABOUT CHRISTMAS COLD CEREAL?
www.snoopy.com
12/24
© 1999 United Feature Syndicate, Inc.
SCHULZ

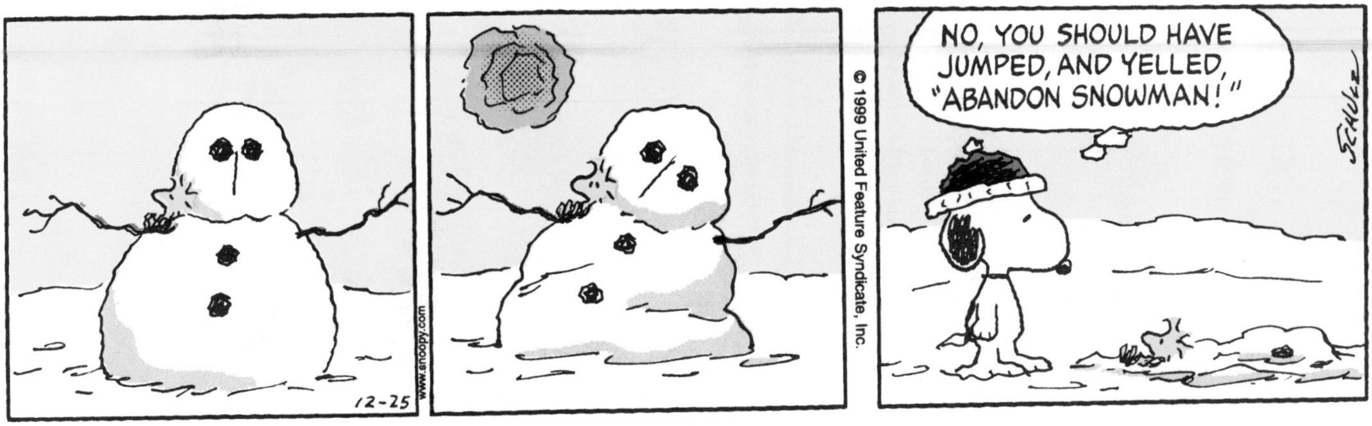
NO, YOU SHOULD HAVE JUMPED, AND YELLED, "ABANDON SNOWMAN!"
12-25
www.snoopy.com
© 1999 United Feature Syndicate, Inc.
SCHULZ

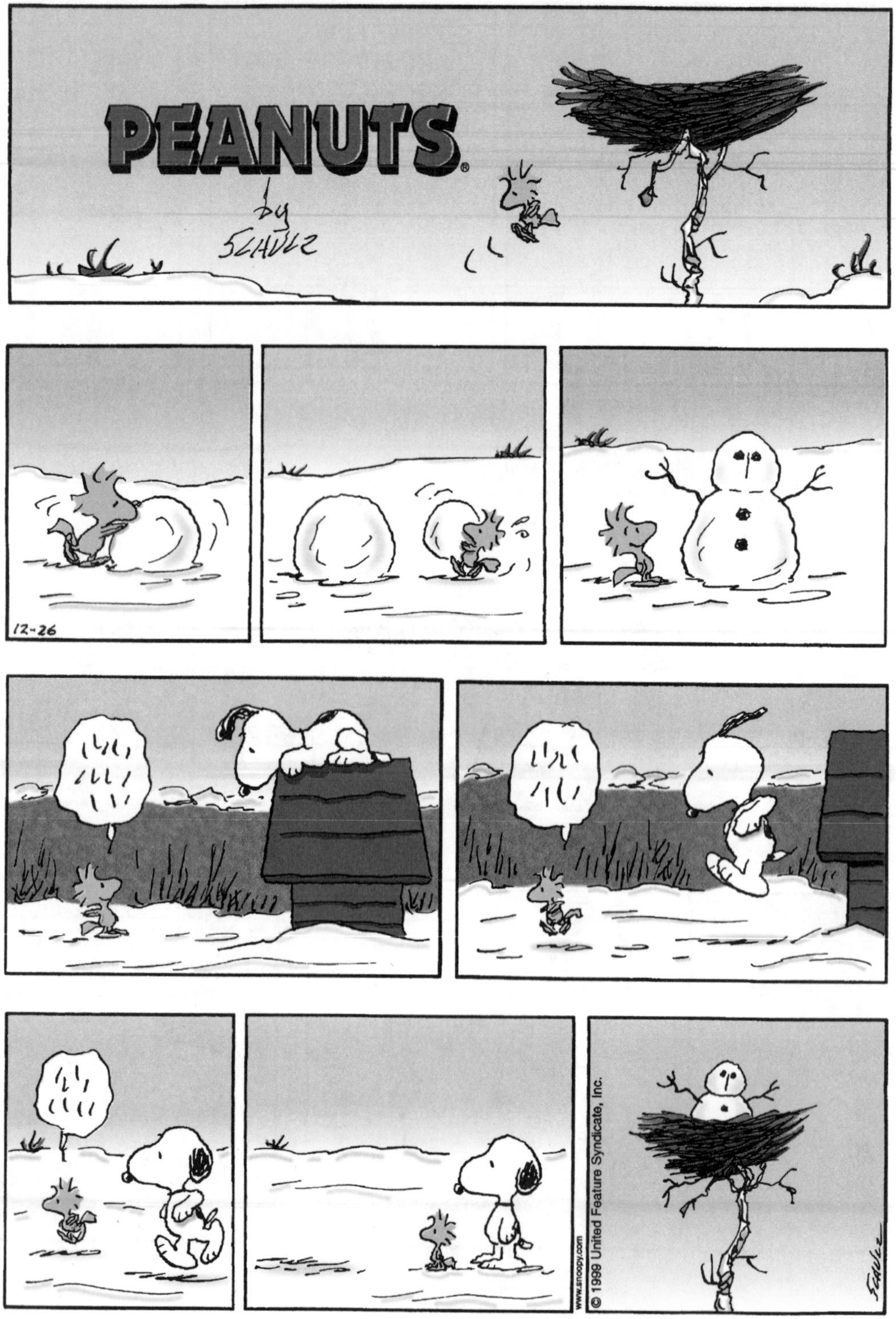
PEANUTS
by SCHULZ
12-26
www.snoopy.com
© 1999 United Feature Syndicate, Inc.
SCHULZ

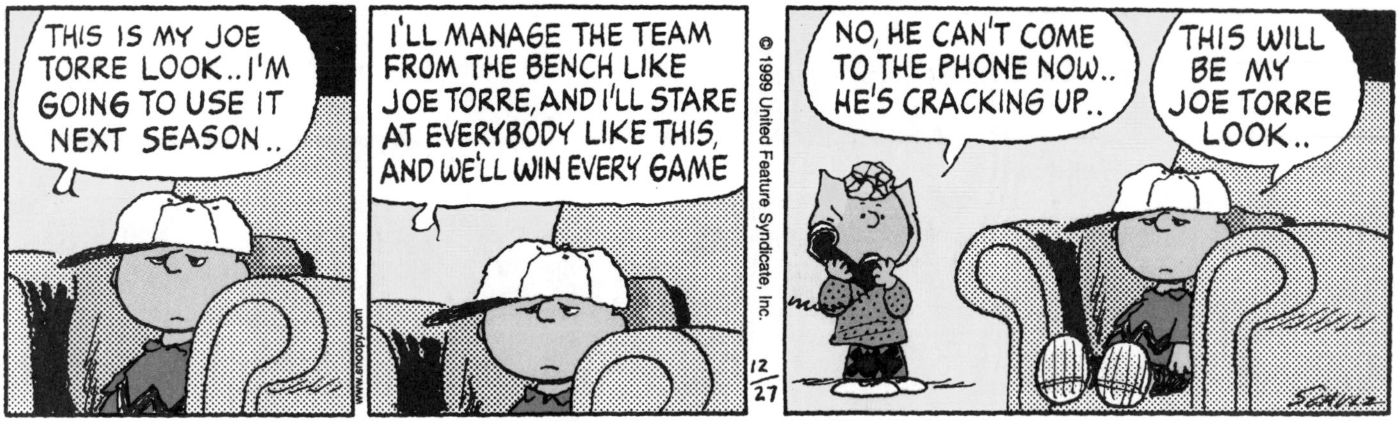
THIS IS MY JOE TORRE LOOK.. I'M GOING TO USE IT NEXT SEASON..
I'LL MANAGE THE TEAM FROM THE BENCH LIKE JOE TORRE, AND I'LL STARE AT EVERYBODY LIKE THIS, AND WE'LL WIN EVERY GAME
© 1999 United Feature Syndicate, Inc.
12/27
NO, HE CAN'T COME TO THE PHONE NOW.. HE'S CRACKING UP..
THIS WILL BE MY JOE TORRE LOOK..

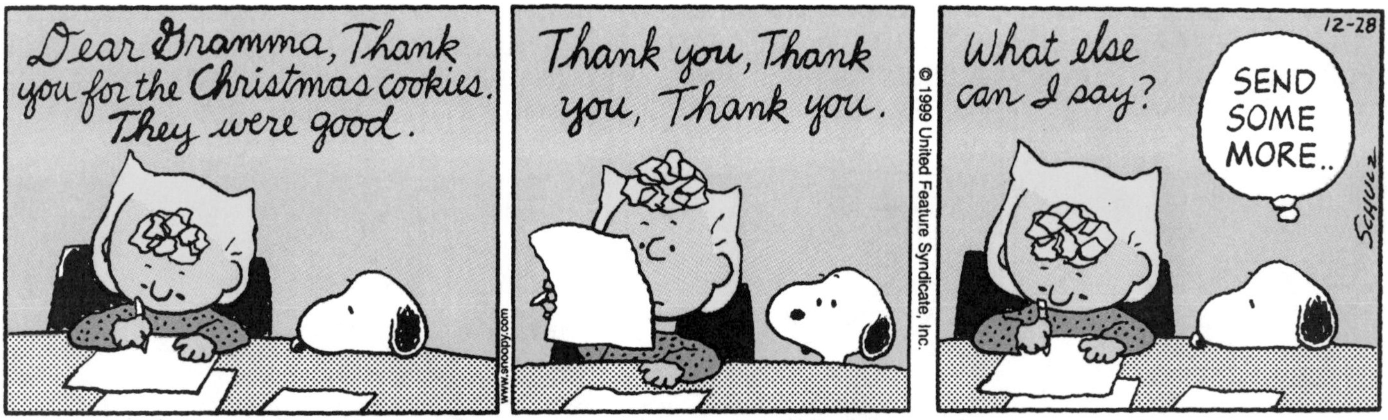
Dear Gramma, Thank you for the Christmas cookies. They were good.
Thank you, Thank you, Thank you.
© 1999 United Feature Syndicate, Inc.
12-28
What else can I say?
SEND SOME MORE..

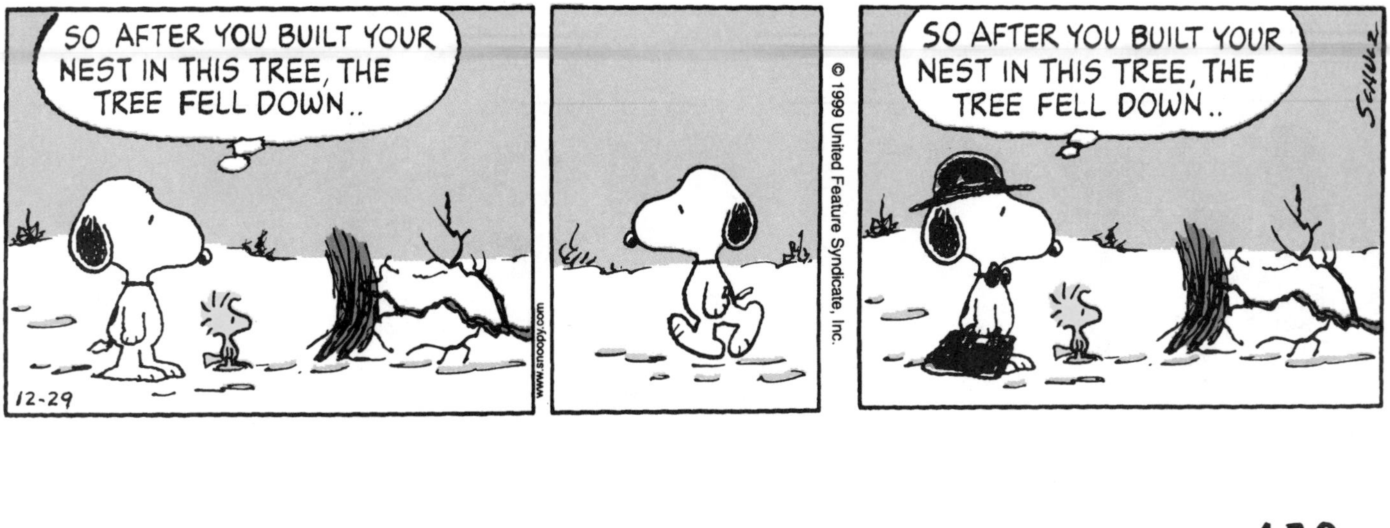
SO AFTER YOU BUILT YOUR NEST IN THIS TREE, THE TREE FELL DOWN..
12-29
© 1999 United Feature Syndicate, Inc.
SO AFTER YOU BUILT YOUR NEST IN THIS TREE, THE TREE FELL DOWN..

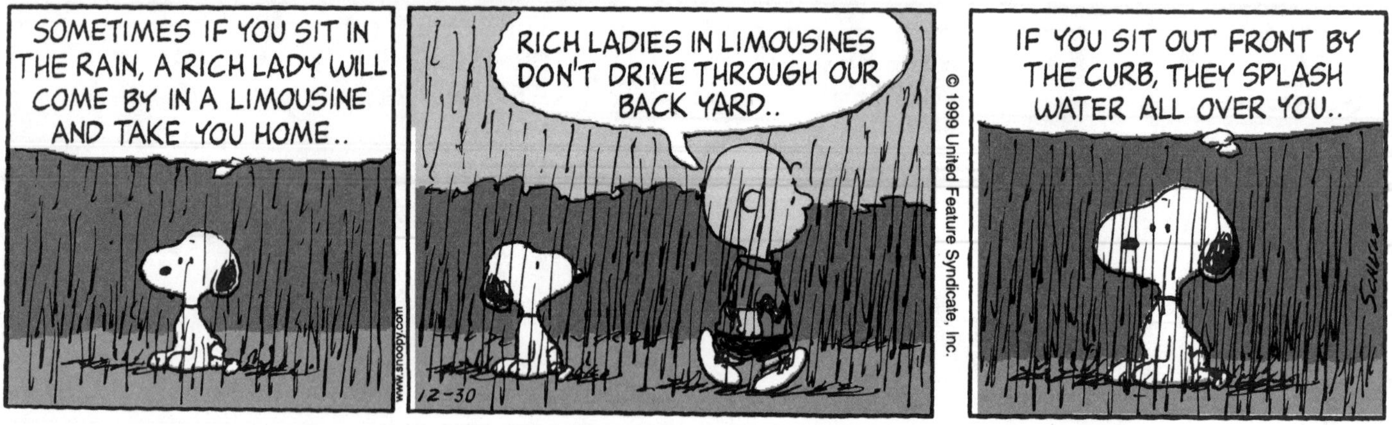
SOMETIMES IF YOU SIT IN THE RAIN, A RICH LADY WILL COME BY IN A LIMOUSINE AND TAKE YOU HOME..
www.snoopy.com
RICH LADIES IN LIMOUSINES DON'T DRIVE THROUGH OUR BACK YARD..
12-30
© 1999 United Feature Syndicate, Inc.
IF YOU SIT OUT FRONT BY THE CURB, THEY SPLASH WATER ALL OVER YOU..
SCHULZ

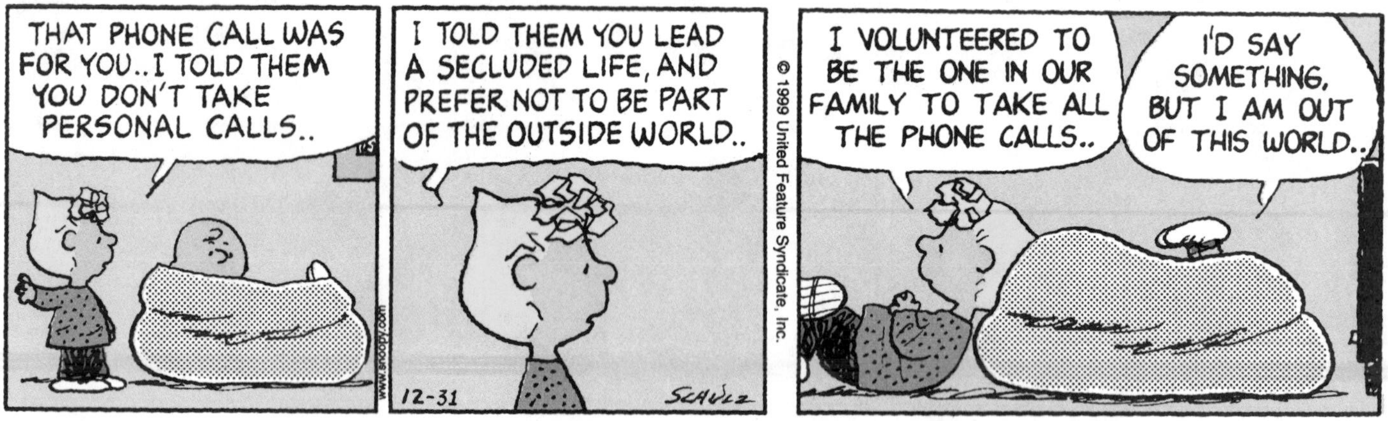
THAT PHONE CALL WAS FOR YOU..I TOLD THEM YOU DON'T TAKE PERSONAL CALLS..
www.snoopy.com
I TOLD THEM YOU LEAD A SECLUDED LIFE, AND PREFER NOT TO BE PART OF THE OUTSIDE WORLD..
12-31
SCHULZ
© 1999 United Feature Syndicate, Inc.
I VOLUNTEERED TO BE THE ONE IN OUR FAMILY TO TAKE ALL THE PHONE CALLS..
I'D SAY SOMETHING, BUT I AM OUT OF THIS WORLD..

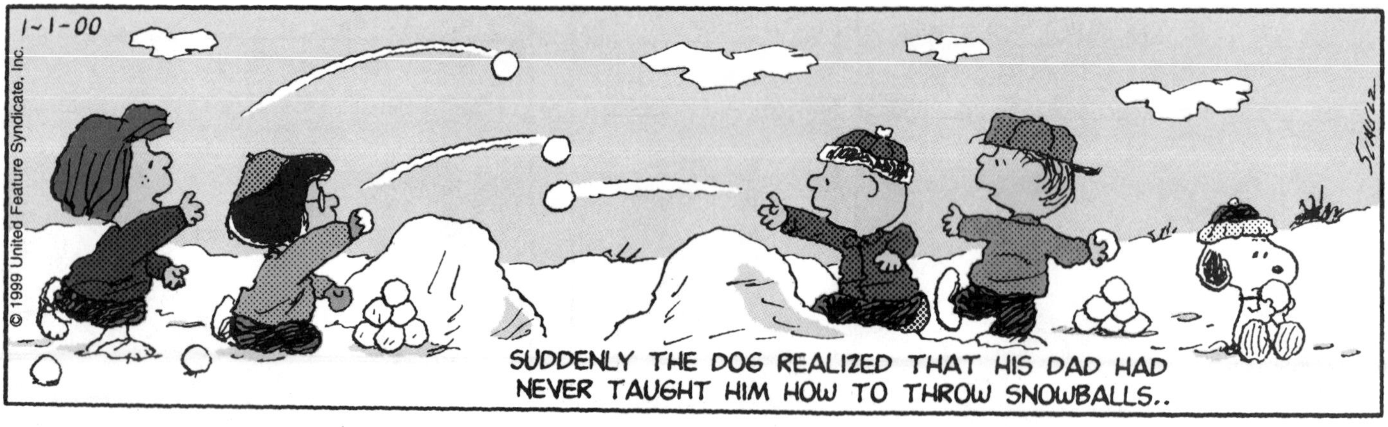
1-1-00
© 1999 United Feature Syndicate, Inc.
SCHULZ
SUDDENLY THE DOG REALIZED THAT HIS DAD HAD NEVER TAUGHT HIM HOW TO THROW SNOWBALLS..

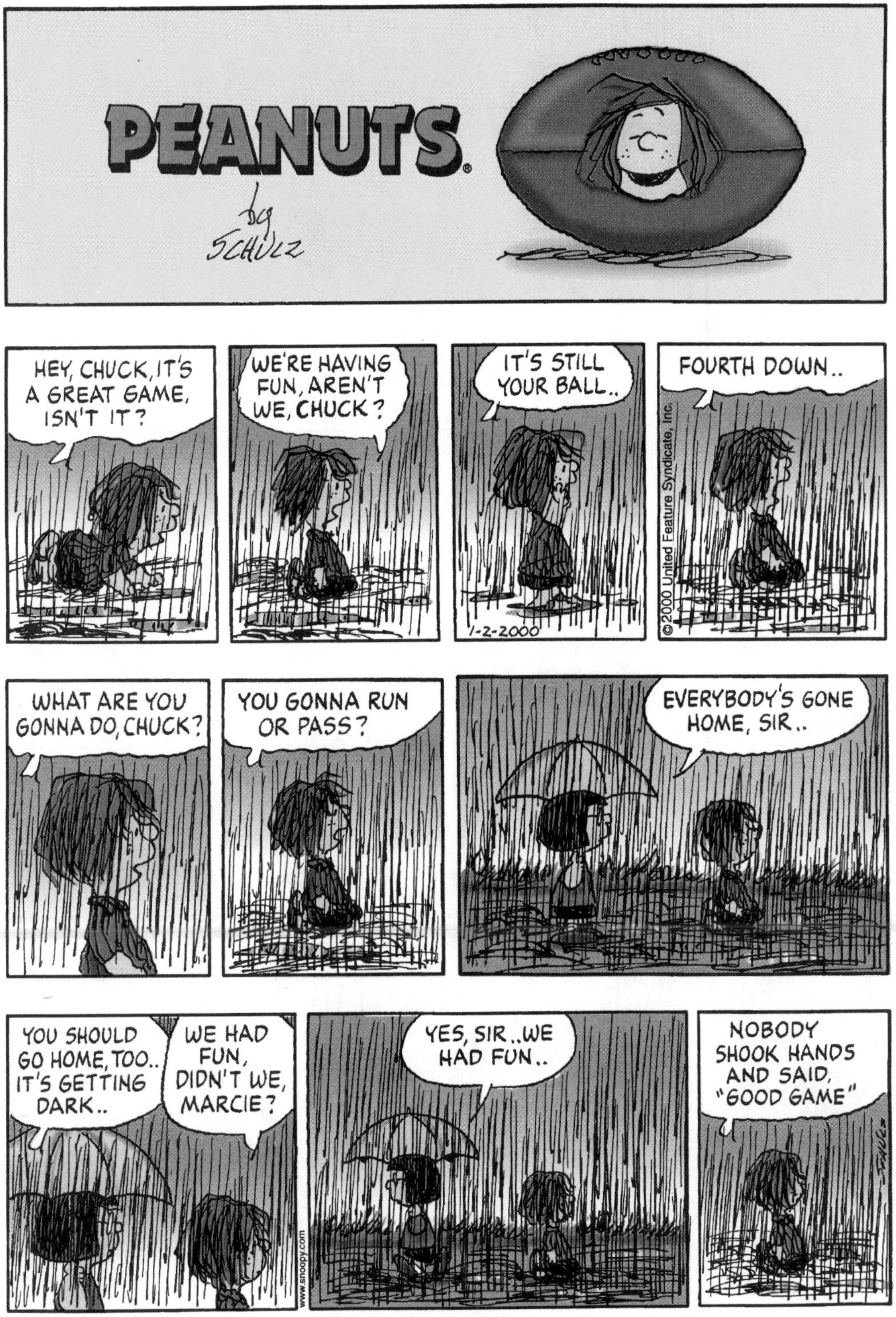
PEANUTS.
by SCHULZ
HEY, CHUCK, IT'S A GREAT GAME, ISN'T IT?
WE'RE HAVING FUN, AREN'T WE, CHUCK?
IT'S STILL YOUR BALL..
1-2-2000
FOURTH DOWN..
© 2000 United Feature Syndicate, Inc.
WHAT ARE YOU GONNA DO, CHUCK?
YOU GONNA RUN OR PASS?
EVERYBODY'S GONE HOME, SIR..
YOU SHOULD GO HOME, TOO.. IT'S GETTING DARK..
WE HAD FUN, DIDN'T WE, MARCIE?
www.snoopy.com
YES, SIR..WE HAD FUN..
NOBODY SHOOK HANDS AND SAID, "GOOD GAME"
SCHULZ

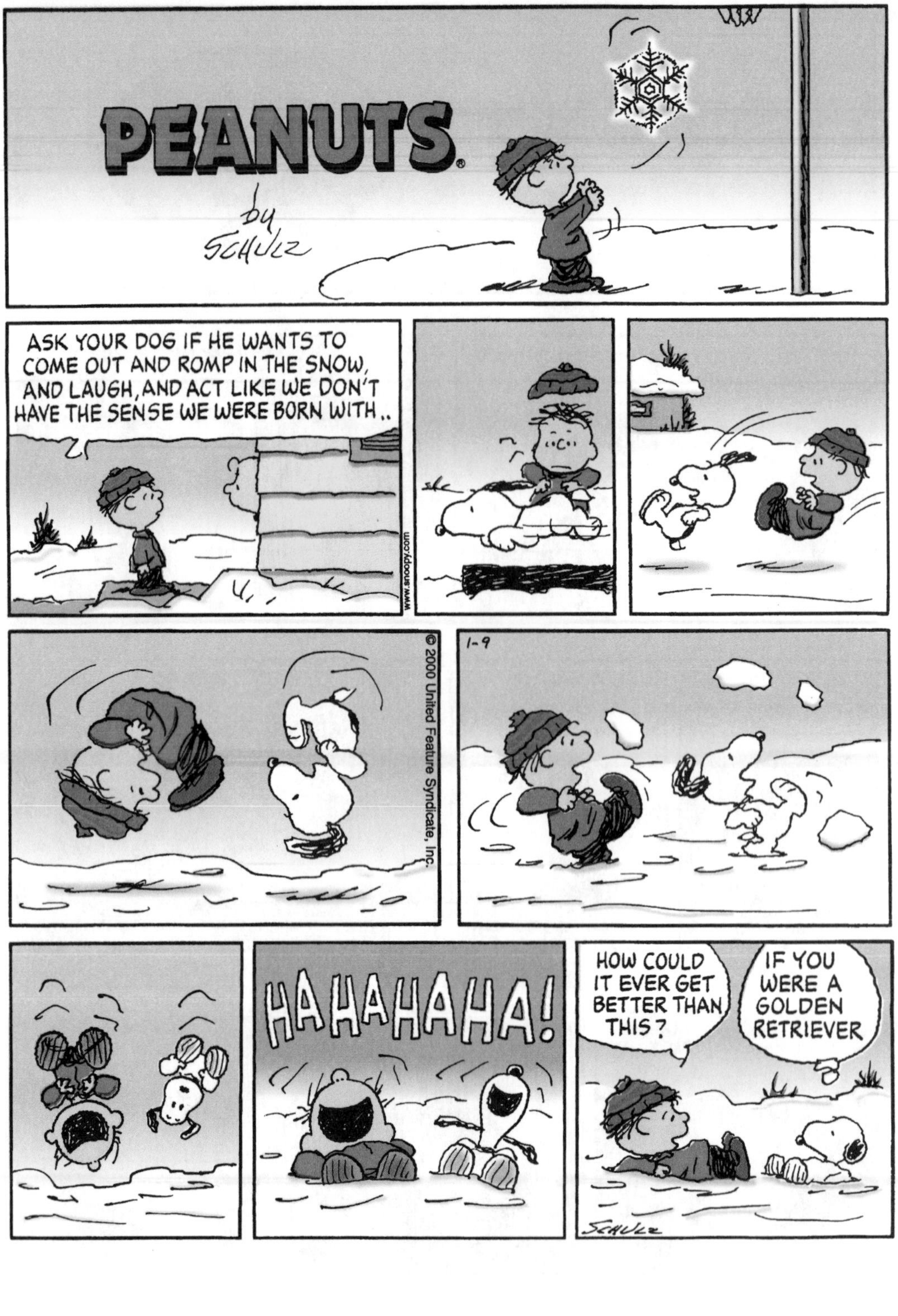
PEANUTS
by SCHULZ
ASK YOUR DOG IF HE WANTS TO COME OUT AND ROMP IN THE SNOW, AND LAUGH, AND ACT LIKE WE DON'T HAVE THE SENSE WE WERE BORN WITH..
www.snoopy.com
© 2000 United Feature Syndicate, Inc.
1-9
HAHAHAHA!
HOW COULD IT EVER GET BETTER THAN THIS?
IF YOU WERE A GOLDEN RETRIEVER
SCHULZ

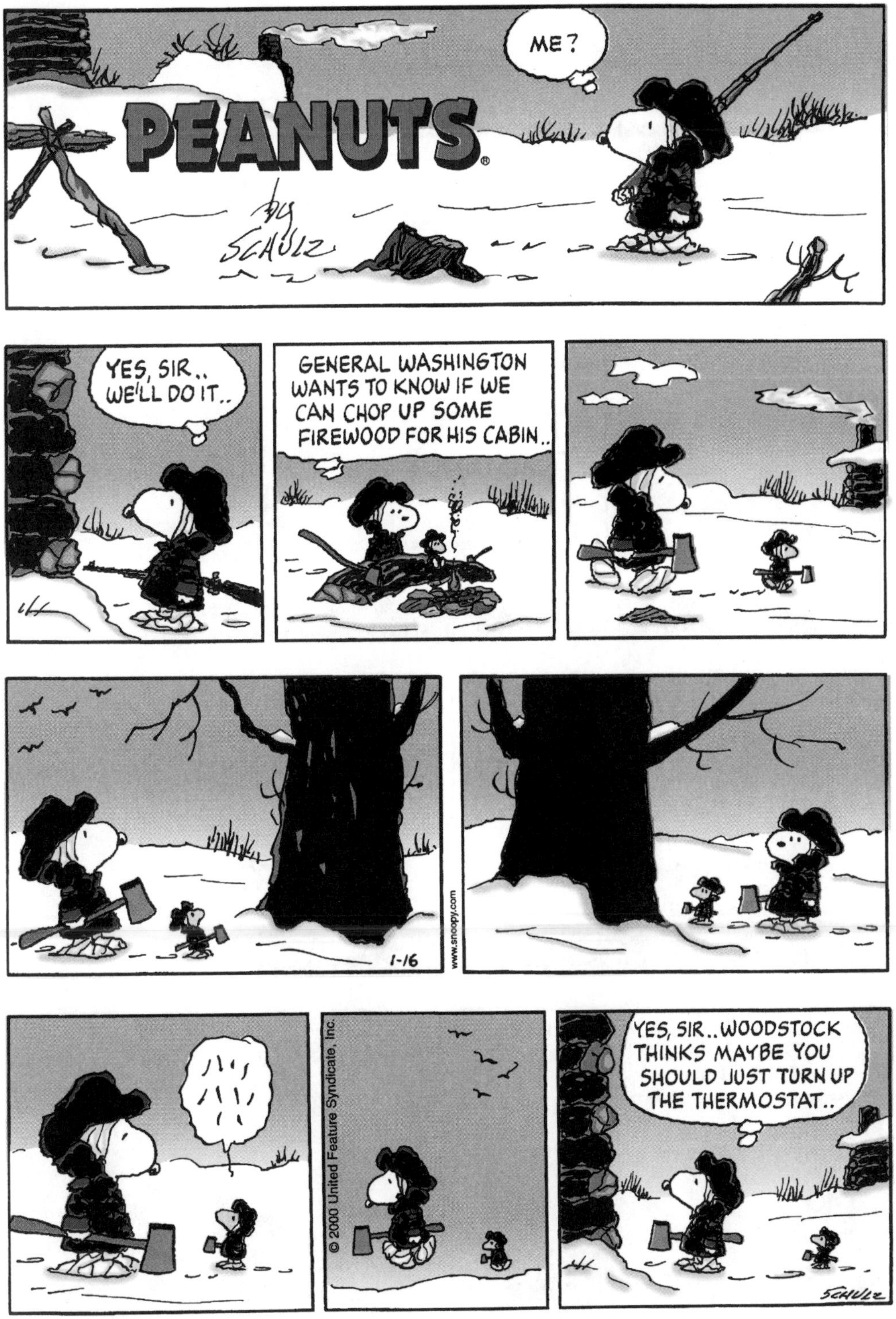
PEANUTS
by SCHULZ
ME?
YES, SIR.. WE'LL DO IT..
GENERAL WASHINGTON WANTS TO KNOW IF WE CAN CHOP UP SOME FIREWOOD FOR HIS CABIN..
1-16
www.snoopy.com
© 2000 United Feature Syndicate, Inc.
YES, SIR.. WOODSTOCK THINKS MAYBE YOU SHOULD JUST TURN UP THE THERMOSTAT..
SCHULZ

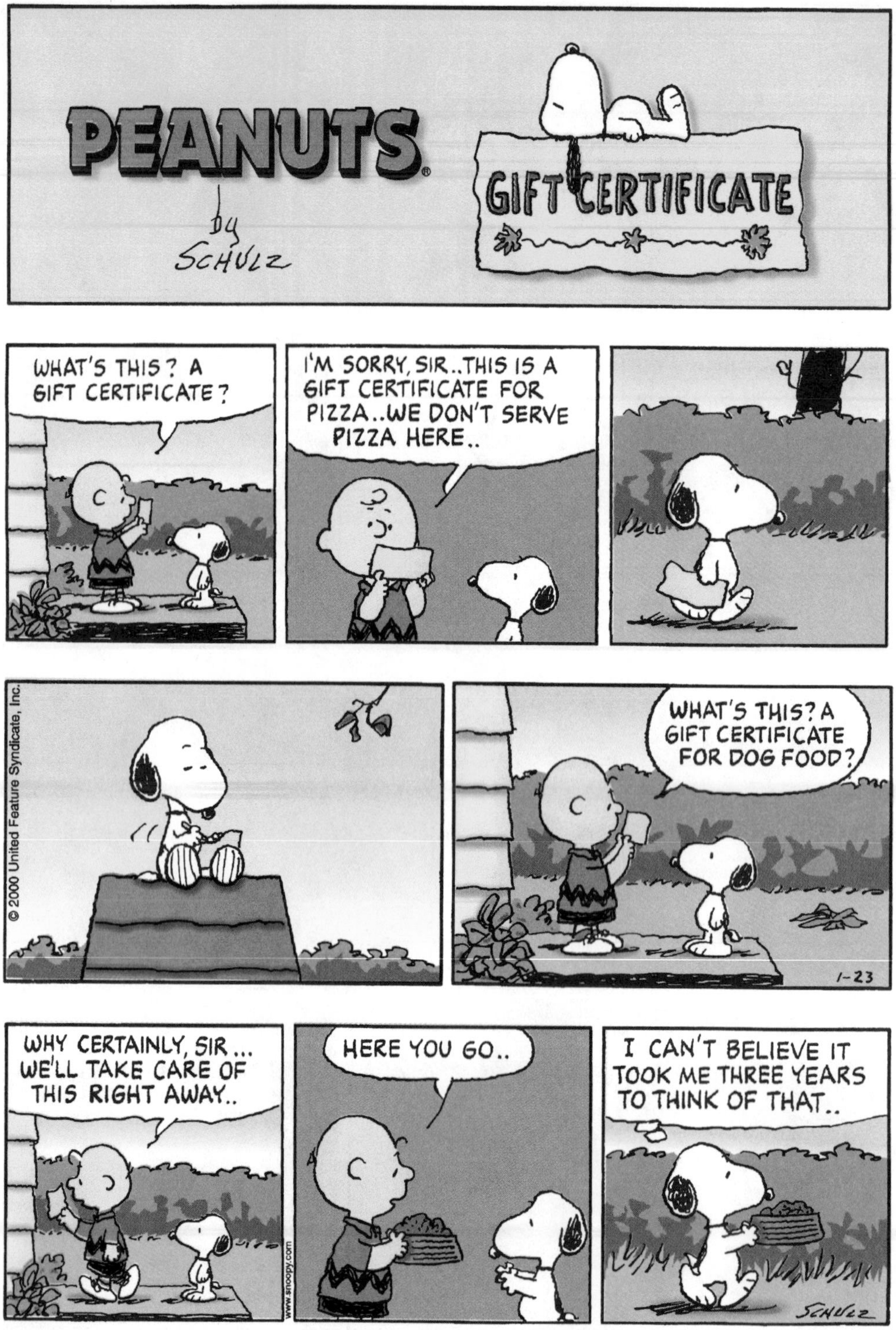
PEANUTS
by SCHULZ
GIFT CERTIFICATE
WHAT'S THIS? A GIFT CERTIFICATE?
I'M SORRY, SIR..THIS IS A GIFT CERTIFICATE FOR PIZZA..WE DON'T SERVE PIZZA HERE..
© 2000 United Feature Syndicate, Inc.
WHAT'S THIS? A GIFT CERTIFICATE FOR DOG FOOD?
1-23
WHY CERTAINLY, SIR... WE'LL TAKE CARE OF THIS RIGHT AWAY..
www.snoopy.com
HERE YOU GO..
I CAN'T BELIEVE IT TOOK ME THREE YEARS TO THINK OF THAT..
SCHULZ

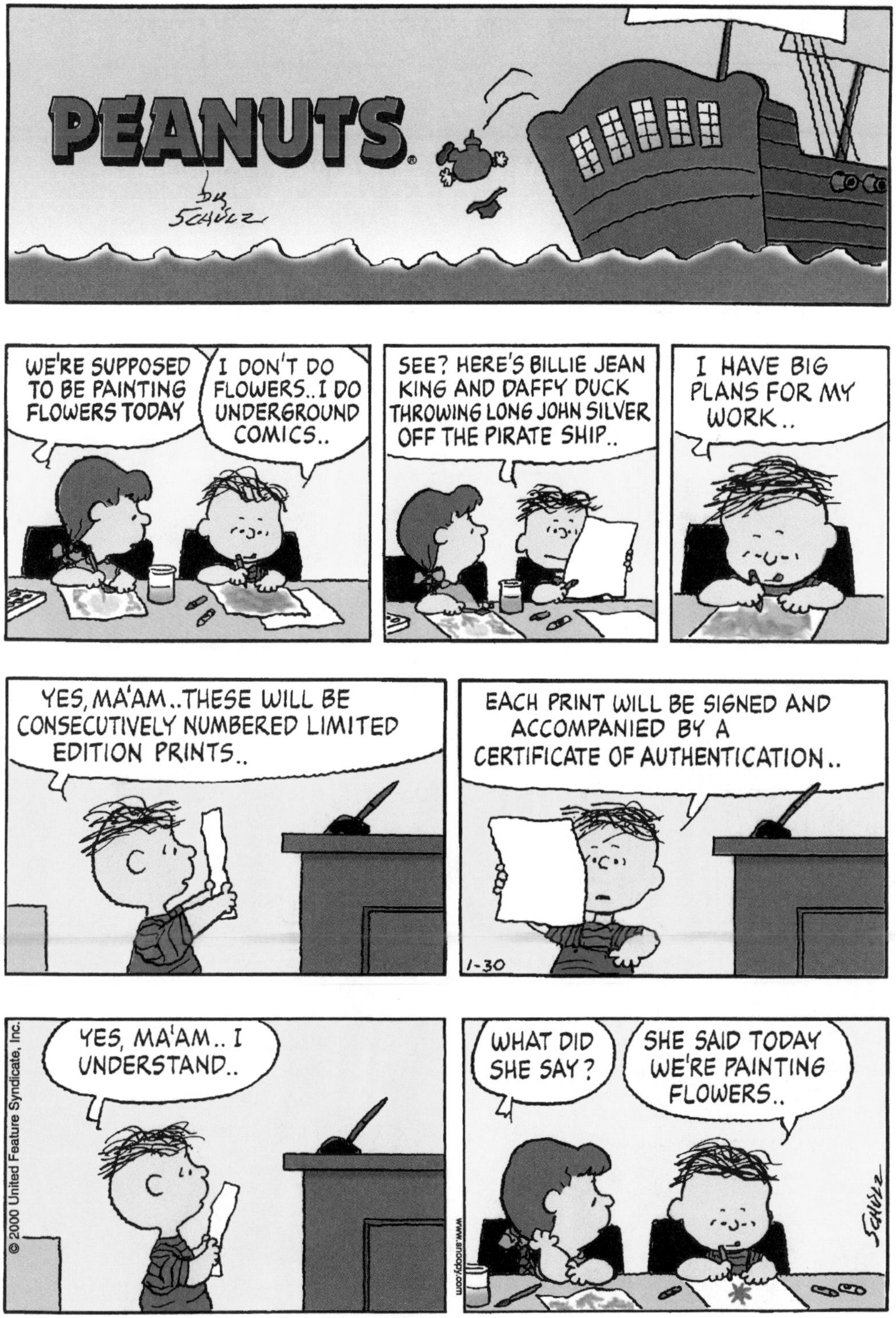

PEANUTS
by SCHULZ
WE'RE SUPPOSED TO BE PAINTING FLOWERS TODAY
I DON'T DO FLOWERS.. I DO UNDERGROUND COMICS..
SEE? HERE'S BILLIE JEAN KING AND DAFFY DUCK THROWING LONG JOHN SILVER OFF THE PIRATE SHIP..
I HAVE BIG PLANS FOR MY WORK..
YES, MA'AM.. THESE WILL BE CONSECUTIVELY NUMBERED LIMITED EDITION PRINTS..
EACH PRINT WILL BE SIGNED AND ACCOMPANIED BY A CERTIFICATE OF AUTHENTICATION..
1-30
YES, MA'AM.. I UNDERSTAND..
WHAT DID SHE SAY?
SHE SAID TODAY WE'RE PAINTING FLOWERS..
SCHULZ
www.snoopy.com

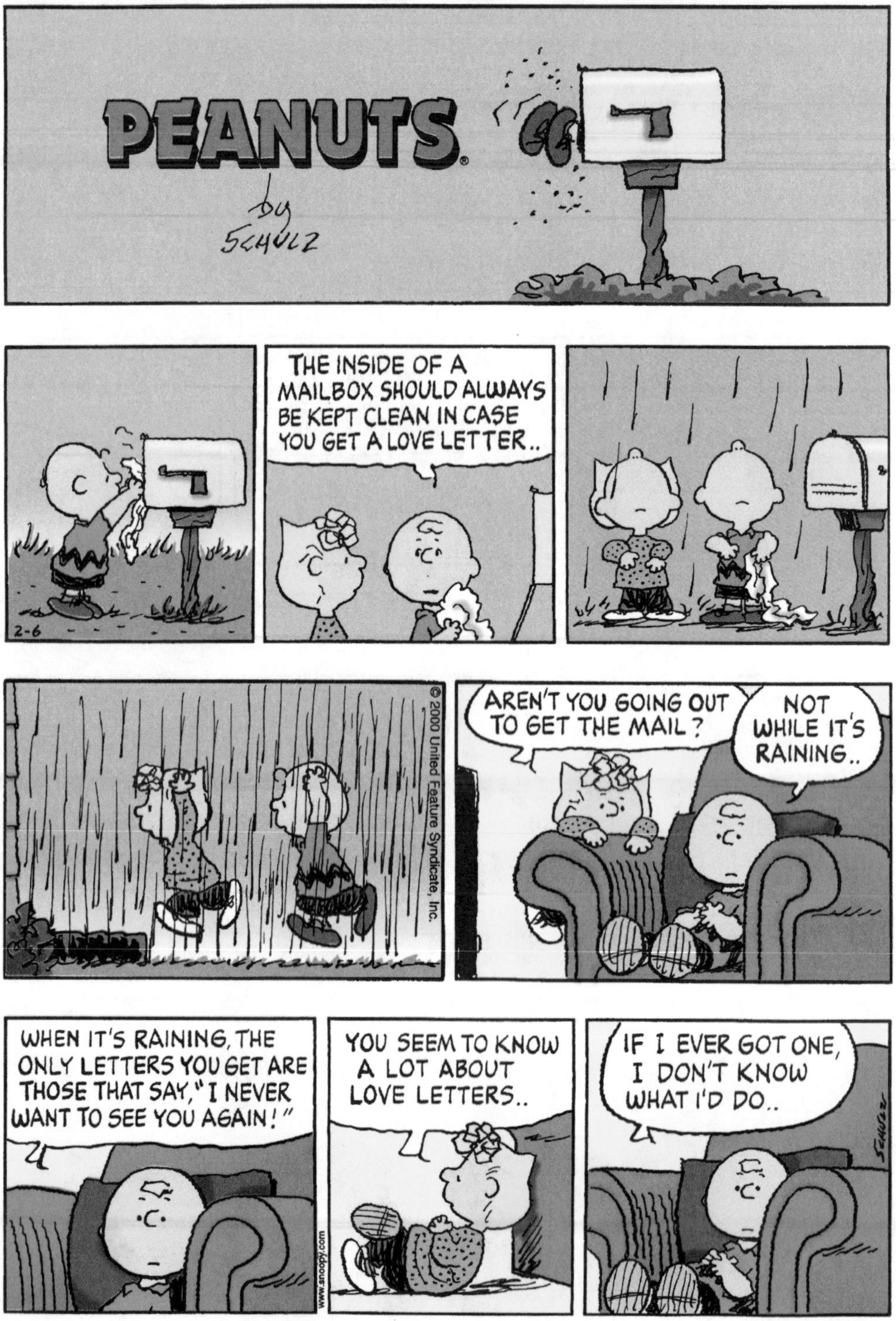
PEANUTS
by SCHULZ
2-6
THE INSIDE OF A MAILBOX SHOULD ALWAYS BE KEPT CLEAN IN CASE YOU GET A LOVE LETTER..
© 2000 United Feature Syndicate, Inc.
AREN'T YOU GOING OUT TO GET THE MAIL?
NOT WHILE IT'S RAINING..
WHEN IT'S RAINING, THE ONLY LETTERS YOU GET ARE THOSE THAT SAY, "I NEVER WANT TO SEE YOU AGAIN!"
www.snoopy.com
YOU SEEM TO KNOW A LOT ABOUT LOVE LETTERS..
IF I EVER GOT ONE, I DON'T KNOW WHAT I'D DO..
SCHULZ